From Hollywood

From Hollywood to Disneyland

Walt Disney's Dream Park and the Influence of American Movies

ROBERT NEUMAN

McFarland & Company, Inc., Publishers
Jefferson, North Carolina

This book has undergone peer review.

ISBN (print) 978-1-4766-8625-7
ISBN (ebook) 978-1-4766-4880-4

LIBRARY OF CONGRESS AND BRITISH LIBRARY
CATALOGUING DATA ARE AVAILABLE

Library of Congress Control Number 2022045875

© 2022 Robert Neuman. All rights reserved

*No part of this book may be reproduced or transmitted in any form
or by any means, electronic or mechanical, including photocopying
or recording, or by any information storage and retrieval system,
without permission in writing from the publisher.*

Front cover image: Tom Sawyer Street, Paramount Ranch,
dressed for *The Arkansas Traveler* (1938, Paramount).
Bison Archives and HollywoodHistoricPhotos.com

Printed in the United States of America

*McFarland & Company, Inc., Publishers
Box 611, Jefferson, North Carolina 28640
www.mcfarlandpub.com*

Table of Contents

Acknowledgments

This book came about thanks to an unexpected realization I had while watching one of my favorite movies, Frank Capra's *It's a Wonderful Life*. I had always assumed that the action on Genesee Street, the main thoroughfare of the film's fictional locale of Bedford Falls, New York, was shot on location in a real American town somewhere. The brisk movement of traffic down the street, the meticulous detailing of the shopfronts, and the scenes that unfolded behind those façades in fully outfitted interior spaces all seemed so real. Viewing and re-viewing the movie over time, however, I noticed that the height of the commercial fronts was not full scale and that any sense of how far the street extended into the distance was blocked by trees in the central median. These, I discovered, were telltale markers of the typical movie studio set. What a surprise to learn later that the false fronts of Genesee Street ranked among the most imposing Hollywood backlot stages ever built.

How could I have been deceived by something so patently false? How could the transition from chaste Bedford Falls to tawdry Pottersville seem so believable? Or those snowy drifts and oversize Christmas bells dangling in the wind? Why did James Stewart and Donna Reed appear to inhabit an actual street?

The answers to these questions led to the illusionistic art of motion picture set design and the level of cinematic reality achieved by skilled studio art directors during Hollywood's Golden Age. As I re-watched the film, Genesee Street reminded me of another remarkably compelling streetscape of false fronts that projected a similarly idealized image of America: Main Street, U.S.A., the entryway into the magical realms of Disneyland in Anaheim, California. The planning of the world's first destination theme park began only a few years after the premiere in 1946 of *It's a Wonderful Life*, and "Genesee Street" stood on the RKO Studio Encino Ranch backlot, a mere ten miles from the Disney Studio in Burbank. Was that pure coincidence, or could there be a connection?

That question led to this book. From the beginning, in his efforts

vii

to "sell" Disneyland to the public, Walt Disney emphasized the park's relationship with Hollywood and candidly acknowledged the design contributions of his team, many of whom had worked as art directors at the big motion-picture studios. But, as well known as those facts are today, few writers have investigated the relationship between movies and Disneyland. My own studies naturally opened with Main Street, U.S.A., and its Hollywood counterparts, and I am grateful to Derham Groves and Loretta Lorance for inviting me to present my initial ideas at the Popular Culture Association meeting in 2007 and to Kathy Merlock Jackson for publishing them in both *The Journal of American Culture* (2008) and the collection *Disneyland and Culture* (2010). Subsequently I have presented papers on the other four sectors of the original Disneyland of 1955 at annual meetings of the Popular Culture Association, the College Art Association, and the Northeast Popular Culture Association. I am indebted to the session chairs who provided a forum for feedback.

Although my primary teaching and research area at Florida State University is the Baroque and Rococo era, I am thankful to a succession of three department chairs who without reservation supported my interest in cinema and theme parks: Patricia Rose, Paula Gerson, and Adam Jolles. Dean Peter Weishar of the College of Fine Arts and colleague Mk Haley of Walt Disney Imagineering lent support and resources. Students in my undergraduate and graduate classes on Disney and Hollywood contributed much to the development of this book, as did many research assistants and Jean Hudson in the media center.

Among Disney scholars, Robin and Janet Allan, Paul F. Anderson, Michael Barrier, Roland Bettancourt, Brent Cowley, Matt Crandall, Didier Ghez, Priscilla Hobbs, Mary E. Lescher, Karal Ann Marling, Todd James Pierce, and Keri Watson provided assistance. I owe a special debt to Garry Apgar, who helped to shape my arguments and shared materials and information from his archives. Heartfelt thanks are due to Ceil Bare for her rigorous contributions as editor. I could not have discussed the relationship of Disneyland to the legendary Hollywood studios without the masterful backlot surveys of Steven Bingham, Michael Troyen, Mark Wanamaker, and their colleagues. I also wish to record my debt to the brothers Leon and Jack Jantzen, whose fanzine *The "E" Ticket*, published from 1986 to 2009, provides the foundation for all Disneyland studies. At McFarland, Layla Milholen facilitated a blind review with two anonymous scholars that deeply impacted the manuscript; she also showed infinite patience in guiding the project through production.

Warmest thanks go to fellow Disney devotees Deanna Lamb, Felicia Lamb, Chris and Jamie Newcomb, Steve Salyers, and Amy deWolfe.

Acknowledgments

Acknowledgments   ix

Long ago John Elliott convinced me that Disney was an appropriate subject for scholarly inquiry. Family and friends have never stopped encouraging me: Bonnie Bennett, Irja and Greg Bonafede, Bobbie and Segundo Fernandez, Kathy Z. Gillis, Mitsy and Gary Granzow, Mary Ann Hartman, John Jakobson, Barbara Johnston, John and Sue Love, Lena and Preston McLane, Jeanne Mills, Lisa Mitchell, Milt Neuman, Clare Pennington, Randy Richter and Dan Covey, and Nancy Rivers.

To all of you: my profound gratitude. *It's a Wonderful Life* indeed!

Preface

In late December 1954, *Time* magazine devoted a cover story to the man who had breathed life into a mouse named Mickey and created multiple feature films, from the animated classic *Snow White and the Seven Dwarfs* to his current live-action and soon-to-be Oscar-winning release *20,000 Leagues Under the Sea*. Walt Disney, *Time* affirmed, was "one of the most influential men alive."[1] Seven months later, in mid–July 1955, he unveiled on national television a new form of mass entertainment that would take the world by storm: the destination theme park.[2] But the term "theme park" did not yet exist.[3] In early July 1955, when a reporter asked "just what" Disneyland was, Walt replied: "It's a fabulous playground. Something of a fair, a city from the Arabian Nights, a metropolis of the future, a showplace of magic and living facts." The reporter boiled it down to a single word: "wonderland" (Fig. 1).[4]

Disney's goal was to distinguish Disneyland from garden-variety summertime carnivals, itinerant funfairs, and year-round urban playgrounds like Brooklyn's famed Coney Island, whose roots went back to the end of the nineteenth century, around the time the expression "amusement park" entered the language.[5] In his late teens, in Chicago, Walt likely visited what was described as "one of the largest amusement parks in the world," the White City.[6] He had fond memories of a similar venue: at age nine, his family moved to Kansas City, "a block and a half from the amusement park," he told Hollywood columnist Hedda Hopper, shortly after Disneyland opened. "I loved it and I could get in for 10 cents."[7] The source of his joy was Fairmount Park, which his sister Ruth Disney Beecher remembered as a fairyland.[8]

By the mid–1950s, however, amusement parks like these had lost their former luster, due to rowdy crowds, lack of upkeep, and the unsavory presence of tacky freak shows, louche midway barkers, and loose morals. A caricature of just such a place was the setting for the 1929 Mickey Mouse animated short *The Karnival Kid*, in which Minnie co-starred as a shimmy dancer.[9]

1

Figure 1. Walt Disney (left) with staff artist Peter Ellenshaw, who painted the aerial view of Disneyland shown on the first *Disneyland* TV show, October 27, 1954 (Earl Theisen Collection/Getty Images).

The family-friendly pleasure ground conceived by Walt in the late 1940s and early 1950s resembled nothing ever seen before.[10] His peers in the movie business and, more importantly, prospective financial backers were skeptical. Even his wife scoffed at the idea. Walt recalled that Lillian Disney had questioned the wisdom of building an "amusement park." "They're so dirty," she sniffed. His response: "I told her that was just the point—mine wouldn't be."[11]

Origins

One of the earliest documents related to Disney's plans for a park, a Memorandum created just before Labor Day, 1948, lists dozens of possible shops or buildings (town hall, doll store, Western museum, among others), eateries, and attractions (horse car, pony ring) suitable for a not yet named playland. This embryonic scheme was divided into two principal parts, a Main Village, patterned after Henry Ford's living-history outdoor museum, Greenfield Village, near Detroit (visited by Walt in 1940 and 1948), and a Western Village, comparable to the Ghost Town at Knott's Berry Farm in Buena Park, near the eventual site of Disneyland in a semi-rural exurb south of Los Angeles.[12] In the Memorandum he consigned typical fair midway attractions to an adjunct Carnival Section.[13]

By March 1952, Disney had recast this vision as a kind of kiddieland, sometimes referred to as the Mickey Mouse Park, that he wanted to build on a sixteen-acre plot adjacent to his studio in Burbank, straddling Riverside Drive and Griffith Park.[14] The Burbank Board of Parks and Recreation rejected the proposal, but Walt persevered and started looking for another—bigger—spot for a more ambitious version of the project. In December 1952, he incorporated a private company, separate from the studio, ultimately called WED Enterprises after the first letters of his full name, Walter Elias Disney. In an interview Walt described WED as what "you might call ... my workshop away from work."[15]

As early as February 1953, mention was made of Disneyland in two influential monthly magazines. *Popular Science* announced Disney's intention to construct a "miniature historic America that is to cover a 50-acre tract in Los Angeles,"[16] and, in an article co-signed by Lillian Disney, *McCall's* revealed that Walt was "working on a Disneyland amusement park to be built somewhere near Hollywood, with rides and displays and even live animals."[17] The latter article made one of the first connections between Tinseltown and Disneyland.

A cadre of experienced Hollywood art directors and set designers was recruited to formulate a rudimentary blueprint, first and foremost, these three men: Dick Irvine, Marvin Davis, and Bill Martin, all formerly employed by Twentieth Century–Fox.[18] Another Fox veteran, Nat Winecoff, was hired as executive assistant and tasked with drawing up documents to attract investors in this increasingly costly scheme.

Finding money to realize the project proved to be an immense obstacle. Other studio bosses in the early 1950s feared that television would eclipse movies as the dominant mass entertainment medium. They wanted little or nothing to do with their upstart competitor. Walt, on the other hand, saw the "tube" as an opportunity—and a way to get his pet project off the ground. In September 1953, his brother Roy, the studio's chief financial officer, flew to New York to meet with CBS, NBC, and ABC to pitch a Disney TV series and—simultaneously—convince at least one of the three to invest in the park, which was still something of a hazy pipe dream. To help the network executives visualize what it was all about, Disney cajoled sketch artist Herb Ryman into drawing the now famous *Aerial View of Disneyland*.[19] In the end, only ABC took the bait, offering a contract to produce an hour-long weekly series and partial financing for Walt's brain-child.[20] Walt Disney was a master of synergy, and one of his most shrewd decisions was to name the show *Disneyland* and pattern its anthology format after the park's four major realms—Adventureland, Frontierland, Fantasyland, and Tomorrowland.

His timing was impeccable. Disneyland's target market was the post-war, middle-class American family: increasingly prosperous parents, who had weathered the Depression and World War II, and their baby-boom off-spring, all ready, willing, and able to hit the road for Disney's funland.[21] Based on a survey by the Stanford Research Institute, the site selected was Anaheim, a small town of 20,000 in fast-developing Orange County, next to the Santa Ana Freeway, thus ensuring easy access by car.[22] To accommo-date an anticipated heavy volume of traffic, WED acquired enough land to build an immense parking lot, capable of holding up to 12,175 vehicles.[23]

To manage crowd flow in and out of the grounds, Disneyland had a single entrance, unlike the average amusement park at that time. "Guests" were funneled through the turnstiles, beneath the berm, down Main Street, U.S.A.—a nostalgic recreation of a small-town main drag, circa 1900—to a central Hub, also called the Plaza.[24] The four "lands" of the fan-shaped layout radiated out from the Hub, visually orienting vis-itors toward Adventureland, Frontierland, Fantasyland, and Tomorrow-land. Spotless, orderly, and staffed by polite, clean-cut personnel—many of them high school kids—each land had a consistent theme. Every ele-ment, from the rides, restaurants, and décor to the signage and costumes, was unified conceptually to help tell stories compatible with its overarch-ing theme. Small-scale passenger coaches pulled by old-fashioned steam engines circled the periphery along a 1.2-mile track atop a high berm that masked the interior of the Magic Kingdom from the outside world.[25]

Disney had a genius for giving a fresh twist to existing modes of entertainment. He rejected thrill rides like the roller coaster, tilt-a-whirl, and drop tower that were mainstays of American amusement parks. How-ever, he and his designers did borrow, and revitalize, certain features, like the electric lights that illuminated Coney Island's nocturnal skyline, the odd castle or quaint European village, and occasional staged display of "foreign" peoples.[26] One wonders if he also didn't transform the name of one of Coney Island's subdivisions, Dreamland, into Disneyland.[27]

Equally important, Walt absorbed the lessons of the world's fair tra-dition, dating back to the second half of the nineteenth century, that laid heavy emphasis on progress through science, technology, and modern modes of transportation. The themed panoramas and vintage locomotives Disney witnessed in person in August 1948 at the Chicago Railroad Fair—a reduced version of a world's fair—helped inspire the Memorandum he wrote soon after he returned home to California.

An interest in miniatures and scale models likewise fired his imagination.[28] In 1947, Walt bought several electric train sets as gifts for children and for himself, and by 1950, he had installed a working scale-model steam engine, with flat-bed cars and caboose, on a half-mile track around his estate in fashionable Holmby Hills.[29] This in turn begat the narrow-gauge railroad that encircled Disneyland. In 1951, in a model-train shop in London, he chanced to meet a former Warner Bros. art director, Harper Goff, whom he hired as a set designer on *20,000 Leagues Under the Sea*, among other films, and gradually integrated into the team working on the park.

From Hollywood to Disneyland

This book focuses on another influence on the structure and design of the park: the work product and methods of operation developed in Hollywood from around 1930 to the early 1950s, the so-called Golden Age of American cinema. The five chapters that follow, devoted to Main Street, U.S.A., and the four "lands," will provide evidence that Disneyland's unique qualities as a theme park owe a significant debt to motion pictures and motion-picture production. Although many writers talk about the place's debt to American cinema, their references are limited, repetitive, scattered, and in many cases incorrect.

Crucial to my argument is the idea of the Disneyland experience as "cinematic," a term often used to mean that in essence the visitor enters a movie, and filmic means, such as establishing shots and close-ups, are used to draw the viewer through the park. "Live action" cross-dissolves blur the transition from one realm or attraction to another through subtle changes in color, architectural detailing, plantings, and music.[30] The cinematic connection was touted in advance publicity, as in an article in *Billboard*: "Motion picture techniques will be used widely...."[31] John Hench, a story artist who joined the studio in 1939 and shared an Academy Award with Disney animator and special effects artist Josh Meador for Best Effects on *20,000 Leagues Under the Sea*, popularized the notion of Disneyland's cinematic effect. He joined the planning unit in 1954. In a documentary aired on the Disney Channel in 1984, Hench mused that the park was very similar to the movies in its use of a long shot—a beautifully composed panoramic view, then a medium shot—a closer view—and finally a close-up.[32] On another occasion, Hench stressed that the use of film techniques created a new experience in the "third dimension."[33]

The word cinematic also implies creating a narrative structure, whereby the visitor is part of a story. Rather than sit passively watching a Western or jungle picture in their local theater, Walt's "guests" were drawn into the "story" as spectators, walk-through participants, and, even subliminally, one might say, as artless "voyeurs." The activation of memory and manipulation of the senses—sight, sound, touch, and smell—effected by the designers made for a more complex, more visceral experience than the cheap-thrill rides of old-style funfairs.

The relationship to movies does not end there. From 1954 the animated opening titles of the *Disneyland* TV program depicted the park's entrance with searchlights moving across the darkened sky, as if heralding a glamorous event like the night in Los Angeles at the Carthay Circle Theatre where *Snow White and the Seven Dwarfs* had its gala premiere in 1937. Moreover, various elements seen upon the park guest's arrival bring to mind a trip to the movies: the colorful silk-screened posters at the entrance recall film posters outside a theater; the first view of the Main Street Railroad Station atop the berm is the park's marquee; and the floral Mickey welcoming guests on the embankment below the station resembles the Mouse's portrait on the title card of the old Mickey Mouse cartoons.[34] Just beyond these visual markers, the names stenciled on Main Street shop windows function as screen credits for the park's creators.

The cinematic analogy with theme parks was explored in the now classic study on Walt Disney World, *Vinyl Leaves* (1992) by Stephen Fjellman, who proposed, "The organizational principles at WDW are cinematic." He went on to explain, "Attractions, lands and worlds are put together in acts and scenes. We are led step-by-step through Disneyfied stories, whether in single attractions or in larger areas of the parks." Continuing the cinematic analogy, Fjellman wrote, "One must understand WDW as a carefully edited place."[35] Other historians, like J.P. Telotte, have extended the analogy, particularly in discussing post–Walt attractions in such places as EPCOT and Disney's Hollywood Studios.[36]

While giving the cinematic qualities consideration, my analysis differs in its emphasis on the visitor's experience as a trip through a Hollywood backlot. I am concerned with the "brick-and-mortar" fabric of the park and how it provided a simulation of touring the production studios of the Big Eight—Metro-Goldwyn-Mayer, Paramount, Twentieth Century–Fox, Warner Bros., RKO, Columbia, Universal, and United Artists. In 1973, Christopher Finch raised—in passing—a closely related point. "What makes Disneyland radically different from other amusement parks," he said, "is the fact that it is designed like a movie lot. The skills that go into building film sets are the same skills that went into Main Street and Frontierland."[37]

Although it is no secret that Walt, frustrated by the architectural firm engaged to design the attractions, went out and hired experienced Hollywood art directors, the techniques they used and the sources they tapped have until now not received full attention from historians. Various writers have touched on the corollary concept that as people tour the park, they are in effect passing through a series of stage sets.[38] But these histories have not stressed the degree to which early publicity promised the public an "insider" experience that was denied at the closed gates of the major studios. The designers' pedigrees as studio art directors were repeatedly stressed in publicity. The July opening was accompanied by an exhibit of art directors' paintings, sketches, and models on loan from other studios.

Walt made few pronouncements on the precise debt to Hollywood. Early on, he described Disneyland as a miniature film set and as based on "motion-picture creativeness."[39] In an essay published in 1965, he explained the analogy further: "In a sense, Disneyland is a stage—a most unusual stage. Members of the Disneyland audience, unlike the audience at a motion picture or a Broadway show, do not simply look on. They participate in the drama, the adventure or comedy. They walk onto the stage. They move through the sets. They touch the props. They examine the set dressings."[40]

Why was it important to make this connection public? One of Walt's goals was to provide a venue that would satisfy tourists coming west to visit Los Angeles. During the development phase, when he forecast that movies and TV shows would be filmed and broadcast at the park, he said, "Everybody appears to be curious about how movies are made."[41] His animation studio offered little excitement for the average tourist, and the big studios had closed their gates to the public since the advent of sound technology. Thus, the Magic Kingdom provided the backlot experience craved by millions of Americans who had fallen for the Tinseltown mystique, and the park's appeal extended beyond its creator's reputation as a producer of quality animation and live-action fare. The place might just as well have been called Hollywoodland. Indeed, the full name, Disneyland, U.S.A., is a variation on the common moniker Hollywood, U.S.A.

Publicity stressed the opportunities to see movie celebrities at leisure with their families. The studio system had been built in part on the manufacture of "stars" and a steady diet of gossip columns and fan magazines, which created a desire to see and meet fan favorites.[42] Nonetheless, the likelihood of seeing an actor at Hollywood and Vine, Schwab's Pharmacy, or on the fabled streets of Beverly Hills was nil. Actively lamenting the disappointment felt by tourists who could not find the hoped-for glitz, Walt considered an alternative.[43] As a drawing card, this feature of the park was touted from the time of the opening day telecast, when guests such as Frank Sinatra, Sammy Davis, Jr., and Danny Thomas were captured on camera enjoying themselves on various rides. Subsequently, a monthly round-up of famous faces, which extended beyond acting folk to world leaders, was actively publicized by the press department. The themed lands, moreover, offered up costumed staff (later appropriately called "cast members"), some of whom acted out specific scenarios, like Sheriff Lucky, who engaged in shootouts in Frontierland. "Hooray for Hollywood!" quickly shifted to "Hooray for Disneyland!"

Pursuing these ideas in greater depth, this book proposes the first systematic investigation of Disneyland's debt to the movies. My goal is to provide a fact- as opposed to a theory-based assessment of Disney's vision in relationship to filmmaking methods, founded on heretofore unexamined or underexplored documentation and reportage. My book engages with previous social and cultural histories, the most important being the foundational studies by Karal Ann Marling and Steven Watts and the subsequent publications of Deborah Philips, Lauren Rabinovitz, and Gary S. Cross and John K. Walton.[44] The calculated application of motion-picture narrative and movie-making methods to the Magic Kingdom's appearance and function is what really separates it from amusement-park precursors. Nor was this an accident. Disney was blessed with an innate gift for storytelling, a rare knack for story selection and—during pre-production of his classic films—editing, tweaking, and massaging stories once they were greenlighted.

Historians have erred in viewing narrative aspects of Disneyland exclusively as a by-product of Walt's own motion picture and television productions.[45] The Dumbo, Peter Pan, Mad Hatter Teacup, and Mr. Toad's Wild Ride attractions in Fantasyland neatly fit that narrow interpretation. But what about the Jungle Cruise in Adventureland, the Mark Twain riverboat in Frontierland, and Tomorrowland's Space Station X-1? They had no prior connection with any Disney film. By emphasizing the impact of non–Disney movies and set-design methods on the park's creation, my text comprises material that has never been presented before.

Furthermore, this book is unique in that, while acknowledging Walt as the all-knowing inventor of his pleasure ground, it shifts responsibility away from him to non–Disney sources and offers alternatives to the traditional biographical interpretation of the place (e.g., phrases like "Walt Disney recreated his own life's journey").[46] This is clear, for example, in the Main Street, U.S.A., chapter, where I challenge the widely-held belief that the street is based on Walt's boyhood home of Marceline, Missouri. Disneyland's themed attractions are steeped not just in his own oeuvre but also in distinct, pre-programmed narratives that movie-goers had grown accustomed to over the previous half-century. The various sectors are each founded on a familiar motion picture genre. Main Street, for instance, is a walk-through incarnation of a small-town film set. Frontierland plays off cinematic Westerns and Southern epics. The rocket ride in Tomorrowland brings science fiction pictures to life, and Fantasyland captures the spirit of fantasy pictures like *The Black Pirate* and *Knights of the Round Table* as well as *Snow White, Dumbo,* and *Alice in Wonderland.* My emphasis in no way undercuts Walt's brilliance in conceiving his fun park. Like all great artists, he had an uncanny ability to absorb and repurpose visual stimuli and to anticipate what his audience wanted.

As part of the studio system, the Big Eight developed cinema genres that supplied ready-made, time-tested templates for producers, directors, and writers, and what is more, saved money since the backdrops and back-lot settings they required could be reused ad infinitum. Audiences happily accepted genre-specific retreads built around a familiar plot, set in a familiar period, and starring a recurring cast—depending on which studio made which film. I also introduce the topic of authenticity: Disney-land publicity guaranteed visitors an "authentic" experience in the various lands, just as big-studio publicity touted Hollywood movies as authentic recreations of the past, even though the recreations were recycled stereotypes.

Expressing American Ideals

The thrust of this book is that Walt Disney conceived his pleasure ground as something different from the standard amusement park and hired skilled film set and sketch artists to create what was essentially a sprawling, walk-through backlot set. The net result was a gathering place that embodied the same mythic settings, meaningful narratives, and high-minded ideals commonly expressed on the silver screen. Blending nostalgia, optimism, and fantasy, this place is perhaps *the* quintessential example of American mythmaking.[47] Its realms and rides are deeply rooted in a system of cultural beliefs, values, and—yes—prejudices. For better or worse, there is a dark side to Disneyland. Along with everything that is warm and fuzzy and comforting about the dream park, it mirrored a postwar conviction that leisure, self-indulgence, and consumer spending are what the Pursuit of Happiness is all about.

Walt had helped his countrymen face and survive the Great Depression through the plucky can-do spirit of his iconic alter ego, Mickey Mouse, and the brave, selfless virtue and work ethic of the Seven Dwarfs.

A few short years later, however, during World War II, he started making propaganda films for the government and served as a cultural goodwill ambassador to South America. Disney the moviemaker assumed an ancillary role as part-time educator.[48] This new-found mission made its presence felt at Disneyland, which he called "above all, a place for people to find happiness and knowledge."[49] Steven Watts has summarized the creator's particular genius:

> Walt Disney operated not only as an entertainer but as a historical mediator. His creations helped Americans come to terms with the unsettling transformations of the twentieth century. This role was unintentional but decisive. Disney entertainment projects were consistently nourished by connections to mainstream culture—its esthetics, political ideology, social structure, economic framework, moral principles—as it took shape from the late 1920s through the late 1960s.[50]

In the mid–1950s, the park and its namesake TV show entertained and comforted both viewer and visitor and elevated "Uncle Walt" to the status of full-blown celebrity, a home-spun, avuncular family man and patriot soft selling mainstream bourgeois values.

Disneyland provided a blank canvas upon which its master builder could project his personal values and an apolitical but fundamentally conservative brand of Americanism. The *Disneyland* series gave Walt a soapbox from which he could proclaim his philosophy.[51] In late May 1957, during one of his frequent promotions on TV, he called it a monument to American ideals.[52] Six weeks later, he told Hedda Hopper that there was "an American theme behind the whole park."[53] During the ceremonial raising of the Stars and Stripes on opening day, Goodwin Knight, the Republican governor of California, voiced a like-minded strain of patriotism. Small wonder that the *New York Times* reported, "For some brief periods, the ceremonies took on the aspect of the dedication of a national shrine."[54] In the mid–1950s, a period in which fear of "the bomb" on the left and fear of the "Red Menace" on the right troubled millions of his compatriots, Walt Disney offered his core audience—the white middle class—a reassuring image of the past in the form of a tidied-up Western frontier and a sanitized small town from granddad's day and an optimistic vision of the future based on exploration of the new frontier of space.

During its Golden Age, Hollywood defined American myths for the public. In the twenty-first century, it is hard to imagine a time when watching a motion picture in a large theater was a shared communal experience. Families, in big cities especially, went to the movies as often as twice a week. Between 1915 and 1945, some four thousand of the great movie palaces sprang up in cities across the country, along with many more modest cinemas in outlying neighborhoods and small towns.[55] In the mid–1940s, the average weekly attendance was ninety million.[56] Projected on a giant screen, moving images exerted a powerful impact unequaled by still pictures on the printed page or paintings hung on the walls of a museum.

Moviemakers knew they had superseded revered authors, educators, historians, and churchmen as the principal curators and disseminators of national legend and mythology.[57] This brought with it the mantle of responsibility. Many producers, directors, and script writers understood that movies, notwithstanding their bottom-line commercial function as a popular entertainment, constituted a powerful medium for projecting shared civic ideals. Motion pictures promulgated a broad range of social and ideological messaging, aimed primarily at God-fearing middle-class adults and impressionable youth—stirring such things as patriotic fervor, devotion to kith and kin, and nostalgia for an Edenic past. The Jewish émigrés or their sons—Louis B. Mayer and others—who founded the big studios were frequently applauded as champions of America and the "self-evident truths" she stood for.

My argument in this book draws from a considerable body of published material about the film industry's role in shaping the national consciousness in the years leading up to and immediately following World War II—especially those studies that deal with set design. One historian rightly referred to movie sets in the Golden Age as "bell jars ... tightly sealed worlds" that stood in for a shared reality.[58] Those jars sprang to life, in living color, thirty miles southeast of Hollywood in Anaheim.

The men who helped their boss design Disneyland mined a celluloid tradition of pitching an often romanticized past and a rose-tinted, imagined future. By adopting sets, props, costumes, and themes typical of standard film genres, they added ready-made visual content to his park. As historian Vivian Sobchak put it, "Because these elements of visual content appear again and again in film after film, they have become visual conventions or icons, pictorial codes which are a graphic shorthand understood by both filmmaker and audience."[59] The goal was to bring past and future to life, reimagined as only Disney could. Reimagining America filtered through the lens of cinema, he retold in action-packed, three-dimensional form stories that were embedded in the nation's cultural heritage and thus received unquestioningly by the preponderance of his "guests."

This book is confined to the years of the park's gestation, 1948–1955, and its first twelve months of operation, beginning in July 1955, a time frame that reflects Disney's vision. Three writers have added immeasurably to our knowledge of this subject: Todd Pierce delved into Walt's relationship with C.V. Wood, Disneyland's first general manager; Jim Korkis profiled the artists and staff who collaborated in its creation; and Alastair

Dallas reimagined the challenges faced by Disney and his people along a reconstructed day-to-day timeline.[60]

In addition to the contributions of these three individuals, I have examined a wide variety of primary sources from this period. Some are well known, having been reproduced in books or posted online, but surprisingly few have been the object of sustained, comprehensive study. These sources include newspaper and magazine articles, television shows and motion pictures (online and on DVD), PR handouts, and souvenirs— supported by an abundance of film-history scholarship.[61] For example, the monthly souvenir newspaper sold on Main Street, *The Disneyland News*, has been overlooked as a valuable resource for firsthand commentary on the park's design and content in its early days.[62]

I also bring to the table an art-historical and socio-cultural perspective, applied to the park and to scores of feature-length and short films from Hollywood's Golden Age. This perspective, I believe, has enriched my reading of cinematic structures and images as they relate to Disney's "fabulous playground."

The Magic Kingdom was not solely a vacation spot or tourist destination. It was a place for ordinary people to gather, explore, and share their common cultural heritage as Americans—a legacy previously transmitted in many cases almost entirely via the silver screen. To paraphrase Gloria Swanson's immortal line in *Sunset Boulevard*, that legacy and its subtle, complex relationship with Disneyland may at long last be ready for its close-up.

Introduction

This book explores how, to what extent, and why Disneyland was shaped by the Big Eight American movie studios of Hollywood's Golden Age: Metro-Goldwyn-Mayer, Paramount, Twentieth Century–Fox, Warner Bros., RKO, Columbia, Universal, and United Artists.[1] I consider the Magic Kingdom's ties to filmdom's capital in the following five chapters, each of which is devoted to one of the park's sectors at the time of the July 1955 opening. But first, it is essential to clarify Walt Disney's relationship with these studios, both as a movie fan and as an independent producer in Hollywood. This chapter also defines the "Hollywood mystique" by considering its origins and what Tinseltown, more as an idea than as a place, meant to Disney and American audiences. Because this book proposes that the park was designed along the lines of a studio backlot, we must review the nature and function of the typical backlot, with an emphasis on the lots of two of the majors, Universal and MGM. The design of cinema sets was entrusted to art directors and sketch artists; thus, I include a brief review of their key positions in the production pipeline and the principles they followed. We will see that, despite the avowed emphasis on authenticity in film sets, soundstages and backlots routinely presented an alternative reality derived from established cinema genres. This is significant because, in creating park attractions, Walt's artists followed the studio art directors' lead in designing buildings and landscapes that mirrored the movies' contrived reality.

Walt and Hollywood

Walt Disney enjoyed enormous respect among his Hollywood peers for his colorful characters, cartoon shorts, full-length animations, and occasional live-action features, but he never attained the same level of respect as the men who presided over the Big Eight. Shortly before his death in December 1966, he was praised by an interviewer as "an artist, writer, businessman, inventor, naturalist, educator"—but not as a motion-picture producer.[2] In fact—as odd as it may seem today—during his lifetime the question arose repeatedly of exactly what he did as head of the business that bore his name. Looking back, we can see clearly that his role was that of producer—a very hands-on producer—intimately involved in the many aspects of his entertainment empire and continuously providing input and ideas in the various departments.[3]

In the mid–1950s he was busily overseeing a full slate of cartoons and live-action pictures, building Disneyland, and getting the *Disneyland* and *Mickey Mouse Club* television series off the ground.[4] He had become, in the words of one historian, "arguably the preeminent cultural impresario of postwar America."[5] But he never claimed that his job was comparable to that of the big studio bosses, and for good reason, perhaps. After all, he did not have to deal with high-maintenance, highly paid, flesh-and-blood film stars. As Alfred Hitchcock joked, "Walt Disney ... has the best casting. If *he* doesn't like an actor, he just tears him up."[6]

According to the veteran Hollywood reporter and Disney biographer Bob Thomas, when Walt was asked to produce the annual Academy Awards telecast, he refused. "I've never considered myself a big producer like Louis B. Mayer or Darryl F. Zanuck," he said. "I'm not in their class."[7] However, like David O. Selznick, he was an independent producer whose output, though relatively slight, was of exceedingly high quality and critically acclaimed.[8] He received a record twenty-six Academy Awards and fifty-nine nominations. In contrast, individuals working for MGM garnered countless Oscars over the years, but MGM's renowned chief, Louis B. Mayer, a co-founder of the Academy, received just one, an honorary award in 1951 for distinguished service to the industry.[9]

Despite—or because of—his aw-shucks, hayseed persona, Walt benefited from the goodwill, professional and personal, of colleagues and contacts in movieland's capital. For example, an MGM producer offered him the rights to Felix Salten's book *Bambi: A Life in the Woods*, thinking it more suitable as animation than live action. Disney and Samuel Goldwyn (a big admirer) even considered co-producing a Hans Christian Andersen biopic.

When he needed a director for live-action sequences in *The Reluctant Dragon*, Disney borrowed Alfred Werker from Fox. Mary Pickford wanted to team with Walt in a film version of *Alice in Wonderland*. And just as he liked to screen film classics in his home, Pickford and the studio bosses projected Disney's movies in theirs. Direct social interaction took several forms. Throughout the 1930s, Walt played polo with such Tinseltown royalty as Leslie Howard, Spencer Tracy, and Will Rogers, and during the war, guests at a party he arranged for the British author

Roald Dahl included Charlie Chaplin, Greer Garson, Dorothy Lamour, and Basil Rathbone.

One of the burdens that independent operators like Walt had to bear was total dependence on the majors for film distribution. In 1932 he signed a contract with the independent production company, United Artists—formed shortly after the end of World War I by Charlie Chaplin, Mary Pickford, Douglas Fairbanks, and D.W. Griffith—to distribute his Mickey Mouse and Silly Symphony cartoon shorts. Seeking wider release of his animated feature *Snow White and the Seven Dwarfs*, in 1936 he moved up a rung, aligning himself with RKO, a more powerful studio that had its own theater chain.[10] In 1948 the Disney brothers, Walt and Roy, weighed the possibility of entering a full partnership with RKO, and in 1952 Howard Hughes offered to sell the studio outright to them.[11] Instead, the following year, they organized their own distribution company, Buena Vista.

Although Walt is usually portrayed as a loner facing a unique set of problems in the late 1940s and early 1950s, they were the same problems his fellow studio heads faced: a decline in ticket sales after the war, rivalry from television, loss of income from British and European markets due to taxation and quota systems, rising production costs for labor and materials, a government antitrust lawsuit against monopolistic ownership of theater chains, and the intrusive terror of House Un-American Activities Committee hearings on Communism in the film industry. Disneyland Park was conceived at a time when Hollywood studios large and small were beset with tough challenges, and prospects for their survival were uncertain.

Among the movie chieftains he knew, Walt's professional life most closely paralleled that of his friend and fellow polo player, Darryl F. Zanuck, who had started in the business as a writer and production head at Warner's (from 1924 to 1933) and vice president in charge of production at Twentieth Century–Fox (1935 to 1956).[12] Disney was born in 1901, Zanuck in 1902, and in their late teens, both served in Europe during the Great War. Disney and Zanuck also were story men at heart, famed for their editing skills and ability to act out a story to win over skeptics at story meetings. They were pioneers in the introduction of sound—Zanuck for *The Jazz Singer*, Disney for *Steamboat Willie*. They developed pictures with Latin American themes to support the Good Neighbor Policy. In the 1950s, both sought to make the big screen even bigger for audiences: Zanuck introduced widescreen in the form of CinemaScope, and Walt was an innovator of 360-degree projection. Lastly, like other Hollywood moguls, Disney had an impressive corner office suite, located on the third floor of the Animation Building. It consisted, in fact, of two offices, a formal one for receiving guests and a private one intended as a workspace.

The latter was described by an outside observer as "furnished with divans and lounging chairs in gay colors, centered with a big coffee table which serves as a desk, and flanked on one side by the soda fountain with its soft pastel lights."[13] The suite had a separate bedroom (Walt often worked until late at night), but unlike Zanuck's suite, there was no casting couch.

The preponderance of film moguls during Hollywood's Golden Age were European Jews who embraced what they perceived as core American values and passionately promoted them in their pictures.[14] Disney and Zanuck likewise celebrated American ideals. But they were sons of the Heartland—Walt was born in Chicago and grew up in Missouri, Zanuck was from rural Nebraska—and they had an inbred feel for what average folks wanted. At the annual Golden Globes ceremony in 1954, Disney received the Cecil B. DeMille Award for "outstanding contributions to the world of entertainment." Fittingly, the following year, Walt presented the same award to Zanuck.

Disney not only made movies, but he was also a consumer of movies. Born in Chicago seven years after the invention of the motion-picture camera by the Lumière brothers, he "admitted," as one journalist put it, that he was a "dyed-in-the-wool movie fan from early childhood."[15] In fact, he and the motion-picture industry grew up together. In 1958, he recalled how he had witnessed films grow from "from a mystifying trick—an amusing plaything first known as 'the flickers'—to a great art-craft."[16]

In 1923, having failed to keep his first modest studio in Kansas City afloat, and convinced that he had entered the field too late—the animation industry then was centered in New York—he struck out for California, hoping eventually to become a live-action director. From the moment he got to Hollywood, he was seduced by its mystique. He explored the various lots and finagled entry into Universal, wandering the sets until late at night.[17] He also roamed the Warner, MGM, and Paramount lots. But the best he could do was win a role as a cowboy extra in a Western, and that modest gig was rained out.

In a letter dated June 1, 1924, to his buddy and fellow animator Ub Iwerks back in Kansas City, he thanked Ub for agreeing to join him out West. In a postscript, Walt enthused: "I wouldn't live in K.C. now if you gave me the place…. Hooray for Hollywood!"[18] Disney went on to build two studios that mirrored their larger counterparts: a makeshift Hyperion complex in the Los Feliz section of L.A., and, in 1939–1940, the Burbank facility. Industrial designer Kem Weber, who had worked as an art director at Paramount, conceived not just the buildings and "street plan" of the new campus, but the fittings and airline-style furniture inside them. From his early *Alice Comedies* and Mickey Mouse shorts through the feature-length cartoons of the late 1930s and 1940s, Walt consistently borrowed stories, themes, and cinematic techniques from live-action films. His state-of-the-art studio in Burbank possessed its very own theater, where non–Disney movies were screened for the staff as a kind of perk and for relaxation, but also to keep them up on the latest developments among the "big boys."

Walt made motion-picture history through his innovative adoption of new techniques in sound, color, and the use of storyboards. Whenever possible, he opted for quality. He engaged top-flight character actors for voice work, notably Billy Bletcher and Cliff Edwards. Bletcher's career dated to the silent era, with appearances in *Our Gang* and *Three Stooges* comedies. He and Disney staff writer/voice artist Pinto Colvig voiced the Munchkins in *The Wizard of Oz*, and Bletcher provided the spoken dialogue for Mickey's arch-nemesis Pegleg Pete and the Big Bad Wolf in *Three Little Pigs*. Cliff Edwards, a.k.a. "Ukulele Ike," a Missourian like Walt, was a former vaudevillian who had a hit recording of "Singin' in the Rain" in 1929, and also had a memorable supporting role as a wise-cracking reporter in the Cary Grant–Rosalind Russell screwball comedy *His Girl Friday* (1940). For Disney, Edwards voiced Jiminy Cricket in *Pinocchio* (1940), for which he recorded the Oscar-winning Disney anthem "When You Wish Upon a Star" that later served as the weekly musical intro to the *Disneyland* TV series.

Disney's animated shorts often owed an unabashed debt to live-action film stars. In the first Mickey Mouse cartoons, Mickey's roles were patterned after screen idols Buster Keaton (*Steamboat Willie*, 1928), Douglas Fairbanks (*The Gallopin' Gaucho*, 1928), and Charlie Chaplin (*The Barn Dance*, 1929). In *Mickey's Gala Premiere* (1933) the Mouse attends the star-studded premiere of one of his own cartoons at Grauman's Chinese Theatre. When Walt made his first feature-length cartoon, *Snow White and the Seven Dwarfs*, he stepped up his game by having footage shot of live actors or models as reference tools for the men assigned to animate the human characters. For his second "princess film," he had every scene in *Cinderella* involving human characters filmed in live action in advance of the animation, by pre-editing the story to keep costs down.

Walt's first feature film with live-action segments—*Fantasia* aside—was *The Reluctant Dragon* (1941), an informal tour of the Burbank studio. Live-action segments were an integral part of Disney's 1940s package films, including the Donald Duck and Mickey Mouse vehicles *Saludos Amigos* (1940), *Make Mine Music* (1946), and *Fun and Fancy Free* (1948). And of course, there was *Song of the South* (1946), the combination live-action/cartoon musical drama in which Uncle Remus, played by James Baskett, interacts with Br'er Rabbit and a cheerful animated bluebird.

In a bid for diversification, Walt added all-live-action features to his repertoire, beginning with *Treasure Island* (1950)—the first color

adaptation of the Robert Louis Stevenson novel—starring English actor
Robert Newton as Long John Silver. Walt's ambitions in the realm of live
action peaked with *20,000 Leagues Under the Sea* (1954), helmed for the
first time by a non–Disney director: Richard Fleischer, who went on to
direct *Doctor Dolittle*, *The Boston Strangler*, and *Tora! Tora! Tora! 20,000
Leagues* required collaboration with other studios for special effects and
use of soundstage facilities. The film's cast of James Mason, Kirk Douglas, Peter Lorre, and Paul Lukas was matched in star quality in the Disney canon only by Julie Andrews, Dick Van Dyke, and a stellar lineup of
supporting players—Glynis Johns, Ed Wynn, Arthur Treacher, Reginald
Owen, and Jane Darwell—in *Mary Poppins*, a decade later.

In short, despite his naysaying, Walt Disney functioned as a Hollywood producer who had close ties with the film community and kept a
sharp eye focused on filmland productions.

The Mystique of Hollywood

Disneyland's success depended on the spell Tinseltown had long cast
on the nation, along with Walt's three decades-long reputation as a master of family entertainment. An article published in the *New York Times*
three months before the Magic Kingdom opened its gates emphasized that
Hollywood was more of an idea than a locale, and, the *Times* said, the park
was the newest entity in that fabled imaginary space.[19] Thus we must consider here the origins and status of this unique dreamscape in relation to
Disney.

As studios moved west from the East Coast in the 1910s and 1920s,
their consolidation in the greater Los Angeles area, from downtown,
Edendale, and Westwood to Burbank, Glendale, and Culver City (on
the other side of the Hollywood Hills), gave rise to a proposal by actress
Louise Glaum that the words "Made in Los Angeles" should appear on
screen in every film created there.[20] Publicity generated by newspapers and
magazines established Hollywood as the focus of a glamorous mystique
characterized, as recent writers have observed, by "a gleam, an ethereal
artificiality, a magic that captivates by rendering its subject as unreal but
imbued with a golden luster."[21] By 1923, the year the original "Hollywoodland" sign was erected, the name Hollywood had supplanted Los Angeles
as the center of motion picture production in America.[22]

Popular magazines, like *Sunset*, *Scientific American*, and *Photoplay*,
piqued reader interest in the movies with abundant coverage of star celebrities and insider secrets on how pictures were made. *Ladies' Home Journal* posed the question, "Were you ever filled with the desire to go straight

through the screen and see just what is behind it ... just as Alice went through the looking-glass?"[23] Overheated prose like this, which purported to demystify the studio system, served instead to (intentionally) heighten curiosity among average folks in a fantastic world they might never see in person.

It is ironic, then, that four of the Big Eight were not physically located in Hollywood. In 1937, the chamber of commerce of Culver City, home to several studios, tried to steal the name "Hollywood," but was fended off by the real Hollywood.[24] A satirical piece in the *Los Angeles Times* argued, correctly, that the first studio founded in Hollywood was not built until one year after its incorporation into L.A.[25] But the mystique would not die. MGM, one of the Culver City complexes, flashed the line "Made in Hollywood, U.S.A." in the closing credits of its pictures from 1949 to 1958, among them, most famously, *An American in Paris*. The phrase did double duty: it bolstered the mystique of American moviemaking, and it pledged, for all the world to see, allegiance to the often-jingoistic Yankee ideals celebrated in its films.

The Rise of the Backlot

If, as I propose, Disneyland took its form from the backlot, then it is worth considering how this space, devoted to filming within studio walls, came about. The major studios occupied acres of real estate housing everything from administrative buildings, commissaries, dispensaries, and technical workshops to soundstages and standing sets simulating both contemporary and historical locations. In cinema's Golden Age, there were three basic options for filming: the interior stage, which afforded total control of light and sound; the backlot, a series of semi-permanent sets that assured relatively predictable outdoor conditions; and off-site locations, sometimes on studio-owned ranches, that provided the greatest authenticity whenever a natural setting was needed.[26] Executives preferred staying close to home and kept location shooting to a minimum for very sensible reasons: the cumbersome nature of sound and camera equipment, the cost of sending actors and crews out on location, and a desire to keep an eye and a firm hand on wayward directors.[27]

During location shooting in Missouri for the Fox picture *Jesse James* (1938), Zanuck sent an urgent message to director Henry King, forcefully arguing the advantages of filming within studio walls:

> After reviewing everything that has been shot to date, I am definitely convinced that the entire location trip was, to a great extent, a financial mistake.... There is nothing in the way of scenery or backgrounds that we could not have

photographed near here at far less expense and trouble. The Universal [Studio] Western Street or our own street could have served just as well as what I have seen on the screen and photographed twice as fast. The railroad station is very interesting and effective, but could have been built anywhere.... From here on, *we will duplicate and fake everything that we possibly can at the studio.*[28]

As early as 1925, when Disney was getting started, the Fox backlot contained, according to the *Los Angeles Times*, "a Western street, New England street, Spanish street, old English street, French ruin street, two haciendas, detached farm houses [and] a reproduction of Johnstown, Pa., as it appeared in 1889 when a great flood swept it into oblivion."[29] In 1950, an article in *American Artist* magazine described how the Fox lot had grown exponentially to include a couple of square miles not far from Beverly Hills (Fig. 2). The writer marveled at the way the dusty streets of a Western town led to a pristine New England square, and from there to a cobblestoned European village located next to the streets of New Orleans, Greenwich Village, and Chicago. Nearby lay an African jungle and the Everglades. These open-air sets could be changed almost overnight into places from a different country, time, or season.[30]

Disney animators paid tribute to these dream factory backlots in

Figure 2. Twentieth Century–Fox Studios. View looking south, early 1950s, with Santa Monica Boulevard in the foreground. Backlot sets and soundstages on the right (Photofest).

the hilarious 1936 short *The Autograph Hound*, in which Donald Duck—like Walt before him—crashes the gate of "Hollywood Studios" looking for film stars, and stumbles through an incongruous series of sets representing a New York City street, an ice-skating rink, the Egyptian desert, a Baghdad market, and the road to Mandalay. We will see in later chapters how this jumble of fake locales perfectly suited Walt's vision for his wonderland.

MGM, Queen of the Backlots

A major source of ideas for Disneyland's imaginary realms was MGM, whose backlot rivaled the others in size and design quality. Its origins lay in the earliest purpose-built complex, Ince/Triangle Studios, founded in 1915 by Thomas H. Ince, D.W. Griffith, and Mack Sennett.[31] A self-sufficient community, its Culver City backlot included a Dutch village complete with windmill and canal, an Irish village, Canadian stockades,

Figure 3. MGM Lot 3 at the intersection of Culver Boulevard and Overland Avenue. At far left Tarzan Lake, Small Town Square, and Andy Hardy Street. In center right, New York streets (Photofest).

Southern log cabins, and Sioux camps.[32] In 1921, the property was sold to Samuel Goldwyn, who immediately increased the size of the lot. Two years later, a *Los Angeles Times* photo spread was among the first to use the term "back lot" to describe Goldwyn's outdoor sets.[33]

In 1924, Metro-Goldwyn-Mayer acquired the Culver City property from Goldwyn. Ultimately, it comprised 175 acres, divided into sectors by city streets. The Irving Thalberg Building, which housed the administrative offices, was located on Lot 1, site of the former Ince Studio, along with sound stages, and the camera, prop, art, and research departments. Lot 2 featured the vast New York streets, Andy Hardy Street, an adjacent Small Town Square, plus various European and Asian districts (Fig. 3). Lot 3 had a man-made jungle, three Old West streets, and the most celebrated of all backlot sets, the nostalgic St. Louis Street. Four smaller satellite lots completed the group.[34] Continually remodeled by MGM for a string of movies, many of these generic locations—main street, town square, railroad station, jungle, Western town, medieval castle, among others—were in essence recreated at Disneyland.

Universal City as a Precursor of Disneyland

Founded as an unincorporated municipality forty years before Disneyland began operation, another early purpose-built motion picture lot was Universal City, which I propose may reasonably be seen as an ancestor of Walt's dream park. Before there was "Uncle Walt," there was "Uncle Carl"—Carl Laemmle, founder of Universal, who tended to the needs of his employees. Like Disneyland, Universal City was built on a 415-acre tract of agricultural land—in this case, barley—and like Walt's protective berm, which shut out the real world, Universal's exterior wall separated the marvels within from the San Fernando Valley without. Whether visitors passed through Universal's main gate or Disneyland's tunnel, either way they felt the awe of exclusivity. Contemporaries dismissed both projects as follies, but when they were proven wrong, they hailed Laemmle and Disney as visionaries. As his biographer put it, "When Carl Laemmle entered Universal City on that March morning in 1915, a magician entered wonderland"—a sentiment comparable to the plaudits heaped on Walt and his wonderland.[35]

Universal's inauguration in March 1915, attended by luminaries, dignitaries, and spectators—20,000 strong—established a Hollywood tradition of mobilizing massive crowds for PR purposes. One journalist called it "an event that can never again happen in the history of the world."[36] Disneyland's inaugural festivities, attended by Governor Goodwin Knight, co-hosted by a future president of the United States, Ronald Reagan, and broadcast over network television, certainly gave Universal's grand opening a run for its money. Roughly 28,000 guests attended, over half of whom had counterfeit tickets or scaled the berm.[37]

Universal City was one big movie set.[38] An article in the *Washington Herald*, "A City Built as a Background for Pictures," had this to say: "Every style of architecture that the world has produced is to be found in some street or house. Each of the four walls of every building is done in a different style of architecture," so that they could be dressed quickly for the next shoot. "All available wall space is utilized as a permanent background whenever possible.... Greek, Roman, Gothic, Byzantine, Tudor, Victorian and modern architecture are evident."[39] What's more, Universal had space left over for the huge standing medieval Paris set used to film the silent Lon Chaney epic *The Hunchback of Notre Dame* (1923), the first large-scale backlot city ever constructed.

Well before Disneyland, Universal had its own city hall, fire department, bank, post office, restaurants, waterfront, and Mississippi steamboat. Like Walt's park, it had a railroad (a specially constructed spur of the Southern Pacific), a tribe of Indigenous peoples, and a zoo stocked with lions, leopards, monkeys, and elephants.[40] (At first, Walt wanted to use wild African animals in Adventureland, but ultimately settled for mechanical versions.) In addition, like Disneyland, Universal was a teetotaler's paradise. As one press report put it: "Universal City is absolutely 'dry.' The sale of any liquor is prohibited, and no one is permitted to bring intoxicants upon the premises."[41]

Most important of all, to satisfy a demand for a genuine experience of watching motion pictures being made, Laemmle instituted the first public tour of any American or European studio.[42] The Universal tour allowed locals and tourists alike to peep behind the wizardly curtain of motion picture production.[43] Like spectators at a ball game, anyone with a quarter in his pocket could purchase a grandstand seat facing an actual movie set and cheer on the actors. An extra nickel bought a box chicken lunch. Small wonder the Universal tour became a major attraction for visitors to the West Coast, and a steady source of revenue and publicity.[44]

It was eliminated in the late 1920s, when sound filming demanded "quiet on the set." Spurred by the success of Disneyland, however, Universal-International revived the tour in 1956, albeit in a different format, as one of many sights on a Tanner Gray Line Motor Tour past Hollywood landmarks including the exterior of the Disney Studio in Burbank. Gray Line riders did not, however, have access to Universal's soundstages. At best they caught a glimpse of the backlot from a bus window. In a curious connection with Disneyland, though, a rare record of Universal's tour survives in home movies shot by one Robbins Barstow in July 1956. Barstow and his family had won a free trip to Disneyland as part of a nationwide contest sponsored by Scotch Tape. Visiting Universal the day before the Magic Kingdom, he fixed his camera on Universal's backlot sets, which, on film, were virtually interchangeable with the "sets" he shot at Disneyland. Both places boasted a castle, small-town street, town square, Western Street, and jungle. In short, the Universal studio, a "world that contained all other worlds"—that Walt had seen up close in person as far back as 1923—was the perfect template for Disneyland.[45]

Most studios kept their doors shut to tourists. But during the Golden Age, they cultivated their film-capital mystique on the silver screen. The silent theatrical short *MGM Studio Tour* (1925), for instance, is noteworthy for its early reveal of how movies made their way through the production pipeline, and, a generation later, the one-reeler *Hollywood Wonderland* (1947) toured the Warner Bros. lot.[46] Short theatrical releases promoted tourism, such as *Life in Hollywood* (1947), whose commentary featured these words: "Yes, there's lots to see and do in this wonderful city of Hollywood, a magnet drawing thousands upon thousands of people from all walks of life, … an endless movement of rhythmic feet toward the center of the world, Hollywood and Vine."[47] In the eleven-year period between 1928 and 1939, approximately sixty-five dramas, comedies, and musicals set in Tinseltown featured intimate, generally fanciful views of stars, stages, and backlots, and the word "Hollywood" figured in the title of nearly half of them.[48]

Disneyland was created by Walt partly to please the legion of fans eager to tour his cartoon factory. Over the years, he greeted a veritable Who's Who of celebrities, from Igor Stravinsky and the Regionalist painter Thomas Hart Benton to Eleanor Roosevelt—all eager to see how the place worked. He produced two filmed tours of the Hyperion studio and one of the Burbank campus. The first was shown to distributors of *Snow White and the Seven Dwarfs* (*A Trip Through the Walt Disney Studios*, 1937), to whet their appetites, and the second was a preview of *Snow White* for general audiences, *How Walt Disney Cartoons Are Made* (1938). The third Disney "tour film," *The Reluctant Dragon* (1941), tracked humorist Robert Benchley as he traipsed around the buildings in a whimsical search for Walt.

Walt regretted that his studio, which employed no live stars, had very little to offer the average visitor.[49] Disneyland, on the other hand, could provide a full backlot experience, complete with movie narratives, costumed "cast members," and the occasional glimpse of Walt himself or filmland celebs relaxing with their families. Pre-opening publicity claimed that the park "will resemble a giant motion-picture set" and "will serve as a permanent back lot [sic] for Disney productions."[50] The Hollywood connection all but guaranteed—to use a phrase from the trade paper *Variety*—that the Magic Kingdom would be a boffo success.

Art Direction

In hiring designers for his new park, Walt Disney quickly learned that professional architects were unable to interpret his ideas. Thus, from within his own company and from a few Hollywood studios he recruited art directors and sketch artists who could adapt time-tested methods of motion picture production to satisfy his needs. We shall meet these artists over the course of this book; for now, it is useful to survey the production model they practiced.[51]

In 1933 the *Los Angeles Times* interviewed Fox art director Max Parker, who made it clear he was *not* "an artist with a flowing tie who draws pretty pictures." On the contrary, an art director in Hollywood like himself, Parker explained, "is a trained architect and draughtsman, a mine of exact historical information, a specialist in the ... materials and paints, a practical engineer and a financial estimator all rolled into one. Besides all that he is the man who 'visualizes' the writer's story and the director's dramas before it is acted."[52]

The crucial role played by art directors was the focus of an August 1944 *Life* magazine article aptly titled "Movie Illusions: Hollywood Technicians Create Reality Inside Studio": "One reason for paying movie technicians five-figure salaries is their ability to bring the world onto a studio lot. Almost 90% of Hollywood's footage is shot inside sound stages against backgrounds cleverly compounded of wood, plaster, paint, and ingenious lighting. Expensive, time-consuming trips to the exotic corners of the U.S. and the world began to be a thing of the past even before the war made them impossible." The article emphasized that art directors "must be able to organize quickly, and fairly cheaply, the myriad details which go into the manufacture of a German town, an Alaska tundra or a fake submarine. For all these versatile abilities they are very highly paid."[53]

The advent of sound, introduction of bulky camera equipment, and need to precisely regulate temperature and light, had by the late 1930s obliged Hollywood to operate on-site almost exclusively. The sound-proof shooting stage and all-purpose backlot in close proximity offered maximum control over the many increasingly complex aspects of moviemaking. Art direction, as the September 1950 article in *American Artist* made clear, contributed mightily to the process. The author counted an average of ten art directors, five assistant art directors, five sketch artists, and forty draftsmen at each of the major studios.[54]

In an essay published a few years earlier, Cedric Gibbons, head of MGM's Art Department, explained what the role of all these "talents" was. He emphasized that a film's settings must support the story, convey aspects of the characters, tell the audience how to feel, and even take on the aspect of a character. The ideal, Gibbons said, "is *not* to build sets which will impress, but which will support and enhance the action and mood of the story. The audience should be aware of only one thing—that the settings harmonise with the atmosphere of the story and the type of character in it."[55] Along the same lines, a seven-minute short, *The Art Director* (1949), produced by the Academy of Motion Picture Arts and Sciences, explained to a general audience the stages in the development of sets, from the initial analysis of the script and inspirational sketches to the creation of scale models and preparation of blueprints.

Walt's people absorbed at least some of the holistic creative spirit evoked by Gibbons, and art directors had been hired by Disney even before the gestation of Disneyland. The distinguished British artist, book designer, and art director, Laurence Irving, who worked in Hollywood in the 1930s, recalled being "made welcome at Walt Disney's studio, where two accomplished designers who had worked with me on *The Iron Mask* were among the group of artists" Disney "had enlisted to make moving pictures in the true sense of the words." Irving mentioned David Hall by name, who painted the "lyrical forest backgrounds" for *Bambi*, and Harold Miles, who created "charming" interiors for *Pinocchio*.[56]

Process and Principles

The *American Artist* article explained the position of Fox art directors in the development of a film:

> When the finished script is turned over to the art department, the supervising art director and head of the department, Lyle Wheeler, reads it, probably makes a few notations, and assigns it to one of his art directors. After reading the script and discussing it with Wheeler and the director of the picture, the [unit] art director makes a series of small rough sketches (about 3 × 4 inches) visualizing scenes, sets, camera angles and lighting effects.... The roughs are turned over to sketch artists for elaboration.
>
> Studio sketch artists work closely with the art director. Some of them are painters of considerable ability and reputation who exhibit and win prizes in

national shows. Herbert Ryman, whose continuity sketches for *The Black Rose* are reproduced [in the article], has won awards for portraiture and watercolors.... They take the art director's roughs—which may be quite detailed in one case, very vague in another—and using them as guides, produce detailed drawings or paintings of each shot and sequence in the script as it is expected to appear on screen.[57]

Esteemed by art directors as a well-traveled man of the world, Herbert (Herb) Ryman was employed as a freelance artist at both Fox and Disney. In 1953 he was temporarily retired when out of the blue Walt asked him to draw the first *Aerial View of Disneyland*. That kicked off three decades of work by Ryman on special projects and concept art for the Disney parks.

Models and Miniatures

The article in *American Artist* reported on one other aspect of scene design. Prior to the construction of backdrops, studio woodworkers created small scale models of each set based on architectural plans and sketches approved by the art director. Fox employed five full-time model

Figure 4. Art director Carl Jules Weyl with a model of Nottingham Castle for Warner Bros.' *The Adventures of Robin Hood*, 1938 (Bison Archives and HollywoodHistoricPhotos.com).

makers.[58] Art directors, like Carl Jules Weyl at Warner Bros., would pose for publicity photos with these models (Fig. 4). In the same vein, Walt Disney would later pose with Disneyland attraction models.

Cedric Gibbons emphasized the usefulness of models during production:

> These models, built to a scale of about a quarter of an inch to the foot, would delight any child's heart. Every detail is included. Colours are applied, draperies are hung, furniture, rugs, and other miniature props are placed in their proper positions. This model is the centre of a final discussion between the producer, director, art directors, and other technicians involved. Suggestions or objections are made which could not possibly have been foreseen from the original drawing. When the final sets are constructed, therefore, no changes are ever necessary.[59]

Well before Disney moved into live-action film, his animators and background artists used models (produced initially in the Character Model Department) to help visualize characters and setting.

Sometimes miniature, reduced-scale buildings and landscapes were installed in the rear of a stage set. According to the 1944 *Life* article, "When Warner Bros. bought the rights to *The Doughgirls* it had no hesitancy about deciding to create a miniature Washington [D.C.] in the studio ... [with] well known structures like the Washington Monument and Jefferson Memorial."[60] "All Warner Bros. sets," same-size or reduced-scale, *Life* said, were crafted on-site,

> on the studio lot in a humming, 125,000 sq. ft., factory fitted out with hundreds of woodworking and machine tools, a forge, and a foundry. Here carpenters, painters and metalworkers turn out everything from submarines to period furniture with rapid and versatile craftsmanship. Working within time limits of two or three weeks for set construction they have become adept at short cuts, using cast plaster to simulate carved wood or marbleized wallpaper for a palace floor. Rocks for outdoor scenes are made from wood framing, chicken wire and plaster.[61]

In the following chapters we will see how Disney's artists adopted the Big Eight's techniques of visualizing attractions during the design process, first in drawings and sketches, and then in models. Even before it opened, Disneyland was famous for the reduced scale of its attractions. The press usually exaggerated the actual proportions, as in the *New York Times* notice: "Disneyland involves five fairyland 'worlds,' scaled to two-thirds normal size."[62] Walt himself cautioned, "Don't call 'em [the railroad trains] toys or miniatures. These are scale models, slightly reduced, of the real thing."[63] As we proceed, we too will differentiate between miniatures and models.

Authenticity and Research

The ultimate aim of film art direction was to devise an "invisible style" in which every detail created the illusion of verisimilitude and enhanced the narrative without calling attention to itself. This was a major consideration Disneyland's art directors shared with their motion picture peers. Early press releases stressed the park's realistic simulation of the American past. Few words, if any, appeared with greater frequency in Disneyland publicity than "authentic." The *Mark Twain* was an "authentically recreated paddle wheeler," Frontierland's stagecoaches were "identical to those used in the West prior to the coming of the railroads and automobiles." For dining, there was the "authentic gay nineties restaurant," the Red Wagon Inn, on the central Plaza.[64] Hollywood similarly used claims of authenticity as a marketing tool. As early as 1912, the ad campaign for *Custer's Last Fight* touted the months of research that went into producing a historically accurate movie.[65]

The key component was research. If a story had a historical theme, the first thing the art director did, according to Gibbons, was delve into the period: "Questions can be easily answered from the vast collection of research material, both in our own files and in those of the Studio Research Department, or from our previous experience with a picture of that era."[66] Each studio had a research department and library, with extensive files of indexed material, and staff able to field questions from producers, directors, and prop men regarding period details.[67] Louis van den Ecker, who began his career in 1923 as a technical advisor at Paramount, described the facilities at the Big Eight during Hollywood's Golden Age: "The pursuit of authenticity begins with the research libraries maintained by all the major studios. Some of these contain as many as 30,000 books and bound magazines, files of clippings, photographs, and drawings, and extensive card indexes of illustrative material appearing in periodicals. The staff of a research library includes from ten to twenty permanent employees, most of whom are trained librarians."[68] Disney built up its own research library starting in the mid–1930s, for use by story men, animators, and staff, who, if need be, consulted materials at other studios as well.

Realism also depended on careful prop selection. According to Gibbons: "As soon as the set is assembled, the prop man begins to 'dress' it. He has previously made a careful study of the script, and, in the case of period pictures, has done enough research to ensure that the props used will be absolutely authentic. It may have been necessary for him to send abroad for certain pieces, to borrow them from museums, or, in the case of props no longer in existence, to have them built in the studio cabinet shop."[69] A single specialist acted as prop man for Disneyland, Emile Kuri, who had established himself in the business before he was hired by Walt for the live-action *20,000 Leagues Under the Sea* and then moved to the Disneyland unit.

Tricks of the Trade

Ironically, as studios strove for ever more authentic cinematic storytelling and realism, they withdrew from the real world to the artificial realm of the soundstage and the backlot. Indeed, one of classical Hollywood's triumphs was its mastery of heightened verisimilitude through an abstraction of the real world, rendered plausible by progressively sophisticated filming and editing techniques.

Although most designers strove for veracity, total authenticity was impossible—and besides, the literal copying of models was not always desirable or necessary. The camera lens has a limited field of vision and perceives objects differently from the human eye.[70] It cannot register "real world" effects of scale, proportion, or height. So, art directors and set designers devised a range of illusionistic gimmicks or tricks of the trade.[71] Film-set or backlot architecture is fragmentary and, in many cases, one-dimensional, limited to what is seen onscreen. It is usually smaller than life-size—and upper floors of buildings needn't be human scale or enclose actual interior space. Gibbons (once more) remarked on the unique skills of his staff: "We have developed a corps of skilled technicians who, in the space of a few hours, can build a cottage and 'age' it so that it will appear to have stood for centuries. Or a ship, or a jungle, or whatever we may need."[72]

William Cameron Menzies, production designer for *Gone with the Wind*, discussed another trick: "Texture is a rather interesting subject. All our straight plaster structures are cast in sheets nailed to a frame, and then pointed or patched with plaster. Brick, slate roofs, stone work, and even aged and rotted wood are casts taken from the original thing, made in sheets and applied."[73] The use of perspectival foreshortening— or forced perspective—was common in sets intended to give a sense of depth, as noted by one commentator: "For *The Yearling* (1946) Gibbons and Paul Groesse perfectly combined exteriors shot in the Florida Everglades with sets they constructed in Culver City, some of which filled the sound stages from wall to wall and had to be built in diminishing 3-dimensional perspective."[74] In an article titled "Hollywood Sets Would Fool Mother Nature: Scenic Experts Make Land, Sea, and Sky Look More Realistic Than Reality," columnist Hedda Hopper cited a wonderful example of how heightened realism in motion pictures was obtained. The leaves in the forest of the Shirley Temple fantasy, *The Blue Bird*, Hopper wrote, "are real but they're sprayed with a mixture of glue to keep them from shedding, varnish to give them highlights and artificial color for a prettier panoramic picture. Oddly enough, the cost of a studio tree is twice that of a real one, but they can be altered and moved at whim."[75]

Not all films call for strict authenticity, and many possess their own unique form of reality. Production designer Ken Adam (*Goldfinger, Dr. Strangelove*), commenting on one of the classics of the Golden Age, said, "One thing that I think works in *Casablanca* and which I've lectured a lot about—in terms of what I've been trying to achieve as a designer—is the film's creation of its own form of reality ... in departing from actual reality.... And in a strange way, that's what happened in *Casablanca*. Having been to Casablanca, I can say that it is nothing like that. But! It suited the atmosphere of the film, because you are carried away by it, and it seems absolutely right in terms of the story."[76]

In 1965, five years after Cedric Gibbons's death, George P. Erengis explained how Gibbons's historical settings for the Leslie Howard–Norma Shearer version of *Romeo and Juliet* (1936) were created:

> No actual Veronese square was reproduced on the backlot, no particular Italian garden was transplanted shrub by stone, no exact wall or street was duplicated. Instead, there was stylization and elements of Capulet-Montague Verona were simplified, clarified, and intensified, and the reproduced corridors, vaulted ceilings, colonnades and archways, the grillwork, casements, and balconies, were all correct in spirit. The results, although disparaged in some quarters as being "too MGM-ish," worked.[77]

The same illusionistic principles were applied—and were successful—at Disneyland. One of the most remarkable things about the park's design is that the art directors employed these tricks of the trade not only to simulate a backlot environment that was originally created to suit the eye of the movie camera, but also to produce a charming and whimsical "Disneyfied reality" that would please the eye of the park guest.

A New Reality

The establishment of canonical movie genres, coupled with a uniform visual shorthand in storytelling and revolving-door reuse of stage sets and backlot sets, expedited production and fattened the corporate bottom line. Working within tight budgetary and time constraints imposed from on high, art directors in Hollywood created hyperreal versions of reality via recurring tropes and myths that audiences accepted—or, in any event, did not reject—as real.[78] The Western, jungle adventure, historical drama, and biopic were particularly susceptible to standardization. These cinematic constructs, however artificial, threw open an instructive picture window onto a rich array of history and material culture from times gone by. By 1950, books be damned! The average American's take on famous people, castles, fortresses, the Wild West, tropical jungles, and space travel very likely came from motion pictures. The pre-conceived notions and expectations that audiences had about these things were part and parcel of the mental baggage they brought to Disneyland.

Once again, fortune smiled upon Walt Disney, as it did repeatedly over the course of his career. The languishing of the studio system circa 1953 freed up many talented art directors. Just as the Big Eight were trimming their workforce, Walt needed artists who could meet the challenges posed by walk-through themed entertainment. Unsurprisingly, his coterie of new hires followed the hierarchical organization and established modes of production developed during Hollywood's Golden Age. Walt loved movies and knew as well as anyone how they were made. But the deceptive spatial and backlot effects required to make Disneyland unique might have been impossible to attain without the skilled professionals whose services he engaged to make it happen.

1

Main Street, U.S.A.

Main Street, U.S.A., endures as one of Walt Disney's most innovative and influential creations (Fig. 5). Main Street lacks the word "land" in its name, thus differentiating it from the other themed realms of Disneyland. Walt was especially fond of this microcosmic recreation of small-town life, circa 1890–1910, which, he once said, represented the "heartline of America."[1]

I disagree with latter-day critics who characterize the street as primarily a commercial corridor.[2] Main Street is, to be sure, packed with tempting places for people to spend their money. In the early going, income generated by the businesses lining its sidewalks helped to finance the park.[3] But its core raison d'être is not mercenary. Just two city blocks long, Main Street serves as a gentle transition—quaint, cute, and cozy—from the "real" world beyond the berm to the larger, action-packed realms of fantasy, adventure, and science fanning out from its end point at the central Plaza. In addition, in 1955 it greeted both young and old visitors with an environment perceived as representing a simpler, happier period in our history.[4] The reduced scale and colorful, old-timey shops exude a sense of playfulness and a subliminal sense that the visitor is "in control."

When it was created in the mid–1950s, Main Street stood in marked contrast to the country's declining city centers and Topsy-like suburban growth.[5] In the words of Richard Francaviglia, its "archetypal and shared" look and feel, on the cusp between the gaslight era and the advent of electricity, satisfied a deep "nostalgic longing."[6] Presented as a less troubled, bygone age, its pavements reaffirmed basic middle-American ideals. At the same time, children, less aware of this nostalgic past, were entranced by the unique opportunities for play and exploration afforded, often at no cost, in the shops and arcades.[7]

Literature on Disneyland repeatedly expresses the notion of Main Street as an autobiographical evocation of the main street of Marceline, Missouri, Walt's boyhood home. From 1906 to 1911, the Disney family lived on a farm a mile and half north of the town and then briefly within the

Figure 5. Main Street, U.S.A., Disneyland, Anaheim, California. View north-
ward toward the Plaza and Sleeping Beauty Castle. Vesey Walker leads the Disneyland Band. Publicity still, *Disneyland, U.S.A.* (*People and Places*, 1956)
(author's collection).

town. I counter this prevailing point of view by showing that this connection has been the product of the Disneyland publicity department. Before
1955 Walt revealed no deep feelings about Marceline's main thoroughfare.
Disney did not invent the idea of Main Street, of course, and since the turn
of the twentieth century a firm tradition in theater, literature, popular
magazines, postcards, paintings, and photographs had celebrated downtown corridors.[8]

I show, however, that Hollywood's conception of Main Street, as
it appears in movies of the classical period, had a crucial impact on the
park's designers. Constructed and filmed on studio backlots close by the
Disney operation in Burbank, these faux streets exerted a greater influence
on Walt's walk-through march down memory lane than any faint recollections he had of Marceline.

What is significant is Walt's timing. He conceived Main Street,
U.S.A., just as post-war suburban growth was hastening the decline of the
traditional civic spirit that had prevailed prior to World War I.[9] In the late
1980s, Griffin Smith, Jr., remarked that small towns were still remembered
"as places of contentment and stability ... places where people had a sense

of common purpose and shared values." Small-town America had peaked in 1910, Griffin wrote, when nearly 20 percent of the nation lived in communities of fewer than 10,000 residents.

By 1940, over half the populace lived in urban communities of more than 50,000.[10] After World War II, the numbers rose higher, as Americans left the small towns. Suburban life ushered in a new era of family self-sufficiency, leisure, dependence on the automobile, and conspicuous consumption. Neither the cities nor the suburbs possessed the sense of community provided by the small town with its walkable streets.

Thus, Disney's Main Street shone like a beacon for the values expressed in small-town-themed movies made by directors like Preston Sturges and Frank Capra. The Main Street, U.S.A., formula was not only repeated in Disney parks in Orlando, Tokyo, and Paris, but it also contributed to the revitalization of real-life Main Streets across America, many of which had fallen into relative ruin by mid-century—their beautiful brick façades boarded over in ghastly attempts at modernization. This country-wide interest in restoration still stands as one of Walt's greatest legacies.[11]

Disneyland's Main Street resonated with visitors because the old-timey narratives played out there—in the soda fountain, the bank, the music store, and elsewhere—were familiar cinematic tropes.[12] The theme-park visitor, surrounded by cast members costumed as Keystone Kops, a barbershop quartet, or a saleswoman of ladies' undergarments, was transported not so much back to 1900 as to the Golden Age of Hollywood. Disney designers used the vocabulary of the movie set to produce key markers throughout the street, from building types to signage, that conveyed a wealth of meaning to the movie-going public about the values and ideals embodied by small-town America. Disney hired costume designer Renié Conley, formerly of RKO and Twentieth Century–Fox, to create the themed apparel worn by park staff.[13]

Consideration in this chapter of how Main Street functions in long shot, close-up, and social context in several representative movies from these years provides insight into Disney's design choices and reveals specific visual tricks borrowed from the repertoire of motion-picture set-design techniques. In addition, a look at several fully realized street sets on Hollywood backlots from the years preceding Disney's Main Street offers a framework for interpreting ideas embedded in the park's entryway.

An Authentic Small Town

Disneyland's Main Street, U.S.A., has always signified more than a commercial street. The original plans for this sector called for five elements to be experienced sequentially: a Train Station, Town Square, Main Street proper, Plaza (or Hub), and a Residential Neighborhood. Together these would make up a complete albeit tiny, small town. The Residential Neighborhood was never built, but its presence was always implied. By 1955, in ordinary parlance, the phrase "Main Street" defined not just the "main drag" of a town but also the concept of a small or medium-size urban community. In a sense, adding "U.S.A." to the name was redundant since Main Street was already a global symbol for the United States. For example, in the MGM war-time propaganda short *Main Street Today* (1944), the words operate metaphorically, insofar as the film urges all citizens to contribute to the war effort, regardless of gender, class, or race. Disney could just as easily have named his "main drag" "Small Town, U.S.A." or "Every Town, U.S.A."

Three articles in the first issue of *The Disneyland News* (July 1955) made claims for the authentic nature of the sector. The first, titled "Complete American Small Town of 1900 Era Reproduced Here," asserted that Main Street faithfully duplicated every type of building or store prevalent in a turn-of-the-century village.[14] The second, "Main Street Is Historic Replica," emphasized not only the authenticity of the design, but the educational potential for visitors who had never experienced actual small-town life.[15] The third article, a guest editorial, focused on the nostalgia evoked by the multitude of details, like the clanging of the horse-drawn street trolley, which brought back vivid memories of the town the writer recalled from his youth.[16] To be sure, the seeming authenticity was compromised to some degree by the lessees of the shops, modern businesses that contributed financially to the park while benefiting from their presence. As we will see in this chapter, notions of authenticity were further tempered by a reliance on Hollywood set design in the creation of the street.

Walt's designers carefully calibrated the layout of distinct spaces along the park's principal avenue. Visitors entering pass through the gate and beneath the Victorian-style station of the Santa Fe and Disneyland Railroad. Although most photographic views of Main Street are directed north toward the Castle, the Train Station, high up on the berm, forms an imposing backdrop when seen looking back from the street (Fig. 6).

Once inside the park, visitors immediately find themselves in Town Square, flanked in the initial year of operation by the Police Station, Town Hall, Fire Station, and Bekins Van and Storage on one side, and by a Bank of America office, Town Square Realty, the Opera House, Show Business in Disneyland, and Maxwell House Coffee House on the other. The Town Hall, Police Station, and bank—traditional components of civic plazas— suggest stability, order, and cohesiveness.

Figure 6. Main Street, U.S.A., Disneyland. View southward toward Town Square and Main Street Station. To the left, the Swift Market House and a horseless carriage. August 1958 (author's collection via Michael Sumrell).

The Town Square is the springboard for Main Street's axial corridor bordered by replicas of small-town American commercial buildings. It is intersected by Center Street, half-way down its short two-block length. The buildings on the west side, starting, in order, at Town Square, originally housed the Emporium, Crystal Arcade, Upjohn Pharmacy, Carnation Ice Cream Parlor, Sunnyview Farms, Puffin Bake Shop, Penny Arcade, Candy Palace, and Coca Cola Refreshment Corner. On the east side stood the Wurlitzer Music Hall, Wonderland Music Company, Fine Tobacco, Main Street Cinema, Jewelry Store, Yale and Towne Lock Shop, Swift Market House, Gibson Greeting Card Shop, Ellen's Gift Shop, Blue Bird Shoes, Kodak Camera Center, Timex Clock Shop, Grandma's Baby Shop, Intimate Apparel, Ruggles China and Glass, and the (fictive) Plaza Hotel and Apartments.[17] The resulting aggregation of businesses was surprisingly akin to a real Main Street.

The merchants, in cooperation with WED, the Disneyland design organization, strove to create a vintage atmosphere on the interiors. For example, the Upjohn Pharmacy was a veritable museum, allotting minimal space to the company's current products. According to early PR, company personnel had scoured numerous cities nationwide to amass over a thousand antiques for display in authentically recreated display cases.[18]

The chief historical element lacking was a soda fountain, but the neighboring Carnation Ice Cream Parlor supplied that amenity.

At the end of the street lies another public square, the Plaza, from which the themed "lands" radiate, and beyond the Plaza, the storybook towers of Sleeping Beauty Castle. The castle is the "wienie," in Walt's parlance, that entices the spectator down the street through the themed narrative of Main Street.[19] Although usually characterized as a point of transition, the Plaza, with its trees, benches, and lawns, completes the small-town ideal by doubling as the public park—a place to sit down, rest, meet family members, or indulge in a sweet treat.

Main Street as Spectacle

Main Street America has always been a place of spectacle. In Nathanial Hawthorne's short story "Main-Street" (1849), a showman unrolls a scenic panorama of a street as he recounts the history of the town's denizens.[20] A century later, Hollywood envisioned Main Street as a stage set, a background against which the lives of its citizens would be played out. Similarly, visitors at Disneyland could commingle with cast members to revisit the past.

Although designed chiefly for pedestrians, over the years Main Street has accommodated light traffic ranging from horse-drawn trolleys, surreys, and a fire wagon, to horseless carriages and a double-tiered omnibus. At certain times of day costumed performers enliven the setting in the form of a barbershop quartet or an organ grinder with a monkey, while the alluring aroma of fresh pastries and cookies wafts from the bakeshop.[21]

A significant aural element was provided by the Disneyland Band, which invoked a feeling of the Good Old Days by performing regularly in the street and around the Hub.[22] Old-time music also emanated from the Wonderland Music Store, where visitors could purchase sheet music in the "Disneyland Main Street Series" and sing to the accompaniment of a large collection of vintage piano rolls. Mechanical instruments, such as the Welte orchestrion in the Penny Arcade, with its automated pipes and drums, further enhanced the ambiance. Taking a cue from Hollywood, early projects put forward the idea of a soundtrack. Although not carried out, thought was given to installing hidden tape recordings suitable to the street's second floor businesses, such as the sounds of a music lesson or a dentist drilling.[23]

On special occasions visitors became costumed performers. For the first Easter celebration in 1956, guests donned historic costumes from a private collection to participate in Main Street's first Easter Parade. They were joined by members of the Southern California Horseless Carriage Club who drove down the street in their vintage cars, all dating from around 1900 to 1915.[24]

Early Concepts

How did Walt Disney conceive Main Street? It is well known that his artists researched a number of amusement parks and recreated historical towns, from Knott's Berry Farm in Buena Park, California, to Coney Island in New York. A few buildings were loosely based on specific prototypes. A former sketch artist and set designer at Warner Bros., and one of the first artists to propose designs for Disneyland's Main Street, Harper Goff, sought inspiration for Walt's Town Hall from the City Hall in Goff's hometown, Fort Collins, Colorado.[25]

The source most discussed by historians is Marceline's principal commercial thoroughfare, Kansas Street. Richard Francaviglia calls Main Street "an autobiographical statement by Disney himself,'" and Karal Ann Marling suggests that "all of Disneyland is Walt Disney, but the most personal, idiosyncratic part of the autobiography written there in buildings, streets, and sidewalks is Main Street, U.S.A."[26] Steven Watts describes it as "nearly a replica, although highly idealized, of Marceline's main street, as photographs of the latter make clear."[27] But in truth old photographs of the town portray a very different, grittier reality: a broad, unpaved muddy road cluttered with utility poles, raised wooden sidewalks, and plain street fronts.[28]

In a letter published under his name in the *Marceline News* in 1938 Walt himself initiated the mythologizing of his childhood that would remain constant throughout his life. "I'm glad I'm a small town boy and I'm glad Marceline was my town," he (or, more likely, a hireling writer) said—even though he was much more of a big-city boy, having grown up in Chicago and Kansas City. In the letter in the *Marceline News*, Walt fondly recalled his adventures on the farm—but similar details of the town and its main street are lacking.[29] He did not make a return trip to Marceline until 1946.[30]

It also should be remembered that big cities have their neighborhood main streets as well, and Walt may have recalled Fullerton Avenue in Chicago (near the family home on Tripp Avenue) and Prospect Avenue in Kansas City (near the Disney home on Bellefontaine Avenue).

The Marceline connection with Main Street dates back to the inaugural days in July 1955, when a *Look* magazine writer, already defining Disneyland as autobiographical, commented, without specifically referencing

Marceline, "Here is a replica of Main Street in a small American town as Walt remembers it from his childhood."[31] One year later Diane Disney Miller and her co-author Pete Martin, in the serialized *Saturday Evening Post* biography "My Dad, Walt Disney," evoked the same relationship, based on her father's fond accounts of the family's Missouri farm: "I suspect that Main Street in Disneyland is his dreamlike re-creation of Marceline's main stem as he remembers it."[32] That same year, Walt traveled back to Marceline to dedicate the Walt Disney Municipal Park named in his honor. However, in 1956 he confessed to the syndicated columnist Hedda Hopper that he didn't "remember much about the town."[33]

Furthermore, early guidebooks, such as the one published in 1964, two years before his death, make no mention of Marceline.[34] Harper Goff, when later asked whether Main Street was based on Marceline, swiftly debunked the myth: "Well, that's a good story."[35]

Without denying the role played by these much-discussed sources, it is useful to search for Main Street's origins by returning to Walt's earliest projects for a theme park. The initial written evidence for an amusement park, the internal Memorandum drawn up in August 1948 for a Mickey Mouse Park, shortly after his trip with Ward Kimball to the Chicago Railroad Fair and Henry Ford's Greenfield Village in Michigan, called for a Main Village, a Western Village, and a Carnival Section. The first of these was described as a small town built around a village green, close to a rail station, with civic monuments like a town hall, fire and police stations, a post office, and a combined movie/opera house. Disney also included a list of potential stores, such as a pharmacy with a soda fountain, clothing, music, and magic shops, and a restaurant.[36]

The earliest conceptual drawings, dating from 1951, for a venue located on a parcel of land across Riverside Drive from the Disney Burbank studio, included a small town with a main street adjacent to a train depot, the whole rendered in a modest, clapboard style.[37] Seeking approval from the Burbank Board of Parks and Recreation in March 1952, Walt referred to this sector as a turn-of-the-century Midwestern town.

In a detail overlooked by historians, the *Burbank Daily Review* indicated that the planned kiddieland would also incorporate "a complete television center, with theater, stages, sets, and technical equipment."[38] In short, early in the development process the Disneyland prototype was conceived like a studio backlot. Whereas other major Hollywood studios already had working backlots, some on occasion open to the public in the form of a guided tour, as in the case of Universal Studios, Disney was not yet producing live-action films on the Burbank lot, and the animation facility was not considered a viable tourist attraction.

Once the Burbank site was rejected, the backlot tour concept was kept in place for the new Anaheim location chosen in August 1953.[39] When Disney joined forces with ABC in March 1954 to produce the *Disneyland* TV series in exchange for assistance with funding, together they informed the public that "the Disneyland amusement park is an ambitious project, which would serve two purposes—as a film production center and as a tourist attraction for which admission would be charged."[40]

When the Anaheim site was announced publicly on May 2, 1954, the *New York Times* reported that the future park "will resemble a giant motion-picture set" and function as "the principle center of the weekly one-hour TV show."[41] In its April 18, 1955, issue *Newsweek* reported that "the park, containing three-dimensional records of every idea Disney ever had, will plug all other Disney enterprises and will serve as a permanent back lot for Disney productions as well."[42] Similarly, *Woman's Home Companion* called the site "a living set for television.... When it's finished, you'll be able to visit this TV set. You will enter on 'Mainstreet' [sic]."[43] As it turned out, a few months after the opening, ABC announced that it would broadcast a daily half-hour radio show, *Walt Disney's Magic Kingdom*, from the park, but only in 1962 was a production facility constructed behind the Opera House façade.[44]

Throughout the various early phases of the project, the small-town element remained a constant. Walt envisioned a small town as a kind of portal or prologue to the park comprising the above-mentioned five successive elements—the train station, town square, main street, city park, and residential district. The idea was to recreate a familiar pattern experienced over the preceding first half of the century by most Americans, for whom a visit to a small town consisted of arrival by train and movement through the downtown to their destination, a neighborhood home.

Perhaps because train travel is now largely outdated, discussion of the Main Street Station has tended to focus on its position as the park's frontispiece, experienced chiefly upon arrival from the outside and as a stopping-off point on the peripheral berm, rather than as an integral part of Main Street itself. However, prior to World War II, small towns were most easily accessible by train, and many of them (Marceline included) were built as service points for the railways.[45] In considering Disneyland's rail line, writers invariably focus on Walt's hobby of model railroading, but it is equally important to regard the station as integral to Main Street—formally, spatially, and conceptually.

The planned residential section was likewise intended as an integral element of Main Street. Concept drawings in 1953 by Dale Hennesy and Harper Goff depict a neighborhood area at the end of Main Street with grand houses conceived in the Second-Empire style.[46] Four of these houses, with their elegant mansard roofs, face the Plaza in the famous

Aerial View of Disneyland drawn by Herb Ryman in September 1953 to accompany the pitch kit Roy Disney took to New York.[47] Other than as an intrinsic part of Disney's small town, it is hard to imagine how these houses might have functioned, though brief consideration was given to using some of them as guest accommodations.[48]

Although envisioned, these homes were never built. Later, one grand house materialized as the Haunted Mansion in a new "land," New Orleans Square, planning for which began in 1957. Additionally, a project conceived in 1957, Edison Square, a turn-of-the-century cul-de-sac of urban row houses to be located off Main Street, went unrealized. By conceptually reuniting the five elements comprising the path into the park as originally conceived, we can define the relationships between Main Street and Hollywood's portrayal of small towns in terms of both the particulars of set design and broader issues of content.

The Small-Town Film

Analogies between Disneyland's small-town sector and set design appear throughout the literature. For example, Marling has said, "Main Street is a movie set, a section of backlot foolery." Her emphasis, however, is on the notion that the visitor enters a fictitious place scripted like a movie or a TV show, where *The Walt Disney Story* is playing.[49] Indeed, the connections with cinema are often phrased in terms of Main Street being "like a movie," through the use of devices such as narration, continuity, and cross-dissolves.[50] Yet scant attention is paid to Main Street's relationship to the genre of the main-street film.

Walt Disney's choice of the small town as an American archetype was by no means original. His interest is related to Hollywood's depiction of small towns in the movies, described by Emanuel Levy as "a permanent staple of the American cinema from the very beginning. Their preeminence has derived from their prevalence in other cultural forms: books, short stories, and stage plays."[51]

Like Disney, producers and directors chose this subject as the locus of essential American values symbolized by the flag on the village green, the family home, the civic center, and locally owned businesses.[52] The movies rejected the Main Street of Sinclair Lewis's novel (1920), a provincial backwater and site of small-mindedness, in favor of a more positive image, one that represented social harmony and timeless virtues. The small-town film enjoyed success during the war and postwar years because its nostalgic evocation of the family unit confirmed America's place in the world.

Among over 160 movies from the 1930s and 1940s that involve aspects of the genre, I have chosen representative examples to demonstrate how elements of the American small town, both in isolation and in relation to each other, typically function in film.[53] They appear in a variety of ways: as a backlot set, as a flat backdrop on a soundstage, or as a real-life locale. Sometimes they are not visible at all but are referenced through dialogue. The point is that through set design and staging, Hollywood created archetypes of the small town that came to stand for a shared reality. The various tropes and forms would later reverberate during the creation of Disneyland's small town.

The classic small-town movie, *Our Town* of 1940, was shot on a sound stage to maintain the abstract and universal content of Thornton Wilder's play (1938), admired by Walt Disney.[54] The principal thoroughfare of the fictional Grover's Corners, New Hampshire, is little more than a backdrop painting seen in an extreme long shot in the opening frames of the film. But its importance to the town and its relationship to the railway and residential neighborhoods are immediately indicated by the Stage Manager/ Mr. Morgan (played by Frank Craven), addressing the audience directly: "Running right through the middle of town is Main Street. Cutting across Main Street on the left is the railroad tracks...."

Mr. Morgan makes the point that residents can tell the time by the arrival of the trains. "Next to the post office is the town hall; jail's in the basement.... It's a nice town, know what I mean? ... Along Main Street there's a row of stores with hitching posts and horse blocks in front of 'em. The first automobile is going to come along in about five years." In other words, the film covers approximately the same idyllic period, 1901 to 1913, as the period represented by Disneyland's Main Street, where both horse-drawn and motorized vehicles exist side by side.

In *Our Town*, Main Street also appears in close-up, notably in the form of the drugstore, where George and Emily (William Holden and Martha Scott) drink strawberry ice-cream sodas while Mr. Morgan laments the arrival of the new gas-powered traffic: "I'm telling you, you have to look both ways before crossing Main Street these days.... I can remember a day when a dog could [lie] on Main Street all day long without anything to disturb him." Typically in small-town pictures, the drugstore is the chief meeting place for people of all ages.[55]

In the opening monologue the Stage Manager also identifies the steeples of all the churches of various denominations. There was a church in an early concept sketch for Disneyland drawn by Harper Goff (c. 1952–53), and a "Little Church around the Corner" appears at the end of the crossing street in Herb Ryman's 1953 schematic aerial view.[56] However, deeply skeptical of organized religion, Walt evidently decided there was no visible place for God in his Edenic but secular "happy place."[57] For that matter, churches in small-town films operated less as houses of worship than as places for community interaction. Relatively few scenes take place in a church, and those that do often emphasize socializing and gossip, or the culmination of a romance in the bonds of matrimony.[58]

In the RKO movie *Alice Adams* (1935) starring Katharine Hepburn, two key scenes take place on a nameless main street. Instead of an establishing shot as in *Our Town,* the street is shown in a succession of close-up details of shop fronts. Street signage is used to convey information to the audience, quickly and silently, regarding the setting and the conflict faced by the title character. In the opening shot the banner draped across the street announces the name and age of the small town: "75th Jubilee Year: South Renford, the Town with a Future." Next, the camera moves in close-up from left to right across the names of three main-street businesses: "South Renford News, Circulation 5000," "Vogue Smart Shop," and "Samuels 5–10–15 ¢ Store."

The following medium shot encapsulates Alice's desire for upward mobility as she exits through the open glass doors of the five-and-dime store, whose cheap trinkets are all she can afford, to the closed, forbidding front of the Vogue dress shop, representing the elite but restricted world to which she aspires. The camera moves further to the left to Nashio Florist, where the flowers are too expensive (the word "corsages" on the front acts as a verbal cue to the narrative). Later, when Alice returns to main street to seek a job at Frincke's Business College, the flight of eighteen steps emblazoned with names of blue-collar occupations contrasts with the front of the nearby barber shop and shoe-shine chair occupied by Arthur (Fred MacMurray), emblematic of his position in leisured society (Fig. 7).

Class restrictions notwithstanding, the special character of the American downtown is its embrace of all classes of society. A short stroll takes the couple into the residential neighborhood, past grand elegant homes to her "little place." In *Alice Adams*, even the smallest details of Main Street, as Disney understood, serve as useful means of conveying telling features of the American experience.

Shadow of a Doubt (1943), Alfred Hitchcock's personal favorite among his body of films, was shot mostly on location in Santa Rosa, California, population roughly 13,000. Santa Rosa was chosen due to war-time restrictions on set-building. One historian, however, has claimed that a studio backlot set would have looked more authentic than the real thing with its random disorder and overload of detail—an argument many art directors would have readily endorsed.[59] In typical big city vs. small town fashion, the movie—co-written by Thornton Wilder—opens with a dull, grayish sequence in a seedy rooming house in Philadelphia, set to the strains of Franz Lehar's *Merry Widow* waltz. The action then shifts to the

Figure 7. *Alice Adams* **(1937, RKO). Katharine Hepburn (Alice) and Fred Mac-Murray (Arthur) during filming on an RKO set (RKO/Kobal/Shutterstock).**

sunlit imagery of Santa Rosa's charming downtown, focusing on a traffic cop, whose repeated appearance on screen symbolizes small-town stability and order.

Early in the narrative, Santa Rosa is cast as the center of good invaded by evil as depicted by Uncle Charlie (Joseph Cotton), who arrives at the local train station, having come from Philadelphia. The station appears again at the end of the film, with Charlie's forced exit from town and the climactic struggle on the train itself. Thus, the station is a pivotal element within the small town, operating as the point of connection between the closed world of domesticity and the larger world outside. Uncle Charlie underlines the importance of the residential district in his farewell speech: "But I want you all to know that I will always think of this lovely town. It's a place of hospitality, kindness, and homes—*homes*." In his early vision for Disneyland, Walt, like Hitchcock, combined key elements of the small town in complementary roles.

Sometimes, when Main Street is physically absent from a small-town film, a line of dialogue conjures up its essence, as in Frank Capra's *Mr. Deeds Goes to Town* (1936). Deeds and Babe (Gary Cooper and Jean

Arthur) commiserate on a park bench in the midst of a corrupt New York City, talking of how they miss their respective birthplaces. "I'm from a small town too, you know," she says, "probably as small as Mandrake Falls. Oh, it's a beautiful little town too. A row of poplar trees right along Main Street. Always smells as if it just had a bath. I've often thought of going back."

The residential area of Deeds' hometown is seen from the windows of his house; automobiles and horse-drawn carriages are both visible outside on the street.[60] The train station as usual denotes the juncture between big city and countryside. It is the point of arrival for the city slickers and the point of departure for Deeds, who never wanted to leave in the first place ("I don't think we have any suitcases!"). In other words, *Mr. Deeds* and other films of the period, produced on Disney's own turf in Hollywood, Burbank, or Universal City, used images of the small town to depict the same American cultural values that Walt, a child of the very end of the Victorian age and a survivor of the Great Depression, sought to affirm in Disneyland.

Techniques of Art Direction

As a Hollywood producer, Disney was familiar with the ideal of small-town life that was a recurrent theme in American movies. He also knew the studio backlots where fictitious towns stood alongside Western and medieval sets. These lots comprised a kind of proto-Disneyland. Their false fronts and assorted exotic locations, often packed into a single site, offered him a ready-made vision of what he hoped to achieve in Anaheim. Disney's backlot mentality is evident not only in his aim to broadcast television shows from the park but in his naive desire to build the attractions cheaply, like stage sets—not realizing that public building codes would drive up the cost of construction.[61]

The big-studio pipeline for creating movie sets (as described in the Introduction) provided a template for Disneyland's art directors in building Main Street. They followed the established system, from library research and conceptual drawings to cardboard models and construction blueprints. The contributing designers were illustrators, continuity sketch artists, and architects formerly employed at the major studios: Harper Goff (Warner Bros.); Herb Ryman, Marvin Davis, Dick Irvine and Sam McKim (Twentieth Century–Fox); and Wade Rubottom and Harry McAfee (MGM).[62]

An article in the September 1955 issue of *The Disneyland News* attributes the overall design of Main Street to Rubottom, a former associate art director whose credits include *The Women, The Philadelphia Story,* and *The Shop Around the Corner.* He came on board WED, the creative unit, in November 1954. The *Disneyland News* article cites his membership in the Society of Motion Picture Art Directors, and quotes him saying, "Designing Main Street was much like doing a set for a motion picture."[63]

The main goal, Rubottom said, was to create the flavor of an American small town with numerous realistic touches to help develop a narrative. Lighting posed a particular problem. Old-time shop interiors featured low lighting from vintage fixtures, whereas both movie sets and modern commercial interiors required brilliant lighting. Rubottom solved this dilemma by incorporating old-fashioned fixtures with concealed and indirect lights. The demands of the site required flexibility, as in the case of the Plaza Pavilion Restaurant, a "two-faced" building. It gave onto the Hub on one side and Adventureland on the other, necessitating a subtle transition from Americana to Polynesia.

The initial design stage required research comparable to that for a movie, with the help not only of the Disney studio library, but other movie studio resources as well. Concept drawings led to the creation of a scale model. In fact, the first three-dimensional glimpse of the Disneyland theme park—shown to the world during the premiere of the *Disneyland* TV program eight months before the opening—was of the model of Main Street, photographed close-up in a tracking shot accompanied by sound effects to convey the sensation of moving down the street.[64]

From the playbook of set design these artists borrowed numerous tricks.[65] Forced perspective is the single technique used at the park to receive much comment from writers. The scale of architectural sets in movies rarely matched the scale of their counterparts in the real world. For reasons of economy, fake buildings were usually constructed smaller than normal, with the understanding that on film such differences were not noticeable. Upper floors were progressively smaller than lower floors, an effect that registers on film as greater height.[66] Like a movie set, therefore, the structures on Main Street are smaller than they would be in real life, and the upper floors proportionally compressed compared to those below. The lower floors are approximately nine-tenths their "true" size, the second floors eight-tenths, and the third floors seven-tenths.[67] There was no single rule regarding scale throughout Disneyland, but contemporary publications consistently made broad statements about the downsizing.[68] Walt Disney himself claimed that every element of Main Street, U.S.A., was five-eighths actual size—which was certainly not the case. More important, however, he interpreted the reduced scale as an effort at playfulness, to give the street the aspect of a toy, and to reflect in the spectator's imagination the less grown-up world of an earlier generation.[69]

Furthermore, stage sets for movies are invariably fragmentary—only what will be seen by the camera is fully finished. This procedure was partly the result of spatial and budgetary limitations. Likewise, on Main Street, only those areas that are visible to the spectator are decorated in period style. Roofing, second floor interiors, and backstage areas are not. Some of the doors are fixed and cannot be opened, and upper-floor window trimmings disguise storage areas.

Once inside a storefront, the visitor can move from one shop to the next without going outside. Inner walls were eliminated, similar to the way moveable walls on a film set allow the camera to shoot the actors with greater freedom. Just as materials used for sets, like plaster and canvas, are often inexpensive but visually convincing alternatives to masonry and brick, on Main Street a new substance, fiberglass—strong, cheap, and lightweight—fools the eye in much of the detailing.[70] The successful illusion created by a new type of fake brick called Quikbrik for the façades prompted The Disneyland News to publish a corrective in its third issue. In response to a request from the bricklayers' union, the paper informed the public that numerous types of *real* brick were in fact used in construction, giving as examples the foundations of the Red Wagon Inn and the Plaza Pavilion on the Hub.[71]

Movie architecture is an exaggeration of reality. Unlike the human eye, the camera lens cannot differentiate between what is important and what is not, and being monocular, it tends to flatten things. The creators of Main Street took a cue from the art of set design, in which certain elements, like the edges of windows and doors, are emphasized to give a more accurate impression, and textures are intensified for the sake of contrast. The celebrated art director William Cameron Menzies said that if you are filming on location, "like a picturesque European street, you can achieve an exact reproduction—but that will still be minus the atmosphere, texture, and color. So it is always better to replace it with a set which gives the *impression* of the street as it exists in your mind, slightly romanticized, simplified, and overly textured."[72]

Architectural detailing in movie sets—doors, window surrounds, columns, balustrades, railings, etc.—is normally composed of recycled rather than newly built materials, not just to save money but also in the interest of "getting it right." Much of the detailing on Main Street sets consisted of "props" salvaged from other films. Disney PR people consistently boasted about the treasure hunt across America to acquire period artifacts, from lighting fixtures and wrought-iron cresting to "street furniture" like hitching posts, benches, and the century-old, cast-iron gas lampposts that illuminated Main Street, purchased from three different cities, all in order to satisfy Walt's passion for authenticity.[73]

Upon hearing that a Gay Nineties–era mansion in the ritzy St. James district in L.A. was slated for demolition, Disneyland's props man Emile Kuri and a crew salvaged many pieces, from ornate woodwork to leaded glass. Architectural fragments ended up in Main Street's contribution to fine dining, the Red Wagon Inn, which offered complete dinners from $1.65 in a setting advertised as an actual restaurant from the fin-de-siè-cle Gilded Age: "Gay memories become glamorous realities in the air conditioned Red Wagon Inn."[74] Kuri had enjoyed a distinguished career as Hollywood set decorator, having worked on such films as *Spellbound*, *It's a Wonderful Life*, and *Shane*; he received Oscars for *The Heiress* and *20,000 Leagues Under the Sea*, his first picture for Disney. He continued as set decorator with the Disney live-action films, including *Mary Poppins*.[75]

Color was another element of studio set design that tended to be unnaturalistic to compensate for distortions imposed by lighting and the camera. For example, paler colors on upper stories give the illusion of height. Set designers also used a subjective palette to enhance the mood of a scene. Walt Disney fully understood the impact of color. A pioneer in color film, he was approached by the Technicolor company for exclusive use of the three-strip process, first appearing in his Oscar-winning *Silly Symphony* short, *Flowers and Trees* (1932), thus giving him a competitive edge over other cartoon studios.[76] He knew that color ensured greater realism, provided emphasis, and most important, added a strong emotional component. Thus, during the design of Main Street, Walt himself supervised the development and use of a palette with a range of over two hundred custom colors, stronger and more varied than anything seen on any "flesh and blood" Main Street of 1900.[77]

Finally, as in *Alice Adams* on film, physical signage served to identify businesses all along Main Street. In addition, over time, employee names were stenciled on upper-floor windows to celebrate their service to the company or the part they played in Walt's life. Walt's designers credit him with an acute sensitivity to the potential impact of words, type fonts, and graphics; he was familiar, they said, with every sign, large or small, throughout the park.[78]

The architecture of set design in Hollywood was intended to enhance the actions of the characters, support the storyline, and trigger an emotional response consistent with the story. In much the same way, Walt's men at WED rearranged the particularities of their street "set" to create an idealized version of a Main Street that never existed, thus striking a dramatic or nostalgic chord and encouraging strolling and shopping.

The Small Town on the Hollywood Backlot

Aside from passing commentary, writings on Disneyland have not given serious consideration to the small-town backlot sets that preceded and influenced Disney's Main Street. Close examination of several examples will illuminate design choices later taken at the Magic Kingdom.

One of the more identifiable of their number was a small-town set on the Paramount Ranch, northwest of Los Angeles, which also boasted a frontier town, American and European urban backgrounds, and various outdoor locations. The town set was called Tom Sawyer Street after the David O. Selznick production starring Tommy Kelly filmed there in 1937. In Selznick's screwball comedy of the same year, *Nothing Sacred*, the set acts as the fictional town of Warsaw, Vermont, to which the leading man (Frederick March) travels from New York via train. Extensive views of the street are also visible in *The Arkansas Traveler* (1938), in which an itinerant printer (Bob Burns) arriving by train saves a small-town paper by exposing the duplicity of a wealthy local. Numerous horse buggies and

Figure 8. Tom Sawyer Street, Paramount Ranch, dressed for *The Arkansas Traveler* (1938, Paramount) (Bison Archives and HollywoodHistoric Photos.com).

automobiles may be seen cruising down the street. As at Grover's Corners, the locals can tell the time by the train whistles. An early title card and dialogue throughout the movie argue for the superiority of life in the small town over the big city (Fig. 8).

This small-town set was updated for two Preston Sturges films, *The Miracle of Morgan's Creek* (1944; art dir. Hans Dreier and Ernst Fegté) and *Hail the Conquering Hero* (1944; art dir. Haldane Douglas and Hans Dreier). According to legend, Sturges wrote the script for *Morgan's Creek* specifically to save the charming set from demolition.[79] The same downtown buildings and their defining signage can be seen in the two films. The most elaborately counterfeited structures are the Regent movie theater, with its neon marquee, and the pharmacy, whose awning, neon sign, and wooden placards advertise everything from drug prescriptions and cigars to sodas and candies. Although the narrative is set in the present, *The Miracle of Morgan's Creek* derives much of its ambience from the presence of both horse-drawn and fuel-powered vehicles on the street.[80]

The Main Street set was one block long, with six to eight businesses on each side. Transverse streets blocked the axis at the ends. Thus, in *The Miracle of Morgan's Creek* the *Bugle* newspaper office and adjacent fire department terminate one vista, as may be observed in the scene where Trudy (Betty Hutton) drives Norville's car over the curb in front of the Regent Theater. For *Hail the Conquering Hero* these buildings were replaced by the façade of a large white clapboard church forming the backdrop of the march of the citizenry down Main Street in the movie's climax. Their destination is the train station lining the cross street on the opposite end, similar to the transverse position of the Main Street Station at Disneyland. It is at the station that a group of uniformed Marines, who alter the life of the little town, arrive early in *Conquering Hero* and depart at the end. Station exteriors were created on a soundstage.

Significantly, Sturges employed long tracking shots to reveal the relationship between Main Street and the residential sectors on either side. For example, in *Morgan's Creek*, Trudy and Norville (Eddie Bracken) converse while strolling from a picturesque neighborhood of middle-class homes to the downtown cinema in an uninterrupted shot lasting four minutes—a technical feat at the time. In *Hail the Conquering Hero* Libby and Forrest (Ella Raines and Bill Edwards) walk from downtown to her house in a lengthy two-minute shot. The director used the fluid camera movement across the set to present an integrated picture of the characters' hometown environment, and to convey the idea that the town is small enough to be traversed on foot. The fact that it is the same set in both movies is unimportant. Like Disney, Sturges' goal was to create an illusion of the typical American town whose size allows all of the inhabitants to know each other and develop a strong sense of community. The extraordinary, comic events that beset the protagonists are played against the good humor and eccentric behavior of the small-town citizens.

The best-known Hollywood Main Street is Genesee Street in Frank Capra's *It's a Wonderful Life* of 1946, which used parts of an earlier set named Modern Street on the RKO ranch in Encino, California (art dir. Jack Okey; Fig. 9). Shown through all four seasons, the street, with its tree-lined median, is the centerpiece of the utopian town of Bedford Falls, New York.[81] Other scenes take place at the train station and in a charming residential neighborhood. The film opens in 1919, with the usual visual cue in the first minute of the horse-drawn carriage vs. the automobile moving down the street. Stretching three blocks, Genesee Street was comparable to Disneyland's Main Street in length and its use of forced perspective. Seventeen of the twenty-seven generic businesses and institutions facing the street—from the bank and police station to the bakery and emporium—would also line Disney's Main Street.[82] Some of the shops, such

Figure 9. Modern Street, RKO Encino Ranch, c. 1934, also called Cimarron Street, before being dressed as Genesee Street in Bedford Falls, New York, in *It's a Wonderful Life* (1948, Liberty Films) (Bison Archives and HollywoodHistoricPhotos.com).

as Gower Drugs and the World Luggage and Sporting Goods Store, were fully outfitted and filmed behind the façades. Capra's props man, Emile Kuri, would later perform the same job at Disneyland. Capra treated the street as one of the characters, especially in the transformation from the welcoming thoroughfare of Bedford Falls to the main drag of Pottersville, a dystopian nightmare of bars, dance halls, and strip joints lit by menacing neon signage.

Walt Disney and Frank Capra shared a populist point of view and an old-fashioned code of conduct. Capra paid homage to Disney in several movies. In *It Happened One Night* (1934) Clark Gable sings "Who's Afraid of the Big Bad Wolf?"; in *You Can't Take It with You* (1938) James Stewart evokes a fantasy world by referencing Walt Disney's name, and the basement inventors toil to the sound of "Whistle While You Work." Their friendship became a partnership when Walt, deeply engaged in making propaganda films for the war effort, provided animated footage for Capra's *Why We Fight* series in 1942–43.[83] Capra spent time on the Disney Studio lot, and it is tempting to think that a few years later Walt may have visited the Bedford Falls set, located only ten miles to the west. Perhaps that is why the marquee of the Bijou Theater on Genesee Street heralds a Donald Duck cartoon!

MGM's Small Towns

MGM's small-town set was located on the eastern side of Lot 2. The centerpiece—Andy Hardy Street, also called New England Street—was a residential neighborhood composed of a row of private houses (Fig. 3). Much used, the street appeared in such films as *Father of the Bride* (1950) and *Small Town Girl* (1953), and in the *Dr. Kildare* TV series. Immediately adjacent, Small Town Square consisted of a line of commercial buildings and a small lawn that might accommodate such props as benches and a flagpole. The square could be dressed to suit narratives set in any period from the eighteenth century on. MGM built three train stations of different sizes nearby, connected by rail tracks. Located between Andy Hardy Street and Small Town Square, the Small Town Railroad Depot witnessed the repeated comings and goings of characters in a variety of films. A smaller station—Railroad Terminal #2, located on the south side of Hardy Street—represented a small, rural station. The railroad tracks converged on a third, larger, big-city station set, dubbed Grand Central Station.[84]

These backlot locations, combined with soundstage interiors, comprised the world of Carvel, the hometown of Andy Hardy in one of the most successful series of small-town movies—fifteen films released between 1937 and 1946. The domestic interaction of the characters was acted out in homes along Andy Hardy Street, but conflicts and plot development took place at Small Town Square, typically in the Carvel Drug Company, where Andy and Betsy (Mickey Rooney and Judy Garland) enjoyed ice cream sodas.

Metro mogul Louis B. Mayer personally oversaw the series.[85] Head of the studio from 1924 to 1951, Mayer impacted output in a way comparable to that exercised by Walt Disney at his studio. A Russian who emigrated with his family at an early age, Mayer grew up on the second floor of a commercial building—literally on Main Street in Saint John, New Brunswick. Like Walt, he endured a difficult childhood, involving rigorous work and physical abuse. Like Walt he formed a vision of solid American virtues and left his personal stamp on MGM's small-town films. "He did this," in the words of Neal Gabler, "by fashioning a vast, compelling national fantasy out of his dreams and out of the basic tenets of his own dogmatic faith—a belief in virtue, in the bulwark of family, in the merits of loyalty, in the soundness of tradition, in America itself."[86]

Mickey Rooney confirmed the crucial role played by set design in Mayer's films. "Creating this … utopia was all part of L.B. Mayer's master plan to reinvent America," Rooney said. "In most of his movies… Mr. Mayer knew that he was 'confecting, not reflecting' America…. He wanted values to be instilled in the country and knew how influential films could be." His pictures "helped Mr. Mayer cast a spell on America, on its values and attitudes and images."[87]

Mayer approved construction on Lot 3 of a second residential street, called St. Louis Street. This was the locus of director Vincente Minnelli's 1944 picture, *Meet Me in St. Louis* (art dir. Lemuel Ayers, Cedric Gibbons, and Jack Martin Smith; Fig. 1.10). Developed by celebrated MGM producer Arthur Freed, the film was based on the *New Yorker* stories by Sally Benson, a co-writer for *Shadow of a Doubt*. Despite St. Louis's status as a city, the director emphasized that he treated the setting as a slice of small-town Americana.

Central to the story is the question of whether the Smith family must leave its quiet, provincial existence and move to New York, where everybody is "cooped up in a tenement."[88] In fact, whereas almost all previous movie musicals glamorized the big city or the theater, only a handful had focused on small-town life. The original plan was to dress up the Andy Hardy Street, but Minnelli's vision called for creating from scratch a spectacular street graced with grandiose Victorian houses better suited to the early 1900s.[89] He considered the Smith house and Kensington Avenue to be characters in the movie on a par with the actors.[90] Within a few opening seconds of the film, the requisite contrast between horse drawn vehicles and automobiles makes its appearance on the street.

The Second-Empire style of the Smith house, with its sloping mansard roofs, blocky towers, asymmetrical massing, and ironwork cresting, had been used in movies before. But Minnelli revitalized the look, partly through the set-design tricks of exaggerated color and scale, for which he is justifiably famous. The house also exemplifies forced perspective: although the side walls were quite shallow, on film they come across as steeply foreshortened.

Meet Me in St. Louis was Minnelli's first color film, and it defined the palette of the movie musical in the same way that Disney had influenced color cartoons in his *Flowers and Trees*. (Both were shot in Technicolor.) Each of the four seasonal sections of the movie opens with a view of the house and street transformed from an old-fashioned black-and-white still photo into a dazzling, multi-hued moving image, particularly vivid with the contrast of the white clapboard and red roof tile repeated in the candy-cane-striped awnings. As mentioned above, Disney's artists chose the

Figure 10. *Meet Me in St. Louis* (1944, MGM). Vincente Minnelli, standing on a camera crane, lower right, directs a sequence on St. Louis Street on MGM's Lot 3 (Bison Archives and HollywoodHistoricPhotos.com).

Second-Empire style for the large houses proposed (but never built) facing the Plaza. It is a style that gave magnificence, authority, and a touch of French sophistication to three key structures ultimately built at Disneyland: the Main Street Station, City Hall, and the Emporium.[91] Additionally, the original ornate décor inside several Main Street shops, with their sparkling crystal and ornamental bric-a-brac, were conceived in the Gilded Age mode of the richly detailed interiors of *Meet Me in St. Louis.*

Minnelli's film is one of several Hollywood productions that rode the 1940s wave of nostalgia for a more innocent time and place. MGM contributed many of these films, such as the Garland musical *In the Good Old Summertime* (1949), set in turn-of-the-century Chicago, but with views of St. Louis Street. The Freed Unit used the *Meet Me in St. Louis* template for *Summer Holiday* (1948), a musical retelling of the Eugene O'Neill play set in a small Connecticut town, *Ah Wilderness!* As in *Meet Me in St. Louis,* the family in *Ah Wilderness!* is introduced on screen to the tune of "Our Home Town," composed by Harry Warren and Ralph Blane, a song that might well have served as the anthem for all small-town movies. Mickey Rooney plays Richard Mills, the middle son, in the film, not without irony, since the house inhabited by the Mills family had been his "home" on Andy Hardy Street.

Nostalgia at Fox and Warner Bros.

Meanwhile, at Twentieth Century–Fox, studio boss Darryl F. Zanuck was also drawn to Midwestern themes. Like Disney, Zanuck was a storyteller who shaped movies at both the script and editing stages. All three moguls—Mayer, Disney, Zanuck—were self-professed lovers of "corn"—sentimental stories that taught basic American values.[92] Zanuck's penchant for nostalgic turn-of-the-century stories led critics to label the studio "19th Century-Fox." Like Walt, Zanuck was the product of a Midwest upbringing, in this case Nebraska. From the 1930s through the early 1950s he produced multiple pictures focused on the family unit in a pastoral setting, many of them Technicolor musicals. The Fox studio's backyard sets—New England Street and Square, Midwestern Street, and Train Station—accommodated these films.[93] In *Mother Wore Tights* (1947) traveling vaudevillians, played by Betty Grable and Dan Dailey, sing "Kokomo, Indiana," another paean to small-town virtues. One of Zanuck's last films in the genre, *Wait Till the Sun Shines, Nellie* of 1952, laments the decline of rural life.[94]

Warner Bros. followed the *St. Louis* template in family dramas like *Life with Father* (1947), featuring lavish Victorian interiors rivaling those of Minnelli. As late as 1953, as Disneyland was being envisioned, Warner released the Technicolor musical *By the Light of the Silvery Moon,* in which Leon Ames (Doris Day's on-screen befuddled father) repeats his performance as Garland's befuddled father in *Meet Me in St. Louis.* The interior sets again recall those of Minnelli, but instead of building the house exterior on a backlot set comparable to St. Louis Street, art directors chose the inexpensive trick of a matte painting of the family residence, partially obscured under the opening credits. Gordon MacRae, as Bill Sherman returning from World War I, sings yet another tune praising small-town life: "My Home Town Is a One-Horse Town (But It's Big Enough for Me)."[95]

Disney's Movie Main Streets

In the late 1940s Walt Disney had only begun to make live-action movies, but the film often cited as a personal favorite, *So Dear to My Heart* of 1948, includes an early version of Main Street, U.S.A., set in the year 1903 (art dir. John Ewing). The movie's make-believe locale, a small Indiana town called Fulton Corners, was built on location near Porterville, California, north of Los Angeles. The view from the train station encompasses a dirt street leading to the main street bordered by Grundy's Mercantile Store, the Feed Store, a blacksmith shop, and a structure whose bell tower signals a schoolhouse or, more likely, a church.

The characters never inhabit this street—it was a simple mock-up serving as a background. They do, however, enter the Grundy shop. Because of limited space at the studio, an actual interior was constructed behind the store front. The shops at Disneyland would similarly consist of real spaces behind what were in essence false fronts. Remarkably, the set designers found an old, closed-up hardware store in Porterville and purchased its entire inventory for use as historic props.[96] The train in the movie, No. 99 of the Evansville and Indianapolis Railroad, was a vintage engine rented from Paramount that Walt hoped to reuse in Disneyland along with the rail-station set, patterned after a real depot back east. After completion of the film, he gave the set to animator and train buff Ward Kimball but later wanted it back to use at the park. At that point, Kimball had invested too much energy into turning the set into a real building. Thus, a new design for the Frontierland Train Station was prepared, based on the set for *So Dear to My Heart* and its historical model.[97]

Disney also created turn-of-the-century small towns in his cartoon shorts and feature-length animation. In *The Nifty Nineties* (1941), Mickey and Minnie Mouse cavort in period dress to the sounds of a barbershop quartet. One month before the opening of Disneyland, the studio premiered its first CinemaScope feature cartoon, *Lady and the Tramp*. Tramp resides on Main Street and sleeps at the railroad depot, while Lady lives in a neighborhood like St. Louis Street. A true American melting pot, the town features a notable number of immigrants, to judge from the dialects of the dogs and cats and the offerings of the downtown eateries, most famously Tony's Italian restaurant. Tramp may yearn to escape from the strictures of a dog collar and the provincial town, but ultimately, he finds bliss at home in the family unit. The title page of a children's book published the same year, *Walt Disney's Main Street Coloring Fun*, features a drawing of the two dogs strolling down Disneyland's commercial avenue.[98]

Hollywood on Main Street, U.S.A.

Hollywood established a strong presence on Disney's Main Street, U.S.A. No small town would be complete without its movie house, and a reviewer in *The Disneyland News* praised the choice of Film Classics of the Ages projected continuously and simultaneously on six screens in the horseshoe-shaped auditorium of the Main Street Cinema. Four silent shorts on the program, accompanied by piano-player music, represented different genres: an aviation adventure, *A Dash Through the Clouds*, with Mabel Norman (1912); a Western with William S. Hart, *Dealing for Daisy, or The Gambler's Love* (1915); a Keystone Kops comedy, *The Noise of Bombs* (1914); and a drama, *Shifting Sands*, starring Gloria Swanson (1918). Winsor McCay's *Gertie the Dinosaur* (1914) represented the origins of animation, while the sixth screen featured hand-tinted slides with such admonishments as "Ladies kindly remove hats" and "If you spit on the floor at home, feel free to spit on the floor here, for we want you to feel at home."[99]

There was also a Hollywood connection on Town Square: the Show Business in Disneyland Shop run by Jimmy Starr, motion picture editor for the *Los Angeles Herald and Express*, who provided a guest editorial for an early edition of *The Disneyland News*.[100] Inside, park visitors could admire an exhibit of costumes and props from the Silent Era and purchase guidebooks and maps of Hollywood, autograph books, photos and postcards of the stars, fan magazines, and such park souvenirs as a miniature director's chair and a camera-on-tripod cigarette lighter.

Finally, and most important, Main Street offered the possibility of seeing Hollywood stars in the flesh, one of the principal goals of a trip to Los Angeles but forbidden by the closed nature of the studios. The park publicity department made this a top priority. A front-page headline on *The Disneyland News* of March 10, 1956, announced: "Disneyland Top Celebrity Attraction; 'Magic Kingdom' Hosts Entertainment

Figures, Film, TV Personalities."[101] The article claimed that television and movie actors flocked by the hundreds to the park, where without fanfare they could be spotted relaxing, queuing for attractions, and taking in the sights. The paper also boasted that more stars could be seen in the Magic Kingdom than at Hollywood and Vine, the fabled crossroads of the entertainment world. In photo essays like the one titled "Hollywood Comes to Disneyland," the *News* published the names and photographs of famous actors like June Allyson, Dick Powell, Esther Williams, and Lorraine Day, and even some stars who passed unnoticed in public, like the grown-up Shirley Temple and her two daughters.[102]

Equally exciting, starting in late 1955, was the opportunity to meet and chat with stars made possible by the daily radio broadcast *Magic Kingdom*.[103] In the early months of the park, artists from the Disney Studio could also be found on Main Street. The Disney Artists Exhibit, located between the Red Wagon Inn and the Plaza Apartments, showcased watercolor and oil paintings by studio employees. Additionally, four studio artists were regularly stationed inside the Exhibit, sketching portraits of guests and drawing cartoon characters for fans.[104] Appropriately, animation art on display included Disney's newest feature, *Lady and the Tramp*.

A Small-Town Revival

Small-town subjects in movies in the 1930s and 1940s served to reinforce the idea of the quintessential moderate-size community, with its train station, civic center, main street, and safe, happy homes, and, in so doing, to validate the hometown experiences of an older generation. But by the early 1950s, the genre was on the wane.[105] The recycling of tropes from films like *Meet Me in St. Louis* had run its course, and, to meet the threat from television, studios turned to more exotic, spectacular fare. One of the later idealized Main Street/residential pairings filmed on a studio backlot appeared in RKO's *Two Tickets to Broadway* (1951), in which the adoring townsfolk of Pelican Falls, Vermont, give a rousing sendoff to a small-town girl (Janet Leigh) who seeks showbiz fame in New York City— not in movies or theater, but, ironically, on television (Fig. 11). Meanwhile, the nationwide move to the suburbs was altering the habits of a new generation, leading to greater insularity, although suburbanites still retained a deep-seated need for the community experience and for reaffirmation of American ideals in the seemingly endless days of the Cold War. Disney met these needs by reviving the small town and placing it front and center at the entrance to his theme park.

Figure 11. Backlot set dressed as Pelican Falls, Vermont, for *Two Tickets to Broadway* (1951, RKO). Photographed June 30, 1954 (Bob Steele/Valley Times Collection/Los Angeles Public Library).

In the 1950s and into the 1960s, many park guests were Californians transplanted from the Midwest. A walk down Main Street was right up their alley. In short, like the inspired efforts of the big-studio art directors who had crafted a nostalgic view of a bygone America on film, the collaborative genius of Disney's creative team made Disneyland's visitors feel right at home.

2

Frontierland

Addressing visitors, Disneyland's first souvenir brochure promised that "Frontierland is where you will actually 'live' America's colorful and historic past."[1] In a similar vein, the first guidebook announced:

> Our country's exciting past is accurately reproduced in Frontierland....
> Museum authorities devoted their knowledge and skill to the accurate repro-
> duction of Conestoga wagons, Concord stages, Western buckboards, and a
> 105-foot paddle wheel river boat. Cabinet-makers carved and painted the accu-
> rate reproductions that furnish the buildings.[2]

A year later, another guide affirmed: "America's frontiers, from Revolutionary days to the great southwest settlement, live again in Frontierland. You'll actually experience the high adventure of our forefathers who
shaped our glorious history."[3]

Despite multiple pledges of verisimilitude like these, this chapter
will show that Frontierland owed an immense debt for how it looked and
worked to one of the most popular and enduring of entertainment genres
during Walt Disney's adult life: the motion-picture Western. Hollywood
made its own claims to visual and factual authenticity, but conventions
and stereotypes established early on begot a fundamentally mythic cinematic spin on "how the West was won."[4] Disneyland's Frontierland was in
many ways the heir to a conceptual construct that, in fact, predated classic
"Cowboys and Indians" films and had deep roots in nineteenth-century
history, fiction, and stage drama.[5]

Aptly located west of the Hub, Frontierland occupied roughly a third
of the park's developed terrain in 1955. Though its thematic timeframe ran
mainly from 1840 to 1860, flags and pennants flying over various sections
alluded to a longer arc in the nation's history, as far back as 1790 and as
recently as 1876.[6] Then, as today, guests passed through the rough-timbered towers of a cavalry fort onto Frontier Street, the commercial corridor of what purported to be a typical Old West town.[7] Straight ahead
they could glimpse the riverboat landing where passengers boarded the

sternwheeler *Mark Twain.* Off to the left, near the dock, the saloon—
dubbed Slue Foot Sue's Golden Horseshoe after the rootin'-tootin' cow-
girl in the "Pecos Bill" segment of Disney's *Melody Time*—and tiny,
bustling New Orleans Street beckoned. A variety of landscapes peeled off
from there: the Painted Desert, open plains, and the Rivers of America
that encircled Tom Sawyer Island, a long, sinuous isle thickly planted with
trees. A plantation-style Southern restaurant sat on the west bank of the
river, and further along, an Indian Village. High-tech thrill rides like Big
Thunder Mountain Railroad that later generations associate with Frontierland did not yet exist. In its first incarnation, four-legged beasts powered
all of the rides, including stagecoaches, covered wagons, a mule pack train,
buggies, and buckboards.

As with Main Street, U.S.A., the metaphor of Frontierland as walk-
through movie set is not uncommon in theme-park literature. Three
historians—Richard Francaviglia, Michael Steiner, and Karal Ann Marling—have, in passing, compared the sector to a studio backlot.[8] I propose to take this idea a step further and examine the sector in the context
of specific films and the dream factories that created them. Ultimately,
motion pictures and Frontierland, as envisioned by Disney, shared the
same patriotic goal. For example, an intertitle card in the 1923 silent epic
The Covered Wagon paid tribute to "the lion-hearted men and women who
carved a splendid civilization out of an uncharted wilderness." Using similar rhetoric on opening day, July 17, 1955, Walt called Frontierland "a tribute to the faith, courage, and ingenuity of the pioneers who blazed the
trails across America."[9] In this chapter, I trace Hollywood's impact on
Frontierland in terms of four concepts: backlot and stage design, dramatic
action and movement, sense of place, and the actors or cast members who
would populate its fanciful space.[10]

Walt as a Westerner

The general perception that Frontierland represents a personal statement by Walt Disney is grounded in fact.[11] Walt was born and raised in
Illinois and Missouri, two states that once marked the eastern fringe of
the frontier. He came into this world shortly after a young professor at the
University of Wisconsin, Frederick Jackson Turner, presented a groundbreaking paper at a meeting of the American Historical Association at
the 1893 World's Columbian Exposition in Chicago. Turner's thesis, "The
Significance of the Frontier in American History," related the drive westward to a growing sense of national identity fired by ideals of determi-
nation, individualism, and a consensual commitment to democracy. His

disregard for Indigenous populations was typical of his time: he called the frontier "a meeting place between savagery and civilization." Turner's thesis impacted not only historical writing but also literature and popular culture, including the movies—and ultimately, Frontierland—in their embrace of a factually fluid vision of the Old West.[12]

Walt Disney and others of his generation could still relate directly to the frontier. As a youngster in Marceline, he met Buffalo Bill Cody and was invited to sit in his buggy.[13] In an article in *True West* magazine, Walt confessed: "Boyhood memories are the reason for my fondness for Frontierland.... It was a thrill for a boy to grow up in Missouri after the turn of the century ... when elements of the frontier were still visible."[14] Park publicity played up these connections. *The Disneyland News* added a colorful touch to Walt's family history when it stated that one of his mother's ancestors had moved from New York State to Ohio in 1810 because they had heard that "Indians" were friendlier in the Midwest.[15]

Stories of the Old West had made an appearance in Disney films well before the mid–1950s. At the start of Walt's animation career in L.A., several of the *Alice Comedies*, a series of fifty-seven silent shorts from the mid–1920s, bore titles like *Alice's Wild West Show, Alice's Tin Pony, Alice in the Wooly West, Alice at the Rodeo,* and *Alice in the Klondike.* Four 1930s Mickey Mouse cartoons were Wild West-themed: *The Cactus Kid, Pioneer Days, The Klondike Kid,* and *Two-Gun Mickey.* In 1951, Donald Duck starred in *Dude Duck,* a satire on the craze for dude ranches, and in the 1952 cartoon short *Two Gun Goofy,* the Goof overpowers Black Pete, Mickey's archvillain of yore.

Two feature-length Disney animations had frontier connections. *Peter Pan* (1953) has its now much-regretted Native American camp sequence. In the "package" picture *Melody Time* (1948), the "Johnny Appleseed" segment draws inspiration from "a real-life person," who, as the narrator concedes, "has given way to legend." In a second segment, the tuneful tall tale of "Pecos Bill" details his bromance with his horse Widowmaker and the sad if improbable fate of his girlfriend, Slue Foot Sue, who is propelled to the Moon by her wedding-day bustle.

Authenticity in the Western Film

Movie history is bound up with the Western, starting in 1894 when Thomas Edison filmed Buffalo Bill Cody and sharp-shooter Annie Oakley using his patented kinetoscope process.[16] Jean-Luc Godard called the Western "the most cinematographic genre in cinema."[17] Action-packed, scenic, and comparatively easy to shoot, the Western ensured a steady return on its production cost. And it provided ideal content for both big-budget pictures with big-name stars and the bargain-basement adventures cranked out by Poverty-Row independents. Virtually every great leading man of the Golden Age had top billing in at least one shoot 'em up, from Gary Cooper, Humphrey Bogart, and James Cagney to Jimmy Stewart, Henry Fonda, and Glenn Ford. Growing up in the Midwest, Disney must have seen some early Westerns. In Hollywood in the 1920s and '30s, he witnessed at close hand their steady growth and ascent in popularity.

Two sure-fire storylines developed. The first glorified early nineteenth-century trans-Appalachian pathfinders and backwoodsmen like Daniel Boone.[18] A second strain focused on the hazardous trek of wagon trains across the Great Plains. Both strains supported the so-called foundation myth: a pop-culture dramatization in sound and image of the onward march of civilization by intrepid pioneers who battled outlaws, savage natives, rogue bankers, and assorted scoundrels in pursuit of freedom and a place in the Western sun to call home.[19]

Hollywood studio publicity employed much the same language used for promoting Disneyland to promise an authentic experience for the moviegoer. Take for example the trailer for John Ford's *She Wore a Yellow Ribbon* (1949), which asserted: "You'll live the robust days of frontiersmen, their nights of danger, their laughs, their loves. You'll feel the penetrating chill of savage war cries, the piercing of an arrow shot from an ambush, of Indians of all nations banded together for one last war on the advancing white man."

Authenticity could be guaranteed by attention to detail in costuming and props, the use of vintage vehicles, hiring extras adept at riding and roping, or folding historical figures and events into the narrative mix.[20] Such was the demand for realism that experienced wranglers, and even a few rogues, applied for work.[21] Still, any meaningful attempt at historical correctness was undercut by time-worn tropes. From at least the 1860s, literary fiction, theatrical melodramas, dime novels, and Wild West shows had all mythologized the frontier. Moving pictures merely took a pre-existent mythic West and made it flicker.[22]

Furthermore, authenticity is relative. An audience can gauge reality only by comparison with what it trusts to be true.[23] By 1955, clichés and stereotypes in Western films were so firmly ingrained that Frontierland could only pass for real by borrowing, appropriating, or stealing them—lock, stock, and barrel.[24] The elements in Walt's Wild West wonderland had infinitely more in common with fictions witnessed in a neighborhood movie theater than any of the mundane or grittier aspects of daily frontier life a scholar might document in print.[25]

Art Direction at Disneyland

The supervisor for Frontierland in its infancy, George Patrick, a former art director at Twentieth Century–Fox and ghost-town aficionado, began his career on the Marilyn Monroe comedy *Love Nest* (1951).[26] He designed the Western *The Siege at Red River* shortly before going to work for Walt in November 1954. After a few years at Disneyland, he took his talents to television, hiring out on numerous Westerns.[27]

Another recruit from Fox, illustrator Sam McKim, found that his job tapped into lifelong passions: "I had worked in Westerns as a kid, and I'd been around cowboys off and on, and I always liked the West. I used to read, when I was a kid, Western pulps; you used to buy those two for a nickel.... I used to like early West, and pioneer stuff, mountain men as well, as well as the cowboys and Indians stuff. I was fortunate enough to hit upon some of this stuff in my assignments, like the stagecoach."[28] McKim and fellow sketch artist Harper Goff contributed early concept drawings for Frontier Street.[29]

According to the 1955 Disneyland press kit, an effort was made to seek out artisans with expertise in nineteenth-century construction techniques. But the fragmented nature of Frontierland, evoking diverse times and places, meant that architectural styles jostled cheek-by-jowl. This made it hard to strike a balance between overall visual harmony and making individual structures appear convincing.[30] Moreover, a practical need to combine historic elements with modern amenities—electricity, lighting, plumbing—to guarantee visitor and employee safety, further complicated the pursuit of absolute authenticity.[31]

In Hollywood, after the stage flats went up, set dressers applied a veneer of verisimilitude. So too at Disneyland. Details such as cresting and railing were scrounged from old buildings scattered throughout the West and Southwest.[32] Set decorator Emile Kuri was a master at this sort of thing. At Paramount, for the great 1950s Western *Shane*, he chose props that gave the saloon, general store, homestead, and barn a persuasively unique flavor. Kuri located items for Frontier Street that not only looked good but tapped movie tropes that evoked familiar aspects of frontier life and Old West virtues.[33]

Prop men at the major studios could access a vast in-house stock of furniture and objects, antiques as well as copies or replicas. Walt's people had no such luxury. They had to turn to dealers and private collectors. Their most notorious "find" was Lafitte's Anchor, which allegedly had been attached to a pirate ship commanded by Jean Lafitte in the Battle of New Orleans.[34] Props from Disney films also found a well-publicized second life at the park. Watercraft from the Davy Crockett series on the weekly *Disneyland* TV show were recycled as the Mike Keel Boats river ride.

Frontier Street and the Studio Backlot

Walt Disney wanted a frontier town in his dream park from the out-set.[35] As we have seen, Disneyland's origins have been traced in part to Walt's 1948 live-action film *So Dear to My Heart*, set in idealized turn-of-the-century Kansas, with powerful echoes of frontier life. He even hoped to build a traveling exhibition around a mechanized scale model called "Granny Kinkaid's Cabin," derived from a scene in *So Dear to My Heart*.[36]

Disney's 1948 Memorandum mentions a Western Village, with a general store, stagecoaches, a farm and an old mill, and a Native American encampment. The store would sell Western toys and costumes. Walt also thought about having a small theater for showing cowboy movies, and a museum dedicated to the West.[37] His proposal to the Burbank city council in 1952 included an attraction called "Granny's farm" as well as a frontier town and a Mississippi paddle wheeler.[38] These embryonic projects for Disneyland aimed to educate Americans about their heritage and what the past looked like, as well as to entertain them.

Disneyland Park was built with the idea that education and entertainment (and a dash of consumerism) would be elements central to Frontier Street, located next to the cavalry Stockade and Block Houses at the entrance to Frontierland (Fig. 12). On the right-hand side of the street stood the Frontier Trading Post souvenir shop, Miniature Horse Corral, and combined Blacksmith Shop and Marshal's Office. The left side was dominated by the Davy Crockett Frontier Museum and Pendleton Woolen Mills Dry Goods Store, among other offerings.[39]

"The Western town" in general, as pop-culture authority John G. Cawelti has explained, came "to center about the image of the isolated town ... surrounded by the vast open grandeur of prairie or desert and connected to the rest of the civilized world by a railroad, a stagecoach, or simply a trail." "The rickety wooden buildings with their tottering false fronts," Cawelti continued, "express the town's position against the surrounding desert. Nonetheless we do not see the town solely as an isolated fort in a hostile country ... but as the advance guard of an oncoming civilization."[40] This is how Disney imagined Frontier Street.

Like the rest of Frontierland, Frontier Street was conceived as a motion picture set, not a museum piece—a fanciful version of the real thing, to better engage the visitor. Because entertainment trumped realism, just as Main Street had no houses of worship, Walt's Old West main

Figure 12. Frontier Street, Frontierland, Disneyland. South row, with the Pendleton Shop and Slue Foot Sue's Golden Horseshoe, August 1956 (from the collection of Dave DeCaro).

drag lacked some of the commercial amenities of a functioning town. There was no bank, no post office, no grocery, or butcher's shop.

"The repeated use of nearby locations, backlots, and town sets for the studio-made Westerns and B-westerns" at the height of Hollywood's Golden Age, Richard Slotkin has noted, "created a special kind of 'Western' space." But, Slotkin added, "it was also studio space"—a space born of necessity.[41] Studio sets and backlots solved a huge technical problem: heavy cameras and sound recording equipment required stable conditions. Backlots generated extra income, too, when rented out to smaller studios lacking the plein-air facilities enjoyed by Fox or Metro-Goldwyn-Mayer. Charges for redressing were minimal. Fronts were repainted, architectural details altered, and signage and dressing changed, depending on the production. As one writer put it, "On these mean streets, thousands of gunmen died with their boots on after shootouts with men in white hats."[42]

The undisputed queen of the backlots was MGM, whose Culver City studio covered 175 acres. Here, among Parisian boulevards, European villages, and urban American streets, MGM could boast the world's biggest Western location. Lot 3 was "one of the greatest lots in the picture business," according to production manager Edward Woehler. "We had the big lake, we had the big waterfront street, we had the St. Louis Street, and we had three Western streets." In fact, there were four: Monterey Street, Western Street, Billy the Kid Street, and Ghost Town Street—plus Fort Canby and Fort Scott, analogous to Frontierland's Stockade and Block Houses.[43]

Fox had its own Western backlot set, Tombstone Street, built in 1931, which, with minor changes, accommodated many popular "oaters." Henry Fonda starred in five Westerns shot on Tombstone Street.[44] One of the smaller studios, Columbia managed to fit into its cramped quarters a very convincing Western Street that could be restyled as a Southern or Midwestern location (Fig. 13).[45] Paramount also had a frontier location on its backlot. Hemmed in by city streets in downtown Hollywood, the studio had to erect a fake mountain made of chicken wire and plaster to block out neighboring buildings.[46] Although Warner Bros. had no permanent Western set on its Burbank lot until the mid–1950s, it produced its share of cowboy pictures by redressing its urban street sets or using the two sets on its Calabasas Ranch, where the terrain was perfect for Wild West action.[47]

Unlike the majors, the independent studios initially shot their B Westerns in abandoned ghost towns. As their fortunes increased, they built cheap sets and recycled them in film after film, much like their

Figure 13. Western Street, Columbia Ranch, Burbank, 1951 (Bison Archives and HollywoodHistoricPhotos.com).

constant reuse of stock footage of Indian attacks and chase sequences. Disney had no Western street on his own studio backlot until 1958, when he began making miniseries like *The Nine Lives of Elfego Baca* for the *Disneyland* TV show. Thus his first Western "backlot" would be in Frontierland. Like the buildings of Main Street, U.S.A., Frontier Street was built according to a reduced scale. Here too, the designers applied the cinematic principle of foreshortening to the upper floors, whose interiors were too short to be habitable, but exteriors were believable to the viewer's eye.

Movie set techniques of a slightly different sort were used for a second town in Frontierland, Rainbow Ridge, a fictitious mining town recalling the California Gold Rush of the mid-nineteenth century. Bill Martin, an art director who left Twentieth Century–Fox for Disney in 1953, built the diminutive town as part of Disneyland's first expansion in June 1956. As a mining town, Rainbow Ridge recalled another inspiration for Disneyland, the ghost town assembled at Knott's Berry Farm in nearby Buena Park.[48] Since it acted strictly as a scenic backdrop to the loading area of a new ride, called the Rainbow Caverns Mine Train, Rainbow Ridge was not accessible to guests but was viewed from a distance. Hence, the set-design technique of miniaturization came into play. An article in *Life* magazine (1944) titled "Movie Illusions," with the subhead "Cities Are Built on Movie Stages," explained, "If necessary Hollywood technicians can build a whole complicated city inside one of their stages.... Such projects always involve a problem of scaling.... [Buildings] had to appear in correct relation to action ... in the foreground."[49] In the case of Rainbow Ridge, the buildings were greatly undersized. *The Disneyland News* confirmed the small town's relationship to stage design, particularly in the attention to detail and the aura of enchantment that was typical of Disney's cinematic output.[50]

Belly Up to the Bar, Boys

Early park PR touted the authenticity of Disneyland's Golden Horseshoe saloon: "In the turbulent days of the Old West, every newcomer to town headed first for the dance hall. Here in Frontierland is an exact replica of just such a place—the 'Golden Horseshoe.'"[51] Four days prior to opening day, the Golden Horseshoe Revue strutted its stuff for Walt, Lillian Disney, and 250 friends invited to celebrate the couple's thirtieth wedding anniversary. One of the guests, director-producer Mervyn LeRoy, called Disneyland "the eighth wonder of the world." A "modest Walt" grinned as he explained to syndicated *Los Angeles Times* columnist Hedda Hopper how he did it: "All it took is money, Hedda, and fortunately my partners were very generous with that folding stuff."[52]

Every frontier town, it seems, had a saloon, initially little more than a tent or a shack, but often, in established communities, a grand show-place. Drinking, gambling, and socializing comprised the main activities (taverns and hotels provided food and lodging). Large saloons might accommodate dancing and civic meetings. Big or small, they were primarily a male preserve. Although a woman sometimes owned or ran the place, women were employed solely as hostesses, performers, or prostitutes. At best, the saloon had a small stage relegated to a corner. Serious music or drama were seldom on offer. These were reserved for towns with a theater or "opry" house. Disneyland's Opera House, on Main Street's Town Square, was properly situated in a more developed locality.

Frontierland's saloon—officially designated Slue Foot Sue's Golden Horseshoe—contrasts with the historical type. The word saloon is absent—beer and hard liquor, gambling, and billiards, too. In other words, the Horseshoe did not function like the typical saloon in early one-reelers like *Cripple Creek Barroom* (1898) and *The Great Train Robbery* (1903), or films of more recent vintage, wherein certain plot devices—brawls, shoot-outs, sexual intrigue—were acted out.[53] The ubiquitous musical element of Western movies, however, required a prominent stage. Cinema art directors adapted what historians call the concert-saloon, a rarity in the Old West but a popular building type in low-end districts of Eastern cities.[54]

The form was fully developed in Hollywood by 1939 with the appearance of the Last Chance Saloon in the James Stewart–Marlene Dietrich film *Destry Rides Again* (1939). The *Destry* set was larger than the standard Hollywood saloon to allow for fist fights and square dancing. A raised stage literally elevated Dietrich's numbers, including her signature song, "See What the Boys in the Back Room Will Have." A second example of the concert-saloon figured in the 1946 MGM Judy Garland musical *The Harvey Girls*. The Alhambra Saloon has a bar that serves drinks, a staircase leading to the women's quarters (the movie never hints at sex for sale), and a stage as a platform for a song-and-dance act performed by Angela Lansbury and a dozen scantily clad chorines.

Warner's 1953 musical *Calamity Jane* uses a similar set for its Golden Nugget Saloon, with steps to one side that lead upstairs to hotel rooms. Doris Day as Calamity sings and dances across the set from bar to balcony to stage. Some writers claim that Walt asked Harper Goff, a former Warner set designer, to obtain plans for the Golden Nugget to aid in the design of the Golden Horseshoe. Goff reportedly duplicated the plans, and the Golden Horseshoe indeed echoes key features of the Golden Nugget—its white and gold Rococo décor, the second-story gallery with turned balusters, and the charming semicircular box seats framing the stage.[55] The exterior façade is similar as well. But the differences are striking: inside the Golden Horseshoe, the proscenium arch is curved, not rectilinear, the gallery extends around the entire upper level, and the ceiling displays a magnificent tracery skylight. The Disney version retains the flavor of the Warner set but is by no means a clone of its putative model.

The interior of the Golden Horseshoe lacks the usual touches of grand saloons, both historic and cinematic: pictures of bare-chested prizefighters and recumbent nudes.[56] There was one further exception: "the longest little bar in the world" served Pepsi-Cola, and no booze.[57] A show-biz model for this particular lapse in Old West reality existed in the person of William Boyd, the straight-shooting lead in the *Hopalong Cassidy* series of cowboy films and TV shows from the mid–1930s into the 1950s. Whenever he bellied up to the bar, he ordered sarsaparilla instead of liquor.

The Golden Horseshoe Revue was further indebted to Hollywood in terms of live entertainment. Its in-house chorus line, the Golden Horseshoe Girls, kicked up their high heels to the rousing strains of Offenbach's cancan, a dance imported from France and popular in 1950s films like the Oscar-nominated drama *Moulin Rouge*.[58] The cancan had crossed the Atlantic by 1860 and in due course into silent pictures. In the 1954 remake of *Destry Rides Again*, femme fatale Mari Blanchard and six prancing showgirls perform "If You Can Can-Can" while raising their skirts to show off their gams.[59] The action is mostly set inside a saloon that conforms to the cinematic norm: long bar on the right, balconies on either side, a stage framed by columns. Thus, by the 1950s, the "Western cancan" had become an indelible trope without which the Golden Horseshoe Revue would have seemed inauthentic.

Action! All the World's a Stage

Movement was a defining principle of Frederick Jackson Turner's Frontier Thesis, as summarized by historian and Mark Twain scholar Henry Nash Smith in 1950: "One of the most persistent generalizations concerning American life and character is the notion that our society has been shaped by the pull of a vacant continent drawing population westward through the passes of the Alleghenies, across the Mississippi Valley, over the high plains and mountains of the Far West to the Pacific Coast."[60] Movement—the element that most defined motion pictures and gave the medium its nickname—was also the dominant element of Westerns. Many early Frontier films were essentially "chase" pictures, accommodating audiences' thrill at seeing movement across the frame. Likewise, early publicity defined Frontierland in terms of movement: "Frontierland tells the story of a young and enterprising nation and of the people moving westward by riverboat and keelboat, by stagecoach and covered wagon."[61] The vehicles were touted as accurate reproductions of the originals (Fig. 14). Like the Hollywood studios, Disneyland had its own stables and wranglers who bred horses and pack mules to carry or pull Frontierland's greenhorn guests along its highroads and byroads.[62]

Vicarious experience at the movies heightened visitor expectations of Frontierland's Stage Coach ride. The vehicle, according to publicity, had been "immortalized over the world by countless Hollywood motion pictures."[63] In emulation of a long tradition of "stagecoach" movies, not historical reality, Disneyland visitors could "delight to early day adventures aboard a stage as it swings through the Painted Desert, hotly pursued by renegade Indians and outlaws."[64] One classic film in particular, John Ford's *Stagecoach* of 1939, the movie that revived the A Western after a temporary slump and made John Wayne a star, put a fresh spin on the standard clichés of Western travel while influencing a later crop of movies (Fig. 15). The high drama in the movie, Ford's tale of disparate travelers—a young gunslinger, a gambler, the prostitute with a heart of gold, a crooked banker, an alcoholic sawbones, and an upright Army officer's wife—derives from the contrast between the claustrophobic confines of

Figure 14. Frontierland attractions, Disneyland: Conestoga Wagon, Stage Coach, and Pack Mule rides, with artificial rock formations. Publicity still, *Disneyland, U.S.A.* (*People and Places*, 1956) (author's collection).

Figure 15. *Stagecoach* (1939, United Artists), filmed in Monument Valley near the Arizona–Utah border (United Artists/Photofest).

the vehicle and the expansive landscape outside the coach. The events that befall the group—attack by Indians, horse theft, crossing a treacherous river—were the subject of countless films. Before motion pictures, the stagecoach hold-up was one of the "authentic" set pieces popularized by Buffalo Bill's Wild West show. A *New York Times* review of the Frontierland ride emphasized its relationship with the silver screen: "A stagecoach ride through Disneyland's fabricated desert is not just motion and scenery. The stagecoach is so authentic in construction, appurtenances, and decorations that it could serve tomorrow in a John Ford movie. It challenges even the adult sophisticates to imagine they are bucketing across the plains a century ago."[65]

Another Frontierland vehicle, the Conestoga wagon, was on show in many Westerns. Disneyland PR promised guests the thrill of riding actual vintage wagons.[66] Numerous Hollywood movies focused on wagon trains. When Walt was twenty-two years old, the Paramount silent *The Covered Wagon* was the first epic Western to attempt through abundant detail to simulate the settlers' westward odyssey. The film follows two wagon caravans that unite in Kansas City and persevere through heat, cold, hunger, and Indian attack to complete their cross-country trek to Oregon. The filmmakers' quest for a documentary effect included a search for genuine period vehicles, many passed down in families or preserved in private collections.[67] The production underwent hardships akin to those of the original wagon trains. In the famous sequence of an arduous and risky river crossing, two horses used in the production drowned.

The advent of sound had a major impact on audiences. Raoul Walsh's epic *The Big Trail* (1930), like many Westerns of the 1930s, gave a palpable sense of historical experience in its retelling of "the assembly of the covered wagon train, ... the train fording a swollen river in a storm, and the dismantling of the wagons so that they could be hauled over mountains."[68] The movie also features one of the most compelling scenes on film of Natives attacking the big circle of wagons.[69] Popcorn in hand, Americans sat through hundreds of films like these, with titles like *Roll Wagons Roll*, *Wagon Master*, and *Wagons West*.[70] (There was also *Covered Wagon Days*, which is not about wagons!)

Disney tackled the wagon-train theme in two features. In the package film *Melody Time*, the artfully conceived "Pioneer Song" sequence ("Get on the Wagon Rollin' West") uses the motif of a Conestoga train to visualize Johnny Appleseed's conflicted aspirations as a frontiersman. In March 1955 Disney announced a Frontierland subject for the *Disneyland* TV show "Children of the Covered Wagon," touted as a fact-based adventure about "a pioneer caravan over the Oregon Trail."[71] This project developed into the feature film *Westward Ho the Wagons!* set in Wyoming, but shot on the Conejo Ranch at Thousand Oaks, northwest of L.A.[72] In short, moviegoers, whose Western appetites had been whetted by the movies, could experience the same adventures in Frontierland.

I've Been Working on the Railroad

In addition to horse-drawn rides, another form of mass transportation—by rail—provided exciting views of Frontierland's landscape. From the time of the 1948 Memorandum, Walt intended to have an old-fashioned train in his theme park. A confirmed train buff, as a teenager he worked as a "news butcher" aboard rail lines served by the Van Noy-Interstate News Company, based in Kansas City.[73] Two of the Nine Old Men, Disney's long-time core group of animators, Ward Kimball and Ollie Johnston, who had trains in their backyards, inspired Walt to craft and install on his Holmby Hills estate a one-eighth-scale model, dubbed the Carolwood Pacific Railroad.[74] These combined interests sparked the idea for a Donald Duck short, *Out of Scale* (1951).[75]

WED Imagineers built two 5/8-scale steam locomotives to circle around Disneyland.[76] According to the narrator for the featurette *Disneyland, U.S.A.*, "These two iron horses are exact replicas of the old-timers that spanned the continent a century ago."[77] Originally there were just two stops on the circuit. A passenger train served only the Main Street Station. A second engine, with cattle cars in tow, served the Frontierland Station, a copy of the depot in *So Dear to My Heart*.[78] The latter route privileged Frontierland among the park's realms, for reasons made clear in the *Disneyland, U.S.A.* film narration: "In winning the West, it was the railroads that clinched the victory and welded our country together with bands of steel."

The steam locomotive was a force unto itself in many Hollywood Westerns. The major studios rented or purchased vintage engines for pictures like *The Great Train Robbery*, *The Iron Horse*, and *Union Pacific*.[79] The twelve-minute silent *The Great Train Robbery* from the Edison Company owed its long-lived influence to sophisticated editing techniques and innovative use of set pieces forever identified with the Western: a dance hall scene, fisticuffs and gunplay, masked bandits commandeering the train, and the cold-blooded murder of a passenger. Its impact was even felt in Disney's silent *Alice Comedy, Alice's Tin Pony*, about an attempted payroll robbery of a cartoon train pulled by a little engine that really could.

In the landmark saga *The Iron Horse* (1924), director John Huston treated reverentially the construction of the first transcontinental railroad. Its devotion to detail and cast of thousands remain impressive today. Telling a similar story in *Union Pacific* (1939), Cecil B. DeMille brought a new sense of spectacle to the traditional set pieces, which in *Union Pacific* included a train holdup and train wreck in a snowbound pass. Railroad Westerns became routine thanks to pictures like *Santa Fe* (1951) and *The Denver and the Rio Grande* (1952)—which featured a spectacular head-on crash that destroyed two real engines.[80] Walt contributed to the genre with his live-action feature *The Great Locomotive Chase*, produced in 1956 during Disneyland's first year of operation. He borrowed two antique engines for the movie, the William Mason from the Baltimore & Ohio Railroad Museum, and the Inyo, one of a pair purchased by Paramount in 1937 and much used in films, including *So Dear to My Heart*.[81]

In view of Walt's fondness for trains and musicals, mention should be made again of MGM's *The Harvey Girls*, starring Judy Garland as a young woman who travels by rail from Ohio to New Mexico to be married and ends up serving passengers in a Harvey House Restaurant. According to director George Sidney, for backlot scenes set in the fictional town of Sandrock, MGM purchased a steam engine from the Virginia and Truckee Railroad, which in 1869 had started a line to service the Comstock Load.[82] In order to synchronize screen action during shooting (which involved a large cast), the locomotive was powered by steam, gas, and electricity. The shoot was so complex that actors close to the wheels of the engine were

scalded by hot steam shooting out in time to the music. The film's popularity derived from its signature song, "On the Atchison, Topeka, and
the Santa Fe," performed in an unusually long, nine-minute segment that
served to introduce many of the characters.[83] Thus, in 1946, MGM had its
own vintage railroad nearly a decade before Walt had his.

"Mark Twain!"

In addition to travel on land, Frontierland provided travel by water
along the Rivers of America. Docking near the New Orleans area prior to
its voyage through the historic American past and nostalgic Old South,
the *Mark Twain* Riverboat served as one of the park's icons, visible in early
conceptual sketches as the "wienie" that would draw visitors through
Frontierland's gates (Fig. 16).[84]

Walt credited the inspiration for the *Mark Twain* to his childhood
experiences. A juvenile fascination with riverboats may also explain why
an old-fashioned paddle wheeler figured prominently in the first Mickey
Mouse sound cartoon, *Steamboat Willie*, a good-natured riff on the Buster
Keaton silent film *Steamboat Bill, Jr.* In his article "Frontierland," Walt
declared, "I go back a long way with stern-wheelers; back to the Missouri

Figure 16. *Mark Twain Riverboat*, Frontierland, Rivers of America, Disneyland. Tourist snapshot, December 1955 (author's collection).

River in the 1910's," when two vessels were still operating out of Kansas City. In describing Frontierland's *Mark Twain*, he emphasized his desire for authenticity, but also the cinematic element of reduced scale "to give a fantasy-like appearance."[85]

Its dedicatory name was appropriate: Samuel Clemens grew up in Hannibal, Missouri, directly east of Marceline. He was a master pilot on the Mississippi for two years, and, significant for our discussion of westward movement, traveled by stagecoach to Nevada to work on the Comstock Lode.[86] Steamships are common in Twain's writings, such as the autobiographical *Life on the Mississippi* (1883). He took his pen name from the measure used by boatmen—two ("twain") fathoms deep on the sounding line or "mark"—indicating a depth safe for passage.

The Disneyland publicity machine claimed that the *Mark Twain* was the first paddle wheeler built in over a half century.[87] In fact, the steam-powered sternwheel tugboat *Portland*, used in publicity for the James Stewart Western *Bend of the River* (1952), had been built in 1947. Because of their connection with the frontier and the Mississippi River, all manner of steamboats appeared in Golden Age films, in matte paintings, mock-ups, partial sets, stage interiors, and real boats, historical and new. In the early 1950s, for example, the vintage vessel *The Henderson* appeared in *The Kentuckian* (1955) and *Band of Angels* (1957), as well as *Bend of the River*. Universal used a prop boat, *The Enterprise*, in *The Mississippi Gambler* (1953) and the following year loaned it to Fox for *The Gambler from Natchez*.

It is possible that Walt was also inspired by the *Cotton Blossom*, built expressly for MGM's 1951 version of the Jerome Kern–Oscar Hammerstein musical *Show Boat* (art dir. Jack Martin Smith; Fig. 17).[88] Described as the most expensive MGM movie prop up until that time, its elegant design by art director Jack Martin Smith incorporated a double curved staircase at the prow, used in the film's opening number, shot on the lake in Lot 3—a plausible stand-in for Ol' Man River. Concealed diesel engines and underwater cables guided the boat, and oil tanks provided the black smoke streaming from the two stacks for a convincing visual effect.

The *Mark Twain*, whose beautiful upper deck resembles the top level of the *Cotton Blossom*, likewise functions as a showboat. In publicity photos and on film in the mid–1950s, such as *Disneyland, U.S.A.*, the Disneyland Band proudly performs on the foredeck. On Disneyland's inaugural day, it shared another connection with the Kern–Hammerstein musical. Irene Dunn, who christened the craft with a bottle reportedly containing waters from the major rivers of America, had starred in the 1936 version of *Show Boat*. In truth, the *Mark Twain* was a combination of studio

Figure 17. *Show Boat* (1951, MGM), *The Cotton Blossom* on MGM's Lot 3 Lake (Bison Archives and HollywoodHistoricPhotos.com).

prop, built on the Disney Burbank soundstage, and glorious amusement park ride. It was powered by a diesel-fired boiler, not by burning wood or coal, and guided by a hidden underwater rail.[89] No unsightly black smoke would billow from the elegant stacks of Walt's version of an old-time sternwheeler.

The *Mark Twain* has endured to this day, while the *Cotton Blossom* suffered a reversal of fortune. Used as a backdrop for promotions and rented to other studios, such as Columbia for *Cruisin' Down the River* (1953), it remained on Lot 3 until 1970, when it was sold to Worlds of Fun in Kansas City. There, ironically, it served as a theme park attraction until, a quarter-century later, it expired of old age.

A Sense of Place: Locating the West

In discussing Turner's Frontier Thesis and the pioneers' attitude toward the North American empire, Henry Nash Smith placed emphasis on "the physical fact of the continent": "The American interior is presented as a new and enchanting region of inexpressible beauty and fertility. Through stately forests and rich meadows roam vast herds of animals which own no master, nor expect their sustenance from the hands of man. A thousand rivers flow into the mighty Mississippi."[90] Frontierland offered its share of natural beauty: wooded spaces represented the eastern frontier, including the Tennessee hill country of Davy Crockett; the Rivers of America, plied by the *Mark Twain*, evoked the mighty Mississippi; and a faux desert connoted the American southwest.

Coach and wagon rides required a specific type of landscape to feel authentic. What would comprise such a landscape? Cultural historian Margaret King cited Disney's True-Life Adventure films, such as *The Living Desert* (1953), as inspiration for Frontierland's locales, whose "attractions were faithful, three-dimensional extensions of the Disney nature films. They featured a mix of live domestic animals and Audio-Animatronics 'wild' animals set against constructed, landscaped, and carefully edited 'natural' settings."[91]

A more influential source was the Hollywood Western. By 1955 the "Old West" had for the most part been reduced to the American southwest, recognizable from elements seen "in film after film," according to Diana Reep: "the burning sands, rugged mountains, sagebrush, winding streams or raging rivers, and the familiar buttes and mesas of Monument Valley."[92] To save money, thousands of features, B Westerns, and one-reelers were shot on studio ranches near Los Angeles. The Corriganville Movie Ranch, for one, provided the requisite hills, boulders, and scrub oak, plus an on-site Western Street and cavalry fort. An important prototype for Frontierland, the Corriganville spread in Simi Valley was open on weekends for fans to meet their Western heroes and witness a stagecoach or bank holdup every Sunday at noon.[93]

The soundstage, of course, remained an attractive production option. As a *Life* magazine story about the Warner Bros. film *The Petrified Forest* (1936) put it, "The extent to which Hollywood relies on its illusion masters is illustrated by the fact that, although the real Arizona desert is less than 400 miles away, Warner's preferred to construct an imitation one inside stage 21."[94]

With Hollywood's version of the West well established, Walt assigned art director Bill Martin to design a "backlot" desert for Disneyland called the Painted Desert.[95] It was not intended to replicate the badlands area of that name in Arizona—the designation was generic.[96] But it inevitably called to mind *The Painted Desert*, the 1931 film that gave Clark Gable his first speaking role, and the 1938 B-Western remake, *Painted Desert*. As *Life* had done for *The Petrified Forest*, an article in *The Disneyland News* enumerated the steps in the process required to create the landscape. Real

Joshua trees, some transplanted from the Mohave Desert, the *News* also reported, stood in as "props."[97]

Though interior and exterior scenes were routinely shot on soundstages, A Westerns often earned their "A" by going further afield to shoot. Utah and Arizona were favored surrogates for more distant states like Texas. One individual above all established our enduring mental image of the Old West. John Ford transformed the towering rocks and vast expanses of Monument Valley into pictorial symbols of nature's austere grandeur and the hardships faced by settlers in their westward trek (Fig. 15). "TV westerns you can make on the back lot," John Wayne told a reporter. "But for the big screen, for the real, big-scale out-door drama, you have to [go] where God put the West."[98]

John Ford made Monument Valley the mythical Western landscape par excellence. Ironically, as a space unsuitable for habitation, Monument Valley was more backlot than authentic location. It lies, as film historian Edward Buscombe put it, "in an empty quarter on the way to nowhere in particular, and few visitors make the detour. It has ... essentially no existence in the popular mind except as a movie set."[99] Monument Valley became so closely identified with the Western that even studio-bound movies confected ersatz versions of it. *The Harvey Girls* included process shots seen from a moving train, and for *Annie Get Your Gun* (1950) artists painted a 250-foot-long backdrop depicting the Valley's familiar buttes.

Thus, within Frontierland's Painted Desert, Disney built his own mini-Monument Valley of artificial rock arches, cliffs, and stacked boulders—all reasonably convincing from afar, despite their drastically reduced scale. A grove filled with saguaro cactus added another ubiquitous Western symbol to the site. Directly or indirectly, Disney absorbed and transmitted from Ford the idea that travelling west—by coach, wagon, train, or on horseback—was emblematic of America's drive to expand and consolidate the nation.[100]

At the same time, the Painted Desert was one of Disneyland's first areas to poke fun at itself and at the Westerns that inspired it. On a certain level it is a cartoon landscape based on the broad strokes of the painted backgrounds in the "Pecos Bill" sequence in *Melody Time*. Two musical numbers sung by the Sons of the Pioneers anticipate the exaggeration and fantasy of the area. In "Blue Shadows on the Trail," a subtly evocative number, two animated tumbleweeds tumble their way through a stylized, nocturnal desertscape to the strains of a lyrical tune. The more dynamic stanzas in the "The Ballad of Pecos Bill" are accompanied by outlandish images to show Bill single-handedly creating the Western landscape: "He brought rain from Californy" for the Gulf of Mexico, "he got a stick and dug the Rio Grande," and "he gave those redskins such a shakeup that they jumped out of their make-up; that's how the Painted Desert got its name."

The precariously balanced rocks in Frontierland, which threaten to spin and fall on the viewer, are akin to the hilarious devastation wrought by Donald Duck on one of nature's great wonders in the Cinemascope cartoon short, *Grand Canyonscope* (1954). Likewise, the anthropomorphic cacti in the Painted Desert, one of which attempts to thumb a ride, have their ancestors in the surreal cacti that dance with Donald in the finale of Disney's *Three Caballeros* (1944). In short, in addition to recreating on a reduced scale Hollywood's clichéd conception of the Western landscape, Disney introduced punning humor from his cartoon catalog.

In the Footsteps of Tom and Huck

Unlike most of Disneyland's attractions, which provided an unvarying, one-size-fits-all experience to each guest, Tom Sawyer Island, located in the middle of the Rivers of America, offered multiple routes and opportunities to explore on one's own.[101] Guided by paper maps handed out at the raft landings, visitors sought out the many features keyed to Twain's narrative.[102] They reached the island on one of two diesel powered rafts, the "Tom Sawyer" and the "Huckleberry Finn." Once on shore, guests made their way past waterfalls and streams to whatever features caught their fancy: the Old Mill, the Suspension Bridge over Smuggler's Cove, Point Lookout, Injun Joe's Cave, and others. Midway down the island, Fort Wilderness, with its blockhouses and log ramparts, was said to date back to 1812. Beyond the fort lay the one area that could not be reconnoitered: "Indian Territory," whose "terms of treaty prohibit entry."[103]

The Tom and Huck stories derived from Twain's fond boyhood memories of Hannibal, which, like Marceline, claimed to be the quintessential American small town. As Disney recollected in his "Frontierland" article in *True West*, the two towns are situated relatively close to each other, and Walt recalled having explored natural caves like the one in which Tom and Becky get lost.[104]

To many contemporaries the Twain books seemed perfect sources for a Disney motion picture, animated or live-action. In a copy of Tom and Huck's adventures presented to Walt on the day Tom Sawyer Island opened to the public, the proprietor of the Becky Thatcher Book Shop in Hannibal penned this message: "Dear Mr. Disney, I hope that this small gift may inspire you to make these immortal stories into the most wonderful and popular movies that have ever been made."[105] Little did Mr. Disney's admirer realize that Walt had long dreamed of doing just that. Byron

Haskin, who directed Disney's *Treasure Island* (1950), said that Walt "had always been in love with Mark Twain's Tom Sawyer." However, an unwritten agreement among studios for material in the public domain gave priority to the first in line. Walt "wanted Tom Sawyer in the worst way," Haskin recalled. But "David Selznick had prior rights as producer."[106] Moreover, it was a crowded field. By 1955, nine American film adaptations had focused on Tom and Huck. Walt may have seen one or more of three silent versions released in 1917, 1918, and 1920. In 1930, an early talkie from Paramount had been a box office success.

The most influential version was David O. Selznick's *The Adventures of Tom Sawyer* of 1938, by virtue of inspired casting, brilliant Technicolor, and masterful camera work by cinematographer James Wong Howe.[107] Selznick was one of the Hollywood moguls who had much in common with Walt Disney. Like Walt, he was an independent producer committed to creating a small number of prestige pictures per year based on historical literary properties. Selznick, like both Disney and Zanuck at Fox, was a perfectionist who took a hands-on approach to crafting films, from script decisions through cutting and editing. He was famous for his involvement in writing, casting, and directing, even making decisions on costume and color.

The first instance of the impact of Selznick's *Adventures of Tom Sawyer* on Disney is the narrative and art direction of Disney's *So Dear to My Heart* of 1948. Both movies offer a slice of nostalgic Americana in the form of an enchanting idyll about childhood innocence. Walt dressed his youthful hero, Jeremiah Kincaid, played by Bobby Driscoll, in a Tom/Huck costume, and his escapades occurred in an idealized Missouri setting. Two years later Hedda Hopper reported that Disney wanted "to star Bobby Driscoll in 'Tom Sawyer,' but David Selznick has the property tied up, and heaven only knows how much he wants for it."[108] While the book was in the public domain, rights to the name "Mark Twain" were held by Clemens's heirs, and Selznick had taken great pains to secure them.[109] Meanwhile, MGM had its own arrangements with the Clemens estate with respect to world copyright for a film of *The Adventures of Huckleberry Finn*.

Be that as it may, Walt never gave up on an idea with potential. Despite his inability to produce a film version, he realized his desire to bring the Twain stories to life by creating Tom Sawyer Island. The second connection between Selznick's *Tom Sawyer* and Disney is apparent in the design of one of the "scarier" amusements on Tom Sawyer Island, Injun Joe's Cave. This shows the influence of the most impressive sequence in Selznick's movie, toward the end, in which Tom and Becky lose their way in the cave and are pursued by the villainous Injun Joe. In Twain's book this adventure is but one out of thirty-five episodic chapters. However, episodic storytelling functions poorly in the movies.[110] Instead, the film builds steadily toward a crescendo, achieving an emotional punch with a lengthy cave sequence featuring expressionist effects, dramatic lighting, and powerful music (Fig. 18). Footage of bats flying overhead and Becky's

Figure 18. *The Adventures of Tom Sawyer* (1938, Selznick International Pictures). Tom (Tommy Kelly) and Becky Thatcher (Ann Gillis) in the cave sequence (United Artists/Photofest).

hysteria was so intense that cuts were made in this sequence to avoid overly frightening children in the audience.

Selznick hired renowned art director William Cameron Menzies to design the cave sequence, which was shot on a soundstage for both inside and outside views. Menzies began by creating detailed storyboards, a practice recognized by Walt's peers as a Disney innovation. According to studio publicity, the 60,000 square foot set, adorned with stalactites and stalagmites, was constructed of 30,000 feet of lumber, 90 tons of plaster, and 120 bales of sisal fiber.[111] Special lighting apparatus was required to give the sense of complete darkness lit only by candles. Selznick rewarded Menzies with a special mention on screen for his work and gave him the title of production designer for *Gone with the Wind*. Menzies's associate, art director Lyle Wheeler, received an Oscar nomination for his contributions to the movie.

Injun Joe's Cave on Tom Sawyer Island was equally elaborate. Advance publicity promised tunnels leading to rooms hung with stalactites and painted with decorations evoking the story.[112] One detail in particular in the attraction, called the Chamber of the Bottomless Pit, confirms the influence of the Selznick film. In the book Twain barely mentions Tom's approach to two "pitfalls" of uncertain depth, whereas in Selznick's movie Tom is menaced at the edge of a high precipice by Injun Joe, who in a dramatic moment falls suddenly to his death into a deep chasm. This was a major change from the book, in which Joe flees from his encounter with Tom and subsequently dies when trapped in the cave. Like the pit in the movie, Disney's Bottomless Pit was pure Hollywood illusion—in reality, it was only about seven feet deep. In addition to the Bottomless Pit, Disney's cave featured eerie sound effects, specifically a mournful howl in the dark that could be interpreted as either the wind or Joe himself.

The Disney attraction was an outsize fabrication that both internally and externally echoed Menzies's cave, being designed and constructed according to studio methods—with framing, chicken wire, and plaster. Art director Vic Green partnered on plans for Tom Sawyer Island with Disney artists Herb Ryman and Claude Coats, and Emile Kuri was on hand for the set decoration. As at the big studios, Walt's design team included a landscaper for the exteriors: Bill Evans knew how to compose natural shrubbery quickly for the greatest scenic effect. As he noted, "For my projects, for landscape, Walt would say, 'Hey Bill … 'I need a jungle! or, 'I need a Hannibal, Missouri, river shore!' or something … and it would take me a few days to get that."[113]

Disney and Selznick shared the conviction that a high-quality film provided lasting monetary value through periodic rereleases. Selznick rereleased *The Adventures of Tom Sawyer* in 1954. Thus, as production on Disneyland ramped up, the movie was fresh in the minds of Disney's designers as well as the moviegoing public.

Though the construction of Tom Sawyer Island may have approached in complexity what it took to stage Selznick's film, Disney's "casting" of a youth to impersonate Tom Sawyer in Frontierland was much simpler than Selznick's method of casting the movie's hero. The hype generated by Selznick's nationwide search for "Tom" was matched only by his subsequent casting of Scarlett O'Hara.[114] According to studio publicity, some 25,000 boys were interviewed, and hundreds given auditions, with the prize going to a twelve-year-old non-actor from New York.[115] However, at Disneyland, the lad picked to "be" Tom Sawyer got the job almost all on his own. Initially, when the island was unveiled, two youngsters from Hannibal were on hand to represent Tom and Becky at the ceremony. Subsequently, a local twelve-year-old boy, who had been selling *The Disneyland News* on Main Street, kept pestering Walt to give him the "part" on a more permanent basis, and his persistence paid off.[116]

Actors: Wanted Dead or Alive

Costumed characters, like the youth given the role of Tom Sawyer, brought Frontierland's stage set to life. The first park brochure promised that leather stockinged frontiersmen and "Indians" of various tribes would be on hand to greet visitors at the stockade gates[117] The men handling the horses, mules, and wagons made up the largest group of players. All the recognizable cinematic suspects were present and accounted for: cowboys, Native Americans, dance-hall girls, a marshal, a gunfighter, a wagon master, a mustachioed bad guy, and townsfolk. A visual shorthand like that employed on film was used to identify types: "A tall Stetson and a bandana make a cowboy," as cultural historian Karal Ann Marling put it, "a fedora and a suitcase make a speculator; a vest makes a saloonkeeper."[118]

There were no cattle in Walt's Wild West, but there were plenty of buckaroos. The cowboy hero, seen in over two thousand B movies between 1930 and 1954, embodied stoic frontier virtues.[119] Many of Frontierland's cast members were experienced ranch hands—men who, like those of an earlier generation, were drawn to Hollywood to represent themselves on the silver screen.[120] Meeting a flesh-and-blood cowpoke was nothing new for many Disneyland guests. Vacationers in the mid-fifties were mingling with cowboys on dude ranches across the West. The July 1955 issue of *Travel* magazine featuring the article "The Newest Travel Lure: Disneyland" also contained reports on "Dude Ranch Recreation," "Oklahoma's Cherokee Strip," "Alaska's Modern Day Gold Rush," and "East Coast's

Only Ghost Town." Frontierland put a glittery Tinseltown gloss on an up-close-and-personal experience Americans already had a hankering for.

Walt also revived the stories of folk heroes who embodied the nation's enterprising spirit.[121] On his first *Disneyland* broadcast, "The Disneyland Story," Walt stood before a large U.S. map and pointed toward pictures of sixteen fabled individuals, real and imaginary, from various regions across the country—Paul Bunyan from the Midwest, for instance, and John Wesley Powell out West. Some of these heroes, like Hiawatha and Johnny Appleseed, had already appeared in Disney cartoons. Others, like Mike Fink and Zorro, would come to life in movies or on TV. Walt explained the deeper purpose of these projects to Hedda Hopper: "I think this is a good time to get acquainted with or renew acquaintance with the American breed of robust, cheerful, energetic and representative folk heroes."[122]

Popular TV and movie cowboys could also be glimpsed at Disneyland. The August 1955 issue of *The Disneyland News*, which bore the front-page headline "World Visitors Enjoy Disneyland; Guests from Foreign Nations, All Parts of America Include Hollywood Stars," featured a photo of Roy Rogers and his wife and co-star, Dale Evans, "enjoying Disneyland's replica of the Old West, Frontierland."[123] Rogers, the "King of the Cowboys" and well known Western movie star, had appeared onscreen with the vocal group Sons of the Pioneers in the "Pecos Bill" sequence of *Melody Time*. Another celebrity, Clayton Moore, who enjoyed great success in the early television Western *The Lone Ranger*, appeared in character in Frontierland wearing his black mask to publicize the Warner Bros. film *The Lone Ranger* (1956). Similarly, actor Hugh O'Brian, star of the TV series *The Life and Legend of Wyatt Earp*, exhibited his quick-draw skills at the Golden Horseshoe.

Frontierland's characters included the bad guys too. The outlaw was a staple of the Western film, the product of mythologizing the real bank and train robbers recognizable from their black hats and tailored clothes. Their infamous deeds worked as counterpoint to the forces of law and order. Walt's realm would have been unimaginable without a daily shootout between Sheriff Lucky and Black Bart.[124] The gunfight was the set piece of countless Westerns—and, like so much Western lore, it had entered the realm of Hollywood fiction.[125]

One more character deserves mention. A sign over the Blacksmith's Shop proclaimed a legend in the making: "Willard P. Bounds, Blacksmith and US Marshal." *The Disneyland News* explained that this was a memorial to a real-life hero who helped open the frontier as an "Indian scout."[126] The historical Bounds was in fact Walt's father-in-law. Additionally, his wife Lillian's paternal grandfather was an early settler in the Northwest

Territory and later joined the California Gold Rush.[127] Simply put, the cast of players included occasional touches of a more personal sort.

King of the Wild Frontier

Disneyland's opening coincided with a national craze revolving around the Tennessee-born folk hero and Indian fighter, Davy Crockett—a $300 million business touched off by Walt's mini-series for the Frontierland component of the *Disneyland* television show.[128] The first episode, "Davy Crockett, Indian Fighter," aired December 15, 1954, the second, "Davy Crockett Goes to Congress," on January 26, 1955, and the third, "Davy Crockett at the Alamo," February 23, 1955. Audience response was so strong—an estimated ninety million Americans tuned in—that Walt turned on its head the general rule that a film should circulate commercially before it was seen on TV. In late May 1955, he successfully released *Davy Crockett: King of the Wild Frontier*, an edited down, ninety-minute theatrical version of the three shows.[129]

Throughout the "Crockett craze," the men who played Davy and his sidekick, Georgie Russell—Fess Parker and Buddy Ebsen—appeared in Disneyland parades and special events with Parker sporting Davy's trademark coonskin cap and fringed buckskin jacket, the juvenile apparel that fired the merchandising frenzy. (An estimated ten million caps alone were sold.)

Just inside Frontierland's gates, life-size wax figures of Parker and Ebsen had pride of place in the Davy Crockett Museum.[130] In true Hollywood fashion, the rusticated log exterior of the Museum bore no logical relationship to the adobe décor inside, publicized as an authentic replica of the Alamo, where Crockett died during the famous siege.[131] Amid displays of merchandise, show props, and an exhibit of the history of firearms sponsored by the National Rifle Association, visitors could, in a precursor of theme-park Character Meet and Greets of today, pose for souvenir photos with the wax dummies.[132] A year later, they were moved to Fort Wilderness on Tom Sawyer Island and placed in a tableau representing Davy and Georgie reporting to General Andrew Jackson during the Cherokee Indian campaigns of 1813. These silent witnesses to one of pop culture's biggest fads anticipated by ten years the Hollywood Wax Museum, which brought to life popular film scenes.

Disney wanted to make a Davy Crockett film as far back as 1946, when he invited the American Regionalist painter Thomas Hart Benton to the studio to develop ideas for a cartoon short subtitled "The Hunter of Kentucky" as a segment in a package film.[133] Though the Disney–Benton collaboration, whose goal was to produce "a distinctly and unmistakably American form—comic opera of the backwoods," was short-lived, Crockett remained on Walt's mind. Davy's name popped up briefly as an example of a folk hero in *Melody Time*. In the prologue to the "Sleepy Hollow" section of 1949's *The Adventures of Ichabod and Mr. Toad*, Crockett and Daniel Boone are cited as fabulous American characters. In 1954 a cartoon treatment of Crockett was still in the works as a *Disneyland* TV show, before a decision was taken to go with live-action.[134]

Davy Crockett represented for Disney the epitome of deeply felt American values. In 1954 the timing was perfect. Crockett had rarely been depicted by Hollywood since the era of silent pictures. As a young man, Walt may have seen the most impressive of five films made between 1909 and 1926, *Davy Crockett* (1916, presently lost), starring Dustin Farnum. Crockett also appeared as a minor character in movies about the Alamo from 1911, 1915, and 1937. Subsequent films, for some reason, focused on Davy's "relatives": *Son of Davy Crockett* (1941), and the 1950 picture about his nephew, *Davy Crockett, Indian Scout*.

The real Crockett, who had a brief career in Congress, may have donned a deerskin shirt on the campaign trail to convey a backwoods persona, but he never wore full buckskins or a coonskin cap.[135] These accouterments were theatrical inventions absorbed by the movies since the Dustin Farnum silent film.[136] In the mid–1930s, two screen stars solidified the image of the frontiersman in tasseled buckskin and raccoon cap: Randolph Scott as Hawkeye in *Last of the Mohicans* and George O'Brien as *Daniel Boone*. The Disney version of Davy Crockett owed more to films like these than to "straight" history—and Frontierland followed suit.

The Indian Village and Indian War Canoes

Walt long intended to have an Indian Village in his park.[137] Early publicity stated that Indigenous peoples weaving blankets and selling pottery would be positioned at the entrance to Frontierland's log stockade.[138] The original Village, populated by "genuine redskins," was located near the south end of the Rivers of America, between the train depot and Aunt Jemima's Kitchen. An expanded, "completely new Indian Village," located further north along the river's west bank, opposite Tom Sawyer Island, opened in mid–June 1956, to help mark Disneyland's first anniversary.[139]

An article in *The Disneyland News*, "A Visit to Frontierland's Indian Village: Tribal Lore Told, Ancient Crafts Shown," explained the didactic and entertainment value of the attraction and emphasized its authenticity.[140] Separate teepees were devoted to displays like the crafting of beadwork and ceremonial pipes, or regalia worn by the chief and medicine man. The teepees surrounded an elevated circular stage, on which were performed ceremonial dances with such evocative names as the Buffalo Dance, Bow and Arrow Dance, Feather Dance, and Horse Tail Dance.

The attraction followed the ethnological model of villages created for the World's Columbian Exposition of 1893 in Chicago and other international fairs. Their transparent purpose was to show the "savage" nature of Indigenous peoples—a characterization suggested by the word "primitive" used in Disneyland promotional material. Frontierland's Village included a captive buffalo, a demonstration of sand painting, and a Burial Ground. Twenty individuals from sixteen tribes—the Apache, Shawnee, Winnebago, Choctaw, among others—were employed. An abundance of stereotypical trappings (feathered costumes, teepees, beating tom-toms) played directly to Hollywood clichés.

Indian War Canoes in the waters that surrounded Tom Sawyer Island, powered by the guests themselves—paddle in hand, accompanied by two "Indians"—enabled paleface parkgoers to participate in a racial narrative as "braves" on a pretend mission to attack Fort Wilderness. They could also switch roles and mount the ramparts to fire back at the attackers.[141] Rough-timbered Fort Wilderness provides another example of how set design impacted Disneyland architecture. Stockades and corner blockhouses made of logs were uncommon in the West. But in the movies, the picturesque prevailed: hence the faux wooden fort erected at Kanab, Utah (a.k.a. Little Hollywood), for *Buffalo Bill* (1944), a biopic starring Joel McCrea and Maureen O'Hara. And so it was in Frontierland.

On the northern tip of Tom Sawyer Island stood the (perpetually) Burning Cabin of a pioneer presumably murdered by "Indians."[142] The motif of "Indian attacks" is another example of "authentic" history that was well developed before it was ever seen on film (as in *Stagecoach*). Since the 1880s, such recreations had served as showstopping tableaux in Buffalo Bill's Wild West show. Misconceptions, perpetuated since the arrival of Europeans, were readily absorbed by Hollywood. Early on, Native Americans sometimes appeared in a positive light. Over time—inescapably—they fell prey to bias and were portrayed in pictures in one of two ways: as noble savages or bloodthirsty brutes attacking wagon trains, harassing settlers, or kidnapping white women.

Still, historians have pointed to a considerable range of imagery in the Hollywood Western: in a single picture, like *The Covered Wagon*, one tribe might be friendly, another exploitative, a third murderous.[143] This ambivalence toward "Indians" is in full view in *Buffalo Bill*, where Cody defends the Native Americans and opposes hunting buffalo. In a famous story session memo, Darryl Zanuck reminded his writers of "our ignoble treatment of the American Indian." But the movie shows drunken natives on the attack and the spectacle of buffalo hunting. Cody and his childhood friend, Yellow Hand, greet each other, saying "How." Navajos hired for bit parts reportedly laughed at the outlandish costumes and war paint they had to wear. Amazingly, some film critics complained that the film's presentation of Indigenous Americans was too soft.

The year 1950 marked something of a turning point, with the James Stewart film *Broken Arrow*, which showed greater sympathy toward tribes and a sincere interest in their customs. The same year saw the founding of the National Film Committee of the Association on American Indian Affairs, which advocated for better treatment of Indigenous peoples in film.

Pre-park Disney imagery of Native Americans was limited to a couple of animated cartoons, starting with the 1937 *Silly Symphony, Little Hiawatha*, a gentle spoof of Longfellow's "The Song of Hiawatha." In 1948 Disney announced plans—never materialized—to produce a full-length animated version of the poem, for which he dispatched a sketch artist to the wilds to gather material.[144] *Peter Pan* (1953), one of Walt's classic feature-length cartoons, projected a more degrading image than *Little Hiawatha*, epitomized by the musical number "What Makes the Red Man Red?"

Disneyland's treatment of Indigenous peoples is something of a mixed bag. We must look to Disney's television and live-action theatrical films of the 1950s to evaluate the Indian Village. The *Davy Crockett* TV series combined hackneyed movie stereotypes with traces of authenticity: like the eponymous hero of *Buffalo Bill*, Davy is a close friend to some natives and battles and outsmarts others. For *Westward Ho the Wagons!* Walt (like Zanuck) insisted on downplaying the Indians' attack on the wagons and playing up their cooperation with the settlers. A pair of Disney films from 1958 took the point of view of Native Americans. *The Light in the Forest* treats a white youth raised by American Indians whose culture he prefers, and *Tonka* is the story of a Sioux brave and his beloved horse caught up in the Indian Wars.[145]

In sum, while Disney came to embrace a more enlightened attitude, his Indian Village mirrored Hollywood's own ambivalence.[146] It leaned heavily toward the fierce Plains Indians warrior type, with no reference to the American Indian Wars, the Trail of Tears, or the removal of tribes to reservations. Even so, in Walt's favor, it is worth noting that Frontierland's "Indians" were primarily Indigenous peoples, not costumed players, and they participated in design and performance decisions.[147] Meanwhile, back on Main Street, one of the oldest of Western clichés, the wooden cigar-store Indian, still holds its ground on the sidewalk where the original Fine Tobacco shop was located.[148]

Aunt Jemima and the Old South

Before it was decided to dedicate Tom Sawyer Island to its adventurous namesake, thought was given to placing miniature versions of Deep South-themed historical and fictional sites along the banks of the Rivers of America.[149] One such idea, derived from Disney's *Song of the South* (1946), was to feature representations of Uncle Remus and singing Black laborers on a cotton plantation. This idea was discarded. Instead, a full-scale Creole-style mansion was erected on Frontierland's western boundary: the Chicken Plantation restaurant, which specialized in fried chicken dinners. Also, extending south from the Golden Horseshoe, Disney installed New Orleans Street. Its quaint cast-iron balconies and shuttered French doors sheltered two more eateries: the Casa de Fritos, sponsored by Frito-Lay, serving Mexican fare, and, near the border of Adventureland, Aunt Jemima's Pancake House, sponsored by Quaker Oaks.[150] New Orleans Street was a precursor to Disneyland's French Quarter–style New Orleans Square, the larger "sub-land" that opened in July 1966.

Promotional blurbs stressed the sector's thematic unity. Plantation architecture, the strains of Dixieland jazz, and the inviting scent of down-home cooking brought to multi-sensory life a place of "wondrous beauty, of moonlight and magnolias, and mint juleps."[151] An innovative aspect of the park was the theming of dining venues to complement nearby attractions, with a special emphasis on "atmosphere" through evocative décor.[152]

The landscape designer for Disneyland's Dixie, Ruth Shellhorn, described the role played by greenery in creating the desired effect:

> The New Orleans section faces a park along the river, where lawns and magnolias, crapemyrtles, and oleanders give it a feeling of the Old South. Although Spanishmoss [sic] was out of the question, the waving branches of weeping trees along the river add to the atmosphere. There are paved patios for outdoor seating, and iron grillwork, railings, and a gazebo which juts out into the water. Much of this ironwork came from Old Southern buildings.

She also unashamedly acknowledged the sector's ahistorical mix, à la Hollywood, of building types: "Here the studio technique of combining two styles of architecture in one structure is cleverly employed. As one looks toward the Chicken Plantation, the architecture is seen to be that of New Orleans; but as one stands across the bridge in front of the Western Railway Station and looks back, it is that of Arizona and New Mexico."[153]

PR flacks hailed the Chicken Plantation as a faithful recreation of an antebellum mansion—the epitome of Southern hospitality—replete with French-style furnishings.[154] Most Americans were familiar with the mythical space of the Old South primarily through the movies. Between 1929 and 1941, the action in some seventy-five feature films took place in states below the Mason-Dixon line.[155] Every big studio had a plantation house on the premises, appropriately dressed for historical or contemporary subjects. Tara from *Gone with the Wind* remained on the RKO Forty Acres lot until the 1950s, when a private collector in Georgia took the dilapidated remains off its hands. MGM's Southern Mansion, constructed for *The Toy Wife* (1938), survived until 1978. Fox had its Colonial Home, utilized extensively for exterior shots in *The Foxes of Harrow* (1947), and Universal had, by Tinseltown standards, an almost "antique" Colonial Mansion, built in 1927.[156]

Nonetheless, a permanent New Orleans "street" was a rarity on a Hollywood backlot. It was easier to refashion a standing urban set by adding signage and lacy balconies to achieve the required look. Robert Haas designed one of the most detailed of these temporary sets for Warner's *Jezebel* (1938), which opens with a tracking shot in the Vieux Carré (identified in a screen title "New Orleans, 1852") along a busy cobblestone street market with simulated cast-iron balconies. Warner Bros. built an indoor New Orleans Street for *A Streetcar Named Desire* (1951), then moved it to the backlot. Used for filming into the 1970s, it gained in "authenticity" as it deteriorated from exposure to the elements.

Typically, a single movie might have New Orleans street scenes filmed both outdoors and indoors on a soundstage. For *The Foxes of Harrow*, art directors created a *plein-air* set of the French Market and an indoor set of the French Quarter. Similarly, for *The Flame of New Orleans* (1941) a large soundstage set combined elements of both the French Quarter and the Garden District, while a backlot setting recycled an old European village set utterly inconsistent with the architectural style of the Crescent City. When Disneyland's New Orleans Street was dedicated in September 1955, its Hollywood connection was underscored as Dorothy Lamour broke a bottle filled with water from the Mississippi and the Gulf of Mexico against Lafitte's Anchor. She declared that the street looked exactly like the city of her birth.[157]

Walt's New Orleans Street forms the backdrop to the final musical segment set in Frontierland in "Dateline Disneyland," the park's televised premiere, in which a Dixieland band, trumpet players, and sultry jazz dancers conjure up the Big Easy during Mardi Gras. Joining the party are two Black cast members, a tap-dancing youth, seemingly transported from street-side busking in New Orleans' French Quarter, and Aunt Jemima, the hostess of the Pancake House, outfitted in her trademark checked dress, bandana, and apron. They were the only people of color visible on the opening day telecast, aside from Sammy Davis, Jr., who trailed Frank Sinatra in an Autopia car. In its early years, Disneyland's customer base was overwhelmingly white middle class. Articles in *Ebony* and *Hue*, focusing on Black children touring the park, suggest that Black patrons were welcome. However, the *Negro Motorist Green-Books*, which offered advice to Black travelers, made no mention of the Magic Kingdom.[158]

The tapping youth in "Dateline Disneyland" was one of many New Orleans stereotypes meant to impart a semblance of authenticity.[159] Another was the presence of Aunt Jemima—a variant of the Mammy stereotype—who for many years was a fixture of the Magic Kingdom. The woman best known for personifying Aunt Jemima in Frontierland, Aylene Lewis (hired in 1957), apparently saw nothing offensive about her work. She reportedly relished her experience and claimed to be on friendly terms with Walt.[160]

Part of the backstory of Walt's Pancake House Mammy is that for nearly sixty years, dozens of women had appeared as Aunt Jemima at fairs, conventions, and local gatherings all across the country. Paper placements in the Pancake House reproduced World War I era artwork by famed illustrator N.C. Wyeth (father of Andrew Wyeth) that promoted Jemima's legend—depicting her days as a slave on a Louisiana plantation, her formulation of the "Aunt Jemima Pancake Flour" recipe, and her participation in the Columbian Exposition of 1893. *The Disneyland News* was not alone in recounting the legend as if it were historical truth.[161]

The Mammy stereotype embodied by Aunt Jemima had emerged in minstrel shows and was largely familiar to Americans through motion pictures, beginning with *The Birth of a Nation* in 1915. The most famous personification of the type was actor Hattie McDaniel, a child of formerly enslaved parents. McDaniel won an Academy Award for Best Supporting Actress as the house servant "Mammy" in *Gone with the Wind*. She replicated this role as Aunt Tempy in *Song of the South*, which was severely rebuked by *Ebony* in 1947 in an editorial that castigated the Uncle Remus character as an "Uncle Tom-Aunt Jemima caricature, complete with all the fawning standard equipment thereof."[162]

Walt never accepted *Song of the South*'s failings, and for years he looked for ways to resolve the critical pain and box office disappointment of its initial release. Six months after Disneyland opened, a full-hour *Disneyland* TV show, "A Tribute to Joel Chandler Harris," advertised the imminent rerelease of the film, which again got a hostile reception in the press.[163] In the end, although Br'er Rabbit appeared on the "The Disneyland Story" program as one of the sixteen legendary characters appropriate to Frontierland, *Song of the South* had little further association with Disneyland until Splash Mountain was conceived in the mid–1980s.[164]

Reinvigorating the Frontier Myth

Disneyland's opening coincided with a period of change for the Western film. The genre had taken a darker, "psychological" turn, with complex, emotionally damaged protagonists driven by inner demons, as in John Ford's *The Searchers* (1956). The higher cost of making epic pictures and lower returns meant that fewer went into production. As early as 1950, Darryl Zanuck was bemoaning their decline, and in 1958, only a few years after Disneyland opened, Fox president Spyros Skouras held a press conference on Tombstone Street—a spot aptly chosen—to announce the demise, demolition, and redevelopment of the studio's backlot.[165]

In the late 1940s, independents like Republic began selling off their back catalogs to television for use as programming filler. That sealed the fate of the B-series Western, the last of which was made in 1954. But "Cowboys and Indians shows" for kids, like *Hopalong Cassidy*, were a huge hit on the small screen. Bill Boyd's "Hoppy" set off a merchandizing mania that prefigured the one triggered by Fess Parker's Davy Crockett. In 1955, the "adult" Western cracked the primetime lineup on TV, starting with *Gunsmoke, Cheyenne*, and *The Life and Legend of Wyatt Earp*. The number of Western programs peaked at thirty during the 1959–1960 season. Their popularity probably fueled interest in Frontierland, but oversaturation in the early 1960s contributed to their permanent decline.[166] The Hollywood Western suffered highs and lows in Disneyland's early years—but Frontierland was never adversely affected. Walt's Wild West remained wildly successful.

Walt Disney did not respond to the new psychological Western. At age 54, he was fully committed to the virtues exemplified by the old-fashioned shoot-'em-ups of the 1930s and 1940s. Motion pictures featuring heroic, manly men like John Wayne, Randolph Scott, Jimmy Stewart, or Joel McCrea would eventually bite the dust. But Frontierland carried on their legacy, as an expression of a core concept of Turner's Frontier Thesis—the belief that America's greatness sprang not from its European roots but from the taming of the frontier. The entertainment gospel according to Hollywood and Walt meant that the stouthearted men and women who accomplished that feat should serve as models for future generations—especially in times of trouble. The inevitable corollary was that they reinforced an age-old notion of cultural conflict between "savages" and so-called civilization.

But we may well ask: Wasn't Turner's thesis outdated by the 1950s? In fact, it was not. Significantly, it was the subject of an influential book published in 1950, *Virgin Land: The American West in Symbol and Myth*, in which Henry Nash Smith argued for the original and persuasive character of Turner's essay.[167] Smith brought Turner's interpretive take on the frontier to the attention of new generations and restored its standing in academic circles, where it held firm until the 1970s. Americans, recovering from the calamities of World War II and seeking to negotiate the Cold War, found strength and purpose in the myth of the frontier, with its emphasis on liberty, courage, and individualism—the basic hallmarks of American identity and culture. Smith opens his text with the question "What is an American?"[168] Disney in effect responded by recreating the Old West not only as a means of entertaining, but also of inculcating the ideals expressed in Golden Age movies.[169]

Just as the Western film, fashioned on the backlot, had crystallized a set of visual and narrative ideals, so too Disney, inspired by midcentury nostalgia for the great American past, absorbed the conventions of Hollywood to provide visitors to Disneyland with the iconic settings, the exciting movement, the sense of place, and the cast of characters that had been the stock-in-trade of Western films. In short, the "authentic" Western on the silver screen came vividly and authentically to life in Frontierland.

3

Adventureland

While Main Street, U.S.A., is firmly rooted in turn-of-the-century nostalgia, and Frontierland takes visitors back to the great American West, circa 1840–1880, Adventureland covers both eras, from the mid-nineteenth to the early twentieth century. Located southwest of the central Plaza, Adventureland was described in Disney publicity as a wonderland of lush foliage of nature's own design that transported visitors to foreign locales inhabited by "life-like wild animals" and "savage natives."[1]

When Disneyland opened in July 1955, visitors entered Adventureland through a portal surmounted by crossed elephant tusks with a human skull dangling between them. There was just one ride. Originally called the Explorer's Boat Ride and alternately referred to as Rivers of the World, Jungle River Boat Ride, and Jungle River Boat Safari, it has been known since the late 1950s as the Jungle Cruise (Fig. 19). According to early publicity, guests departed from a Tahitian Village on a tour of the Rivers of the World, where robotic lions could be seen lunching on a dead zebra, crocodiles and hippos rose suddenly from beneath rivers, and cannibals awaited each new boatload of passengers. Publicists claimed it was the only ride on earth that let visitors safely explore uncharted territory.[2]

Today, the Jungle Cruise enjoys the cachet of being one of the few surviving original rides in Disneyland. Adventureland's other draw was its tropical settlement and bazaar on the banks of a jungle river, where souvenirs from far-flung places like India, Kenya, and the South Sea Islands were available for purchase.[3]

As with Main Street and Frontierland, the semblance of authenticity was a selling point for Adventureland. Seven boats, the *Congo Queen*, *Swanee Lady*, *Amazon Belle*, *Ganges Gal*, *Nile Princess*, *Mekong Maiden*, and *Irrawaddy Woman*, took travelers on a journey through realistic settings where they could gaze upon life-like creatures in the wild. According to *The Disneyland News* in September 1955, no less a personage than

Figure 19. Jungle Cruise boats and landing, Adventureland, Disneyland, 1955 (from the collection of Dave DeCaro).

Nazli Sabri, the Queen Mother of Egypt, confirmed the "authenticity" of the ride, especially its recreation of the Nile.[4]

According to Disney PR, Adventureland was an outgrowth of Walt's *True-Life Adventures* documentaries. But there was more to it than that. Conceptually, there were multiple sources: real-life Victorian-era colonialism; illustrated stories in American and English magazines for boys; travel narratives and best-selling non-fiction like Frank Buck's *Bring 'Em Back Alive* (1930) or Alfred Aloysius Horn's *Trader Horn* (1927); and unsavory "white bwana"–type heroes and explorers.[5] In addition to these influences, I argue that there was a Hollywood connection as well, mentioned only in passing by Disney historians. In this chapter I explore the ways in which Adventureland's thrills and chills were grounded in jungle movies—from *Tarzan the Ape Man* to *The African Queen*—as well as the more prosaic genre of the travelogue.[6] We will see that, to a surprising extent, Disney's art directors, some recruited from other Tinseltown studios, found inspiration in old film scripts, backlot sets, and even Hollywood's private zoos. During four decades of motion pictures, certain underlying conceits, such as the White Hunter, the "savage" native, and the jungle as a place of danger and romance, had become so deeply embedded in the public's consciousness that their appearance in Adventureland was inevitable. Walt himself confirmed Adventureland's association with Hollywood. On

one occasion, upon debarking from one of the boats, he complained that
the ride proceeded too rapidly, comparing his experience to watching a
movie with the middle reel missing.[7]

Development

During development of the park, Adventureland promised to be a
minor sector among the Magic Kingdom's realms. Marvin Davis, a former
assistant art director at Fox who joined Disney in 1953, drafted numerous potential layouts for the park. One such plan, dated September 25,
1953—one of the first to incorporate the Hub layout—listed an area called
"True-Life Adventure," *sans* the word "land."[8] Located on the eastern
(right-hand) side of the Hub (the Plaza), south of the "Land of Tomorrow,"
this forerunner of Adventureland was entered through a tropical garden
lined with shops. Immediately south of the entry corridor was a True-Life
Adventure Theatre. The main attraction was an Explorer's Boat Ride moving in a continuous loop along a meandering jungle river. Situated directly
opposite Davis's draft version for Adventureland, on the other side of the
Hub—where the sector eventually was located—were a Pony Ride and Circus Land.

Created under Walt's supervision in September 1953, Herb Ryman's
Aerial View of Disneyland shows Adventureland still located on the east
side of the Plaza, entered via an iron and glass shed named the Crystal
Palace. This structure reveals the designers' deep reach into history, in
this case the huge building in London's Hyde Park, site of the very first
world's fair (The Great Exhibition, 1851), which enclosed full-sized elm
trees within its spacious cast-iron and plate-glass confines. Ryman's drawing confirms that a canopied explorer's boat was already in the works, and
it shows crocodiles sunning themselves on an outcrop in the river, monkeys cavorting on their own island, and a pyramid-shaped ruin with a bird
perched on top. Eventually, the idea of live animals gave way to mechanical replicas.

One curious proposal was to have the cruise boat cross an imaginary
equator, where a three-dimensional figure of Neptune would pop up out
of the water. This is one of the earliest mentions of an automated figure
in Disneyland. The Roman god of the sea had been the star of a Disney
Silly Symphony cartoon, *King Neptune* (1932), and the same character rises
at the Equator in the cartoon short "The Cold-Blooded Penguin" in the
package film *The Three Caballeros* (1944). But the physical presence of a
mythological god in Adventureland sounded a false note, and the idea was
dropped.[9] Also at this stage, it was not the boat's guide who announced the

ports of call, but a pre-recorded voice emanating from strategically placed speakers. Suggestions were also floated for tiny villages along the shore in keeping with Disney's *modus operandi* throughout the park: miniaturization. Main Street, U.S.A., as we have seen, adopted the Hollywood set technique of varying scales; the Disneyland trains were reduced in size, and in Frontierland the mining town of Rainbow Ridge was visualized as a scale model.

By October 27, 1954, when the *Disneyland* TV show débuted, the tropical realm, now called Adventureland, had moved to its permanent position on the west (left-hand) side of the Plaza, while Circus Land moved to the east. The switch is clearly seen in a four-by-eight-foot aerial view in oil and florescent paint by Peter Ellenshaw, reproduced a week later in *Look* magazine ("Here's Your First View of Disneyland"), showing Jungle Cruise steamboats with their red-and-white striped canopies.[10] Former Warner Bros. assistant art director, Harper Goff, who supplied visual ideas for Main Street and Frontierland, spent thirteen months overseeing the layout and planning of Adventureland. An August 1955 article in *The Disneyland News* credits Goff's extensive input and—in accordance with big-studio procedures—the sketches, illustrations, and models he made during the design process.[11]

Riding the Jungle Cruise

Before and after the park opened, Walt shared news about it on TV and in the forty-two-minute theatrical release, *Disneyland, U.S.A*, in his *People and Places* series. A glimpse of the earliest iteration of the Jungle Cruise under construction, still little more than an earthwork, appeared in "A Progress Report" aired on the *Disneyland* TV show on February 9, 1955. This six-minute segment featured a simulated ride in a Rambler Cross Country station wagon—a nod to a co-sponsor of the show—moving along a dry riverbed. Bolstered by intercuts of real animals and footage of their mechanical counterparts being built in the studio, Walt teased the audience with his enticing description of the coming attraction. Viewers learned that a mangrove swamp representing the Everglades and a boat passing by a cannibal village in Zululand were in the works.

Five months later, a "Pre-Opening Report" broadcast on the *Disneyland* show on July 13, 1955, a few days before the park's opening, included clips of the waterproofing of the riverbed and fiberglass cruise boats under construction. On July 17, 1955, "Dateline Disneyland," the televised inauguration, introduced Adventureland almost as an afterthought. It got less than two minutes of airtime, though the pre-recorded views of the boats and animals were intriguing.

Most important for our analysis, seven months after the park began operation, a half-hour "making-of" documentary under the "True-Life Adventure" label was presented on the February 29, 1956, episode of the *Disneyland* TV series, where it was paired with the True-Life Adventure film *Water Birds*. Walt introduced the segment, "A Trip through Adventureland," with a full demonstration of the conception and realization of the Jungle Cruise, from sketches and blueprints to installation of foliage, water, and boats. Then he invited viewers to take the full Jungle Cruise ride, lasting nine and a half minutes. Staff writer-producer Winston Hibler penned and voiced the skipper's narration, subtly modified to make it sound as though he was talking through a megaphone. An orchestral soundtrack for the segment—as in any motion picture or television drama—cued the viewer when to be frightened, when to relax, and when to laugh. The widespread belief that the early skippers' scripts were dull, and that humor was a later addition,[12] is belied by Hibler's lively commentary: jokes and puns were clearly a major part of the ride from the get-go. As "A Trip through Adventureland" likewise shows, the array of tropical lands billed in pre-opening publicity had been reduced once the sector premiered.

A detailed description and analysis of this televised tour reveals the ride's components in the park's first year, before later changes and additions were made. Once the passengers boarded, the explorer's launch took them from the safety of civilization to the calm beauty of the Edenic upper reaches of the Amazon. Nature is tranquil in this paradise of spectacular orchids, lush vegetation, brilliant colors, and sounds of rare birds. A few moments later, the passengers find themselves on the Mekong River in French Indochina. The environment is still friendly, and the soundtrack is lighthearted, as guests laugh at the sight of an ancient abandoned Cambodian shrine with mechanical monkeys mucking about, trying perhaps, as the captain says, "to ruin the ruins. You never can tell about monkey business, you know."

As the cruise arrives in Africa, the music takes a sinister turn. On the Nile, the skipper warns everyone to keep their hands inside the boat as crocodiles menace the craft. Continuing through the Dark Continent, he gestures at a pair of rhinoceroses partially hidden in the grass lining the shore. Clever camera work and cutting make it appear that the rhinos are charging the boat. A trumpeting sound prompts the captain to draw passengers' attention to a "lonesome" female elephant and a bull elephant answering her call. Dispensing animal lore, he points out the characteristic large ears of the African elephant. Next, a close call with the plunging waters of Schweitzer Falls threatens to dampen the proceedings. But this is a minimal threat compared to the sight of two roaring lions hungrily eyeing the group. Spotting a long-necked creature poking its head above the trees, the skipper tells his passengers they can now boast "a nodding acquaintance" with a giraffe—noting, parenthetically, that giraffes lack vocal cords and cannot make a sound.

As the boat moves on, a hippopotamus herd swims toward the craft wiggling their ears. Commenting on a pair of hippos facing each other with mouths wide open, the skipper remarks that they have probably surfaced to laugh at jokes they had shared under the water. Just then, an aged male with curved tusks, Old Snaggletooth, charges the boat (Fig. 20). The guide warns of the impending danger and, grabbing a pistol from its holster, fires at the hippo. The Congo River is next on the tour. The atmosphere grows ominous, as a line of heavily painted natives wielding spears and shields peer at the boat from the foliage. The camera zooms in on a skull mounted on a stake, and the skipper muses that the tingling sensation felt by passengers might be explained by the fact that the headhunters had recently claimed a souvenir from an unlucky tourist seeking a shortcut through the dense vegetation.

Calm is restored and a smooth patch of water evokes memories of a time-honored amusement park attraction, the Tunnel of Love. The camera lingers on a young couple as the narrator, Hibler, says this would be a

Figure 20. Jungle Cruise, Adventureland, hippo pool, 1957 (from the collection of Dave DeCaro).

good time to pause and let young lovers hold hands and gaze fondly into each other's eyes. Thus, the jungle is also revealed to be a garden of love, a happy byproduct of adventure. After this warm and fuzzy interlude, the excitement builds again with a thrilling run through white-water rapids, followed by a glimpse of another crocodile, Old Faithful, checking out the trip's survivors. Satisfied that everyone has come through safely, "alligator tears" come to his eyes.[13] The boat pulls into the dock at the Tahitian Village and back to civilization. Passengers are greeted by a hula dancer and assured in song by a group of Hawaiian musicians that the spell of the tropics means many repeat trips to Adventureland. The same storyline was used for a shortened Jungle Cruise segment of the *Disneyland, U.S.A.* featurette, released in December 1956, in which a few menacing elements were left out, and others, like the shooting of the hippo, were given greater emphasis.

The Travelogue and Nature Documentary

Prior to the twentieth century, travel to faraway places was experienced chiefly through travel accounts of real-life explorers and imaginary characters. With the advent of motion pictures, the printed page yielded to celluloid. Fiction and non-fiction travel films provided vicarious adventures and an escape from the travails of daily life, especially during the Depression, then World War II, and then from the ennui of postwar suburban life. The voice-over techniques of traditional big-screen travelogues provided the basis for the voiced narration of the Jungle Cruise ride on the *Disneyland* TV shows and the *Disneyland, U.S.A.* featurette. Furthermore, the skipper's spiel on the actual ride, peppered with interesting facts and amusing anecdotes, also possessed a documentary flavor. For these reasons, before we examine made-in-Hollywood jungle adventure films, it is worth looking at the history of the movie genres of the travelogue and nature documentary to see how they influenced the Adventureland attraction.

In 1923 a Kansas couple, Marvin and Osa Johnson, began filming a series of travelogues set in Africa. Far from being plodding classroom documentaries, pictures like *Simba, the King of Beasts* (1928) and *Congorilla* (1932) concentrated on dramatic confrontations between animals and humans, popularizing images of ferocious brutes charging the viewer.[14] The Johnsons called the Nile "a river of horror, teeming with slithering crocodiles" and the rhino "Public Enemy Number One." The Congo was a paradisiacal "land where man and beast still live in the Garden of Eden." The films were thrilling of course but stained by a pernicious tone of racism vis-à-vis the natives, common to all types of motion picture entertainment for most of the twentieth century.

The first "talkie" travelogue was the aptly named *Africa Speaks!* (1930), directed by Paul Hoefler and narrated by famed broadcaster Lowell Thomas. Rather than broaden moviegoers' knowledge of the unknown, *Africa Speaks!* sensationalized its subject, exaggerating the elements of danger and intrigue. It opened with a black silhouette of the continent, literally the Dark Continent, and these breathless words: "Africa ... the sinister ... the mysterious ... the unknown! Land of savagery and dangerous adventure ... where nature is without mercy ... and deadly beasts of the jungle are supreme."

Travelogues flourished in the 1930s and enjoyed a post-war surge with films like RKO's *Savage Splendor* (1949). The opening narration of *Savage Splendor* tried to break with earlier stereotypes: "The Dark Continent, they call it. Land of shadows. And yet it blazes with light and color. There is not merely one Africa, but a hundred Africas: varied, changing, unpredictable." Despite this promising beginning, the movie falls back on the old clichés, starting with the word "savage" in the title. Capturing a giraffe by lasso to sell to a zoo, the narrator reminds us, "With all that neck, he has no vocal cords"—a piece of lore repeated in other films and on the Jungle Cruise. Fearsome hippos enter the picture in *Savage Splendor* when the crew discovers a clear pool, a "secret hideout" where no white man has ever ventured. A guard stands on the boat, rifle at the ready, while the narrator explains, "The hippos resented our intrusion; they kept coming up to reconnoiter. We started off cautiously, our gun guide alert. Hippos have immense strength and agility in the water. Like elephants, some of them become rogues and attack without provocation.... One old bull, his twisted tusk a souvenir of bygone battle, added a nightmare touch to the scene." This nightmarish touch would be repeated at Disneyland when the cruise captains drew their guns on the charging hippo, Old Snaggletooth.

Disney tried his hand at the travelogue genre in the early 1940s in the form of a trio of South American package films, starting with *South of the Border with Disney* (1942). It is clear that he sought to emulate the big studios when he borrowed from MGM several documentaries in the *FitzPatrick Traveltalks* series for the purpose of study. From these he also used stock shots of Mexico for his own *The Three Caballeros*.[15] Then in 1948, Disney surprised Hollywood and his distributor, RKO, by reinvigorating the travelogue with the first of thirty *True-Life Adventures* and *People and Places* films released over a twelve-year period. By 1956, *The Disneyland News* claimed that more than three dozen photographers were scattered across the globe, shooting sequences for the two series. All the world had, in effect, become, if not his oyster, Disney's stage.[16]

Writers have repeatedly cited the *True-Life Adventures* as the prime inspiration for the Jungle Cruise ride.[17] No less an authority than Walt himself, in his duties as host of the February 1955 *Disneyland* show about the making of Adventureland, said the original plan had been to recreate scenes from *True-Life Adventure* films. Studio publicists promoted the interrelationship between Adventureland (the cruise in particular) and both the *True-Life Adventures* and *People and Places* pictures.

In its August 15, 1955, issue, *The Disneyland News* reported that Harper Goff had been tasked with designing the scenery of the Jungle Cruise in a manner consistent with the *True-Life Adventure* film, *Prowlers of the Everglades* (1953).[18] A second *True-Life Adventure*—*The African Lion* (released in September 1955)—was also named in the same issue as the principal inspiration for the attraction.[19] This hour-and-fifteen-minute-long film, in production as Goff worked on the Jungle Cruise ride, was presumably known to him.[20] The opening titles acknowledge cooperation by the governments of South Africa, Kenya, Tanganyika (present-day Tanzania), and Uganda, giving it an unofficial stamp of approval from four of the most important countries on the east coast of sub-Saharan Africa. The titles also describe *The African Lion* as a project "three years in the making … an authentic camera record of actual happenings."

James Algar, a studio veteran and Stanford undergrad buddy of Disney legends Ollie Johnston and Frank Thomas, oversaw production of *The African Lion*. Algar had directed the "Sorcerer's Apprentice" segment in *Fantasia* (1940), co-directed the *Wind in the Willows* half of *The Adventures of Ichabod and Mr. Toad* (1949), and later produced the live-action thriller, *Ten Who Dared* (1960), starring Brian Keith and Ben Johnson. More importantly, Algar served as head writer and director for two Oscar-winning Disney documentaries, *The Living Desert* (1953) and *The Vanishing Prairie* (1954). Like earlier films set in Africa, *The African Lion* opens with a map of the continent in silhouette, a solid mass of black with no national borders. The narrator—again Winston Hibler—swiftly deflects any implicit racism in the epithet "Dark Continent." The term came about, he explains, because Africa has long been shrouded in mystery. A cartoon artist's brush then applies color to four stretches of terrain around the periphery of the continent: the northern desert, southern bush country, eastern swamp, and western jungle. The African lion, we learn, roams a broad plain in the heart of the continent interspersed with mountains, lakes, and forests. Thus, the film introduces the African veldt, a primitive "paradise," and liberates the mythic "king of the jungle" from the jungle. Despite its title, every species seen on the Jungle Cruise appears in *The African Lion*—the key difference being that Disneyland's mechanical creatures all inhabited a make-believe jungle. Both the movie and the ride had a massive, trumpeting bull elephant, slithering crocodiles, and yawning hippos. Winston Hibler performed the roles of narrator and co-writer for both *The African Lion* and the Cruise segment on the late-winter 1956 *Disneyland* TV show. His mild but authoritative, paternal voice delivered plain-spoken facts leavened with gentle humor. Commenting in the film on the giraffe's height and long neck, he falls back on the standard lore, emphasizing its unusual characteristic: muteness.

In Disney wildlife movies, the camera is invisible, and the human presence negligible. Taking up themes of the early travelogues, footage in *The African Lion* emphasizes the great cats' relentless hunt for food. Director Algar built his story around seven dramatic kills executed by lions and other animals. Critics have disparaged the *True-Life Adventures'* tendency to anthropomorphize wild animals, even though there is little of that in *The African Lion*. The most significant human touch is the stirring music used to heighten the action. Near the end of the picture a swarm of locusts obliterates the savanna. Exercising a degree of homocentric projection, Hibler calls the plague a living nightmare in which animals wander about like ghosts lost in a dream. Dream versus nightmare juxtapositions like this have a rich history in jungle films. On the Adventureland ride, visitors are active participants in its alternating dreamy and terrifying elements. In short, *The African Lion* is "fair game" as a contributing factor in the attraction's development. But Hollywood jungle films, particularly those set in a fictionalized Africa, provide a better sense of how the ride came about and why its narratives resonated with park visitors.

Trader Horn

The prototypical jungle film *Trader Horn* (1931) inspired in multiple ways an entire line of subsequent movies—and, ultimately, the Disneyland ride. After MGM acquired the rights to Trader Horn's memoir, it conceived the bold plan to shoot the story on location, making it the first Hollywood action picture produced almost entirely in Africa.

Trader Horn opens with titles superimposed on a map of Africa. Giving a false impression of authenticity, officials of four nations—Tanganyika, Kenya, Sudan, the Belgian Congo—are thanked for their cooperation, and mention is made of 14,000 miles of veldt and jungle traversed by the crew. However, with one exception, no cities or countries are identified on the map. "Cameroon" is named, but merely as an unlocalized site. Generic trails and rivers crisscross the map, leading nowhere in particular. Words like "unknown," "cannibal," and "head-hunter" appeal to moviegoers' naïve notions about natives, and pictographs of an elephant, giraffe or gazelle likewise simply evoke the wildness of faraway lands. Notwithstanding these minimal efforts to suggest authenticity, *Trader Horn* perpetrates a received idea of Africa as the Dark Continent, a tabula rasa upon which viewers may project their own fantasies. Twenty-five years later, maps of Adventureland in Disneyland guidebooks displayed a similarly vague landmass and a river to nowhere that repeatedly turns back on itself. Words like "bazaar," "cantina," and "jungle river," and pictographs of a giraffe, elephant, and tribal shield served not to inform, but to spark the imagination.[21]

Trader Horn was a global hit, garnering an Academy Award nomination for Best Picture. In America and around the world, it unleashed a series of jungle-adventure conceits that would be repeated so often in subsequent films that it would have been a blunder if the Jungle Cruise had not tapped into them, since visitors expected these tropes.[22] *Trader Horn's* influential conceits may be categorized here.

- *The perilous river journey.* The film is bookended by a river journey, in which the characters react, going and coming, to the wild beasts they encounter. As in the Jungle Cruise, a crocodile awaits on shore, silent and still, or a cohort of crocs slips into the water, glides toward the boat, and in seemingly authentic footage, an African porter accidentally falls into the stream and is devoured by one of the toothy monsters.
- *The White Hunter.* Trader Horn, played by Harry Carey, epitomizes the white adventurer in Africa (usually English or American), a heroic guide and all-around good guy who dispenses fun facts to his on-screen companions—and the audience—along the way. An extraordinary fifteen-minute sequence resembling a travelogue temporarily interrupts the narrative, as Horn points out various animals to his novice sidekick, Peru (Duncan Renaldo), noting, for example, "Did you know, lad, the giraffe can't cry out, even in his death? No vocal cords!" Horn kills two rhinos and a lion in the film. In a scene in which hippos menace the boat, he regrets the lack of weapons, which had been stolen: "Hippos are gettin' pretty thick. It would be a rare comfort to have a gun this moment." In Disneyland's Jungle Cruise, the skipper is Walt's Trader Horn, dispensing knowledge and shooting hippos.
- *Africa as both paradise and nightmare.* Documentary footage, like the exceptionally fine views of Murchison Falls, enhanced by the earliest use of sound equipment in Africa, conveys its beauty, majesty—and dangers.[23] This seeming paradise can quickly become hellish, especially at nightfall, as sounds of predators on the prowl and the relentless beat of tribal drums are heard. "That's Africa for you," says Horn. "When you're not eatin' somebody,

you're tryin' to keep somebody else from eatin' you!" Horn and Peru also comment on the "beauty and terror" around them, an unwitting reference to Edmund Burke's theory of the Sublime. Horn comments, "Terror can be a form of beauty."

- *Africa as a garden of love.* Just as the skipper of the Jungle Cruise invited couples to express their amorous feelings, the jungle-as-a-garden-of-love trope plays a big part in *Trader Horn*. Peru is smitten by Nina Trent—an archetypal White Goddess—the daughter of an American missionary captured and raised by natives. Their unconsummated ardor is no match, however, for the intense bromances between the film's three central characters. Despite his crusty demeanor, Horn tenderly embraces the much-younger Peru throughout the picture. Horn is equally devoted to "the finest gun boy in all Africa," his servant Rencharo (played by Mutia Omoolu), who is so faithful that he dies in his master's arms fatally wounded by a spear aimed at Horn. Trader Horn will take on other "gun boys," but Rencharo remains on his mind. In the final frame, Horn glances upward toward a double-exposed image of Rencharo in the sky!

- *African natives as servants and savages.* Finally, *Trader Horn* reinforces degrading stereotypes of the Africans who appear on screen exclusively as aggressive tribesmen, porters, or, in the case of Rencharo, a selfless Gunga Din–like minion. Horn refers to inhabitants of a native village as cannibals, "a god-fearing race except in the matter of diet." The males sharpen weapons, while the women—revealed fully to the camera as bare-breasted—do the domestic chores. Human skeletons are omnipresent.

In the remainder of this chapter, we shall see how Hollywood film-makers continuously and repeatedly inserted these early conceits into jungle pictures. At every stop along the way, we will consider the relationship of individual elements to their counterparts in Adventureland. In a unique way, the Jungle Cruise will prove to be the culmination of a quarter century of cinematic adventure narratives.

"Me Tarzan!"

The most successful jungle franchise of all time was based on characters created by the American writer, Edgar Rice Burroughs, introduced in 1912 in *All-Story Magazine*.[24] Some thirty-three separate *Tarzan* films or serials were made between 1918 and opening day at Disneyland in 1955.

(*Tarzan's Hidden Jungle* was released in February 1955.) Their broad distri-
bution and box-office success helped them shape the image of Africa in the
American mind for decades, though not one *Tarzan* movie was filmed in
Africa before 1951. Nor indeed had Burroughs ever set foot in Africa.

Of particular interest are the first two films in the series of six produced by MGM. Co-starring Johnny Weissmuller and Maureen O'Sullivan, *Tarzan, the Ape Man* (1932) was directed by W.S. Van Dyke, who had
directed *Trader Horn* just two years earlier; *Tarzan and His Mate* (1934)
was co-directed by Cedric Gibbons and Jack Conway. The theme of Africa
as an earthly paradise is embodied by O'Sullivan's character, Jane Parker,
who falls in love with its beauty and timeless mystery. Africa is a kind of
plein-air zoo, but it is also an untamed, uncivilized wilderness, fraught
with danger. As Jane makes her way through the jungle, cinematic perils
lurk around every bend, as they do in Adventureland. Only in the safety
of Tarzan's company does this occasionally nightmarish world shift back
to a pleasant dream. The stereotype of the White Hunter, in the mold of
Trader Horn, appears in the form of Jane's father, James Parker (played by
C. Aubrey Smith), and his trading partner Harry Holt (Neil Hamilton).
Their role in *Tarzan, the Ape Man* is to educate Jane (and the audience) in
the lore of Africa and to defend the safari in its search for ivory treasure in
a fabled elephant burial ground.

Audiences were stunned by the number and variety of animal "actors"
in these films. The set pieces in which they confront the human actors
were especially powerful. Early in the story, the expedition constructs
makeshift rafts to cross a river. They are attacked first by crocodiles—one
of which attacks a porter—then by a vast herd of angry hippopotamuses.
The sequence in which the White Hunters fire their guns at the hippos is
particularly vivid, with round after round of ammunition expended. This
action was repeated so often in subsequent jungle movies that it became
another common trope—and inevitably, emerged as a highpoint of Disney's Jungle Cruise.

To give a convincing sense of human-and-beast interaction, post-production cleverly intermingled stock footage of wild critters with fleeting
frames of Weissmuller and O'Sullivan, plus newly shot film of captive animals fighting with their trainers (who also sometimes performed as doubles).[25] Rear projection on a glass surface, common practice by the early
1930s, provided a safe way to integrate actors, animals, and pre-existing
film of African natives into a single sequence. In fact, the *Tarzan* pictures
were conceived in part as a means of profitably reusing excess film shot on
location for *Trader Horn*—which had the added advantage of enriching
the series with much-needed verisimilitude. The animals' performances
were recycled by MGM year after year, in movie after movie—not unlike

the way the Jungle Cruise "animals" replicate their performances for each passing boat.

MGM had its own stable of animals on Lot 3 of the studio. When their noise began to disrupt shooting on nearby sound stages, they were moved to the larger, four-acre Lot 4. The success of *Tarzan the Ape Man* encouraged studio brass to expand its holdings to include zebras, elephants, ostriches, and chimpanzees. The most famous addition was Mary, the rhinoceros, imported from Germany. MGM was the only studio to hire a full-time trainer, George Emerson. He attempted to train Mary for the rhino attack scene in *Tarzan and His Mate*, shot in the so-called Rhino Area on Lot 2, and he trained a young elephant, Baby Bea, for scenes with "Boy" in *Tarzan Finds a Son!* (1939).[26]

Naturally, what appeared on screen was not always real. To be more convincing, some animals required make-up and prosthetics. The Indian elephants, reputedly easier to train than African elephants, wore large fake ears and exaggerated tusks to more closely resemble their African counterparts. The studio also devised fantastic beasts, such as the vampire bats with moveable heads and glowing eyes in a scene cut from *Tarzan Escapes* (1936). The most elaborate construction was the mechanical crocodile that the hero does battle with in *Tarzan and His Mate*. The model maker responsible for these creatures, "Buddy" Gillespie, head of the special effects department, explained the function of the giant reptile: "We built the crocodile and he [Weissmuller] was working in around eighteen feet of water. He finally maneuvered around with this mechanical beast made out of steel and rubber and started to stab into the throat of the crocodile to kill it. We had planted a bunch of little negrazine dye sacks in the crocodile's throat. When it came out, it looked like blood."[27] Gillespie also oversaw the sculpting of miniature elephants with moveable trunks that were filmed and combined with footage of real elephants to make the herd look bigger. In addition to make-believe animals, human dummies were sometimes flung about the set—an instance of truly death-defying stunts!

Extensive use of dummies and other tricks was essential in sustaining the fiction of Tarzan's relationship with African wildlife, whether the beasts were sympathetic, as the hippos and elephants were, or antagonistic—e.g., his fight to the death with crocodiles and lions. In *Tarzan and His Mate*, wounded by an evil White Hunter, Tarzan is carried to safety on the back of a fake hippo. In another scene, he comes to Jane's rescue astride a rhino. A close look reveals Emerson, Weissmuller's double, riding Mary, a real rhino, while Johnny rides Mary's (fake) double (Fig. 21).[28] Tarzan's loyal mascot, Cheeta the chimp, provides comic relief throughout the series, but two circus troupes, the Flying Codonas and the Picciani Family, wore monkey suits for the more difficult stunts involving apes.

Internationally renowned trapeze artist Alfredo Codona performed Tarzan's occasional swinging on the jungle vines and dives from tall heights, while Bert Nelson, a trainer for the A.G. Barnes Circus, doubled for Weissmuller wrestling a lion. Olympic swimmer Josephine McKim doubled as Jane in the nude underwater sequence and her tussle with a mechanical crocodile. Small wonder, then, that *Tarzan* author Burroughs, searching for a metaphor to describe the *Tarzan* films, compared the series to a circus.[29]

Disney originally toyed with the idea of populating the Jungle Cruise attraction with live lions and other creatures, but that proved impractical. Instead, like the big studios, Walt had his men create dummy animals, an approach that his PR people stressed as a Disneyland connection with Hollywood.[30] The apparent realism of Adventureland's beasts surprised visitors, and according to an exaggerated account in *The Disneyland News*, at close range even a safari hunter would take them for the real thing.[31]

Two special effects artists, veterans of other studios who worked for Disney on the giant squid in *20,000 Leagues Under the Sea*, collaborated

Figure 21. *Tarzan and His Mate* (1934, MGM). Johnny Weissmuller and rhino double, March 16, 1934 (*Herald Examiner* Collection/Los Angeles Public Library).

to produce the mechanical creatures that menaced riders. Chris Mueller, Jr., formerly with MGM, sculpted the small maquettes that were enlarged to full-size clay models and cast in life-like fiberglass and latex. Robert A. (Bob) Mattey, formerly of Universal, RKO, and Republic, created the track and mechanical systems that made the sculptures move.[32] In a procedure mimicking that of the big studios, where one person received credit for the work of an entire department, only Mattey's name is mentioned repeatedly in publicity and appears on the "Trip through Adventureland" telecast. Another special effect borrowed from Hollywood was the strategic placement of loudspeakers throughout the ride to broadcast appropriate jungle sound effects.[33]

Few people watching the *Tarzan* series were fooled by these gimmicks. *New York Times* critic Mordaunt Hall, who gave Mickey Mouse his first rave review in 1928, stated the obvious when he said that *Tarzan the Ape Man* "is a cleverly photographed film and, although some adults may doubt that Mr. Weissmuller kills two lions and a leopard with a knife after a prolonged struggle, there is good enough camera trickery for lads and lassies and mayhap a few parents to believe that Johnny Weissmuller took his life in his hands when he agreed to act in this jungle feature."[34] Hall added, "This fantastic affair is filmed with a sense of humor." The critic for the *New York Post* concurred: *Tarzan, the Ape Man* "has a way of making fun of itself, a ruse so disarming that you are tempted to enjoy the picture most when you are believing it least."[35] In short, there was delight to be had in the spectacle of an Olympic gold medalist splashing about with a giant mechanical croc. A long cinematic tradition of faux animals like the ones in the Tarzan films was absorbed into the Jungle Cruise attraction, and their almost nudge-nudge, wink-wink fakeness was a big part of the appeal, operating in concert with the punning anecdotes of the skipper. The droll tone of the films and the ride offered both fun-house fright and amusement.

Backlot Jungles

The landscape in the Jungle Cruise attraction was integral to its illusion of reality, and Disney creators tapped into the Hollywood techniques used for the *Tarzan* pictures to maintain the myth of the Dark Continent. As in *Trader Horn*, the *Tarzan* locales were never specified, and the title-card map from *Trader Horn* was reused ad infinitum as well. MGM chose not to go on location in Africa, opting instead for local sites, notably a location in Ventura County named Sherwood Forest for the Douglas Fairbanks swashbuckler *Robin Hood* (1922) shot there. This was the location for the hippo attack in *Tarzan the Ape Man*. The Toluca Lake section of L.A., near Burbank, a relatively unpopulated area with its own dense vegetation bordering a spring-fed marsh, also provided backgrounds.[36] From its well-stocked nursery and sod farm on Lot 6, MGM's Greens Department trucked in plants as needed, a few of them bogus. Studio craftsmen constructed the Tarzan Tree House, an elaborate six-room bungalow, at Crater Camp in Brent's Mountain Crags in the Santa Monica Mountains. Set dressers even enhanced nature in underwater scenes shot in Silver Springs, Florida, by adding white sand, logs, and vegetation.

The half-acre, cement-sealed lake on MGM's Lot 1, bordered by tropical foliage, provided a convincing background for *Tarzan the Ape Man*. Nearby, the Mutia Escarpment Rocks, a tower of fabricated stones, served for the uphill trek to the elephant burial ground. But as the series grew in popularity, MGM created an alternate space on Lot 2, installing the four-foot deep, thirteen-million-gallon, concrete-bottomed Tarzan Lake, surrounded by a twelve-acre jungle. Anticipating a fourth picture in the series, *Tarzan Finds a Son!*, an even bigger lake on Lot 3, the "Jungle and Lake," with neighboring rock formations, was built in the late 1930s.[37]

MGM was not alone in recreating natural settings for its films. In 1939, show-biz gossip columnist Hedda Hopper described some of the landscapes created inside studio sound stages in an article titled "Hollywood Sets Would Fool Mother Nature: Scenic Experts Make Land, Sea and Sky Look More Realistic than Reality." Describing the temporary transfer of real trees from the Paramount studio nursery to an indoor set for the forthcoming Bob Hope–Bing Crosby–Dorothy Lamour "road picture," *Road to Singapore*, Hopper called Paramount's facility "one of the largest nurseries in the country." She commented as well on efforts at Warner Bros. to improve the look of water in *King of the Lumberjacks* (a.k.a. *Timber*): "In order to make a lake seem more realistic it was necessary to dye the entire body a cerulean blue, because it didn't look rippled when it was just plain water." For a Twentieth Century–Fox fantasy with Shirley Temple, Hopper said,

> Two forests and five groves were built—and not grown—for "Bluebird" [*The Blue Bird*], the work of Nick Kaltenstadler, chief nurseryman of the studio.... In his 24-year career he's built more than 1,000,000 trees for use in movies.... When they first started shooting "The Bluebird" real grass was used. It was replaced several days after shooting commenced because they discovered two things: first, that the intense heat of the lights made the grass grow and, therefore it required mowing before each day's work and, secondly, the artificial grass could be sprayed with a brighter green hue for brighter results in Technicolor reproduction.[38]

Hollywood art directors were fully invested in creating hyperreal landscapes that were "realer" than reality. The major studios constructed artificial Asian waterways just as Harper Goff would do when he created the river route for the Jungle Cruise. A *New York Times* article in 1942, "A Kipling Jungle Is Re-Created," which also cited MGM's Sherwood Forest location, explained the rationale for keeping film production close to home:

> In Hollywood it is cheaper to create a jungle than to go to one of nature's own. Because of the difficulties of controlling lighting, action and sound large-scale location trips have become infrequent. Thus when, more than a year ago, Alexander Korda decided to film in technicolor [sic] the adventures of Mowgli, the wild forest boy, he did not go to India, where Rudyard Kipling had set the tales. Instead, for "The Jungle Book," he went inland forty miles from Hollywood to Sherwood Forest. There with the white magic that only a corps of movie technicians can command, he converted a ten-acre tract into as lush a tangle of tropical flora and fauna as ever flourished this side of the Equator.[39]

Big-studio methods like these were repeated at Disneyland.

Disneyland's Jungle

Walt had no greensman at the studio, so he brought on board Bill and Jack Evans of Evans and Reeves Landscaping, who had designed the garden at Disney's home in Holmby Hills. Responding to Walt's appeal, "Hey, Bill…. I need a jungle!" Evans turned barren earth into a tropical paradise for the Jungle Cruise.[40] Bill Evans attended early design meetings and understood his mission to be the realization of Goff's inspirational sketches. Evans strove to reproduce the popular conception of a jungle as represented on the silver screen: "I've traveled a great deal to tropic regions around the world and jungles can be endlessly monotonous," he said. "So I created a 'Hollywood' jungle, the type an armchair traveler who has never been to the tropics might visualize."[41]

The press kit released to mark the park's inauguration indulged in hyperbole, claiming that trees varying in age from thirty to fifty years were imported to Adventureland from China, Japan, Australia, New Zealand, and South Africa.[42] *The Disneyland News* reported on the extensive importation of exotic vegetation, with emphasis on unusual characteristics, such as fifty-foot tall bamboos, a dragon tree that bleeds red sap if cut, and a "poison plant" used by "savages" to make poison darts.[43] This oft-repeated hype bolstered the purported authenticity of what one writer called a "portrayal of the earth's fast-vanishing wilderness land."[44] In fact, the prop department at Burbank supplied an abundance of fake flowers. Many trees were salvaged from neighborhoods destroyed by the creation of L.A.'s freeways, and orange trees already on-site were uprooted and replanted upside down by the Evans brothers to mimic mangroves. In the *Disneyland* TV show on the making of Adventureland, an artist is shown daubing paint on a tree trunk, and Walt jokes that even nature sometimes needs a little artistic improvement. The goal—as Hedda Hopper so deftly said—was to paint "a prettier panoramic picture" with "Technicolor" results.[45]

Moviegoers, as a *Chicago Tribune* critic put it, had grown accustomed to seeing dummy animals and "the tall trees in the jungles—of Hollywood!"[46] Bernard Hyman, production supervisor for the first two MGM *Tarzans*, specifically attributed their success to "the mystery, the 'Never Never Land' quality which has made Tarzan a thing apart from [the] ordinary."[47] Historian Brady Earnhart went so far as to argue that the *Tarzan* films are constructed in a way that intentionally reminds us they are only movies: "The 'Africa' of *Tarzan* is ... transparently and doggedly fictional ... exempted from any requirement to correspond to what it signifies."[48] An *L.A. Times* critic said of *Tarzan and His Mate*: "Seeing is believing, if you want very much to believe.... After all, 'Tarzan' (whatever the rest of the title) is fantasy, and as fantasy it can be pretty well accepted as not related to anything mundane or logical."[49] Maureen O'Sullivan summed up, in reverse, Disneyland's debt to Hollywood jungle pictures when she commented, a decade after the Jungle Cruise boarded its first guests, that the *Tarzan* movies "were fairy tales—almost Disney-like."[50]

Stanley and Livingstone

An article in the August 1955 issue of *The Disneyland News*, "Stanley's Exploits in Search for Livingston [sic] Brought to Life by Adventureland Boat Trip," claimed that Jungle Cruise passengers experienced a trek into the wild comparable to Stanley's search for Dr. Livingstone in the African wilds in 1869–71.[51] In 1955, a reference to these two figures most likely brought to mind the 1939 Twentieth Century–Fox motion picture, *Stanley and Livingstone*, produced by Darryl F. Zanuck and directed by Henry King. Kevin Dunn has stressed its long-range influence: "Perhaps because the film was released more than sixty years after the actual events, most viewers never questioned the authenticity of the film. In fact, the greatest exposure to the legacies of Stanley and Livingstone, and for the most part African missionaries and explorers, has come from this film." Zanuck's epic, Dunn concluded, "is an important film to analyze due to its tremendous impact as an image shaper, as well as its role as a historical narrative."[52]

During a fictionalized meeting early in the story, James Gordon Bennett, legendary publisher of *The New York Herald*, tries to convince ace reporter Henry M. Stanley (Spencer Tracy) to undertake the search for the good doctor. Standing before a wall-size map of Africa, Bennett does his best to get Stanley's blood coursing: "The Dark Continent: mystery, heat, fever, cannibals, a vast jungle in which you could lose half of America, a land which even the greatest conquerors did not dare to penetrate, ... unchanged, untouched since the dawn of history." In pitching the idea, Bennett describes *The Herald*'s readers and their hunger for an adventure story, but in effect his words also allude to the audience watching the movie in the theater, "the millions, the plain, common everyday people who derive excitement from ... the adventures of the heroic figures in the dark places of the earth." "Dr. Livingstone," he adds, "is a great adventurer, one of the greatest."

Following standard procedure, opening credits for *Stanley and Livingstone* brag about its location shooting in Kenya, Tanganyika, and Uganda for "safari episodes" like the one in which the porters are attacked by hundreds of costumed tribesmen. But the dialogue scenes were filmed in Hollywood. Tracy and his fellow actors never left the Fox soundstages.

Figure 22. *Stanley and Livingstone* **(1939, MGM). African natives, Hollywood-style.**

Sets and rear projections supplied the "wild" backgrounds. Even close-ups of the "savages" with spears and shields, lurking behind shrubbery, were staged indoors, much as Disney's natives were staged, albeit outdoors, in Adventureland (Fig. 22). Unlike the heroes of most jungle films, however, Stanley regards the wildlife he sees as "game," or part of a grand show, not as a threat: "I would call this a hunter's paradise," he says, adding: "What old P.T. Barnum wouldn't give for a few of these specimens! This is the greatest show on earth!" Thus, Darryl Zanuck's "Africa" treats the "Dark Continent" as a spectacle—at least where the fauna is concerned.

Jungle Epics of the 1950s: *The African Queen*

Three early 1950s Hollywood blockbusters, produced at a time when on-location shooting was increasingly common, illustrate how Africa was perceived by most Americans during Disneyland's development phase. Commenting on *King Solomon's Mines* (1950), *The African Queen* (1951), and *Mogambo* (1953), South African-born Oxford historian and African-ist William Beinart, and Beinart's former student, Dominique Schafer, observed that these films "embellish, manipulate, exoticise and renature African landscapes in the pursuit of narrative excitement. They render Africa into a cinematographic terrain that was contained within Hollywood's ... mainstream conventions."[53]

The African Queen is repeatedly cited as a source for the Jungle Cruise.[54] But its impact was greater than previously thought. Produced by Sam Spiegel (and distributed by United Artists), *The African Queen* was the first Technicolor movie shot on location in Africa, and only the third major narrative motion picture made there.[55] The two prior films were *Trader Horn* (1931) and MGM's 1937 version of *King Solomon's Mines*. Cast and crew on those two shoots endured exhaustion and illness, as did everyone involved in the making of *The African Queen*. But that was the point of filming in Africa—not the animals or scenery—according to the director, John Huston. The hardships suffered by the actors would enhance their performance, a judgment that proved correct.

Both Walt Disney and Harper Goff are mentioned as fans of the movie. However, Disney Imagineers Bruce Gordon and David Mumford claim that Goff "tried (and failed) to get Walt to watch the film, but Walt trusted Harper's judgment and told him to go ahead with the idea."[56] Either way, the picture provided the core concept of a perilous river journey for the Jungle Cruise ride. Based on the novel by C.S. Forester, set during World War I, *The African Queen* unites adventure, comedy, and fantasy in a captivating tale of two middle-aged characters—"characters"

in both senses of the word—a Canadian booze hound, Charlie Allnut, and
the puritanical daughter of an English clergyman, Rose Sayer (played by
Hollywood legends, Humphrey Bogart and Katharine Hepburn), who risk
their lives sailing down the Ulanga River in German East Africa intent on
blowing up a German gun boat. Publicity for *The African Queen* emphasized two months of location filming on the Ruki river in the Belgian
Congo, on Lake Victoria, and at the Murchison Falls in Uganda. What is
rarely acknowledged, though, is that roughly half of the picture was shot
on a studio soundstage in England, employing water tanks for river scenes
that on location were unsafe for the actors—scenes that on the big screen
are completely believable.[57]

Goff adopted several motifs from *The African Queen*'s mixed bag of
cinematic tropes. Much of the movie takes place on murky waters in a
beautiful but mysterious tropical jungle. At one point Rose comments on
the beauty of the flowers, and surmises that they may be the first humans
to behold them. Charlie and Rose marvel at wild animals in the water and
on the shore, some threatening, others playful. On three occasions, they
share the thrill of dangerous rapids—and much to Charlie's astonishment,
she is enraptured by their sublimity. Finally, there is the Tunnel of Love
angle: despite diametrically opposed personalities, Rose and Charlie fall
for one another on this rickety, skiff-sized African "Love Boat."

Compared to stars in other African adventure movies, Bogart and
Hepburn rarely interact with local wildlife. As in Adventureland, animals
are always glimpsed from a boat. No doubt, to satisfy audience expectations, colorful bits of stock footage of water birds, lions, elephants, and
a giraffe are spliced into the action. This does not really affect the story.
However, there are three memorable mini-scenes—each mere seconds
long—that engage the couple with indigenous creatures and add comic
relief to the drama. First, Bogie directs Hepburn's attention to some crocodiles slinking from the shore into the water ("Waiting for their supper,
Miss!"). Second, he mimics for her amusement the sounds and twitch-
ing ears of hippos in the water. And third, he imitates the sounds and
rib-scratching antics of chimps on the banks of the river. Though live jungle critters are present in these fleeting frames, the images do not seem to
rely on rear projection but were probably photographed by Huston's crew
on location.

Per the familiar disclaimer, "No animals were harmed during the
making of this film," none was harmed in the making of *The African
Queen*, unless you count a close encounter of the human kind. And that
occurred off-camera, when Huston took Hepburn elephant hunting, and
they were nearly killed by a stampeding herd.[58] All on-screen dangers were
fake. In the famous scene in which a hysterical Rose discovers leeches on

Charlie's body, stand-ins made of rubber were used because Bogart refused to work with the real thing. His shuddering reaction was so convincing it earned him his one and only Oscar for Best Actor. A heightened sense of danger in other, less up-close-and-personal brushes with native wild-life was created during post-production. Synchronized sound effects were added, both musically and—à la Disney's Jungle Cruise—with recorded sounds like a distant lion's roar or trumpeting elephant.

The African Queen benefited from the authenticity its non-speak-ing co-star—the beat-up vintage boat Charlie Allnut is forever silently cursing, kicking, and repairing—brought to the cutting-room table. The Adventureland ride owed a huge debt to the thirty-foot-long craft. Harper Goff's early designs for the Jungle Cruise launch were clearly patterned after the *African Queen*: her steam boiler, smokestack, and make-shift par-tial canopy, beneath which, in the film, Rose permits Charlie to take shel-ter during a tropical downpour. Only at the end of the picture does Rose urge tidying up the *Queen* as a respectful prelude to sinking the German gun boat.

Of course, in finished form, Adventureland's vessels were new and totally safe, with immaculate white fiberglass hulls (an early use of the material) and red and white striped awnings running from stem to stern. This suggests a second model for Goff's ride. In the summer of 1953 Par-amount was shooting *The Naked Jungle*, a Technicolor adventure set

Figure 23. *The Naked Jungle* (1953, Paramount). Steamer boat on backlot set.

in South America at the turn of the century. The female lead (Eleanor Parker) travels up a tributary of the Amazon on a small, open-air motor launch to a cocoa plantation deep in the jungle to meet her husband (Charlton Heston) whom she had married by proxy in New Orleans. The boat's white hull and candy-cane striped awning bear an unmistakable resemblance to Goff's Jungle Cruise design (Fig. 23). Incidentally, though made entirely in Hollywood—the river sequence was largely filmed using rear projection—*The Naked Jungle* is a rare jungle picture set in the southern hemisphere of the Americas rather than Africa—and instead of fending off lions and hippos, the protagonists do battle with blood-thirsty army ants!

King Solomon's Mines

Hollywood's impact on the Disneyland ride is also evident in the 1950 color epic *King Solomon's Mines*.[59] Like the 1937 version, this MGM remake, set in 1897, follows the adventures of Alan Quatermain (Stewart Granger), who is hired by Elizabeth Curtis (Deborah Kerr) to lead an expedition into uncharted African territory to find her husband, who had gone missing while searching for the legendary mines. Here too, the chief characters are initially antagonistic, but gradually fall in love (thankfully, for love's sake, they learn that Kerr's husband died in the course of his greedy pursuit of the precious stones). The picture was shot in brilliant color on location in Kenya, Uganda, and Ruanda-Urundi. An ad in the *New York Times* plugged the film's realism: "Here, for the Technicolor cameras to capture, was compelling beauty, painted by nature's own hand ... all the strangeness, the astonishing tribal ways, the awesome majesty, all the fascination of this fabulous land."[60]

In one telling scene in *King Solomon's Mines*, Elizabeth and Alan pause to admire the beauty around them. She comments, "Lovely, isn't it? It has a sort of majesty. A feeling of forever." Pointing to dangers lurking around them, he retorts, "There's not a square inch that doesn't have war, if you look for it." In a place where, as Granger's character says, everything eats everything else, there are "no souls in the jungle, very little justice, and no ethics." Yet again, the high-contrast, dual concept of the jungle as both paradise and nightmare is forcefully illustrated. Throughout the film, Elizabeth suffers recurrent nightmares—some real, some imagined. Similarly, Disney's Jungle Cruise plays on a dreamy paradise/nightmare duality to heighten the ride's emotional impact.

Those parts of the picture showcasing African flora and fauna, typically, are a montage of quick shots from five different sources: close-up

frames of Granger and Kerr on a sound stage; action shots filmed on location; doubles filling in for the stars in dicey situations; location footage
in Africa; and stock wildlife footage from outside sources. Because these
shots are well matched and glide rapidly across the screen, the effect is
remarkably convincing. This editing technique is analogous to the "quick
cuts" experienced on the Jungle Cruise, where a sequential succession of
views and events unfolds so swiftly and seamlessly that riders have no time
to mentally deconstruct the spectacle passing before them.

Fans of films like *King Solomon's Mines* expected to see a colorful
assortment of jungle critters, and this film does not disappoint. In addition to giraffes, zebras, monkeys, hippos, a hyena, and an anteater, there
are ostriches, porcupines, and impressive footage of a large tortoise in
the near foreground, almost close enough to touch, as the safari caravan
moves along in the distance. More striking are the shots of actors (or their
doubles) standing mere yards from a racing lion or a lumbering rhino,
and a scene in which a furry mechanical bug, lacking the slightest shred
of credibility, terrorizes Deborah Kerr's character. And, in a bit of shtick
right out of a Disney cartoon, as Elizabeth crosses a stream, she mistakes
a crocodile for a log and steps on its back. To save his on-screen paramour,
Quatermain whips out his pistol and fires at the writhing piece of rubber.
At Disneyland, quick-draw action like this has been a high point of the
Jungle Cruise since its inception.

Stewart Granger's swaggering hero, and some-time tour guide
in scenes that are quasi-documentary, is yet another stereotypical,
made-in-Hollywood Great White Hunter. Although he acts jaded and
cynical at first, this of course, is just a plot device that sets up his ultimate
submission to the charms of Kerr's Elizabeth. Quatermain—like Trader
Horn—is also the only source of humor in the film:

> ELIZABETH, FEARING THE LIONS: "How do we know whether they are
> hungry?"
> ALAN: "Well, if they eat you, they're hungry!"

Disney's guide is part Great White Hunter, part educator, and part
stand-up comic, too. Nowadays, the skippers wear khaki safari garb,
but in 1955 they sported white shirts and pants more suitable for service topside on a yacht. For a while, it was white trousers and a Hawaiian shirt. Despite the presence of real-life images of tribal dancing and
music (there was no orchestral score, only beating drums and simple
percussion), native Africans, for the umpteenth time, fared poorly in
King Solomon's Mines, represented as easily frightened porters or savages in war paint carrying shields and spears—just like Adventureland's
automatons.

Mogambo

Number three in this trio of 1950s jungle pictures repeats by-now familiar tropes that would be absorbed into Adventureland. Eager to match the success of *King Solomon's Mines*, the studio sent director John Ford and a crew of 500 abroad to film *Mogambo*, and again pressed its claims for authenticity in the opening titles: "Metro-Gold-wyn-Mayer is grateful beyond measure to the government officials of Kenya Colony, Tanganyika, the Uganda Protectorate and the Republic of French Equatorial Africa, whose limitless co-operation made this motion picture possible." Nonetheless, the story takes place in the usual generic African setting. The titles also credit indigenous peoples that appear on-screen, the "Samburu tribe of Kenya Colony, Wagenia tribe of Belgian Congo, Bahaya tribe of Tanganyika, and M'beti tribe of French Equatorial Africa," though they do not figure in the narrative. At one point, a static line-up of African women and children, worthy of an ethnological display, poses in brilliantly colored garments enhanced by the Technicolor process. Clever editing once more combines live-action filming, stock footage, and dare-devil doubles replacing the stars in action scenes where they might get hurt. Several outdoor sequences involving animals were shot at MGM's London studio, using rear projection.

The jungle in *Mogambo* is another garden of love. Its sensuous qualities trigger passionate interaction among the main characters—Victor Marswell (Clark Gable), Eloise Kelly (Ava Gardner), and Linda Nordley (Grace Kelly). The film's trailer promises "the story of a love affair as adventuresome as the surroundings in which it happens," and vaults the audience into the action: "You travel along uncharted waterways on a suspenseful safari. You venture across the African veldt alive with all manner of wild beasts. Just as the animal stampede in *King Solomon's Mines* created a new high in screen thrills, MGM has now topped this with a blood-chilling spectacle, the battle of the gorillas." Gable plays the White Hunter in *Mogambo*, in this case capturing, not shooting, animals, unless they pose a mortal threat. The obligatory hippo charges a boat, and he readies his rifle but with heroic forbearance does not shoot. The jungle is also nightmarish for Grace Kelly's character, who is saved by Gable from an attack by a black leopard. And, as in *King Solomon's Mines*, instead of an orchestral soundtrack, the film is accompanied by native drums and chants recomposed in the studio. Trapped in such time-worn clichés, early 1950s Hollywood still exerted little effort to advance the public's knowledge of foreign lands. Disneyland's Jungle Cruise took its cue from the movies.

"Savages"

Jungle Cruise thrills and chills peaked near the end of the ride when menacing African "savages" popped up along the shore. In case anyone might take them for real people, guests were reassured that they were made from plastic.[61] Again Disney followed standard studio practice: art directors in Hollywood frequently used dummies as substitutes for wild animals and for humans in scenes where interspecies interaction might be dangerous. During the climactic fight in *Tarzan and His Mate*, for example, dummies of African tribesmen were dropped from trees into a horde of lions, and strategic placement of cuts of meat gave the illusion of a native devoured by a lion.[62]

The "dummies" in Adventureland were positioned facing the guide boats as they passed by. Jungle films routinely featured lines of natives gazing directly at the camera, like the colorfully dressed women and children in *Mogambo*. Nineteenth-century tintypes and turn-of-the-century picture postcards imposed these now hackneyed poses on the popular mind.[63] Disney's Indian villagers and African tribesmen also were presented in a spirit consistent with the way scantily clad, live Indigenous peoples in "human zoos" at World's Fairs were presented: to illustrate the chasm between "primitive" and "advanced" civilizations and implicitly celebrate Euro-American ethnic superiority—based, presumably, on scientific fact and anthropological research.[64] Exhibits of this kind at pre–Disney amusement parks staked no claim to authenticity, offering mere spectacle instead. Likewise, Adventureland's goal was entertainment, pure and simple. A visitor's enjoyment of the Jungle Cruise ride depended largely on his or her willing suspension of disbelief.[65]

A dash of ethnological factuality did creep into the televised "Pre-Opening Report from Disneyland." In a scene devoted to the creation of the park's dummies, narrator Winston Hibler noted that, unlike Adventureland's mechanized animals, which were modeled in clay from small maquettes, the tribesmen were cast in plaster from a live model. With the authoritative voice of an anthropologist, Hibler remarked on the "imposing physique" of the six-foot, four-inch tall, unidentified Black model. In fact, the model was Woody Strode, a former athlete who had turned to acting and had bit parts on TV and in jungle films, achieving fame on the big screen in *Spartacus* (1960).

Degrading images of Africans as "savages," born of European colonialism and the international slave trade, were repeated ad infinitum in literature, art, and films. Three varieties of stereotypical males became stock characters in jungle epics, influencing generations of moviegoers' impressions of sub-Saharan Africans.[66] On the bottom rung were the porters: easily scared and lazy, they must sometimes be whipped into action and are considered expendable. One step up the ladder, the white master's loyal gun bearer is smart and virtuous, but still subservient. Rencharo, for instance, takes the fatal spear in *Trader Horn* to save his master. Finally, there is the third variety, omnipresent in all jungle films: the barbaric type seen on the Jungle Cruise, clothed in feathers, bones, animal teeth, smeared in body paint, wielding a spear and shield. In the 1950s, the popular myths of cannibalism and witchcraft were still being "confirmed" in dubious, sensational American newspaper "reports."[67]

Comedy films of the Golden Age perpetuated the most egregious stereotypes. In *Africa Screams* (1949) comedy-duo Bud Abbot and Lou Costello travel on an expedition to "Africa," where they escape being boiled alive. In one of Paramount's "road pictures," *Road to Zanzibar* (1941), a musical reiteration of the paradise-as-nightmare theme, Bing Crosby and Bob Hope, menaced by cannibals, pretend to be White Gods. The common trope of the Witch Doctor is played for laughs when he responds to their deceit by saying (translated in a subtitle), "If he's a god, I'm Mickey Mouse!" As planning for the Jungle Cruise was underway, another of Paramount's road comedies, *Road to Bali*, released in 1952, featured a sarong-clad, part Scottish, part Polynesian White Princess played for laughs (and G-rated romance) by Dorothy Lamour. During their musical adventure, Crosby and Hope are nearly devoured by cannibals, and Hope's character swims across a stream with a mechanical crocodile snapping at his heels. *Road to Bali* can also be read as an amiable spoof of the semi-erotic White Goddess trope introduced in *Trader Horn* and developed in films like *She* (1935).[68]

Disney's live-action *20,000 Leagues Under the Sea* (1954) includes what is supposed to be an amusing scene in which cannibals chase after two of the principal characters.[69] Turning to cartoon shorts, we see that Mickey himself cavorts with cannibals in *Trader Mickey* (1932) and ends up "in the soup" in a pot of boiling water. In *Mickey's Man Friday* (1935), he rescues a native from cannibals and takes him on as his servant ("You Friday, me Mickey"). The *Silly Symphony* short *Cannibal Capers* (1935) also contains offensive conceits. Thus, it comes as no surprise to hear Walt, as he introduces "A Trip through Adventureland" on the *Disneyland* TV show, identify the Jungle Cruise sculptures as cannibals. A nearby photo op consisted of an iron pot large enough to hold a child, who would learn "how [a] cannibal pot feels, even without fire."[70] At the bazaar, the Island Trade Store displayed an actual shrunken head in a vintage glass jar, and its most popular item for sale was a pair of salt and pepper shakers representing cannibals.[71]

In Hollywood movies, African jungles typically were playgrounds for white adventurers and "accidental tourists." The Jungle Cruise replayed this familiar script in which colonized lands were subject to white domination.[72] The natives in Adventureland were merely part of the scenery, little better than the flora and fauna deposited around them.

Disneyland received almost no coverage in the African American press. A rare exception was a three-page pictorial of an outing by two Black children, published in the March 1956 edition of *Ebony* magazine. Just beyond the gate to Adventureland they stroll by a display of shields and spears topped with skulls. Boarding a jungle launch, they anticipate a journey in which, according to a caption, "Cannibals lurk on river banks, mock elephants, giraffes, [and] other animals roam the jungles."[73] In the final analysis, Disneyland was primarily a white middle-class venue.

Hollywood Zoos

To supplement its backlot stables of animals, Hollywood rented creatures from nearby sources, two of which had histories that were surely known to Disney. One of these sources was the Selig Zoo and Movie Studio, founded by "Colonel" William N. Selig, who helped make Tom Mix a great silent-film cowboy star.

Like Walt, Selig was born in Chicago, had a strong interest in moviemaking, and was responsible for many "firsts." He was the first producer to move his studio to the West Coast and the first to make a jungle film, *Hunting Big Game in Africa* (1909). In 1911, he purchased thirty-two acres on Mission Road, east of downtown L.A., as a home for the beasts that performed in his films. In 1913, the colonel transformed the Selig Wild Animal Farm into what one writer has called "the original motion picture theme park," attracting a paying public eager to watch movies being made. He planted semitropical vegetation and erected structures in styles reminiscent of Africa, Southeast Asia, and South America to house the animals, serve as film sets, and entertain his customers. In 1922, his initial success prompted him to expand his "Farm" into an operation called Luna Park, modeled after Coney Island, that he hoped would eventually hold restaurants, a hotel, and a theater, but financial difficulties forced him to sell the property in the mid–1920s.[74] Nonetheless, Selig conceived the essentials of the motion picture backlot that ultimately filtered down to Disneyland.

A second private zoo was established in 1926 when animal caretaker and trainer Louis Goebel bought five lots just north of Los Angeles on Ventura Boulevard in Thousand Oaks to house African lions he had purchased from the personal zoo of Carl Laemmle, founder of Universal

Studios. As his menagerie expanded, Goebel leased his animals and the property to the major studios for live-action photography. Dubbed Goebel's Lion Farm, it opened to the public in 1929 with a focus on circus acts. In 1945, under new ownership, the site expanded to 170 acres and changed its name to World Jungle Compound. In 1956, in an effort to rival Disney's park in Anaheim, the proprietors enlisted the services of the Stanford Research Institute, as Walt had done, and changed the name again, to Jungleland. Promoted as "Disneyland with Live Animals," Jungleland had its own Safari Land, where visitors could watch wild beasts in a simulated jungle environment. Following the Adventureland template, plans were announced to recreate African, Asian, and Middle Eastern jungles, along with a bazaar selling artifacts from distant places. An aerial map from the 1950s shows a Jungle Boat Ride.[75]

In the end, neither the Selig Zoo nor Jungleland could compete with what Walt had to offer. A small amusement park on Selig's site operated until 1957, and Jungleland closed in 1969. Why pay good money to see wild animals that might be taking a nap, when Walt offered the sure-fire fun of automated lions, elephants, monkeys, and hippos guaranteed to be "up and at 'em" each and every time? All that, and Mickey too, in a controlled, clean, and thoroughly Disneyfied environment!

The Success of Adventureland

As we have seen, although Asia and South America were represented in the Jungle Cruise, its principal locale was Africa, the primary locus of jungle movies. The big studios had created artificial semblances of jungle habitats on their own turf, and Disneyland's designers followed suit in providing a suitable wilderness of tangled vegetation, simultaneously welcoming and dangerous, filled with thrills but also offering a paradisical garden of love. The detailing on the ride reflected a tradition that, despite claims of authenticity, derived from an unbroken line of cinematic conventions. From *Trader Horn* through *Tarzan* and up to *The African Queen*, reiteration of the same clichés—from the perilous river journey and the White Hunter to charging hippos and savage natives—created an unassailable vision of life in the wild. At the same time, the humorous playfulness, the suspension of disbelief in the face of artifice, and the repetition of the most egregious stereotypes made both the movies and the theme park palatable and even irresistible to the public.

4

Tomorrowland

In discussing Tomorrowland, historians and critics usually concentrate on one concern unique to the "land": its inability to keep up with the future.[1] Set thematically in 1986, the year of Halley's Comet's return to the inner solar system, Tomorrowland has always required periodic renovation to keep pace with scientific developments. Walt himself admitted that, among the themed realms of the Magic Kingdom, Tomorrowland posed the greatest challenge due to its emphasis on things that had not yet happened—or might never happen.[2] Although he hired renowned specialists as advisors, bringing the sector to life was not "rocket science." It could not be based solely on testable or predictive explanations about the universe and mankind's place in it. For it to work, Tomorrowland had to rely primarily on the collaborative ingenuity of the boss and his devoted employees.[3]

What historians have failed to note is the degree to which Disney's design team sought solutions for Tomorrowland's rides and exhibits by turning to the world of motion pictures.[4] There the designers found a history of forward-looking cinematic techniques that offered the possibility of further development. Moreover, the genre of futuristic sci-fi movies provided narratives that complemented Disneyland's emphasis on storytelling.

This relationship was clear from the beginning. An eight-page article published in the trade journal *Business Screen Magazine* two months after opening day on July 17, 1955, hailed three "show-stopping exhibits," each in their way a "major technological achievement," involving "some of the most unique motion picture techniques developed in recent years." "At three of Tomorrowland's key exhibits," *Business Screen Magazine* reported, "visitors will be surrounded by motion pictures, projected into space with their help and taken thousands of feet below the surface of the earth."[5]

As we shall see, Tomorrowland's technology depended heavily on cutting-edge, synchronized modes of projecting movies. The first attraction

Business Screen Magazine raved about was American Motors' Circa-rama. One of the earliest modern examples of projection in the round, Circarama used eleven screens in a space forty feet in diameter to envelop the audience completely. The second exhibit, Richfield Oil's The World Beneath Us, featured the latest in flat widescreen technology, Cinema-Scope, combined with a novel configuration of double-projection on a fiberglass dome. The third attraction, Trans World Airlines' (TWA) Rocket to the Moon ride, incorporated films on three separate screens to create the illusion of space travel. "After watching these three shows in Disney's land of 1986," *Business Screen Magazine* enthused, "the natural conclusion almost draws itself: Motion pictures have a great future."

True to Disneyland's *modus operandi* of project creation, the three attractions drew inspiration from new developments of the seventh art. Later in the chapter, I will also show how other Tomorrowland exhibits, such as the Art Directors show, the 20,000 Leagues under the Sea walk-through, and the Art Corner shop, likewise were tied specifically to Hollywood moviemaking. Thus, by analyzing the detailed text, diagrams, and rare photos in *Business Screen Magazine* and then delving into motion-picture history, we will be in a better position to gauge Disney's forward-looking vision in this park sector.

Development and Realization in 1955

But first, a brief review of Tomorrowland's early development and the layout of its spaces will provide context. Compared to its sister realms, planning for Tomorrowland progressed slowly. Walt's August 31, 1948, Memorandum outlining his vision for a Mickey Mouse Park in Burbank stressed the nostalgic past of an American Main Village and Western Village. But an accent on the future as determined by science was soon added to the mix, with a spaceship and submarine among the attractions under consideration.[6] Eventually, in September 1953, after the vastly expanded project shifted to the Anaheim site, plans emerged for a World of Tomorrow, with its glittering promise of wonderful "Things to Come," a publicity phrase borrowed from the title of a 1936 sci-fi movie scripted by H.G. Wells.

Entrance to this rudimentary prototype for Tomorrowland would be via a moving sidewalk flanked by corporate exhibits. Once inside, prospective attractions included a monorail, atomic submarine, flying saucer, and House of the Future. Even food service might be futuristic, with dishes delivered by conveyer belt. The dominant visual element in the World of Tomorrow, and its most powerful magnet, would be a giant rocket ship. Visitors would climb a ramp into the craft for a virtual-reality ride around the Moon. On the Drive Yourself Freeway System, children could delight in operating a car while learning the rules of the road. An area was reserved for driving tests, which everyone would "pass."[7]

Stitching these ideas into a coherent whole, however, proved so challenging that a year later, in September 1954, Walt tentatively decided to put Tomorrowland on hold until after the rest of Disneyland began operation. He reversed that decision in January 1955, convinced that he had to showcase the entire park during opening-day festivities, scheduled for broadcast on network television. The lead designer was Gabriel Scognamillo, recruited on the basis of his experience as a Hollywood art director, whose credits include *Tabor the Great* (1954), a fantasy featuring a giant robot. In the end, *faute de mieux,* WED art directors sought salvation in the modern-day world's fair as a "business model," with the bulk of Tomorrowland's attractions underwritten by corporate sponsors. The idea—born of necessity—was to balance a visionary display of never-before-seen marvels with unabashed marketing of consumer products by the people who helped bankroll the sector. This is why some exhibits in Tomorrowland, down to the present day, have never had more than a tenuous connection to the future.

As opening day drew near, staff scrambled to fill empty spaces, and Walt urged them to use balloons and pennants as camouflage.[8] Oblivious to such trifling concerns, guests approached Tomorrowland—like every other "land"—from the Hub. During the park's first year of operation, they passed through a court of honor with an American flag encircled by forty-eight flags, one for each state then in the union. A monumental Clock of the World, crowned by a small sun-and-moon sculpture and symbolizing the transition from present to future, stood in the center of the court. On its dial viewers could see the exact time of any place in the world.[9]

Walking along the main thoroughfare, visitors could enter at no charge any exhibition hall that caught their fancy. Marvin Davis, the park's chief architect, designed the halls in a conservative modernist style. Smaller buildings like the fast-food Space Bar had a bolder space-age look, inspired by the Southern California "Googie" aesthetic.[10]

Sponsors of the halls provided uplifting educational exhibits intermingled with displays of their products. Structures or exhibits on the left (north) side of the axis included Circarama, American Motors' 360-degree movie; Richfield Oil's The World Beneath Us, a potted history of fossil fuels; and National Lead's Dutch Boy Color Clock. On the opposite, right-hand (south) side were Monsanto Chemicals' Chematron, eight huge test tubes filled with basic natural materials; Kaiser Aluminum's giant telescope, a three-dimensional paean to "The Brightest Star in the World of

Metals"; the American Dairy Association's exhibit on state-of-the-art milking technology; and Crane's "Bathroom of the Future."[11]

Some of the commercial displays bore a resemblance to sci-fi and horror movie sets. Kaiser's telescope was reminiscent of the Space Gun in *Things to Come*, while the Chematron recalled mad scientist laboratories like the one in *The Bride of Frankenstein* (1935). Kaiser sponsored the sole costumed character roaming the realm, "K-7," the Kaiser Aluminum Spaceman, outfitted in a spacesuit, bubble helmet, and oxygen tank. Beyond the exhibit halls rose Tomorrowland's spaceship, the iconic *TWA Moonliner*, and its attendant ride, the Rocket to the Moon. Finally, for the young at heart, pint-sized roadsters in Richfield's Autopia beckoned to kids and adults alike.

Circarama

The first of Tomorrowland's three attractions surveyed in *Business Screen Magazine* was the 360-degree experience called Circarama, housed within an imposing modern-style pavilion past the Clock of the World, on the left side of the sector's main axis leading to the rocket ship. The article opened with a quote from a reviewer in the *New York Times* who had previewed the attraction two weeks prior to the park's opening: "For the most startling innovation in movie presentation, one will have to visit Disneyland…. Walt Disney and the Eastman Kodak Company have hit upon the ultimate in audience participation or envelopment, via a 360-degree screen…. The effect of viewing a motion picture that is going on all around you is fantastic. Particularly overpowering is the sense of motion, or moving with the picture."[12] Indeed, some audience members felt dizzy, some had a sense they were falling, and others simply covered their eyes. A few instinctively tried to slam on (non-existent) brakes. Often the film brought back memories of a trip once taken, or inspired plans to explore new destinations.[13]

The marquee on the pavilion's façade highlighted the "car" in "Circarama," an allusion to its corporate sponsor, the American Motors Corporation, formed in 1954 when the Nash-Kelvinator Corporation merged with the Hudson Motor Car Company.[14] American Motors sponsored half of each *Disneyland* TV episode in season one of the show as well. Inside the Circarama auditorium, current models of AMC automobiles—Nash, Hudson, and Rambler—lined the circular walls opposite Kelvinator kitchen appliances like the Foodarama, "the Rolls Royce of Refrigeration," a forerunner of the frost-free refrigerator.

Circarama's main draw was a film called *A Tour of the West* that was shot by eleven cameras mounted in circular formation on the roof of a Nash Rambler station wagon. The audience stood in the center of the asphalt floor, forty feet in diameter. Eleven 16 mm projectors faced eleven flat screens suspended in a circle above the perimeter. Separating the screens was a six-inch-wide vertical black bar, with a hole through which images were projected across the space.[15]

Business Screen Magazine heaped praise on the technical achievements, with detailed expositions of the problem-solving process, in some instances contracted out to non–Disney specialists. The article called the synchronization of the eleven projectors "an engineering feat," and celebrated the innovative method for correcting burnt-out bulbs and film breakage, potential "mechanical showstoppers." It cited the speakers located beneath each screen for contributing to the surround-sound effect.

Widescreen and the Travelogue

A Tour of the West played continuously at eighteen-minute intervals. Serving as art director was British-born artist Peter Ellenshaw, who had begun his career as studio matte painter with such films as *Things to Come*. In the late 1940s Disney hired him to paint matte backgrounds for his live-action movies filmed in England to use revenue frozen in the U.K. after the war. Ellenshaw moved to Burbank in 1953, where one of his career highlights was as co-winner of an Oscar for Special Visual Effects for *Mary Poppins*. The twelve-minute reel of *A Tour of the West* opened with still images of Kelvinator products and a brief introduction. The *Tour* itself began at the Beverly Hills Hotel from the vantage point of a car moving past lavish homes on Sunset Boulevard. Abruptly, it roared off, to the sound of a police siren, in a high-speed chase (achieved by altering the film speed) down fashionable Wilshire Boulevard. The car exited Wilshire onto a freeway, showcasing L.A.'s new system of roads. Next, the action switched to Monument Valley—copied in miniature, as we have seen, in Frontierland—where Indigenous sheep herders provided a historic touch. The action shifted briefly to a speedboat for a cruise through Newport Harbor, then to the Grand Canyon, ending at nightfall in Las Vegas.[16]

Like Disney's *People & Places* series and, on occasion, his *True-Life Adventures*, Tomorrowland's *A Tour of the West* was a travelogue—a genre pre-dating talking pictures.[17] From the days of early cinema until Disneyland, scenes of America's native splendor stimulated local pride and promoted a sense of national identity. Wilderness areas in national parks and cities fast becoming metropolises, circa 1910–1940—in California especially—lent themselves to travelogues. Whether a title promised *Seeing Los*

Angeles (1912) or *Natural Wonders of the West* (1938), such shorts helped boost tourism in an era when a nascent car culture was making travel in the West easier than ever before. Thus, at a crucial moment, the mid–1950s, Disney's Circarama project, *A Tour of the West*, rounded up touristy subjects, picturesque locales, and breathtaking scenery. As it entertained, the show sparked a postwar consumer desire to see the West, and to acquire new cars and consumer goodies like the Kelvinator Foodarama.[18]

A Tour of the West was a remarkable synthesis of earlier groundbreaking cinematic techniques. A major prototype for Circarama was the "phantom ride," a late nineteenth-century type of short film, in which a camera was mounted on the front of a moving vehicle. This had the dual purpose of imparting a startling sense of forward motion while taking viewers to exotic foreign climes as well as wondrous sites closer to home.[19]

Widescreen and Walt

Why did Disney install Circarama in Tomorrowland? Would not *A Tour of the West* have been more at home in Frontierland? Because Tomorrowland was modeled on the idea of a world's fair, he was likely stimulated by the longstanding association of innovative cinematic techniques with large-scale expositions. The following examples will help to emphasize further Circarama's connections with the past.

For the ultimate prototype for movies-in-the-round, we must go back to the 1900 Paris Exhibition, the site of the spectacular Cinéorama system. Devised by Raoul Grimoin-Sanson, it consisted of ten interlocked 70 mm projectors facing a 360-degree screen measuring thirty feet high. The diameter of the auditorium was 300 feet. Grimoin-Sanson's hand-tinted silent film treated the audience, seated in a faux hot-air balloon gondola, to a mock flight from the Tuileries Garden in Paris to the Grand Place in Brussels. Unfortunately, the heat generated by the arc lights of the projectors posed a fire hazard, and the show was shut down after three days. At the same fair, the Lumière Brothers exhibited color films on a screen measuring 53 feet high by 670 feet wide to an audience of three to five thousand per show. Subsequently, in Paris, at the 1937 International Exposition of Art and Technology in Modern Life, Henri Chrétien projected a composite film (made using two anamorphic lenses) onto a 2,000-foot long concave exterior wall of the Pavilion of Light. Two years later, Fred Waller, inventor of Cinerama, experimented with his Vitavision process at the 1939 New York World's Fair and, in 1949, at the Chicago Railroad Fair, which Disney and Ward Kimball had visited the previous year.[20]

Widescreen's prehistory was known to Disney.[21] One legendary example occurred—again in France—the year Walt introduced Oswald the Lucky Rabbit. In April 1927, Abel Gance premiered his silent masterpiece, *Napoléon*, at the Palais Garnier, home of the Paris Opéra. Gance had developed a three-projector/tri-panel process, Polyvision, for the film's dramatic final reel, alternating between three separate, side-by-side moving images and a single, synchronized widescreen sequence.[22]

Widescreen did not take off, however, until the 1950s, during the gestation phase of Disneyland, as the film industry struggled to compete with the rise of television. Exceptional among novel widescreen formats was the Cinerama process, in which three synchronized cameras were mounted on various moving vehicles (most astonishingly, a rollercoaster). The process was introduced in 1952 with the feature film *This Is Cinerama*, which took the form of a travel film. To the strains of "America the Beautiful," it closed with sweeping views of the Grand Canyon and other marvels of nature. The process was first demonstrated in New York in the same cavernous movie palace where *Steamboat Willie* debuted in 1928. The Broadway Theatre was refitted to accommodate Cinerama's aspect ratio of 2.85 to 1—almost triple the width of the ordinary movie screen. The process involved a six-channel stereo sound system, three projectors, and a deeply curved screen. A subsequent film in the franchise, *Cinerama Holiday* of 1955, took its audience on a visual jaunt to colorful venues in Europe and the United States. For about a decade, the most successful Cinerama productions were travelogues that paraded the wonders of Europe and America before eager eyes.

The drawbacks of a multi-screen projection system led to a proliferation of anamorphic, single-lens systems, including Paramount's VistaVision and Michael Todd's Todd-AO, which squeezed wide-field images onto standard 35 mm film stock. The most popular of these systems was CinemaScope, first seen in the 1953 20th Century–Fox biblical epic *The Robe*. Some idea of the tremendous interest in CinemaScope at this time may be gathered from the volume of publicity generated between July and December 1955 by the movie version of the Rogers and Hammerstein Broadway musical *Oklahoma!* The movie was shot simultaneously in both CinemaScope and Todd-AO, due to a major problem of early widescreen projection: the incompatibility of the two systems and the cost of retooling small-town movie houses.

Disney leaped on the widescreen bandwagon. In November 1953, he released the first cartoon in CinemaScope, *Toot, Whistle, Plunk, and Boom*. Co-directed and animated by Ward Kimball, it won an Oscar in 1954 for Best Short Subject in the animation category. Two Disney films in CinemaScope, the live-action *20,000 Leagues Under the Sea* (1954) and

Lady and the Tramp (1955), the first full-length widescreen animated cartoon, soon followed. In 1956, *Disneyland, U.S.A.*, a theatrical featurette in the documentary series *People & Places*, celebrated Walt's wonderland while revealing its broad vistas—especially when seen from the air. At the end of the decade, Walt pushed the widescreen to "greater widths" by being the first movie producer to use Technicolor's new Super Technirama 70 process. Released in January 1959, *Sleeping Beauty*, the least successful of Walt's three princess films, might have lost more money at the box office than it did without the superlative clarity and lush chromatic hues in its 70 mm Super Technirama roadshow format.

By inserting Disney's Circarama into the context of cinematic history, the writer in *Business Screen Magazine* acknowledged these efforts at various points in the development of motion-picture technology to fill the spectator's field of vision: "Bigger and wider screens are the unmistakable trend of movie presentation. The best way to predict the future of movie presentation, then, was to go to the end of the line—the widest possible screen is a complete circle." Circarama pushed widescreen to its limit, thus earning its place in Disneyland's World of Tomorrow.

Collaborators

No one knows for sure who conceived the idea for Circarama's 360-degree projection system. Its history is fraught with conflicting legends bound up in the collaborative process at the studio and WED. However, Disney, an inveterate, hands-on manager, was likely its primary instigator.[23] Walt's career was marked from start to finish by technical advances in moviemaking. He produced the first cartoon shorts with synchronized sound, the first Technicolor cartoon, and the first successful feature-length animated cartoon. The Disney studio pioneered hybrid live-action/animation, the multiplane camera, and Fantasound, an immersive system for *Fantasia* that synchronized stereophonic sound with moving pictures. Walt even dreamed of a system that would project *Fantasia* onto all four walls of the theater—clearly an early vision of movies-in-the-round.[24]

In describing the technological achievement of Circarama, *Business Screen Magazine* named one member of Disney's crew, Roger Broggie, whose son Michael has claimed that his father developed the system. A cameraman who worked at various Hollywood studios, Roger joined Disney in 1939, where he was appointed head of the machine shop in 1950. Walt, so the story goes, saw *This Is Cinerama* at the Pantages Theater in Hollywood and asked Broggie, since Cinerama had three joined screens, whether he thought a full-circle system was feasible. According to Brog-gie's son, that is how it started.[25]

On the other hand, Oscar-winning documentary producer Leslie Iwerks has asserted that her grandfather, Ub Iwerks, Walt's early partner and co-creator of Mickey Mouse, was instrumental in developing the Cir-carama system, although he is not mentioned in the *Business Screen Magazine* article. Apparently, during a casual conversation in a studio hallway, Walt and Ub pondered the possibility of expanding current widescreen formats to 360 degrees.[26] In the end, Circarama was most probably a team effort, perfected at Walt's behest, by Iwerks and Broggie.[27]

Regardless of authorship, Circarama seemed to presage the future of motion pictures. The press deemed it "the very last word in wide-screen movie projection … visually and kinesthetically overpowering."[28] According to AMC, *Tour of the West*'s sponsor, it had "the amazing ability to create a sense of actual audience participation greater than any yet developed."[29] At the unveiling of the Tomorrowland attraction, Walt intimated that Circarama might have a future beyond the travelogue, in the form of a narrative film exhibited in "a specially constructed theatre—one with chairs the individual could revolve by pushing a button—for a panoramic drama of unique design."[30] Tongue in cheek, a contemporary observer asked, "Is there still another step in wide-screen movie projection? Conceivably a system might be devised in which the audience is suspended in the center of a sphere and visual images are screened all around, above and below. Would it serve a useful purpose? Well, your guess is as good as mine."[31] Be that as it may, immersive entertainment *per se* was Walt's goal throughout Disneyland, and Circarama offered a version of this concept that fully utilized the cinematic medium. The show was a major technical achievement in terms of the visceral thrill it gave its audience—evidenced by the longevity of cinema-in-the-round attractions at parks across the United States and world's fairs here and abroad.[32]

Richfield's *The World Beneath Us*

The second of the three attractions praised by *Business Screen Magazine* was Richfield Oil's *The World Beneath Us*, an automated twelve-minute show viewed by a seated crowd of 125 in an auditorium. Between the audience and a CinemaScope screen lay a 40-foot-wide, scale-model diorama of the 450 square-mile Los Angeles basin, which harbored one of the world's largest oil deposits. The show described the prehistoric underground formation of fossil fuels and modern methods of extraction. The writer for *Business Screen Magazine* was particularly impressed by the "two separate motion picture media—CinemaScope and the 'underground' fiberglass dome show"—embedded in a complex system of moving parts that included various scale models—the latter being one of the Hollywood art-direction techniques we are following in this book.[33]

Part one of the *World Beneath Us* show was a five-minute Disney cartoon in widescreen CinemaScope. Based on research by Walt's artists, it summarized three billion years of geophysical creation, from a shapeless mass of gases to a sphere whirling in space, blanketed with active volcanoes and shattering earthquakes. The dinosaurs followed, and finally "the coming of man." *The World Beneath Us* thus repeated elements of "The Rite of Spring" segment of *Fantasia* that told the story of the Earth's formation and its earliest inhabitants. Animated diagrams and cross-sections of the planet resembled the ones used for instructional purposes in Disney's most ambitious wartime production, the feature-length propaganda film *Victory Through Air Power*, released in July 1943. The narrator of the Tomorrowland film, a new Disney cartoon character, Professor "Rich Field"—dressed in various guises, from caveman to modern tourist, depending on the epoch he was explaining—drove home Richfield's core message when he declared that remnants of earlier life were the basis of petroleum, a commodity essential to modern life.

House lights brightened for part two of the program, and an invisible voice explained the diorama and the upcoming demonstration. Finally, as the lights dimmed, and part three began, the central section of the model, the Long Beach oil field, rose like a table on legs. Below it were toy-size underground shafts, pumping equipment, and storage tanks. A novel configuration of fiberglass motion-picture screens, one flat and the other convex, received images from a pair of projectors hidden behind a half-dome. *Business Screen Magazine* marveled at the ingenuity of this feature, while struggling to describe it: "Probably the oddest shaped movie screen ever devised, the dome has a flat, half-round face at the front, a vertical section of the dome. Thus the front face is actually one of two adjoining screens. The second is spherical, completing a unit shaped something like a quarter of a watermelon." Cast onto the screens were cross-section depictions of "the world beneath us," illustrating a future method for oil extraction that would employ the downward force of gas and water to push oil upward through a circulation system the narrator compared to the workings of the human heart. According to an explanatory brochure given to the audience, this new drilling technique would enable independent oilmen to join forces to ensure a better life for everyone while conserving Earth's riches, an act described as "peacetime patriotism."[34]

The Richfield Oil Corporation sponsored both the *World Beneath Us* attraction and Tomorrowland's highway of the future, Autopia, which I will discuss shortly. A California-based company, Richfield Oil boasted that its fuel was "the official gasoline of Disneyland." The entrance to Autopia, with the company logo of a large eagle perched atop a post, replicated the forecourt of a Richfield service station like the one next door to the Disneyland Hotel. Richfield offered, at no cost to its customers, both a children's comic book, *Adventure in Disneyland*, and the *Official Road Map to Disneyland*, showing highway routes to the park.

Rocket to the Moon

The last of the trio of attractions featured in *Business Screen Magazine* was the ultimate goal of visitors to Tomorrowland, the TWA Rocket to the Moon attraction, which consisted of two elements: the freestanding spaceship, called the *Moonliner*, the land's principal icon, whose function was wholly symbolic as the "wienie," in Walt "talk," that drew visitors down the central corridor; and the Space Port enclosing a pair of auditoriums in which the ride actually took place, with three circular tiers of seating representing the interior of a spaceship (Fig. 24). According to the magazine article, TWA made the most of its sponsorship through national advertising, its motive being "sound institutional promotion."[35]

As early as April 1954 Walt Disney declared that movies would be a vital component in Tomorrowland's signature ride, but he likely did not anticipate the degree to which the cramped interior of the Space Port would require the unorthodox placement of hidden projectors and reflecting mirrors to create a series of persuasive illusions on three screens.[36] In a pre-show area, where visitors gathered to await entry, a rear-projected film simulated a futuristic screen monitor that indoctrinated first-time fliers. Further on, in the spaceship cabin, two large circular screens, called "space scanners," one in the floor and the other in the ceiling, employed rear projection to simulate televised views from the exterior of the ship, from blastoff to the circumnavigation of the moon. Judged within the narrative of the ride, these complex components, hailed by *Business Screen Magazine* as "unique motion picture techniques," built on a firm tradition of movieland technical advancement and, appropriately enough, prefigured the World of Tomorrow. In considering the Rocket to the Moon attraction, we will look at the ride itself first and then at the *Moonliner*. For the relationship with Hollywood, we will focus particularly on two space films, *Destination Moon* (1950) and Disney's own *Man in Space* television series (1955–57).

Figure 24. TWA *Moonliner*, Tomorrowland, Disneyland, 1956 (from the collection of Dave DeCaro).

The Ride

Typical of the publicity surrounding the Rocket to the Moon ride, a promotional brochure in 1955 emphasized its astronautical authenticity, and the park's first guidebook promised a sensation simulating weightlessness.[37] Walt rejected the notion that space travel was science fiction. His vision of tomorrow was, in his words, "science-factual."[38] Since space travel had not yet occurred, Disney was dependent on two sources: scientific advisors and earlier science-fiction films.

Publicists hyped Disney's reliance on scientists during the development phase, as reported in a *Disneyland News* article, "Noted Rocket Moon Authorities Contribute Skills to Space Ride."[39] Among the men collaborating on the ride were Willy Ley, a rocket enthusiast and writer who fled Hitler's Germany in 1936, and aerospace engineer Wernher von Braun, who served the Nazi regime during the war but, once Hitler was defeated, was scooped up by the United States to jumpstart America's rocket program. With his past smoothed over, he became a celebrity as a promoter of space exploration.[40] A third German, physicist Hans Haber, advised Disney on matters of space medicine. This trio had contributed to a series of articles, collectively called "Man Will Conquer Space Soon," published between 1952 and 1954 in eight issues of *Collier's* magazine.[41] The articles, with their detailed illustrations by astronomical view painter Chesley Bonestell, fired the imagination of a generation of space enthusiasts, including Walt Disney.

"Passengers" on the Rocket to the Moon started their journey at the gate to the Space Port, constructed to resemble a pair of observatories, where staff in silver spacesuits and plastic bubble headgear took tickets and ushered them into the Briefing Room. There, the first of three films, a fifteen-minute introduction to the ride, was projected onto the rear of an overhead screen to give the impression of a television monitor. In the video, a narrator posing as a uniformed TWA captain delivered a short oral history of space flight and a preview of how the trip would unfold. The slick combination of animated diagrams, shots of model rockets and planets, and actors dressed up as crew members, was geared toward authenticity. The Briefing Room film was a forerunner of pre-show videos now ubiquitous at entrance queues of theme-park rides as a means of building excitement, providing instruction, and keeping everyone in line occupied—children, above all—while they wait.

"Hostesses" in TWA jumpsuits escorted guests to one of 102 tiered seats in the two separate cylindrical auditoriums where they settled in for the ten-minute "eight-hour journey" to the Moon and back.[42] Following the countdown to liftoff and roar of the tail blast, air motors under the seats and temperature changes in the cabin gave the impression of movement.[43] Next, attention was directed to the two large circular "scanner screens," one in the middle of the floor, the other on the ceiling, showing televised images of where the rocket had been and where it was going. Illustrated in a line drawing in *Business Week Magazine*, the elaborate system of synchronized rear-screen projection and reflecting mirrors showed films that combined animation with footage of realistically rendered paintings and a scale model of a sister ship. The magazine also praised the synchronized sound effects that lent an authentic touch. The calm voice of "Captain P.T. Collins, TWA's flight officer for the trip" on the intercom, reciting facts about space flight, the satellites, stars and planets on view, and Halley's Comet, further contributed to the aura of realism. On the upper scanner screen, passengers caught a glimpse of "Space Station Terra," a tubular wheel measuring 200 feet across with three spokes joined to a central atomic reactor—actually a film of a scale-model fashioned by Wathel Rogers at the Disney studio. A writer in *Reader's Digest*, who took the trip with Walt, gushed, "All this is authentic, made of motion-picture film taken from missiles and satellites, from planetariums and observatories. The effects were so carefully worked out that the sensation of drifting in the stillness of gravity-free space became real too—astounding and blissful."[44]

Then the ship passed over the far side of the Moon, represented on film by a large, sculpted model created by Disney artists from a model in the Griffin Park Observatory. At this point "science-factual" yielded to science fiction, as flares revealed traces on the lunar surface of a structure of distinctly intelligent design. Captain Collins informed the voyagers that the ruins before their eyes represented one of the Moon's greatest mysteries, left presumably by a civilization from beyond the solar system. This spooky tale was accompanied by eerie "alien music." As the *Moonliner* prepared to reenter Earth's atmosphere, a meteoroid shower caused minor damage.

Disneyland's Rocket to the Moon recalled an earlier travel ride that provided a fantastic experience of voyaging to outer space: a Trip to the Moon was created for the 1901 Buffalo Exposition and transferred to Coney Island in 1903. "Passengers" on this pseudo-lunar excursion boarded a ship with bat-like wings and, after a guide's pseudo-science introduction, watched planet Earth grow distant through the use of paintings and projections visible outside the portholes.[45] However, the dramatic incidents on the Tomorrowland ride sprang not only from the collective brow of Disney and his men but also, as we shall see, from the fantasy world of movies.

George Pal and *Destination Moon*

Motion picture treatments of a trip to the Moon influenced the ride narrative, although it should be emphasized that in the first half of the twentieth century sci-fi movies depicting space travel did not comprise a Hollywood genre comparable in number to the Western or small-town film.[46] The best-known precedents, duly credited during the *Disneyland* TV program "Man in Space," were two pioneering silent films, Georges Méliès's *Voyage dans la Lune* (1902) and Fritz Lang's *Die Frau im Mond* (1929). Also notable: between 1936 and 1940, Universal Pictures made three *Flash Gordon* movie serials starring Buster Crabbe. The space genre in movies faded during World War II but gained a new lease on life with the 1950 film *Destination Moon*, produced by George Pal, a former animator of stop-motion shorts called Puppetoons, and directed by Irving Pichel from a script co-authored by science-fiction writer Robert A. Heinlein. The movie received an Academy Award for Best Special Effects and a nomination for Best Art Direction. As noted by science professor David A. Kirby, before Pal "there were no preconceived expectations of what a space movie would look like," but because of *Destination Moon*, "realism and believability ... shaped this new genre for the next 20 years."[47] Thus *Destination Moon* represents the single most important cinematic model for Tomorrowland's Rocket to the Moon attraction.

To begin, Pal preceded Disney in rejecting science fiction and embracing fact-based narrative, as acknowledged by contemporary critics.[48] Like Disney, he was inspired by a magazine publication, in this case a January 1949 *Life* story, "Rocket to the Moon," and before Disney he collaborated with Willy Ley.[49] For sets and matte paintings he brought on board Chesley Bonestell (one of the illustrators for the *Collier's* series). Pal regarded *Destination Moon* as "a documentary of the near future." Publicity for the film posed the question "Would you like to take a trip to the moon?" To explain the principles of rocketry to a 1950 audience, as Walt later did, Pal inserted a didactic animated segment—starring Walter Lantz's cartoon hero Woody Woodpecker (Pal joked, "We couldn't afford Disney").[50] The emphasis on realism resulted in some fairly banal dialog: *New York Times* critic Bosley Crowther commented, half in jest, "There isn't a single beautiful female nor even a Russian scientist anywhere."[51] But the public loved it, and critics were impressed by the apparent "authenticity" of the details.[52]

Previously introduced as a narrative element in *Die Frau im Mond*, the countdown and blast-off sequence was given heightened suspense in *Destination Moon*. It immediately developed into a common trope in postwar space flicks—and naturally was repeated in the Tomorrowland ride.

Likewise, the realistic sounds made by Pal's spaceship, called the *Luna*, were added to the soundtrack of Disney's ride, described as follows: "Faint throbs, pulsing sounds, and an occasional spacey 'up spin' noise could be heard, presumably emitted from the *Moonliner*'s electronics."[53] Americans in the 1950s were anxious about the unknown perils of space travel, like cosmic rays, weightlessness, and meteors. *Destination Moon* played up these fears. The conceit of a meteoroid strike was present in *Rocketship X-M*, a film rushed to theaters in 1950 by a rival studio to capitalize on advance publicity for Pal's picture. Thus, meteors were a must-have in the Disneyland attraction. Like the circular scanners in Disney's rocket, the interior of the *Luna* featured a circular television screen showing, alternately, fore, aft, and ground views, to orient the crew members. The discovery of ancient ruins—on Mars, not the Moon—figured in *Rocketship X-M*. Thus, Walt's men must have studied *Destination Moon* and comparable productions closely. In a message from Willy Ley to von Braun in summer 1954, he explicitly referenced George Pal, and before signing on with Disney, von Braun met with Pal several times to discuss a possible collaboration.[54] Pal's subsequent film, *Conquest of Space*, released two months before Disneyland opened, featured a donut-shaped space station, the "Wheel," orbiting a thousand miles above the Earth, like the one Disney created for the Tomorrowland ride. The trailer for Pal's film described the space station as a "jumping off place for the fantastic rocket ships built in outer space."

The headline of a 1949 *Los Angeles Times* article about *Destination Moon* struck a prescient note: "Hollywood Will Reach the Moon First: Hollywood Nips Science in Race for Moon."[55] In short, Pal delivered the vicarious thrills that Tomorrowland's Rocket to Moon supplied five years later. The trailer for *Conquest of Space* projected a wildly optimistic view of space travel identical to the one Walt would use to sell the ride: "The biggest true story of our century! Before it actually happens! ... And now you will be part of it, rocketing beyond the horizon of our time to join the greatest human adventure of all time."

Man in Space

Another contemporary film that boasted a realistic depiction of future space travel was the live-action segment of Disney's own *Disneyland* TV program called "Man and the Moon," devoted to future space travel. It was developed simultaneously with the Rocket to the Moon ride, although in a separate unit at the studio, and broadcast to the public five months after the ride's premiere.

Disney's deal with ABC—in exchange for helping finance his dream—called for weekly shows organized as televisual anthologies, mirroring Disneyland's division into four main lands. The studio's film library lacked material for Tomorrowland's portion of the shows. That gap was temporarily filled when animator Ward Kimball, one of the elite artists Walt dubbed the Nine Old Men, directed his attention to the "Man Will Conquer Space Soon" series of articles in *Collier's* magazine.[56]

Kimball assumed the dual role of producer and co-writer of a trilogy of one-hour documentaries, collectively called *Man in Space*, that would explain space travel to the public.[57] He brought in as consultants and on-camera narrators three of the German scientists—Ley, von Braun, and Haber—who had written the *Collier's* articles and who served as advisors on the Rocket to the Moon project. (Kimball hoped to hire Chesley Bonestell for the visuals, but his work was too expensive.) Disney would introduce the first episode, also called "Man in Space," stating its aim of uniting cartoon fantasy with hard science. Giving the shows the solid air of a documentary, akin to his award-winning *True-Life Adventures* theatrical films, he sought to differentiate them from contemporary, cheaply made TV space operas like *Captain Video and His Video Rangers* (1949–55) and *Tom Corbett, Space Cadet* (1950–55).

The Tomorrowland ride and the *Disneyland* episodes were inextricably linked in Walt's mind. As a master of synergy, he used his various projects to reinforce and publicize each other. Early on, he affirmed his intent to create a vivid feel for space travel, both on television and at Anaheim.[58] The first two shows in the trilogy were developed jointly but aired nine months apart. "Man in Space" (March 1955) dramatized the challenges of space travel prefaced by a droll romp through the history of rocketry. In "Man and the Moon" (December 1955), a breezy look at humanity's abiding interest in its nearest celestial body preceded the live-action segment, a "real-life" expedition to the Moon. "Mars and Beyond," the third episode, did not air until December 1957. The shows were filmed in color because Walt saw them as potential theatrical releases.

Coupling education and entertainment—an early example of televised "edutainment"—the episodes followed the stylistic lead of Disney's vigorous championing of American air supremacy in his World War II film *Victory through Air Power*.[59] Kimball's programs blended narration, live-action oral presentations, mock-documentary limited animation, and the low-budget whimsy of Cartoon Modern animation.[60] However, the final part of "Man and the Moon" broke with the *Victory Through Air Power* formula. In this twenty-minute sequence, actors in space suits were filmed on a soundstage en route to and orbiting the Moon, which virtually duplicated the footage used in the Disneyland ride.

Less costly to produce than animation, live action—with careful attention to set design, prop selection, and costume preparation—made the "Man and the Moon" sequence all the more convincing. Adding to the realism was the storyline's matter-of-fact tone. Only two instances of imminent heart-stopping danger disrupt the voyage: a meteoroid hit that damages the ship (as in the Disneyland ride), and a near collision with the Moon that forces a quick course correction. As in the Tomorrowland ride, where Captain Collins—to the strains of "alien music"—points to signs of previous extraterrestrial life, Kimball's low-key captain indicates an "unusual formation" on the far side of the lunar surface, accompanied by the brutish sounds of a modernist musical score. Sci-fi critic Gary Westfahl ranked the sequence highly "in the history of spacesuit films" because it did not compromise accuracy despite the imaginative fiction of an ancient settlement or a view of the Moon as yet unseen in real life.[61] As I have emphasized throughout this book, both Disney and Hollywood used apparent realism to give an aura of authenticity to a wide range of fantastic narratives.

The Rocket to the Moon ride and the three *Disneyland* shows shared a common goal. In Walt's intro to the "Man and the Moon" television episode, he displayed photos of the *Moonliner* and the Space Port and told viewers he wanted them to "experience the thrills that space travelers of the future will encounter when rocket trips to the Moon become a daily routine." In April 1955, Disney fast-tracked the Tomorrowland attraction, one year after production had begun on Ward Kimball's space episodes. Kimball and project leader for the Tomorrowland attraction, John Hench, have claimed there was scant interaction between their production staffs. Yet, the projects developed concurrently, and Walt urged the two teams to pool resources, German scientists included. Narratives for the Disneyland ride and the live-action TV segment were noticeably similar—the animated views of the blast off from Earth, orbital flights around the Moon, illumination of its hidden hemisphere, signs of alien life, and the threat of meteoroids striking the rocket. And both projects relied on models of Space Station Terra and the Moon, created—with help from experts—by Disney artists, with ruins on the Moon's far side applied by Kimball.[62]

The *Moonliner*

Like Sleeping Beauty Castle in Fantasyland or the *Mark Twain* Riverboat in Frontierland, the gleaming white *TWA Moonliner* was the potent symbol of Tomorrowland, the "wienie" that would draw visitors into a Disney vision of the future and carry them into space (Fig. 24). Constructed of aluminum over a steel frame and rising eighty feet on retractable legs over a blast pit, the rocket was in fact an elaborate backlot prop, thrust onto center stage.[63] Its elegant contours, first swelling, then tapering, gave an impression of great height—intensified by virtue of being the tallest object in the Magic Kingdom, higher than the spires of Sleeping Beauty Castle. Like so many buildings and objects in Disneyland, it was a scale model—one-third as big as a real spaceship, as indicated on an adjacent placard. A cutaway view posted inside the ride depicted a full-scale rocket that dwarfed the humans within its multi-layered compartments. Hollywood "tricks of the trade" made the *Moonliner* seem much bigger. The man in charge of designing the rocket, John Hench, often cited the importance of linear perspective and foreshortening in manipulating viewer perception throughout the park.[64]

What was the visual source of the design of this single-stage rocket that would take people to the moon? Several candidates have been suggested, the V-2 rocket for one, developed for the Nazis by a team that included Wernher von Braun. However, the V-2—the "Vengeance Weapon"—had disagreeable connotations, having caused thousands of civilian deaths in England during World War II. A second reputed source, the TWA Lockheed Constellation Airliner (a propeller plane), looked nothing like the Tomorrowland craft. Once again, *Destination Moon* provides an answer. Scientists had long argued that a multi-stage vehicle was essential for a Moon mission.[65] *Die Frau im Mond* had such a ship, and the articles in *Collier's* magazine detailed its necessity. In the *Disneyland* TV shows, the massive rocket to the space station orbiting the earth was conceived as a four-stage vehicle. However, for the spaceship *Luna* in *Destination Moon*, art director Ernest Fegté rejected the multi-stage concept in favor of a single-stage rocket, scientifically inadequate, but visually more pleasing (Fig. 25).[66] There were no wings, and the craft had a tall silhouette, gently curved inward at top and bottom.

Film historian Vivian Sobchack recognized the significance of Fegté's bold design choice:

> The ship itself is "good." It is aesthetically beautiful. It is fun to play with. It promises positive adventure, an ecstatic release from the gravitational demands of the Earth, and it can remove us from ourselves and the complexity of life on our planet, taking us to the new Edens and regeneration. In *Destination Moon* ... the silvery sleekness of Ernest Fegté's single-stage spaceship almost palpably glows against the velvet black and star-bejeweled beauty of a mysterious but nonhostile space; it is breathtakingly beautiful, awe inspiring, and yet warmly comforting....[67]

Contemporaries embraced *Luna*'s look. Helen Gould, in the *New York Times*, said: "The long-standing star system is in for some highly

Figure 25. *Destination Moon* (1950, Eagle-Lion Films), Spaceship *Luna* (Eagle-Lion Films Inc./Photofest).

unorthodox competition from the solar system. Hollywood is training the cameras on a new cycle of movies dealing with interstellar space. The stars? Rocket ships."[68] Subsequent big-screen rockets copied *Luna*'s svelte design—as did the *Moonliner*, created, unsurprisingly, by an art director, not an aerospace engineer, although Hench credited von Braun and Ley for providing technical advice.[69] The majestic form of Walt's single-stage rocket, gleaming white with bits of crimson red, fulfilled Sobchack's definition of a spaceship that projects an aura of optimism.[70]

In hindsight, the Rocket to the Moon attraction seems remarkable in that it was created two years before the launch of Sputnik, six years before President Kennedy's call to put a man on the Moon, and fourteen years before Neal Armstrong's "giant leap for mankind" in 1969. A park guidebook declared that, as the nations of the world prepared for such a trip, Disneyland would pave the way.[71]

Space Station X-1

A separate but related attraction, Space Station X-1, was situated inside the northern complex of exhibit halls. Designed to give the impression of looking out from a satellite circling the Earth, this was the only Tomorrowland attraction without a corporate sponsor. Walt's German advisors, who theorized that rocket ships would initiate their journey to the Moon from a space station, contributed significantly in shaping the design. Von Braun explored the concept of a ring-shaped station on camera in the March 1955 *Disneyland* episode "Man in Space."

Guests "aboard" Space Station X-1 stood in the center of a circular room on a revolving platform, peering through a window at a panoramic view of the world no human then had ever beheld. During the three-minute rotation of the platform, the craft appeared to move east to west across North America, from the crack of dawn to twilight and nightfall, the latter enhanced through the use of black light. An article in *The Disneyland News*, "Space Station X-1 Gives Outer Space View of U.S.," emphasized America's grandeur and natural beauty seen from 500 miles out in space (90 miles, in other publicity), compressed in a visual mash-up of landscapes from the Appalachian Mountains, Midwestern farmland, and broad prairies to the Mississippi Delta, the Great Salt Lake, the Rocky Mountains, and Southern California.[72]

The attraction was the latest in a long line of pictorial panoramas that had entertained Europeans and Americans since the nineteenth century. Visitors to the 1900 Paris Universal Exhibition, for instance, could take in two such spectacles, the Trans-Siberian Railroad Panorama, which imitated train travel in Russia, and the Maréorara, an imaginary journey witnessed from the deck of a steamship on the high seas.

There were two basic types of panorama. The first was a circular, 360-degree painting of a landscape, urbanscape, or great battle, viewed while strolling around a central stationary platform. The second was the moving panorama, a long strip of painted muslin or canvas that passed on rollers before an audience seated facing a proscenium stage.[73] Disney's

Space Station X-1 attraction fused the two formats with fixed positions on a rotating platform.

Bridging the nineteenth-century panorama and Space Station X-1 was a half-century of movie-set painting that flourished during Hollywood's Golden Age. Soundstages assured maximum control for filming and were less expensive than location shooting. Large backdrops or "flats" often stood in for outdoor landscapes, domestic interiors, or businesses as a thrifty alternative to full-fledged sets. They were so skillfully integrated into the décor that the transition between foreground props and painted background was imperceptible on screen. By working on a curved canvas, artists could accommodate a turning camera lens and keep the backdrop in focus. Adjustments in lighting could suggest different times of day and atmospheric effects. For example, Warner Bros. artist William McConnell, who worked on *The Maltese Falcon*, achieved fame for the realism of his efforts.[74] For Tomorrowland's backdrop, one of Disney animation's best known background painters, Claude Coats, assisted the designer of the outer space panorama, Peter Ellenshaw.

The Art Directors Exhibit

The need to fill gaps between exhibits in Tomorrowland led to the installation of three attractions that at first glance might not seem (and in fact, were *not*) suited to an imaginary "1986." However, from the standpoint of film, they afforded an inside look at moviemaking craved by tourists to L.A. that the Big Eight studios would or could not satisfy.

The first of these attractions may be the least expected: a traveling exhibition curated by the Society of Motion Picture Art Directors that occupied 2,100 square feet during the park's first three months of operation.[75] The drawings, paintings, photos, sets, and props on display gave a behind-the-scenes glimpse of how the major studios' art departments operated. From conception to realization. The objects on view included continuity sketches for *Marty* and *High Noon*, preliminary artwork for *Guys and Dolls* and *Rear Window*, ship models for *Mr. Roberts* and *Helen of Troy*, and stage sets from *Giant* and *There's No Business like Show Business*. The exhibit called attention as well to recently introduced plastics that were economical alternatives to traditional materials.

Walt took advantage of the exhibition to acknowledge the men whose skills contributed to visualizing, sculpting, and building the Magic Kingdom's different lands. Publicity stressed the fact that the park's chief designers—credited by name—were members of the Society of Motion

Picture Art Directors. As we have seen, those methods were based on those
of their peers at the major studios. Thus, the type of objects on view was
comparable, such as scale models of Disneyland's Main Street, the King
Arthur Carrousel in Fantasyland, and Explorer's Boat Dock in Adventureland. To please an audience interested in how Disney cartoons were
made, production art was pulled from some of the studio's best-known
full-length cartoons, *Snow White and the Seven Dwarfs*, *Fantasia*, *Cinderella*, and *Alice in Wonderland*. Naturally, Disney's newest release, *Lady
and the Tramp* received special treatment. Storyboard sketches, animation
production drawings, and inked-and-painted cels from the film traced
the stages in its development. As with live-action movies shot in Cinema-
Scope, technical advances of the new widescreen medium had obliged layout artists and animators working on *Lady and the Tramp* to adapt to the
new proportions of the wide frame process.

20,000 Leagues Under the Sea

A second exhibit provided Hollywood thrills of a different nature.
Walt had been thinking about a submarine ride ever since his initial
brainstorming for the Mickey Mouse Park. An early proposal for Disneyland included a 20,000 Leagues Under the Sea attraction in Fantasyland.[76]
As realized, the Tomorrowland exhibit was a walk-through of the Academy Award–winning sets from Disney's 1954 movie, *20,000 Leagues Under
the Sea*.

Jules Verne's novel, issued as a book in 1870, had previously been the
source of an innovative 1916 silent film that used advanced technology
to film underwater sequences. Walt's CinemaScope version was equally
advanced. Many Americans first discovered widescreen projection when
they watched his *20,000 Leagues Under the Sea*. Though shooting was
slowed because Fox had only one anamorphic lens available to loan to
Disney, the stunning CinemaScope images of the ocean's waves and panoramic underwater sequences helped make it a hit. A fully storyboarded
live-action production, *20,000 Leagues* was more ambitious than Disney's hybrid movies (combining animation with live-action) from the late
1940s like *Song of the South* and *So Dear to My Heart*, or live-action Disney adventure pictures like *Treasure Island*. This was Walt's entry into live
filming on a scale and budget equal to any other Hollywood studio. And,
for the first time, heading the cast were three top-of-the-bill stars, James
Mason, Kirk Douglas, and Peter Lorre.

Like Warner Bros., which had built a huge maritime studio to
accommodate its pirate pictures (for Studio 21, see chap. 5), Walt

constructed a new facility (Stage 3), with a water tank up to eighteen feet deep.[77] Some scenes were filmed at Fox and Universal, and equipment was rented from MGM. Skilled technicians and stuntmen were recruited from Fox, RKO, and Paramount.[78] Peter Ellenshaw, who contributed to other Tomorrowland attractions, painted twenty-nine mattes for *20,000 Leagues*. The film opened in time for the Christmas 1954 season—a big but winning gamble for Disney. It was an unqualified success, achieving Oscars for Special Effects and Art Direction, the latter awarded to set dresser Emile Kuri, who oversaw props throughout Disneyland and created the décor for Walt and Lillian's private apartment above the Fire Station on Town Square.

Hastily assembled and intended as a six-month exhibit, the 20,000 Leagues walk-through was so popular it lasted eleven years. Disney had already promoted the film in three television shows: the first *Disneyland* episode in October 1954; a making-of special, "Operation Undersea," in December 1954, which received an Emmy for Best Original Show; and "Monsters of the Deep," January 1955. Guests, fully acquainted with the film and its sets from TV and the silver screen, could now physically enter these cinematic spaces and see actual props and production models—a rare opportunity deemed worthy of an article in the *Los Angeles Times*, "Famed Craft Nautilus Shown at Disneyland."[79]

Once inside the exhibit, peering through a window, visitors witnessed the *Nautilus'* final resting place on the ocean floor.[80] Proceeding in counter-clockwise fashion while heeding the voice of an unseen narrator (transmitted by hidden speakers), they passed by a sequence of sets representing the submarine's interior arranged in a circle: the wheel house and chart room, Professor Aronnax's room, Nemo's salon—with its pipe organ, framed artwork, and red-velvet-upholstered furniture—the pump room, diving chamber, outfitting room with diving equipment, and power supply. The jewel in the crown was the eleven-foot-long model of the *Nautilus* created by art director Harper Goff. Goff had convinced Disney to shoot a live-action version of the Verne novel and to reject Verne's concept of a smooth, cigar-shaped submarine in favor of a more expressive sea monster design with jagged scales and glowing eyes.[81]

In Verne's story, electricity powers the *Nautilus*, but in the film, Nemo is reluctant to divulge the mysterious source. Concerned that humankind was not ready to handle it responsibly, he blows up Vulcania, his secret island base. 1950s audiences generally interpreted the erupting mushroom cloud as atomic power, and the voice-over of Nemo at the movie's conclusion repeats his belief that knowledge of this power would come "in God's good time."[82] By 1955, Walt's "good time" had come, and the Nautilus tour was unreservedly advertised as a walk-through of "an atomic-powered submarine."[83]

Disney was optimistic in his view of nuclear power, and the studio undertook a campaign to publicize its benefits. In 1955 he initiated development of a cartoon, *Atoms for Peace*, likely intended for the Tomorrowland section of the *Disneyland* TV show or for a park attraction. In the "Dateline Disneyland" televised park premiere, Heinz Haber demonstrates nuclear fission with a table laid with mousetraps and ping pong balls. While promising the audience a future Tomorrowland exhibit that would demonstrate life during the atomic age, Haber strikes a note of caution, admonishing the audience to "be certain that you use [atomic power] wisely."

A park attraction along these lines never materialized. Instead, in 1959 Disney opened a new Tomorrowland ride sponsored by General Dynamics, the Submarine Voyage, based on the company's first operational nuclear-powered sub, the USS *Nautilus* (launched in September 1954). As for the *Atoms for Peace* cartoon, it evolved into an hour-long program, "Our Friend the Atom," broadcast on *Disneyland* in January 1957.[84] The episode opens with a clip of the mushroom cloud from *20,000 Leagues Under the Sea* and ends with archival footage of a nuclear explosion. Atomic energy is compared to a genie in a lamp: once freed, it cannot be recaptured. However, viewers are told, the genie *can* be controlled—if it is managed sensibly. Haber, who hosted the show and repeated the ping pong ball experiment, warned in his parting words that we must keep the atomic genie as our friend.[85]

Fear of atomic power's dangers, from its destructive use as a weapon to the harm caused by radioactive fallout, haunted the national psyche during the Cold War in what were called "creature features." Moviegoers saw themselves battling aliens from outer space and monsters from the deep, awakened by atomic bomb tests, in pictures like *The Beast from 20,000 Fathoms* (1953) and *It Came from Beneath the Sea* (1955).[86] Historians often count Disney's *20,000 Leagues Under the Sea* among the creature features. Whether the "creature" in Walt's film was the giant squid, Nemo himself, or an atomic bomb, the multilayered plot and production values in *20,000 Leagues* elevated it far above the B-movie level.[87] Nonetheless, at Tomorrowland there was no doubt that the "creature" was the giant squid. Visible through the large viewport of Nemo's salon, the monster was a reminder of the film's most unforgettable sequence, its attack on the submarine. According to contemporary accounts, its wriggling tentacles, sculpted by Disney staff artist Chris Mueller and executed by Bob Mattey, were the high point of the attraction—judging by the frightened squeals of children in the crowd.[88]

The Art Corner

The third attraction in Tomorrowland with a link to Hollywood was the Art Corner, situated on opening day in a tent on Main Street near Disneyland's Hub, but soon moved to Tomorrowland as a space filler in the north range of exhibit buildings, where it remained for eleven years.[89] Seemingly better suited to Fantasyland, the Corner showcased Disney animation art. The Burbank studio was closed to the public, but reasonably priced collectibles from its cartoons were available at the Tomorrowland shop. The Art Corner carried on a tradition of presenting Disney production art as fine art, a practice that started in 1938 when Courvoisier Galleries of San Francisco contracted to sell specially prepared cel set-ups through a nationwide network of dealers.

Displays in the Art Corner also announced the latest Disney releases, and souvenirs mingled with art supplies. Flip books and a suite of six guides instructed amateurs on how to draw Disney characters. A boxed animation kit included a pegged light board, punched paper, exposure sheets, pencils, erasers, and a booklet on animation methods. And there was an official Art Corner beret, a felt cap with stitched Disneyland insignia and a peg on top. Studio artists were frequently on hand to sketch visitors' portraits and teach the basics of character sketching. Many a recent collector of Disney art has wished upon a star to be transported back to the Art Corner, where original celluloids for Disney cartoons could be purchased for a few Disney dollars.

Autopia

In our era of urgent environmentalist concerns, it may be tempting to condemn Disney as a shill who gave entertainment cover to Big Oil and its rapacious messaging. But in Walt's defense it should be remembered that—decades before terms like "sustainable" or "green" energy entered the language—the 1950s witnessed a sharp increase in two-car families, automobile travel, and guaranteed weekend vacations. And, of course, cars were an integral part of Hollywood movies, where an actor behind the wheel of a convertible often symbolized personal independence. From car chases to car crashes, from filling-station pit stops to auto-romance, the durability of onscreen tropes helps explain why Autopia is one of the few original rides still operating.[90]

Richfield's kid-size mile-long track—true to the spirit of Disneyland and Hollywood—touted itself as an authentic model freeway (Fig. 26). With its pint-sized overpasses, cloverleaf interchange, angled freeway lights, and billboards, Disney's reimagining of the familiar fairground bumper-car ride adhered to the park's recurrent reliance on miniaturization. Following the standard practice for park attraction development, the designer of the sporty roadsters, Bob Gurr, a Los Angeles Art Center College of Design graduate, proceeded from drawings, scale models, and a full-size clay mock-up to a plaster mold, from which the fiberglass bodies were cast. Special features were introduced, such as a relatively new item in real cars, the seat belt. As Disneyland's Director of Special Vehicular Development, Gurr solved many transportation problems at Disneyland, and he created the fleet of "vintage" conveyances for Main Street.[91]

So popular was Autopia that its original thirty-nine cars were insufficient to meet the demand. By July 1956, a second fleet was put in service, and the track was improved to handle more traffic. A Junior Autopia, exclusively for children, also debuted in 1956 in an area formerly occupied by the short-lived Mickey Mouse Club Circus. Midget Autopia was introduced in April 1957 for the youngest visitors. More than a thrilling ride for kids and their parents, Autopia symbolized America's cherished freedom of mobility and contained an underlying message. Not only would the attraction instruct youngsters in motor vehicle safety, but it would encourage tax-paying adults to support planning and construction of new roads

Figure 26. Richfield Autopia, Tomorrowland, Disneyland, August 1956 (from the collection of Dave DeCaro).

and highways as a means of spurring economic growth and coast-to-coast consolidation.

With characteristic canniness, Walt understood how important freeways were to the success of his dream. He commissioned the non-profit Stanford Research Institute to find a suitable park site, and, acting on their advice, located Disneyland in Orange County next to the Santa Ana Freeway, a half-hour drive from downtown Los Angeles.

Legend has it that the parking lot beyond the berm, twice the size of Disneyland itself, was the largest in the country. In a February 1955 *Disneyland* television episode, "A Progress Report," Walt showed how easy it was to get to Anaheim on local freeways. Embarking on a helicopter tour from the studio in Burbank, he drew attention to the Hollywood Freeway (completed the year before). Further underscoring the park's ties to Tinseltown, he pointed to the fabled intersection of Hollywood and Vine. The route turned south on the Santa Ana Freeway, which had been a stagecoach trail a century earlier, Disney noted. This comment echoed the theme of westward expansion embodied by Frontierland, located directly across the central Hub from Tomorrowland. The camera hovered over straightaways, interchanges, and ramps—full-sized versions of Autopia's bantam roads—while Walt explained the origin of the term "freeway," meaning no toll charges. The freeway system around Disneyland was still under construction in summer 1955, and alternative routes were devised during the first year of operation to alleviate traffic congestion.[92]

Motion Pictures and the Automobile

Los Angeles' love affair with the automobile fused with the movies' "need for speed" early on, for example, in the car-chase finale of the Keystone Kops two-reeler *Hash House Fraud* (1915) and Harold Lloyd's devotion to a Model T in *Get Out and Get Under* (1920). Passenger cars were the primary mode of transport as L.A. grew into a sprawling metropolis. The four-level downtown interchange nicknamed The Stack, completed in 1949, swiftly achieved the status of urban icon and emblem of the city's feverish postwar expansion of its highway system. By mid-century, Hollywood was contributing in a material way to growth in the auto industry: actors, executives, and lower-level personnel all drove (or were driven) to work in cars. The big studios maintained working garages, gas pumps, and fleets of vehicles to assist production, on- and off-camera.[93] The burgeoning in-state car culture spawned public-service films sponsored by the Automobile Club of Southern California that extolled the joys of car ownership and advised drivers how to cope with unusual situations on the road.

Autopia also had numerous connections to the 1939 New York World's Fair, dedicated to The World of Tomorrow. At the Ford Motors Pavilion, guests could drive life-size versions of the latest models on a multilevel highway, the Road of Tomorrow, constructed around the building—a major precedent for Autopia. Inside the Fair's icon, the monumental Trylon and Perisphere, called the Theme Building, visitors circulated via moving sidewalks around Democracity, a gigantic diorama of an urban community connected to the surrounding landscape via an efficient road system.[94] Further, the concept of a greenbelted metropolis was echoed by a half-hour-long film, *The City*, commissioned by the American Institute of Planners and shown in the Fair's Science and Education Building.[95] This featurette offered an antidote to urban squalor and congested streets by forecasting a utopian vision in which "sunlit factories" and "green cities" might coexist, "built into the countryside." The film was subsequently projected in movie theaters and by civic groups (Fig. 27).

The Fair's number-one attraction was the Futurama installation in the General Motors Highways and Horizons pavilion. At peak capacity, Futurama could accommodate 552 spectators. Seated on a conveyor belt, they "took off" on a simulated plane ride overlooking an immense model

Figure 27. *The City* (1939, Civic Films) (Civic Films/Springer/Photofest).

of a modernistic network of roads linking cities and towns, with hundreds of capsule-sized buildings and cars, some of them moving along futuristic multilane expressways (at one point, according to the narrator, past "an amusement park—1960; man's progress has brought more leisure for amusement and recreation"). At ride's end, the spectators emerged into a full-scale mock-up of an urban intersection twenty years hence, The City of 1960. For those unable to visit GM's exhibit in person, it could be seen in a twenty-three-minute 1940 theatrical film, *To New Horizons*, in which Futurama's Lilliputian roads seemed entirely believable, thanks to Hollywood's skill in photographing miniatures.

The Futurama exhibit-and-ride combo was the work of Norman Bel Geddes, art director for both stage and movies. In 1940, after the Fair closed, Bel Geddes published a book, *Magic Motorways*, that explained how a smartly designed road network superimposed on varying terrains could fulfill four basic goals of highway design: "safety, comfort, speed and economy."[96] In short, both Hollywood movies and the world's fair tradition formed the basis of Autopia, an attraction that appealed to both kids and adults.

Disney and the Car

In January 1955, Disney announced a forthcoming "Tomorrowland" episode of *Disneyland* directed by Ward Kimball, whose didactic mission was to inform while entertaining the viewer.[97] Inspired by the title of Bel Geddes's book, the show was called "Magic Highway, USA." In his introduction to the episode when it aired in May 1958, Disney described an imaginary town, Autopia, where traffic jams are a thing of the past. "Magic Highway" repeated the same approach used in "Man in Space," with an amusing cartoon history of roads, followed by a live "expert" talking about the problems of automotive transport, and an idealized future rendered in Cartoon Modern style, in which freeways unite and foster understanding among peoples of the world. In his introduction to "Magic Highway," Walt said that high-speed roads were the supreme symbol of progress. In other words, in America's never-ending Pursuit of Happiness, highways were a magic carpet conveyance to greater freedom and a better way of life.

The nation's infatuation with cars made its way into several Disney animated cartoons made for theatrical release. In *Lucky Number* (1951), Donald Duck wins a new Zoom V-8 roadster but thinks it's a hoax perpetrated by his three nephews and destroys it. *Susie the Little Blue Coupe* (1952) details the life cycle, from showroom to junkyard hot rod, of a humanized car with windshield eyes. In yet another cartoon, *Autopia*, initially planned as a segment in the "Magic Highway" *Disneyland* epi-sode, later revived as an independent one-reeler, *The Story of Anyburg, USA* (1957), anthropomorphic autos are prosecuted for traffic offenses. An accompanying song, "Autopia" (composed but not used), told of a town "where motorists and motor cars work together, hand in hand."[98] Goofy got into the act in a handful of "car toons," starting with *Victory Vehicles* (1943), in which, faced with wartime shortages, he devises alternatives to gas-powered vehicles, ultimately settling on a pogo stick. In *Motor Mania* (1950), the Goof is a suburban Everyman with Jekyll and Hyde tenden-cies as Mr. Walker, pedestrian, and Mr. Wheeler, maniacal motorist. This cartoon's usefulness as a teaching tool in driver education classes led to two didactic shorts released in 1965, about how to cope with expressway driving: *Freewayphobia* and *Goofy's Freeway Trouble*. Thus, the studio's cartoon output mirrored Tomorrowland's Autopia attraction by encour-aging proper driving skills and celebrating America's expanding system of roadways.

A Great Big Beautiful Tomorrow

Tomorrowland's connections with motion pictures past and present, as heralded in the *Business Screen Magazine* article, gave visitors a preview of the future of the medium. Other exhibits were less related to the World of Tomorrow than to the World of Hollywood, thus providing a unique look into how the studios functioned. Tomorrowland's corporate-spon-sored science exhibits, however, easily turned outdated. Kaiser Alumi-num, in year three of its contract, tried to shut down its "Brightest Star in the World of Metals" exhibit. But widescreen has endured as a staple of moving pictures, and Circle-Vision has become ubiquitous as part of the theme-park experience. More surprising, a rocket ship to the Moon and a space station achieved reality quicker than anyone in 1955 might have imagined.

5

Fantasyland

Unique among Disneyland's four principal subdivisions, Fantasyland—Walt Disney's favorite realm—embodies the boundless domain, neither past, present, nor future, of imagination and childhood dreams.[1] In year one of operation, Fantasyland boasted more rides than any other sector of the park. Passing through Sleeping Beauty Castle from the central Hub, guests entered the castle courtyard to find themselves surrounded by a variety of brightly colored entertainments laid out by the principal art director for the sector, Bill Martin, a former set designer at Twentieth Century–Fox.[2]

Straight ahead, along the main north-south axis, lay three major attractions: the King Arthur Carrousel, the spinning cups of the Mad Tea Party, and the Pirate Ship Restaurant. To left and right, bordering the courtyard, colorful "fabric" tents (made of wood and metal) sheltered Disney's only dark rides.[3] Indoor rides at conventional amusement parks offered random thrills. At Disneyland they adhered to the narrative promise of their names: Snow White Adventures, Peter Pan Flight, and Mr. Toad's Wild Ride.[4] A space destined for an Alice in Wonderland indoor attraction, eventually located next to the Mad Tea Party, was occupied by the Mickey Mouse Club Theater.[5] Three further rides near the park's northern boundary surrounded the Pirate Ship Restaurant: the Casey Jr. Circus Train, Dumbo the Flying Elephant, and Canal Boats of the World (soon recast as Storybook Land Canal Boats).[6]

Writers have always considered Fantasyland the three-dimensional realization of Disney's animated classics, as suggested by contemporary publicity that promised up-close-and-personal encounters with beloved Disney characters.[7] Because a considerable literature details the rides associated with Snow White, Peter Pan, Mr. Toad, Dumbo, and Alice, this chapter deals in a selective way with the impact of Disney's own feature films and cartoon shorts.[8] As in previous chapters, my emphasis is on the land's relationship with Hollywood cinema of the Golden Age. I focus on three attractions occupying the main axis—Sleeping Beauty Castle, the

King Arthur Carrousel, and the Pirate Ship, all of which are connected to Disney while inhabiting the wider cultural sphere of American cinema. In addition, one of the park's most ubiquitous symbols, Tinker Bell, whose home turf was Fantasyland, is of interest here because she was not originally a Disney creation. In conceiving Fantasyland, the park's designers borrowed liberally from the toolkit of the big studio art directors to establish a playground that seemed both familiar and unique to children and adults alike.

Sleeping Beauty Castle

Among the entryways into Disneyland's five realms, Sleeping Beauty Castle occupies a place of special prestige (Fig. 28). Approached from Main Street, its turreted battlements rise increasingly majestically the nearer one gets. To the left and right of the central frontispiece, defensive towers and walls form an enclosure around Fantasyland. The realm is further guarded by a moat. Visitors move toward the interior courtyard by walking over a drawbridge and beneath a portcullis.

Disneyland's most iconic feature (and biggest "wienie"), the castle is Fantasyland's visual anchor and its conceptual cornerstone. Surprisingly, however, for such a universally known structure, many questions regarding its origins and iconography remain to be fully addressed. Whose idea was it to place a European castle in an American amusement park, and who was its principal architect? During the planning stage, which Disney characters' names were attached to the building and why? How did a type of medieval defensive architecture come to embody twentieth-century fairy-tale dreams and wish fulfillment? Finally, in what ways did Hollywood's reinvention of a historical building type impact design decisions at Disneyland? As a means of offering possible answers, the first part of this chapter will investigate early texts and preliminary drawings.

The Castle Emerges

Two veteran motion-picture set designers, Marvin Davis and Herb Ryman, are traditionally credited with the castle concept. All sources emphasize, nonetheless, that Walt Disney himself wanted the castle—"That was his idea, not Herb's," as Davis has said.[9] "Yes, that Fantasyland Castle image was what they used to sell the whole park to the back east 'money boys.' Walt's idea was to look down Main Street at a kind of far off dream with castle spires coming up ... very fanciful."[10]

Figure 28. Sleeping Beauty Castle, Fantasyland, Disneyland. Façade toward the Plaza, October 1955 (from the collection of Dave DeCaro).

Early concepts for a Disney park did not include a castle. The seminal phase in the making of Disneyland began with Walt's 1948 Memorandum describing a project he wanted to develop on a tract of land the studio owned on Riverside Drive in Burbank, facing Griffith Park. The attractions he had in mind comprised a mini-catalog of classic middle-brow Americana: a Main Village, farm, railroad station, Western Village, carnival, and so forth.[11] There was no mention of a castle. Four years later, in 1952, he submitted a prospectus to the Burbank Department of Parks and Recreation Board. (The Board voted the proposal down.) Press reports cited several attractions that would form the core of Disneyland—a submarine, rocket ship, paddle-wheeled steamboat, and "trips through a Wild West village."[12] There was still no mention of a castle or Disney characters.

Of interest here, however, are two concept drawings from the early 1950s attributed to Harper Goff. In the first, we see a horse-drawn stagecoach and "Indian" village along the shore of a lake, with canoes scattered about.[13] On a squarish island sits an unidentified fortress-like structure whose conical towers and watery moat would be appropriate for a castle. Even so, with its boxy interior courtyard and surrounding frontier elements, it represents a log fort with a parade ground and guard towers, joined to the upper reaches of the park by a bridge.

More significantly, a similar, contemporary plan offers curious details in the form of captions written in red pencil in the margins and lines drawn to specific features.[14] Again the theming is primarily American, with such elements as a Main Street, a Western street, Granny's Farm, and an Indian Village. But on the right-hand side, three notations bear the words "Castle," "Dwarfs house," and "Skull Rock." Unlike the other captions, there are no lines leading to specific structures on this plan, so we can only speculate that these represent random thoughts at this point. Nonetheless, they do suggest an initial introduction of motifs from Disney's animated fairy tales, in this case his first feature-length cartoon, *Snow White and the Seven Dwarfs*, and the more recent *Peter Pan*. As such, they anticipate what would become Fantasyland.[15]

Marvin Davis, Master Architect

The first known plans for a castle date from the summer of 1953, concurrent with the search for the acreage needed to build what one writer would describe as "the incredible dream-come-true that is called Disneyland" in Anaheim.[16] By then, three former Twentieth Century–Fox artists, Marvin Davis, Dick Irvine, and Bill Martin, had been engaged to create concept sketches for the park. In addition, Walt charged Davis with drafting hypothetical ground plans and drawings for several attractions.[17]

Davis initiated the conceptual process for the castle by conducting research—the same process to which he was accustomed at Fox. In an interview he recalled, "I was trained as an art director, and we had a very good research library." A researcher assigned to assist Davis gathered "information and background on the castles of Europe: Italy, Spain, London"—and Neuschwanstein Castle in Bavaria, which, he asserted, he didn't copy exactly, "but we sure used the main parts of it as the guide for ours."[18]

Davis created four first generation architectural drawings of the castle that demonstrate his superior skills.[19] He labeled two of the drawings: *Castle Entrance to Fantasyland, Disneyland* bears the date July 21, 1953, and *Side View of Fantasy Land Entrance and Front Elev. of Snow White "Ride Thru"* is dated August 4, 1953.[20] In the same suite, an undated *Developed Elevation, Fantasy Land Castle Courtyard* shows the reverse side of the castle keep (the name traditionally given the residence portion of a medieval castle) and the "Peter Pan Fly Through." A fourth drawing represents the same courtyard portal viewed from within Fantasyland.[21] At this point the building was only referred to as the Fantasyland Castle, without any further descriptive names attached.

These drawings confirm Davis's careful study of his chief prototype, Schloss Neuschwanstein, King Ludwig II's nineteenth-century retreat in Bavaria, a wondrous pastiche of medieval German and French castles. In the *Castle Entrance* elevation, Davis borrowed his model's motif of a semi-circular portico between crenellated towers, topped by a parapet. For the uppermost level, he reconfigured Neuschwanstein's pseudo-Romanesque detailing, but retained its eye-pleasing, asymmetrically positioned towers and their contrasting height and size.

The crucial difference between Schloss Neuschwanstein and Sleeping Beauty Castle lies in Davis's use of movie set-design techniques. At 213 feet, the Bavarian castle is conspicuously taller than its Disney derivative of seventy-seven feet, its towers are separated in deep space, and the castle keep is positioned at the far end of a long courtyard. Davis compressed these elements into little more than a façade. Barely one room deep, with (originally) no interior attraction, the keep in Fantasyland was a one-dimensional movie set of wood, plaster, and fiberglass.[22]

Davis relied on forced perspective, most noticeably in the exaggerated tapering of the tower fortifications, to give the castle an impression of greater height. At each level the ersatz stone masonry blocks are diminished in size. The color palette is darker below and lighter further up, with a pinkish cast in the upper walls and a blue tint in the roofs.[23] Just as Hollywood backlot sets were oriented to receive optimal lighting, Walt had the castle entrance positioned southward towards Main Street to catch the sun's rays from dawn to dusk—making it a constant magnet for tourist cameras.[24]

Herb Ryman, Concept Artist

A month after Davis completed these designs, Walt summoned Herb Ryman to the studio to draw the bird's-eye concept plan that helped Roy Disney pitch the project to the "money boys" in New York.[25] In the mid–1930s, Ryman had worked with Cedric Gibbons on set and costume design at MGM. In 1938, he joined Disney as an inspirational sketch artist on *Pinocchio*, *Dumbo*, and *Fantasia*, and then, in 1944, switched to Twentieth Century–Fox. Ryman said he knew nothing about the park when he arrived for the so-called "lost weekend" of September 1953.

In Ryman's *Aerial View of Disneyland*, the castle keep sits at the furthest, northern perimeter of Fantasyland, not at the front entrance facing the Hub as Davis had imagined and as it would be when the park opened. Details in Ryman's plan were patterned after the Neuschwanstein castle, but as a Hollywood sketch artist, he visualized the castle keep as a backdrop to the land. In contrast, a second perspective drawing, based on Davis's elevations, visualized the castle as the formal entrance to Fantasyland.[26] This second drawing hangs on a wall behind Walt in a publicity photo for the first *Disneyland* TV show, aired by the ABC television network in October 1954.

Ryman's drawings illustrate why, despite a mass of visual material in hand prior to his arrival, Walt felt he needed him for this particular mission. Walt had a genius for spotting and exploiting individual talents of his employees. Marvin Davis was a gifted architect and production designer capable of drawing up the original plans for Sleeping Beauty Castle, but Herb Ryman's artistry could "sell" the park. In tandem with Davis and his crew, Ryman communicated a clear sense of how everything would mesh as a whole and be perceived by the park's guests.[27]

The Architectural Models

In keeping with accepted studio practices, Disney's master *maquettiste* Fred Joerger, assisted by Harriet Burns, constructed two models of the castle, about seven inches and ten inches high, respectively.[28] The seven-inch version—the more faithful of the two to Davis's designs—is seen in a photo of Walt with C.V. Wood, from 1953 or 1954, and in a second photo, from 1959, positioned next to a model of the Matterhorn Bobsleds attraction.[29] Currently on display at the Walt Disney Family Museum in San Francisco, the seven-inch castle—or a gold-painted duplicate—bears a label that reads: "Original Model of the Fantasyland Castle Designed for Walt Disney by Marvin Davis, Built by Fred Joerger, 1953."[30]

Because movie sets could be dismantled to allow for alternative camera angles, models for stage constructions were composed of moveable pieces, and that was how Joerger's ten-inch maquette of the castle was conceived. A studio publicity shot shows Kirk Douglas, co-star of Disney's *20,000 Leagues Under the Sea*, holding one of its towers as he inspects the partially disassembled model.[31]

The larger, ten-inch model was the focus of an oft-repeated incident. One day, as Randy Bright tells the tale, Herb Ryman, while examining the model, judged that the upper half of the inner façade facing the courtyard would be more felicitous if facing outward toward the Hub. "Moving the pieces of the model around like chess pieces," he grabbed "the top of the castle, turned it completely around, and set it back down" turned toward Main Street. The maneuver delighted Walt.[32] Indeed, in its final disposition, the three central towers are reversed compared to both Neuschwanstein and the early Davis drawings, with the large square tower in its now permanent place on the left.

In the final design, on the entrance façade of the keep, two small turrets frame superimposed rectangular windows. These motifs were drawn not from fortified architecture of the medieval period but from French Renaissance châteaux. The French buildings were erected at a time when defense elements, like large round towers, crenellations, and moats, became mere symbolic and decorative accouterments. Just as in the French châteaux, these elements at Disneyland open up the front façade and have the subliminal effect of making it more welcoming. In the end, Sleeping Beauty Castle combines the foreboding and militaristic elements of fortified architecture with the open and inviting details of French sixteenth-century châteaux.

As we have seen in previous chapters, authenticity was a desired goal of both Hollywood set design and Disneyland. Davis confirmed that Walt Disney "was thinking of entertainment all the time, and authenticity too. He could be a real bear on getting things right, so they would be believable."[33] In the case of Hollywood backlot fabrications of the Golden Era, however, it is clear that credibility was always relative. As suggested by film historians Charles and Mirella Affron, "The artificial set releases the art director from the need to replicate the true to life—present or past, tawdry or glamorous. In a legendary Baghdad palace and a legendary Manhattan nightclub, the set designer reflects upon the reality of his or her own art as unabashed edifice."[34] It is significant, therefore, that the chief design source for Sleeping Beauty Castle—Neuschwanstein—was not an authentic medieval building, but a nineteenth-century Romantic evocation.[35]

Nonetheless, to encourage viewers' suspension of disbelief, the Disneyland publicity department invented a medieval pedigree for the castle. Introducing the partially completed building to the American public in the "Pre-Opening Report" on the *Disneyland* TV show, narrator Winston Hibler claims, in response to a request from a viewer wishing to know the castle's design origins, that the building is based on actual plans unearthed in a French archive. Although he admits to subtle changes, he stresses authenticity—for example, the drawbridge actually works, having been constructed according to ancient methods. But then Hibler confesses to the Hollywood touch, pointing out one studio technician adding a realistic paint finish to a plastic stone, and another using a blowtorch to "age" the drawbridge.

Cartoon Castles

Sleeping Beauty Castle is significant in the context of this book because it owes its origins to both the Hollywood backlot and Disney animation. Thus, before considering its ties to Tinseltown's cinematic castles, I focus on Walt's own corpus of animated films to determine how over time the image of a castle conjured up a child's fairyland. Further, we want to consider, in the case of the Fantasyland Castle, which of the Disney stories was referenced.

Disney historian Jeff Kurtti has said, "Nothing is more symbolic of a fairy tale than the image of a castle" and "no symbol is more immediately associated with the Disney Company than a fanciful castle."[36] However, the Disney castle as corporate logo, which we take for granted today, not only for theme parks but also for the company's cinematic enterprise, did not exist in 1955. Thanks to Disneyland, the castle achieved brand status over time. The earliest appearance of what may be called the iconic Disney castle was the black-and-white illustration under the opening titles and end credits of the *Disneyland* TV show in October 1954. Loosely based on designs for Sleeping Beauty Castle, still not constructed at that date, this castle painting signified two Fantasylands—the segment of the TV series and the realm in the park.[37]

During the park's development in 1953–54, the structure is often simply referred to as a great medieval castle. Some sources at that time variously call it the Snow White Castle, the King Arthur Castle, and the Robin

Hood Castle. One of the earliest identifications of Sleeping Beauty Castle appears in the September 1954 prospectus for lessees and sponsors. The following month, in the *Disneyland* TV premiere, Walt stood behind the large castle model, connecting it with his forthcoming animated feature, *Sleeping Beauty*. He promoted the film in the opening minutes of the program, when the camera shows Disney artists sketching Princess Aurora's live-action model. Thus by 1954 Sleeping Beauty had given her name to the building, even though *Sleeping Beauty* would not premiere until 1959. Indeed, by 1955 only two early Disney feature-length narratives had used castle imagery: *Snow White and the Seven Dwarfs* (1937) and *Cinderella* (1950). At the time of the park's opening, Sleeping Beauty was unknown to the public as a Disney character.

Castles in Disney's oeuvre go back to the very beginning of his career in Kansas City. He used the imagery as a signifier of fairy tales in the *Laugh O Grams*, despite their being Americanized versions of children's stories. In *Cinderella* (1922) the prince tracks the heroine's footsteps down the Main Street of a small midwestern town, but opening and closing sequences feature the "two lazy and homely step sisters" relaxing outdoors in a landscape overlooked by a fortified castle that symbolizes their aspirations. Likewise in *Puss in Boots* (1922) the juvenile hero and his cat go to the movies at a Main Street cinema, but the object of his devotion is the princess residing in the local castle.

Disney's pre–Mickey film star, Oswald the Lucky Rabbit, appeared in *Oh, What a Knight!* (1928), a parody of contemporary Medieval films like Douglas Fairbank's hugely successful *Robin Hood* (1922) and John Barrymore's *The Beloved Rogue* (1927).[38] These live-action films in the Medieval genre were instrumental in creating the cinematic conception of a castle as a stage for deeds of derring-do. The Oswald cartoon affirms Walt's personal familiarity with Hollywood castles at an early date.

Castles also appear in Disney's cartoon series, the *Silly Symphonies*. During the parade of nursery-rhyme celebrities in *Mother Goose Melodies* (1931), the landscape background includes a cycled view of a castle; and a splendid castle exterior materializes within a pop-up book in *Old King Cole*. Notwithstanding the ancient origins of the King Midas myth, the central character of *The Golden Touch* occupies a castle whose contents, much to his chagrin, turn to gold.

Mickey Mouse provided indelible images of castles during his career, when he switched from contemporary to historical roles. In *Ye Olden Days* (1933) Mickey, playing Ye Wandering Minstrel, rescues Ye Princess (Minnie) from imprisonment in a castle tower. In *The Brave Little Tailor* (1938) fortified towers and a drawbridge protect the town citizenry from the Giant. *Giantland* was the Mouse's first foray into a Jack and the Beanstalk narrative. In a later version, the "Mickey and the Beanstalk" segment of *Fun and Fancy Free* (1947), two castles provide fairy-tale charm. The majestic white fortress with golden roofs, "shining like a jewel," according to the narrator, from its perch on a hilltop overlooking Happy Valley, is the home of a Singing Harp. Mickey, Donald, and Goofy rescue the harp taken by Willie the Giant to his castle-in-the-sky, accessible to the three peasants via the magic beanstalk. In short, Mickey's all-American resourcefulness and good humor lead him to triumph over obstacles in the storybook context, while the castles conjure up a fantasy setting.

From *Snow White* to *Cinderella*

Because the second concept drawing for the Burbank project had the words "Castle" and "Dwarfs house" penciled in the margin, we can surmise that, at some point, consideration was given to naming the Fantasyland attraction in honor of Snow White. Indeed, early press reports called it Snow White's Castle.[39] Disney's first feature, which reaped huge financial benefits and established the template for the Disney musical fantasy, contains striking views of European castles.

Snow White and the Seven Dwarfs kicks off with a prologue in ornate hand lettering in a bejeweled medieval manuscript, immediately connecting the story with the Middle Ages.[40] Animation commences with the famous shot via the multiplane camera toward a white citadel with red rooftops, perched on a hill, thus establishing the castle as the frontispiece to the narrative and the locale of the fairy tale. The structure is initially revealed to be the home of Snow White, where she toils with a bucket and trills the song "I'm Wishing" by a well in a sunny, verdant open courtyard. A similar establishing shot of the building is repeated in a later sequence, now at nighttime, in the light of the moon, when the structure takes on a frightening aura and the Evil Queen is mistress of the place. These dual aspects of the building, both welcoming and forbidding, would later characterize the Fantasyland Castle.

The film's castle imagery is bookended by the appearance in the finale, to the strains of a heavenly choir, of the Prince's Castle-in-the-Clouds, the locus of Snow White's romantic longings. Earlier, when she entertains the dwarfs by singing "Some Day My Prince Will Come," she acknowledges hopefully, "And away to his castle we'll go, to be happy forever I know." Later, confronted at the dwarfs' cottage by the Witch, Snow White repeats her wish, "And then he'll take me...," before biting the poisoned apple. The castle thus visually signifies her aspirations.

Fittingly, in the original theatrical poster for *Snow White and the*

Seven Dwarfs, a castle hovers over the assembly of characters, a veritable Disney corporate icon *avant la lettre*. The film's fortresses were the creation of Disney's team of European concept artists, such as Gustav Tenggren, hired to bring an Old World ambience to the picture.[41] One of the most stirring sequences from the film is the Evil Queen's rapid descent down a grand spiral stair to her laboratory in the building's bowels. On her departure, the Queen, now disguised as an old peddler, passes by a dungeon, where she taunts the lifeless skeleton of a former prisoner behind bars. In an earlier, rejected storyboarded sequence, the Queen imprisons the Prince in the dungeon, bolts him to the stone wall, and threatens to kill him by flooding the chamber.

In an era predating VHS, DVD, and Disney+, the public would have been familiar with this movie and its castles because of Disney's policy of periodic re-releases. *Snow White and the Seven Dwarfs* enjoyed theatrical reruns in 1944 and 1952. Also, a continuous stream of merchandise, including books, records, sheet music, and games, combined with clips shown on television, extended the life of all the Disney classics. Thus, the prominent role played by the castles in *Snow White* may have contributed to consideration of naming the Fantasyland Castle after the heroine.

Cinderella, the second Disney princess and the one who revived the fortunes of the Studio after the troubled 1940s, would certainly have been a convincing candidate for the naming of a royal building in Fantasyland.[42] The castle in *Cinderella* plays a role equal to that in *Snow White*, so it is worth pondering how well suited a Cinderella Castle might have been at the entrance to the realm.

At the beginning of the movie, an elaborately bound book opens to reveal an illustration of a castle rising above the clouds directly over the words, "Once upon a time in a faraway land, there was a tiny kingdom...." Again the storybook land of the fairy tale is immediately associated with the architectural type. Further, the illustration establishes the spatial relationship between the structure and Cinderella's manor house. From her garret she has a direct view of the building and can hear the striking of the clock on its highest tower. She has mixed feelings about this view. She expresses annoyance when the clock strikes 6 a.m. to set her chores in motion. In the evening, however, when her hopes for attending the ball are dashed, she gazes dreamily at the structure, still rising through the clouds and blazing with nighttime illumination. On some level the castle has become a symbol of her projected desires. She doesn't articulate these directly: when she sings "A Dream Is a Wish Your Heart Makes," she acknowledges that the dream will remain unfulfilled if the wish is revealed. Publicity for the movie featured prominent images of the castle and its clock tower. Bristling with towers and decorated with patterned crenellations and checkerboard surfaces, the frothy confection symbolized the tiny kingdom of the text—"peaceful, prosperous and rich in Romance and Tradition." Curiously, on Disneyland's opening day, Cinderella was largely absent from the realm. Only in June 1956 was a miniature of Cinderella's château introduced into the former Canal Boats attraction, when it was retooled as Storybook Land Canal Boats. The Hollywood ending here is that Cinderella Castle would become the iconic mainstay for the Magic Kingdom in Florida.

Sleeping Beauty

The naming of Sleeping Beauty Castle is considered a prime example of Disney synergy—Walt's genius for cross-promotion to assure a dependable income for the studio—even though *Sleeping Beauty*, the movie, would not be completed until 1959, well after the park was ready to receive visitors. Just as passengers on Snow White Adventures ride, seated as "stand-ins" for the princess, must have asked, in the words of designer Ken Anderson, "Where the hell is Snow White?" many a park guest peering at the castle must have wondered, "Where is Sleeping Beauty?"[43]

Disney registered the title *Sleeping Beauty* in January 1950. An early plot line dates from May 1951, and Mary Costa signed on as the voice of Princess Aurora in 1952. Then the project dragged on for another seven years. In the interim, Walt took every opportunity—on TV and in print—to declare that the film was coming. The first issue of the *Disneyland News* announced that it was slated for release in 1957, and the 1955 Tomorrowland exhibit honoring art directors from the great Hollywood studios included concept and production art from *Sleeping Beauty*.[44]

Like *Snow White and the Seven Dwarfs* and *Cinderella*, *Sleeping Beauty* begins with a shot of an elaborately bejeweled book that seemingly opens as if by magic. Within lies an illuminated manuscript page representing the first of two fairy-tale castles featured in the story. During the introductory song, "Hail to the Princess Aurora," the viewer is swept, along with the townsfolk, into the open, welcoming courtyard and great hall of King Stefan's Castle, the domain of Sleeping Beauty's father.

The original source for the film was Charles Perrault's tale written in the late seventeenth century and set in a vague earlier time. Disney placed the action firmly in a late medieval context, thus reaffirming the American assumption that fairy tales take place in the Middle Ages, an important concept for the Disneyland castle. Prince Phillip provides a clue to the historical era, when, objecting to King Hubert about his arranged marriage, he blurts out the amusing words, "Now, father, you're living in the past! This is the fourteenth century!"

Fantasyland's Sleeping Beauty Castle was conceived roughly simultaneously with King Stefan's Castle in *Sleeping Beauty*, but different artists worked on each project, and the two buildings are not identical. Stefan's open, welcoming domain tends toward a generalized cluster of towers, with an emphasis on a single tall tower wherein the heroine will lie dormant in bewitched slumber. Featuring walls and towers overlooking a promontory, the castle is based on the Spanish Alcázar in Segovia; only slight detailing recalls Neuschwanstein. During their "Once upon a Dream" encounter in the woods, Aurora (Briar Rose) and Prince Phillip cast a blissful gaze from afar at her father's castle, rising in the distance, the locus of their happily-ever-after. In the movie's climactic scene, Phillip hacks an opening in the forest of thorns that has sprung up around the building. The camera focuses on his gaze as he pauses to look upward toward the highest tower, the object of his pursuit. Here again the castle's power as an icon is aspirational.

The castle courtyard offers a stage for several scenes, including the bonfire of the spinning wheels, Phillip's interaction with Hubert, and the Three Good Fairies' putting to sleep and later awakening of the court and townsfolk. The interior of the keep, although not designed as a coherent ensemble of spaces and staircases, does feature some sharply delineated chambers with exquisite Gothic detailing, in particular the great hall, its anteroom, and the banquet hall. In the latter room Stephen and Hubert argue over the plan and elevation of the honeymoon castle, drawn on a scroll, proposed for the bridal couple.

This survey of Disney castles, from Laugh O Grams to King Stefan's Castle, suggests that over time the medieval castle as symbol became entrenched in the Disney lexicon. As a form of shorthand, it immediately signifies that the spectator is entering a fairy-tale realm. Additionally, in a deeper sense, it operates as a site of longing, of wish fulfillment, and of the happily ever after. Gazing upon the towers and turrets of Sleeping Beauty Castle as we approach the entrance to Fantasyland, we too thrill to the expectation that our storybook dreams will come true.

The Dungeon

Certain architectural elements of Sleeping Beauty Castle appear not only in cartoon castles, but also derive their "authenticity" from the kingdom of Hollywood. In particular, the dungeon and the drawbridge have a rich history in live-action films, where they developed as powerful conceits, based on their potential to add drama to the narrative.

For the use of the dungeon in Disney animation, we can turn to the second, and more violent of *Sleeping Beauty*'s two castles—Maleficent's lair in the Forbidden Mountains. Towering on a rocky escarpment, it resembles the citadel of the *Snow White* poster, but with a greater sense of foreboding. In a clever parallel, late in the story both the hero and the heroine are "imprisoned" in castles: Aurora, as the Sleeping Beauty, enclosed on high in the tower of King Stefan's Castle, and Phillip in a cell located in the depths of Maleficent's Castle. In the climactic sequence of the Three Good Fairies assisting his escape, the narrative plays to American fantasies of dungeons in European castles. Using a plot idea rejected from *Snow White*, Disney has the Mistress of All Evil locking the Prince in a dungeon to thwart the possibility of Love's First Kiss. As in *Snow White*, there is the implication of torture and death in the details of manacles, chains, and an execution axe on a chopping block within Phillip's cell.

When designing Sleeping Beauty Castle in 1953, Marvin Davis treated it as a backdrop to the Hub and a portal to the land of fairy stories. Barely one room deep, it contained no spaces designated for an attraction. Proposals only refer to a possible Sleeping Beauty Wax Museum in the castle courtyard, presumably with dioramas based on the film. Pre-opening press releases, however, toyed with the idea of a walk-through attraction within the building, primarily to make the structure more alluring. All of the standard elements of a castle were promised, in particular a large dining hall for the knights and a dungeon with a wheel and rack, as well as a torture chamber. The popular press picked up on these details as early as November 1954, relishing the anticipated "dungeons and torture chambers in Sleeping Beauty Castle."[45] These details were repeated in the opening day press kit, but now with increasing reference to the film: Sleeping Beauty herself will be visible amidst royal panoply.[46] The first souvenir guidebook invited guests to visit Sleeping Beauty slumbering in a beautiful bedchamber.[47] Newspaper accounts around the time of the park's opening continued to mention these spaces in the castle, even though they did not exist. One element in particular, which some writers actually claimed to have seen, received repeated notice: the "dungeon (not yet staffed with an ogre) equipped with kiddie-size implements of torture."[48] Evidently the publicity machine sparked the imagination of young and old visitors. In short, the torture chamber proposed for Sleeping Beauty Castle illustrates the power of film to shape or distort our sense of the past.

Commonly inserted into films of the Medieval genre, the dungeon was a Hollywood conceit that deviated from the historical record (the word dungeon is an English derivation of the French word *donjon*, meaning castle keep). Historically, castle architecture rarely included underground prison cells. This conceit arose in the eighteenth century as a romantic response to the Middle Ages, in both literary form, such as Horace Walpole's Gothic novel *The Castle of Otronto* (1764), and visual form, like Giovanni Battista Piranesi's series of etchings *Carceri d'invenzione* (*Imaginary Prisons*, 1749–50; 1761). Evocative depictions of castles increased in nineteenth-century fiction, such as Sir Walter Scott's *Ivanhoe* (1819), then filtered into other media, initially the theater and ultimately the movies, where they provided spectator-pleasing *frissons*.

In Universal's historical/horror film *Tower of London* (1939), for example, Richard, duke of Gloucester (Basil Rathbone), murders his way onto the throne aided and abetted by his henchman Mord (Boris Karloff). An early scene set in a torture chamber, demonstrates Mord's cruelty as he moves from victim to victim, applying an extra weight on the body of a prisoner stretched on the rack, or throwing water in the face of a manacled prisoner dying of thirst. This is not unlike the dungeon scenes in *Snow White* and *Sleeping Beauty*, which enhance the cruelty of the Evil Queen and Maleficent, respectively. Publicity for *Tower of London* boasted an authentic recreation of the historical site, but no such chamber of horrors actually existed at the Tower of London. Imprisoned royals were kept in apartments, not in underground dungeons. The influence of cinematic medievalizing tropes is visible even at the present-day Tower of London in the form of an exhibition, "Torture at the Tower," showcasing "terrifying instruments of pain"—all of which are questionable replicas. So too, back in 1955, the promise of an "authentic" torture chamber in Sleeping Beauty Castle had become one of the things anticipated in a castle.

The dungeon never materialized at Disneyland, but in April 1957, two years before *Sleeping Beauty*'s theatrical premiere, Disney installed an alternative: a walk-through attraction consisting of display cases based on Eyvind Earle's artwork for key sequences. To provide space on two levels, designers adjusted both exterior and interior elements of the building's fabric.[49]

The Drawbridge

Another component understood by American audiences to be standard in a medieval castle was the drawbridge. It appears in a spectacular action sequence in Disney's *Sleeping Beauty*, Prince Phillip's escape on horseback from Maleficent's Castle. In the dungeon, the Three Fairies use their wands like blowtorches to break the bonds of his chains, and the four race up circular steps. His flight allows us to see the castle's defensive features in action, albeit in an effort to prevent his escape. The Goons stand overhead on the crenellations to hurl boulders, shoot arrows, and pour boiling oil from the battlements. They lower the portcullis and raise the drawbridge to prevent his exit, forcing Phillip's horse Samson to take a flying leap (successfully executed!) toward the entry tower.

The elements of Maleficent's defense system are all present in the Fantasyland Castle. Over the years Disneyland publicity has consistently mentioned that Sleeping Beauty Castle has a working drawbridge. But in fact, this drawbridge has been raised and lowered only twice in the near-seventy-year history of the building, first in July 1955, when it was lowered on the opening day telecast to admit "the children of the world" into Fantasyland, and second in May 1983 for the rededication of the New Fantasyland. Why did Disney go to the trouble and expense of installing a mechanism that was virtually never used—one that, from the standpoint of history, was not even an essential element of the medieval château? Indeed, European castles were often protected by other means, such as wooden palisades and outer gates. The answer lies again in the power of films to create certain tropes. As in the sequence in *Sleeping Beauty* of Phillip's flight, so many movies had incorporated a drawbridge as a plot point, as a dramatic means of either entrance or escape, that its presence had come to guarantee authenticity. (I will provide examples shortly.) Thus, in the average American moviegoer's mind, a drawbridge over a wet moat was an expected component of Sleeping Beauty Castle.

Backlot Castles and Drawbridges: Robin Hood

The castle was an essential element of the Medieval movie genre. Historically speaking, Sleeping Beauty Castle was one of the last artificial fortresses to be built in the Hollywood backlot tradition. As we have seen in the discussion of Davis and Ryman, Disney's art directors brought their knowledge and experience from the big studios to the park's realms. Thus, it is worth investigating a few examples of movie castles to see how they functioned in live-action films, how the audience reacted to them, and how they may have impacted Disneyland.

Depending on budget and shooting location, movie castles comprised a variety of types: entire buildings, partial buildings, scale models, and matte paintings representing a fortress in full or extending a set within the camera frame. On the occasions when a movie was shot in Europe, a real castle might be used, especially for exterior views, but this was rare. Interiors were inevitably created on a soundstage. In short, Hollywood castles are faux castles. MGM art director Cedric Gibbons commented,

One of the chief problems of the art department is to make something look real which is not. Because of the lack of time, it is impossible, for instance, to reconstruct a "mediaeval" castle, using real stones and mortar. It would mean occupying a sound stage for perhaps a year! We must therefore use materials which will appear to be solid rock, and so construct a castle that, when fighting men, for instance, lunge against the wall, it does not "give" but will maintain the illusion of solidarity and antiquity.[50]

During the development phase of Sleeping Beauty Castle, one of the proposed names was Robin Hood Castle. An echo of this early connection with the outlaw of Sherwood Forest appears in the *Disneyland, U.S.A. (People and Places)* documentary, in which park staff wearing Robin Hood costumes and carrying bows and arrows greet guests at the entrance to the building.[51] Because Robin Hood's origins are unknown, and his adventures were propagated by oral tradition and ballads, the legend lends itself to reinvention. In his novel *Ivanhoe*, Sir Walter Scott was influential in placing Robin Hood during the reign of Richard the Lionheart and Prince John. The robber hero was a subject for silent film as early as 1908. Two films that set the template for the Medieval swashbuckler employ castles as important elements in the story: *Robin Hood* with Douglas Fairbanks (1922) and *The Adventures of Robin Hood* with Errol Flynn (1938).

One of the most spectacular castle sets ever built, publicized as the biggest and most expensive at the time, was the ninety-foot tall Nottingham Castle designed by Wilfred Buckland and built at the Pickford-Fairbanks Studio for the 1922 *Robin Hood* (Fig. 29). Fairbanks provided a collection of books and prints for Buckland to use as inspiration—a forerunner of the studio research library.[52] As gigantic as it was, the set provided only those portions of the fortress required for camera work. The viewer never sees an entire castle, except for when the set is briefly combined with a matte painting to show the whole imaginary edifice. Rather than serving as a mere backdrop, it became an integral part of the story. Its great size caused Fairbanks to fear that he would be lost in long shots, but, as it turned out, the building's dizzying heights magnified his acrobatic feats. Downward camera shots from its ramparts gave the viewer the impression of standing on the building. One sequence, in particular, demonstrates not only how a movie set can augment the action, but also serve as a primer in architectural history. In this famous sequence, Robin storms Nottingham Castle singlehandedly, first leaping on the edge of a gigantic drawbridge rising to bar his entry into the fortress, and from there clambering up the bridge's oversize chain as it is hoisted upward. He then scales a high tower, to save Maid Marian from a fatal fall. Scenes like this rendered the drawbridge an active "character" in the drama, showing how a particular architectural detail could be an expressive and even breathtaking element in cinematic storytelling.

For the set representing Nottingham Castle in Warner Bros.' Technicolor *The Adventures of Robin Hood* (1938), art director Carl Jules Weyl's romantic reimagining of Norman architecture so impressed a professional architecture journal that it published a photo of the model (Fig. 4).[53] Weyl won an Academy Award for his work on the picture. Inevitably, during one intense scene, the star, Errol Flynn (Robin, of course), and his companion, Will Scarlet, thunder across the lowered drawbridge on horseback pursued by the Sheriff's men.

The success of the Flynn *Robin Hood* spurred four copy-cat films between 1946 and 1952. Disney released his own live-action film in 1952, shot in England to use funds frozen after the war: *The Story of Robin Hood and His Merrie Men*. He originally planned to create a children's version, casting Bobby Driscoll as a youthful Robin or perhaps a boy in the circle of the Merrie Men.[54] British child labor laws precluded this scheme, and thus Disney went ahead with a more adult version, casting British actor Richard

Figure 29. *Robin Hood* (1922, Douglas Fairbanks Pictures). Nottingham Castle set with tournament tents at the Pickford–Fairbanks Studio (United Artists/ Kobal/Shutterstock).

Todd as Robin. While specifically acknowledging the resonance of the
Flynn version, Disney guaranteed historical accuracy in his film: "We
couldn't touch 'Robin Hood' before doing a great deal of research…. To get
as closely as possible to authenticity we based our story on the old ballads
written about Robin and his men. Then we shot the picture in England,
using the original locale of the ballads as background."[55] The result was
a modest film, lacking the resources of Fairbanks or Warner Bros., but it
was a success thanks to the Disney brand, excellent casting, and a clever
reworking of the story that added "singing" arrows and a singing minstrel.

Some footage was shot in the real Sherwood Forest, while many exterior scenes, including the courtyard and drawbridge of Nottingham Castle, were created on a soundstage. The drawbridge appears prominently
in two scenes. Having disgraced the Sheriff of Nottingham in the town
square, Robin and his men unceremoniously throw him from the drawbridge into the moat. Later, having liberated Maid Marian, the drawbridge
is raised to prevent his departure. Perched on the edge of the bridge, as it
rises to full height, he has two alternatives—being crushed by the closing
bridge or dropping into the moat. He elects to drop. The villainous sheriff, in hot pursuit, is not as lucky. He is caught in the mechanism and suffers death (offscreen)!

Disney aired *The Story of Robin Hood* in two parts on the *Disney-
land* TV show in November 1955 under the Fantasyland heading. This and
other movie drawbridges would render inevitable the one at Disneyland.
Walt enjoyed his own connection with the device: Advertisements for the
"Dateline Disneyland" program read, "As the Pied Piper of 1955, Walt
Disney leads hundreds of children across the drawbridge of the Sleeping
Beauty Castle, where they encounter mounted knights in shining armor,
court jesters, and acrobats."[56]

Ivanhoe

A further example of the backlot castle deserves mention here, because
of its association with Robin Hood and the fact that an entire faux fortress
was constructed. To use funds frozen in the U.K. after the war, MGM, like
Disney, determined to film in England and chose to mount a lavish treatment for Sir Walter Scott's *Ivanhoe* (1952), a novel about a knight who helps,
with the assistance of Robin Hood, to bring Richard the Lionheart back
to England. MGM's publicity department assured potential viewers of the
authenticity of the film. In a newspaper ad titled "Facts You Will Want to
Know about 'Ivanhoe,'" the studio claimed, "'Ivanhoe' was two years in production. Many months of research at the British Museum preceded actual

filming…. M-G-M transported stars and technicians thousands of miles to the actual locales of the story in England. 'Ivanhoe' was filmed in its entirety amid ancient castles, famous battlefields and other historic sites."[57]

Despite the abundance of British castles that might have provided a realistic backdrop, art directors created their own Torquilstone Castle on MGM's Borehamwood Studios backlot in Hertfordshire (Fig. 30). According to *The Atlanta Journal*,

> "They have plenty of old castles still standing in England," the publicity department explained. "But they are old and crumbling now and back in the 13th Century they wouldn't have looked that way. We thought about restoring one but decided it was cheaper to build a new one—turrets and moats and everything." So Hollywood went to work with bulldozers and built the granite-gray turrets and battlements of the castle complete with a 10-foot deep moat, in about one-tenth the time a whole community of Saxon serfs would have taken when Richard the Lion-Hearted was a kid…. "After the addition of a working drawbridge," writes a press agent, "almost a full year was given to careful aging of the castle."[58]

In addition to its barbican, bailey, and round tower, the set contained several requisite elements of a castle: a drawbridge, which rises and

Figure 30. *Ivanhoe* (1952, MGM). Torquilstone Castle set, Borehamwood Studios, Hertfordshire (MGM/Photofest).

lowers at several dramatic moments, a moat, into which marauders fall and splash, and a dungeon, in which the principal characters are incarcerated before a dramatic escape. Since studio publicity repeatedly emphasized the authenticity of the sets, moviegoers naturally assumed they were correct. Combining a variety of sources, real and imagined, the designers of Sleeping Beauty Castle likewise produced a fantasy castle that met the public's expectations.

Chivalric Theming: King Arthur Carrousel

One of the concepts associated with castle architecture is the ideal of medieval chivalry. In the opening moments of *Sleeping Beauty*, for example, during the "Hail to the Princess Aurora" sequence, a procession of equestrian knights bearing lances and heraldic pennants moves majestically toward King Stefan's Castle. So too in Disneyland: on the opening day telecast, "Dateline Disneyland," knights on horseback carried the Fantasyland banner during the grand parade. In his dedication remarks, Walt invoked the realm's recreation of "the age of chivalry, magic, and make-believe." As the drawbridge of Sleeping Beauty Castle lowered, a fanfare of trumpets blown by heralds on horseback announced the official opening of the "land." The chivalric theming continued in the courtyard, shifting from French fable to British legend with references to King Arthur and the Knights of the Round Table. As we shall see, the visual motifs characterizing this area drew from the repertory of Hollywood conventions involving King Arthur and Camelot.

Early publicity referred to Fantasyland's courtyard as the King Arthur Courtyard, where the delights of a medieval fair took place (Fig. 31). The musical soundtrack for the Fantasyland opening included, in addition to classic Disney songs, a tune with the lyrics "Welcome to King Arthur's court, welcome ye knights and ye ladies fair!" Some pre-opening publicity even identified the castle as King Arthur Castle.[59] The connection was so enduring that when Walt died, a cartoon in the *Atlanta Journal* depicted a dejected child watching the Fantasyland Castle rise out of the mist, with the caption "Childhood's Camelot: The Legacy of Walt Disney."[60] Three elements within the courtyard alluded to Arthurian legend: in the center, the King Arthur Carrousel (Disneyland prefers the French spelling); on either side, the simulated tournament tents fronting the dark rides; and adjacent to the castle, Merlin's Magic Shop.

Of these three, I begin by considering the theming of the Carrousel (Fig. 31). As early as fall 1953 it was dedicated to the Knights of the Round Table, thus confirming that well before the public reveal of the Fantasyland

Figure 31. King Arthur Courtyard, Fantasyland, Disneyland, 1955. From left foreground: (1) Mad Tea Party, (2) Mr. Toad's Wild Ride, (3) Peter Pan Flight, (4) King Arthur Carrousel, (5) Sleeping Beauty Castle, and (6) Mickey Mouse Club Theater (from the collection of Dave DeCaro).

Castle as Sleeping Beauty's domain, the castle might be named after King Arthur or Camelot.[61] On early designs for the carousel, shields attached to poles in the shape of lances supporting the umbrella-like canopy atop the ride bore the coats of arms of Arthur, Launcelot, and Galahad, among others, with matching pennants fluttering overhead.[62] The opening-day press kit composed a historical narrative intended to spark the visitor's imagination, according to which the Carrousel enjoined visitors to witness the banners of knights returning to Camelot. Articles in *The Disneyland News* continued this theme when describing the seventy-two prancing wooden horses awaiting knights eager to join the ranks of the mythic monarch's happy band of brothers. Surmounting the canopy was Arthur's gold crown.

　　Disney acquired the vintage 1922 merry-go-round from Toronto's Sunnyside Amusement Park, which was closing. It was originally of the menagerie type, with a variety of beasts, and thus not appropriate to King Arthur. Only the horses were kept, and new ones added, with all posed as active "jumpers," so that the merry-go-round might come closer to "historical truth."[63] As usual, the Disneyland publicity department strove to guarantee the authenticity of each ride experience. An article in *The*

Mickey Mouse Club Annual boasted that Arthur would have been right at home on the ride, which traced its origins to the period when tournaments were a means of keeping knights in shining armor ready for battle.[64]

In July 1955, neither Sleeping Beauty nor King Arthur was an established Disney character. Disney's animated Arthurian feature, *The Sword in the Stone*, would not be released until 1963. He had produced two earlier cartoons in a purely chivalric vein. In *The Reluctant Dragon* (1941) a genteel, mustachioed knight, Sir Giles, engages in a face-saving mock duel with a poetry-loving dragon. *Knight for a Day* (1946) satirizes the conventions of the medieval tournament, with Goofy in multiple roles, winning a joust and the "frail, white, delicate hand of the lovely Princess Esmeralda."[65]

Among properties suitable for animation that Walt acquired in the late 1930s were the rights to T.H. White's best-seller, *The Sword in the Stone*.[66] In 1949, it was reported in England that he was researching the subject for an animated feature. In the same year, in Disney's *Adventures of Ichabod and Mr. Toad*, a camera panning along a library shelf lingers on a leather-bound tome with the words *Tales of King Arthur* impressed on its spine, a subtle spelling out, perhaps, of things to come. The following year, plans were announced for Walt's cartoon treatment of *The Sword in the Stone*.[67]

In 1953 he was still contemplating an animated feature, renamed *The Young King Arthur*, when the studio announced that a live-action version was in the works starring Richard Todd, who had played Robin Hood in one of three previous live-action Disney men-in-tights films.[68] Despite these reports, Walt's interest in the White book waned until, spurred by Lerner and Loews's hit Broadway musical *Camelot* (1960), based on White's revision and extension of his Arthurian novels, he greenlighted *The Sword in the Stone*. That feature cartoon did not appear on screens until eight years after the opening of Fantasyland; thus, it was likely not the chief motivation driving the Arthurian courtyard.[69]

King Arthur on Film

What I propose here is that the impetus for the Fantasyland courtyard arose from a deep-seated Anglo-American fascination with the legendary King Arthur and with chivalry in general.[70] For example, as early as 1790 a Boston supplier of English-milled flour, Henry Wood, called his firm the King Arthur Flour Company.[71] Around 1901, the year Walt was born, there was a surge of interest in Arthur and his magical circle. Between 1903 and 1910, the American illustrator Howard Pyle produced color plates for four popular children's books about Arthur, Sir Launce-lot, and the Holy Grail.[72] Equally influential were illustrated editions by various artists of *Ivanhoe* and Sir Walter Scott's other Waverley Novels. In America, Arthurian legend pervaded the realms of drama, music, and even the Sunday comics—notably, the cartoon strip "Prince Valiant in the Days of King Arthur," created in 1937 by Hal Foster.[73]

Arthur's presence in film dates from a 1904 screen treatment of Wagner's *Parsifal*, directed by Edwin S. Porter. Over the next half-century there would be humdrum fare like the fifteen-part serial from Columbia, *The Adventures of Sir Galahad* (1950), starring George Reeves (best known for his portrayal of Superman on TV), and two well-received adaptations of Mark Twain's time-traveling take on Camelot, *A Connecticut Yankee* (1931) with Will Rogers and *A Connecticut Yankee in King Arthur's Court* with Bing Crosby (1949).

In the 1950s, Hollywood sought to revitalize its customer base with widescreen Medieval offerings like *The Black Shield of Falworth* (1954), *King Richard and the Crusaders* (1954), *The Court Jester* (1955), and *Quentin Durward* (1955). Disney's contribution to this trend was *The Sword and the Rose* (1953), the third in his made-in-the-U.K. string of live-action Technicolor films, based on an 1898 novel set at the court of Henry VIII. It was serialized as a pair of Fantasyland episodes on *Disneyland* TV in January 1956, its name changed to *When Knighthood Was in Flower*, after the title of the book. The announcement of the telecast promised, "Here is all the pomp and majesty that makes history books comes alive! The golden age of chivalry lives again!"

Most important, while Disneyland was under development, three major studios offered Technicolor renditions of the Arthurian legend, among them a run-of-the-mill, low-budget Alan Ladd vehicle, *The Black Knight* (1954), distributed by Columbia.[74] Far more memorable was MGM's first CinemaScope epic, *The Knights of the Round Table* (1953), with Robert Taylor, Ava Gardner, and the proverbial cast of thousands. Screen credits cited Malory's *Le Morte d'Arthur* as its main source, but Tennyson and White were also tapped. *New York Times* critic Bosley Crowther said the "poetic eloquence and grandeur of those distinctly literary works" had been "replaced by a sweep of dramatic action and romantic symbols that is straight Hollywood ... such as to give one an enthusiasm for the potentials of the CinemaScope screen."[75] MGM's retelling of the legend included every essential element of the King Arthur genre, including the sword in the stone.

Advance publicity hailed *The Knights of the Round Table* as "the fulfillment of 10 years of exhaustive planning and preparatory work" and for "delving back through nearly 14 centuries of English history and tradition to determine how knights really behaved when they were bold, and how they made love to antiquity's fair ladies." Director Richard Thorpe claimed he had had a revelatory experience at "Cornwall on the actual site where King Arthur's castle" reputedly stood. "There are even stone remnants of it and … a remarkable assortment of mementoes supposedly associated with the knights, the quest for the Holy Grail, and all else out of the historic and legendary past, including a round table."[76] In the film, knights joust on an exquisitely-green lawn adjacent to Camelot Castle—the recycled Torquil-stone Castle backlot set from *Ivanhoe*, with its fortress and round tower still intact.

For *The Knights'* world premiere, the façade of the Egyptian Theatre on Hollywood Boulevard was "restyled for a change in locale from Egypt to Camelot Castle," and it was announced that "'knights' in costumer's rented armor will patrol marquee and forecourt to dazzle the picture fans lined up in front"—a scenario more or less duplicated at the opening of Sleeping Beauty Castle.[77] MGM studio head Dore Schary summed up the movie's broad appeal: "The picture also has that wonderful magic which transports you into a different world…. The whole feeling of chivalry and knighthood is there, and the picture's appeal will thus, I believe, be far-reaching with all classes of people."[78] Walt Disney must have felt the same way, at the height of Hollywood's Arthur-mania, in bringing to life "chivalry, magic, and make-believe" in Fantasyland's King Arthur Courtyard.

Prince Valiant

In April 1954, Twentieth Century–Fox released its Medieval CinemaScope opus, *Prince Valiant*, starring James Mason, Janet Leigh, and Robert Wagner. Newspaper adverts proclaimed: "YOU storm the castles of infidels with the Viking Christians! YOU fight at the tournaments of Camelot! YOU are a cheering participant in the most beloved story in all adventuredom!"[79] One press report stressed the film's realism: "Director Henry Hathaway spent six weeks in England shooting backgrounds for 'Prince Valiant' and thinks this is the only picture ever made where five real, authentic castles will loom up in the action. Four of them are now government monuments and were lent to the studio for photographing under very strict provisions."[80] Picture-perfect Camelot Castle, however, seen on screen rising above a verdant landscape, was a matte painting. Back in Hollywood on the studio backlot, art directors Lyle Wheeler and Mark-Lee Kirk erected Sligon Castle, from whose dungeon Prince Valiant makes a daring escape.[81] Following general practice, all interiors were filmed on a studio soundstage.

One striking element shared by *The Knights of the Round Table* and *Prince Valiant* is the periodic appearance of smartly dressed young men tooting their horns. Each time a royal proclamation is read or an important event is about to happen, a platoon of heralds materializes to sound a fanfare. Cinematic constructs like these—knightly processions, costumes, page-boy hairstyles, and other conceits—impacted not only the opening of Fantasyland but also *Sleeping Beauty* the movie.[82]

Tournament Tents

At this point I will turn to the second element of theming in the King Arthur Courtyard, the suite of four dark-ride façades surrounding the Carrousel. Marvin Davis originally conceived these as stone and half-timbered fronts comprising a village. Time and budget restrictions prevented this, and Bill Martin devised a simple solution: each of the prefabricated 60- by 100-foot industrial sheds enclosing the dark rides received a simple, flat "fabric" covering resembling a viewing stand at a medieval tournament (Fig. 31).[83] The patterning of these faux cloths consisted of bold colors and shapes. Over each entrance hung a banner with the name of the ride in Gothic script and a coat of arms bearing the face of the principal character (Peter Pan, Toad, Snow White) and appropriate symbols, like Big Ben or the Witch. As a corollary to these tournament tents, the designers added food kiosks, souvenir stands, and ticket booths themed to the idea of small knights' tents, square or round, erected on the edges of tournament fields. These small pavilions were an offshoot of tents proposed by Davis and Ryman as standing at the entrance to Sleeping Beauty Castle. A further complement was the abundance of armorial bearings scattered throughout the courtyard.

How would the public recognize these pavilions as being related to the King Arthur theme, as opposed to, say, circus tents? The answer lies in their ubiquity in Medieval movies. Located at the heart of the Arthurian myth, the tournament functioned as a festival of chivalry, displaying the courtly ideals of honor, love, and above all, valor in battle.[84] One of the specialized types of military games in the thirteenth century was called the Round Table, which involved large numbers of knights jousting in front of spectators in stands.[85]

Tournaments figure prominently in Hollywood's Robin Hood films. The Fairbanks *Robin Hood* opens with a spectacular jousting scene that provided a model for tournament scenes in subsequent movies. Assembled before the joust is an immense crowd bearing hundreds of pennants on tall staffs. Despite the black-and-white film, the art direction overwhelms the eye with patterned fabrics, elaborate detailing, and shields decorated with insignia. In addition to the viewing stand on one side of the tilting field, the scene encompasses the knight's cloth tents and pavilions on the ends of the field (Fig. 29). These tall, cylindrical tents with their striped and checkered decoration also appear in the scenes of Richard's military encampment on Crusade. Kevin Harty has commented, "Clearly, the film does not aim for historical accuracy, ... but the atmosphere of the film is meant to play to an audience's sense of the medieval.... As [director Alan] Dwan commented to *Motion Picture Magazine*, ... '[we] knew that atmosphere was something beyond authenticity and the absence of anachronism.... It was atmosphere that we strived for above anything else.'"[86] In short, these fabric grandstands and tents appeared early in Hollywood films, establishing a visual shorthand for the Medieval genre.

Although studio art directors found inspiration in Renaissance manuscript painting, a major visual source for films was early twentieth-century book illustration. For example, N.C. Wyeth's illustration of a joust, *Sir Mador's Spear Brake All to Pieces, but the Other's Spear Held* in *The Boy's King Arthur* (1922) shows opposing knights on horseback clashing in the foreground, while in the background viewers look on from an elevated stand (Fig. 32).[87] Wyeth was probably looking at representations of jousting in Early Renaissance manuscript paintings, such as *The Tournament of Ingelvert* in *The Harley Froissart*, created in Bruges, c. 1470–72.[88] All of the elements—the striped tents topped by an elaborate finial, the richly patterned fabrics, the decorative coats of arms, the viewing stand, and the charging horses—were reproduced in modern book illustrations.

The tournament trope was entrenched in Hollywood movies, as may be seen in Warner Bros.' *The Adventures of Robin Hood*, starring Errol Flynn. Preliminary storylines for this 1938 Technicolor extravaganza emulated the Fairbanks epic by opening with a joust. Ultimately, an archery tournament was used as a narrative device to lure Robin to Nottingham Castle and launch the action. The film's art direction owes much to the Fairbanks production but also shows the influence of a Wyeth illustrated edition of *Robin Hood* (1917). In a scene that set the standard for gaily hued costumes and tents in subsequent films, the rich hangings at a royal tournament in the Flynn movie perfectly mirror Wyeth's *Robin Meets Maid Marian at the Royal Tourney* in chapter 11 of the book.[89] Thus, in true Hollywood fashion, the film moves further from historical truth toward a constructed reality accepted as genuine by the audience.

Flynn's *Robin Hood* was rereleased in 1948 to renewed box-office success. One of the most popular movies among troops in World War II, it left its mark on several generations as a rerun on late-night TV in the 1950s. As film historian Rudy Behlmer has written, "The characters,

Figure 32. N.C. Wyeth, *Sir Mador's Spear Brake All to Pieces.* **Sidney Lanier,**
The Boy's King Arthur, **1922 (author's collection).**

costumes, castle, and forest are idealized, but then the film is not a document of medieval life; rather, it is a fairy tale illustrated by Technicolor" in response to "a vague nostalgia for a partly mythical age of
chivalry."[90]

By the early 1950s, a tournament scene had become *de rigueur* for
a Medieval film. Between 1953 and 1956, six widescreen epics featured

elaborate jousting scenes. By the time Disneyland opened, audiences were fully conversant with the stereotype. Production values in MGM's 1952 hit film, *Ivanhoe*, especially impressed *New York Times* critic Halsey Raines, who praised it as "a living recreation of twelfth-century feudal England":

> The pennanted pavilions of King John and his retinue signify the presence of royalty at Ashby's famed and sanguinary jousting tournament of 1192 A. D., twenty-three years before the Magna Carta. Scores of circling tents of martial knights carry heraldic emblems, profuse in color and design. The jousting-ground stretches out in front; riders rushing from opposite directions are separated by a list, or four-feet-high banner-covered fence, extending the length of the field. Weapons are thrust in passing at each other across this list, the impact frequently toppling one antagonist.[91]

Director Richard Thorpe reinforced the illusion: "Our research, of course, had been enormous in the effort to obtain a faithful reproduction not only of the essentials of the Scott novel but of the period of the story."[92]

Not everyone was enthralled. The reviewer in the *Los Angeles Times* called the movie "an attractive general filmic tapestry. Reality is a little too much to expect under the circumstances."[93] And a critic in the U.K. commented, "Although produced at Elstree and on English locations, any connection between this and a British film is purely coincidental; it is Hollywood spectacle in conception, treatment and casting."[94]

Twentieth Century–Fox created an equally dazzling jousting-ground for Henry Hathaway's *Prince Valiant*, whose design decisions were based in part on Hal Foster's popular comic feature that combined authentic graphic detail with artistic fantasy.[95] A profusion of striped and checkered tents border the lists along the length of the field. The knights wear chain mail beneath their resplendent surcoats, and the decorative fittings on their horses match the fabric hangings on the grandstands.

Even Disney yielded to tournament fever in his live-action *Robin Hood*. The archery tournament is handled grandly, with the usual accouterments of the cloth reviewing stand and round tents. Compared to the luxurious fabrics that give richness to the aforementioned films, the Disney version emphasizes bright colors and patterns; because these were stenciled onto apparent stage flats, they actually resemble more closely Fantasyland's tournament tents.

Veteran production designer William Cameron Menzies commented that art directors and cameramen can do "a great deal to add punch to the action as planned by the director.... In the case of pageantry such things as scale and pattern, figures, rich trappings against a high wall, through a huge arch are demanded."[96] The patterns on Fantasyland's stands and tents had the same vibrant effect as the fabric hangings in pictures like

Ivanhoe and *Prince Valiant*. Although replaced in the 1983 New Fantasyland makeover by a quaint Old World–style stone village, in 1955 the
look added a dose of "punch" to the King Arthur Courtyard. The bold use
of design elements on the façades bridged the gap between a faithful recreation of medieval pageantry and the stylized décor that prevailed elsewhere in Fantasyland.

With this in mind, another glance at the King Arthur Carrousel is
revealing. We now see that the design of the circular canopy, with its vertical stripes, dangling lappets, and golden finial, may be traced back via
the movies to representations of circular tournament tents in illustrations of Arthurian legends, such as Wyeth's *Sir Mador's Spear Brake All to
Pieces*. Thus, although the carousel design reconfigured the basic elements
of horses, lances, shields, and tents in an unusual and original way, it was
appropriately themed to popular notions of jousting tournaments associated with the Arthurian legend. Although chivalric bridlery had long decorated the carousels of Britain, Disney was unique in applying the imagery
of Camelot to an American merry-go-round.

Merlin's Magic Shop

I now wish to mention the third and final element of Arthuriana
within the castle courtyard, the pair of shops adjacent to the inner castle façade: on the right, Merlin's Magic Shop, brimming with novelties and
souvenirs, and on the left, Fantasy of Disneyland, a kids' clothing store.[97]
Bill Martin designed the picturesque storybook cottages with asymmetrical fronts, half-timbered walls, steeply pitched roofs, and leaded-glass
windows. They strongly resemble the faux European villages built on Hollywood backlots, such as Dijon Street at Warner Bros., which stood in for
Nottingham in *The Adventures of Robin Hood*. Disney had anticipated
a magic shop in his 1948 Memorandum; by 1954 the name of the wizard
Merlin, tutor and advisor to Camelot, had been added in order to complement the King Arthur theme. The shop's interior décor matched the concept of knights and ladies fair, including an interactive Sword in the Stone.
With the help of a hidden device known only to sales staff, a lucky visitor
might release a chrome-plated Excalibur sword embedded in a (plastic)
rock and be pronounced royalty for a day.[98]

Across the way at the shop's twin, Fantasy of Disneyland, items on
offer for "cinema tots thru teens" included a skirt decorated with a sparkling appliqué of a Knight of the Round Table astride a horse.[99] At Disneyland, even an article of child's clothing owed its details to the "cinema,"
not literature or history.

A Pirate's Life for Me!

At the northernmost point of Fantasyland stood the Chicken of the Sea Pirate Ship and Restaurant (Fig. 33). Seen in Herb Ryman's *Aerial View of Disneyland* and touted in opening-day press kits as "the unusual Pirate Ship Restaurant," the ship was omitted in prospectuses, probably to avoid confusion with the Peter Pan Flight ride located in nearby King Arthur Courtyard. Visitors boarded via a gangway over an irregularly shaped pond, and from 1955 until 1982, when it was retired, the Pirate Ship was the focus of many a Kodak moment—especially when the seven sails, in all their red-and-white striped glory, were unfurled.

On opening day, Bobby Driscoll—young Jim Hawkins in Disney's *Treasure Island*, and, more recently, the voice of the eponymous hero in *Peter Pan*—waved to a nationwide TV audience from her deck. Bobby's direct connection to two pirate-themed Disney films reflected a core

Figure 33. Chicken of the Sea Pirate Ship and Restaurant, Fantasyland, Disneyland. Tourist snapshot, June 1957 (author's collection).

ambiguity in the attraction, a confused pairing first apparent in a January 1955 proposal calling the eatery "The Long John Silver and Captain Hook Incorporated Pirate Ship."[100] In the end, it was decided to make it a pirate ship of a generic kind found in any Hollywood high-seas adventure.

The "Tuna Boat," as locals dubbed it, doubled as a fast-food restaurant and hands-on place where young and old could roam the poop deck and give the helmsman's wheel a spin. The Van Camp Seafood Company had prevailed over its rival, Starkist, as the Boat's sponsor, to promote its Chicken of the Sea brand of tuna. Thus, the only fantasy characters associated with the Ship were the mermaid figurehead on the bow and a mermaid relief sculpture on the stern, based on the product logo, and a peg-legged pirate, patch over one eye, who appeared in ads and on site in the person of a costumed vet who had lost a leg in Korea.[101] The lack of a specific narrative for the ship was reinforced in 1958, when Van Camp held a national contest, "Name Our Pirate Ship at Disneyland." Despite lavish prizes, including all-expenses-paid trips to the park, no new name was attached to the boat, the end goal being publicity. Contemporary descriptions made only vague references to the "atmosphere reminiscent of the Spanish Main and Captain Kidd" and "bloody battles ... fought 400 years ago."[102]

From Historical Pirates to the Cinematic Pirate

Just as Hollywood created the "cinematic pirate," so too did art directors create a film version of a pirate ship, the basis for the Chicken of the Sea vessel.[103] In reality, running a sailing ship was a complex business. The vessels were "nests for disease," and life on board was damp, dirty, and dark.[104] On film, these unsavory details were sanitized or glossed over.

Fictionalized accounts and popular prints presenting the sometimes titillating adventures of rogues like Captain Kidd and Edward Teach, a.k.a. Blackbeard, date back to Daniel Defoe's *Robinson Crusoe* (1719), and on film, to the silent days of Thomas Edison's *Three of a Kind; or, The Pirate's Dream* (1901) and D.W. Griffith's *The Pirate's' Gold* (1908). Movie pirates, shorn of their criminal and violent ways, joined the ranks of heroic seamen quick to embark on a mission to right a wrong or see the light and renounce their outlaw life.[105] Such figures had their origins in tales like Lord Byron's poem *The Corsair* (1814), which introduced romantic, even erotic, elements. Beautifully illustrated stories like Sir Walter Scott's *The Pirate* (1822) further contributed to a romanticized image of the buccaneer as a fundamentally "good guy."[106]

Pirates on the silver screen combined sources like these with the allure of dashing leading men like Douglas Fairbanks and Errol Flynn. A milestone in the genre, *The Black Pirate* (1926)—the "earliest of the cinematic pirate classics"—was acclaimed for its spectacular sets and the winning smile and athleticism of actor/producer Fairbanks, who played a swashbuckling hero masquerading as a buccaneer to avenge an injustice and save a damsel in distress.[107] Fairbanks the producer staked a claim to factual authenticity, but in reality he embraced time-honored nineteenth-century literary conceits, breathlessly spelled out in the opening titles like this:

> Being an account of BUCCANEERS &
> the SPANISH MAIN, the *Jolly Roger*,
> GOLDEN GALLEONS, bleached skulls,
> BURIED TREASURE, the *Plank*,
> dirks & cutlasses, SCUTTLED SHIPS,
> *Marooning*, DESPERATE DEEDS,
> DESPERATE MEN, and—even on this
> dark soil—ROMANCE.

One of Fairbanks's consulting art directors for *The Black Pirate* was illustrator and costume designer Dwight Franklin, a disciple of the aforementioned Arthurian illustrator Howard Pyle, who, along with his pupil, N.C. Wyeth, established almost singlehandedly the modern-day image of the seventeenth- and eighteenth-century pirate. Pyle's art combined bold draftsmanship, harmonious handling of color, and dramatic points of view in paintings like *An Attack on a Galleon* and *Walking the Plank*, both reproduced in *Howard Pyle's Book of Pirates*, the motivating force and primary source for the movie.[108]

The methods used to make *The Black Pirate* furnished a blueprint for virtually every pirate action-adventure movie to follow. Filming at sea might yield terrific results but prove treacherous for cameramen. Construction of a navigable replica would be too time-consuming and costly. Though existing ships were sometimes camouflaged with "period" additions, Fairbanks chose to make the most of inherent limitations at the Pickford-Fairbanks Studio. For distant views at sea, the chief art director Carl Oscar Borg supervised the creation of miniature craft big enough to conceal a stuntman yet small enough to be shot in a studio tank. For interior and exterior sequences with actors, elaborately detailed sections of ships were built on a reduced scale, favoring those parts most recognizable to the public: the main deck, rigging, stern, and sails. Since Fairbanks was experimenting with two-strip Technicolor, he gave the ship a weathered appearance, and the sets were "aged" to create the muted look of an antique painting.

Pirate ships did more than provide a backdrop; they were an integral part of the action. In *The Black Pirate*, Fairbanks scrambles across the deck, flits about the rigging, and fights his way all over the place. He even catapults up to the topsail and slashes it in an athletic descent back on deck. One film historian said of *The Black Pirate* that it was "deliberately designed to create a totally stylized, self-contained, mythic universe…. Not based on a classic novel or weighed down with reels of court intrigue, it is entirely a creation of the cinema: a film as light as air…. Like the production design, the story content is rigorously stylized, a distillation of all the pirate myths."[109]

Just as Fairbanks's Robin Hood found a worthy successor in Errol Flynn, so too did his pirate persona. In the sound era, Flynn brought to life two sagas that fused piracy and romance: *Captain Blood* (1935) and *The Sea Hawk* (1940). Warner Bros. shot *The Sea Hawk* in its new Studio 21, the largest soundstage at the time. A vast artificial pool of water allowed stuntmen to fall from the decks and rigging into the make-believe briny. Vessels moved back and forth on submerged tracks, hydraulic jacks created a rocking motion, and a ripple machine and elaborate plumbing infrastructure created different types of waves. A 600-foot-long backdrop completed the picture with a scenic cyclorama of water and sky.

Figure 34. *The Sea Hawk* (1940, Warner Bros.), pair of ship sets in Studio 21 on the Warner Bros. lot (Bison Archives and HollywoodHistoricPhotos.com).

Studio 21 was spacious enough to hold a pair of stage-set sailing ships needed to film two exciting scenes (Fig. 34). In the first, Captain Thorpe (Flynn) and his crew aboard the *Albatross* capture and sink a Spanish galleon. In the second, Thorpe and his men, now galley slaves, free themselves and capture a neighboring vessel. Overseen by art director Anton Grot and his assistant Leo Kuter, the two "ships" reportedly measured between 135 and 165 feet long, but only the portions visible to the camera were finished. Shot from a number of angles by director Michael Curtiz, who was assisted by special effects master Byron Haskin, the sets and action were flawlessly integrated to create a thrilling sense of being on the high seas. As with *The Black Pirate*, when full views were required, models large enough to hold a technician were filmed on the backlot lake.

Treasure Island from Page to Screen

The production values in *The Sea Hawk* represented a high-water mark in the history of the Hollywood pirate ship.[110] The vessels in Disney's live-action *Treasure Island* and animated *Peter Pan* would have been all the poorer without *The Sea Hawk*'s star to steer by. At the same time, the rapport between the Disneyland ship and both the literary and cinematic versions of *Treasure Island* and *Peter Pan* was inevitable and thus deserves our attention. Robert Louis Stevenson's 1883 novel was still in print in 1955, and J.M. Barrie's *Peter Pan* (1901) enjoyed nonstop success both as a book and a seasonal Christmas play.

Stevenson had drawn from a grand tradition of buccaneer and shipwreck fiction. Although aimed chiefly at a male juvenile audience, *Treasure Island*, the book, appealed to a public habituated to previously published tales of piracy and desert islands. Its text was a brilliant synthesis of pirate tropes from various sources, to which Stevenson and talented artists added special touches like buried treasure, pieces of eight, hidden maps, peg-legged pirates, chattering parrots, and a motley crew of supporting characters. Stevenson's engrossing narrative of seafaring life aboard Long John Silver's ship, the *Hispaniola*, moved the plot briskly along. One of the highpoints of the story, popular among the illustrators, was Jim Hawkins's climb up the rigging, from which he shoots his pursuer, Israel Hands.

The action-packed adventure lent itself to the silver screen three times in the silent era. MGM's 1934 sound version was the classic Hollywood retelling until the Disney version. Despite reservations about Jackie Coogan as a pouty Jim and Wallace Beery as a leering Long John Silver, critics and public alike loved the picture, so much so that it was rereleased in 1938. Exterior scenes, some shot on MGM's Lot 1 Lake, created a realistic impression of Bristol harbor and the English coast. Catalina Island, south-west of Long Beach, California, stood in for Treasure Island for location filming.[111] But the most riveting sequences, also inspired by book illustration, "starred" the *Hispaniola*, a repurposed whaling vessel, though photographing the action posed enormous challenges. "The roll of the boat," director Victor Fleming recalled, "made it hard to maintain the balance of the cameras built on parallels over the edge of the boat," and in-studio close-ups had to be intercut with footage shot on the boat.[112]

After the war, MGM allowed its rights to Stevenson's story lapse, and Walt jumped on them. In the postwar era, the high cost of producing quality animation threatened the very existence of the Disney studio, so at first he envisioned a hybrid picture, like *Song of the South*, in which a live-action pirate narrative intermingled with animated yarns spun by Long John Silver.[113] In the end, Walt and Roy turned *Treasure Island* into their first totally live-action feature and filmed it in England to access funds frozen in the U.K. during and after the war.

Bobby Driscoll would play Jim. Director Byron Haskin, who had worked on special effects for *The Sea Hawk*, hired British actors for every other role, including Robert Newton, whose scenery-chewing turn as Long John Silver established the stereotypical screen pirate persona. Filmed in Technicolor on location and complemented by Peter Ellenshaw's inspired matte paintings, *Treasure Island* achieved, according to one writer, "a magnificent piece of bravura" that overshadowed the MGM version.[114] In pursuit of authenticity, Disney insisted that real ships, not miniatures, be used for exterior shots, even though—again—the *Hispaniola* was a fake. Diesel engines were concealed inside a sailing boat refitted with period accouterments based on a nineteenth-century ship model.

A critical and financial success when it premiered in 1950, Disney's *Treasure Island* spawned renewed interest in Stevenson's tale and retellings from other studios. In 1954, Newton and Haskin collaborated on *Long John Silver*, a non–Disney sequel, and Newton milked the role on TV in *The Adventures of Long John Silver*. A follow-up movie version from United Artists set in the twentieth century, *Return to Treasure Island*, was released in 1954. Walt did not immediately rerelease his *Treasure Island* in theaters as he normally would have done. He chose instead to reach a larger audience by airing it in two parts, twice, in seasons one and two of the *Disneyland* TV show, where it appeared under the heading of Fantasyland, not Adventureland or Frontierland. As we saw in Chapter 2, the anchor supposedly hailing from the pirate ship of Jean Lafitte was a major prop in Frontierland. In the planning stage, Tom Sawyer Island was called Treasure Island, and in its definitive design, Pirate's Cove on the island followed Twain's description of Tom and his pals' make-believe attempts to act like buccaneers.[115]

Peter Pan from Stage to Screen

J.M. Barrie conceived *Peter Pan* in both literary and theatrical iterations, from the stage play of 1904 to its novelization *Peter and Wendy* penned in 1911 for an audience steeped in images of pirate gear, shipwrecks, and treasure maps.[116] Barrie envisioned Neverland as an analogue to Treasure Island, and Stevenson's novel influenced his portrayal of Captain Hook and his scurvy crew. The two authors, both Scottish, enjoyed a cordial correspondence, and Barrie acknowledged his debt in subtle allusions in the play.[117]

A great success on Broadway in 1905–06, starring Maude Adams, Barrie's *Peter Pan* was filmed by Paramount in a silent version in 1924, with Betty Bronson as Pan.[118] Critics and Barrie himself found it too stagebound—the flying sequences were brief, overly timid—but it was generally agreed the sequences at sea were remarkable. A sailing vessel moored off the California coast was outfitted as *The Jolly Roger*, complete with bold, vertically striped sails, and cinematographer James Wong Howe's camera captured breathtaking views of the Darling brood on the rigging and Hook walking the plank.

In 1939, after the movie rights were acquired from the Great Ormond Street Hospital for Sick Children, Walt and his team screened the silent film looking for useful ideas. They found particularly compelling the magical rise of Hook's ship from the sea during the departure from Neverland. Preliminary concept art for the Disney film featured the striped sails, and although they do not appear in the completed film, books and games bound commercially to its release all show them. Walt shelved the project during the war and only recommenced the work in late 1949.

The boat in Disney's animated *Peter Pan*, *The Jolly Roger*, conforms to norms long established in major studio productions like *The Sea Hawk*. It is almost always viewed up close. By 1953, viewers had a good idea where on board any action was taking place. The clichéd image of the skull-and-crossbones flag also figures at key points in the cartoon, initially as the crew hoists the white-on-black banner, and in the climactic duel when Hook, trapped within its folds, begs Peter to spare his life and is forced to loudly declare, "I'm a codfish," before he gains his freedom.

Though a box-office success in 1953, the Disney version had not yet attained "classic" status in 1955. Meanwhile, Barrie's play was continuously staged in England. In 1950, it debuted on Broadway in a musical version by Leonard Bernstein, with Jean Arthur as Peter and our old friend, Boris Karloff, in the dual roles of Hook and Mr. Darling. In July 1954, eighteen months after Disney's *Peter Pan* was released, Mary Martin created the greatest role of her career as the "Boy Who Wouldn't Grow Up" in a second musical version of the play at New York's Winter Garden Theatre. The production was made all the more famous because it was broadcast three times on television, the first time around, being shortly before Disneyland opened its gates. In sum, at the time of the park's premiere, *Peter Pan*, like *Treasure Island*, was not considered an exclusive Disney property, and it was more effective to leave the Fantasyland ship's associations with history and film open and fluid.

Disneyland's Pirate Ship Restaurant

In the early and mid–1950s, pirate ships in *Treasure Island* and *Peter Pan* inhabited a larger sphere of swashbuckling sea dogs and thrills and chills on the Spanish Main. During Disneyland's development, a new wave of pirate films reinvigorated several firmly established subgenres, notably the pirate musical, exemplified by MGM's *The Pirate*, co-starring Gene Kelly and Judy Garland, and women-pirate pictures like *Buccaneer's Girl* with Yvonne De Carlo, *Anne of the Indies* with Jean Peters, and *Against All Flags*, featuring Maureen O'Hara as a pirate leader named "Spitfire" Stevens, who, as the *New York Times* noted, winds up as "beautiful putty" in the hands of co-star Errol Flynn.[119] Disney's decision not to tie the Chicken of the Sea ship and restaurant to any identifiable narrative made sense in the midst of this resurgent pirate mania.

Like Hollywood's make-believe vessels, Fantasyland's "tuna boat" was an artificial creation derived from a cinematic stereotype. Art director Bruce Bushman provided concept sketches that suggested setting it on a turntable. The idea of a moving support for motion-picture purposes had been used at Warner Bros. but proved too great a challenge at Fantasyland. Art director Bill Martin translated Bushman's ideas into workable plans.[120] The Disneyland ship, like so much else in the park, was scaled down in size—seventy-five feet long, the central mast about sixty feet tall—compared to ocean-going galleons of old, that were up to three times as long, with masts as high as ninety feet.

The design emphasized those elements most familiar to moviegoers. The fore and aft sections were relatively large compared to the central deck, as they were typically in live-action pirate movies. The crow's nests were oversized, the rigging simplified, and a large skull-and-crossbones flag flew overhead. Boldly striped sails, as in the 1927 silent version of *Peter Pan*, paid tribute to the clichéd look of striped pirate clothing. And, like the 1952 pirate-parody film *The Crimson Pirate*, the ship's silhouette was grossly exaggerated, with a swelling hull and steeply angled stern, further highlighted by a contrasting color scheme of yellow, black, and red. Alas, for guests of all ages, her lines of cannons were strictly for show and inaccessible.

These over-the-top, stylized features befitted the spirit of Fantasyland. By not pegging it to Long John Silver or Captain Hook, the crowd-pleasing vessel evoked the tradition of big-screen buccaneers. In 1960, Walt "plussed" the setting by adding a sandy beach, palm trees, and a large artificial outcropping, Skull Rock, straight out of the animated *Peter Pan*. In 1969, when Van Camp's sponsorship ended, the restaurant was renamed Captain Hook's Galley, aligning it more closely with the Peter Pan Flight ride, in which small-scale galleons cruised over a miniature Neverland via monorail. By then, a new attraction, among the last overseen by Walt before he died, had premiered in New Orleans Square. Pirates of the Caribbean proved to be one of the park's most enduring entertainments and ultimately sired the blockbuster Johnny Depp movie franchise.

Tinker Bell

One of the more "spritely" characters in Disney's *Peter Pan* immediately developed a presence at Disneyland, being reproduced on guide maps, shopping bags, souvenir books, and other paraphernalia: Tinker Bell, the impudent sidekick of the boy who wouldn't grow up. That a cartoon version of a fairy, who was not a Disney creation but was adapted from the work of an Edwardian playwright, would become a symbol of the park and ultimately of the company itself, is one of the more remarkable scenarios in the history of Disneyland.

Tinker Bell's association with the park goes back to the introductory credits of the *Disneyland* TV series. As the show opens, she appears onscreen trailing pixie dust. With a wave of her magic wand, an artist's rendering of the Train Station at the entrance to the park materializes, with Main Street and the castle beyond. Searchlights make an instant connection with Hollywood. In lively animation produced by company stalwarts Les Clark and John Hench, Tink reveals each of the four realms of both the anthology program and the park. She mimics in pantomime an "Indian brave" and Davy Crockett for Frontierland, dives headfirst into a spinning atom for Tomorrowland, floats over a turning globe representing Adventureland, and sprinkles her magic on the Fantasyland Castle. As Walt explains in the first broadcast, "Disneyland the place and *Disneyland* the TV show are all part of the same [concept]," and Tink would inhabit both. She was chosen for this prestigious position because better known Disney characters were already bound to licensing agreements, and Mickey and Donald would be tied to *The Mickey Mouse Club* TV series.

While Tink acted as a symbol for *Disneyland*, she was also a spokesperson for one of the show's first advertisers, Derby Foods, makers of Peter Pan Peanut Butter. Thus, during the opening of the early broadcasts, she also uses her wand to magically create jars and cans of peanut butter. In the *Disneyland* program titled "An Adventure in the Magic Kingdom," telecast in April 1958, the curvaceous cutie even sweeps the boss off his feet, levitating him into the air.

Barrie had described Tinker Bell in print as "exquisitely gowned in a skeleton leaf, cut low and square, through which her figure could be seen to best advantage." On stage, she was portrayed as a darting ball of light. The Paramount silent film of *Peter Pan* is the sole instance before Disney in which Tink, played by Virginia Brown Faire in a flowing semitransparent gown, appears in close-ups as human, albeit with special attributes. Taking several cues from Barrie's description of Tink's mercurial disposition and ability to feel only one emotion at a time, Walt's artists fleshed out her personality as both vain and insecure but ever loyal to Pan. They dressed her in a kind of one-piece green bathing suit, pulled up her blond hair in a bun, studded her slippers with pompoms, and frequently revealed her panties. Thus, with her spunky personality and pinup-girl looks, Tinker Bell possessed an element rare in 1950s Disney animation—girlish sex appeal.[121]

At the time of the movie's premiere, film critics consistently expressed surprise at the pixie's allure, as in the instance of British writer Moore Raymond, who asked Disney about the "bit of sex" spicing up the animated features. To his question about whether actresses Marilyn Monroe and Zsa Zsa Gabor served as models for Tinker Bell, Walt replied that the character was based on Barrie's description of a jealous little pixie, as well as Disney's own observations of his daughters as they grew up. Both Walt and the journalist claimed to be "really in love" with the animated character.[122]

Although she does not carry a wand in *Peter Pan*, printed promos for the film in 1953 show her introducing the Disney version with a wand as evidence of the movie's magic. One of the park's earliest souvenirs was "Tinker Bell's Enchanted Wand—[it] glows in the dark for hours! Only 25¢!" In addition to her ubiquitous presence in souvenirs, the pixie received her own shop when Fantasy of Disneyland closed in 1956 due to poor sales, and the Tinker Bell Toy Shop opened in its place. In 1961 Tink materialized as a costumed cast member. As part of the nightly fireworks, veteran circus performer Tiny Kline reenacted Tink's association with the TV castle by donning wings and "flying" 754 feet down a cable strung between the Matterhorn and Sleeping Beauty Castle.[123]

An early promo for the film promised, "Tinker Bell will fly straight into the heart of every man, woman, and child who looks upon her loveliness."[124] Speaking on behalf of a wide audience, one film critic exclaimed, "Tinker Bell completely won my heart and I shall be desolated if Disney does not bring her back at some future time."[125] Thus, Tink's plucky spirit and sex appeal proved to be universal.

In fact, Walt pitched the entire realm of Fantasyland to a universal audience—Disneyland was not created solely for children or for Disney fans. His artists aspired to a broader vision, one that appealed to movie lovers of all stripes and to devotees of popular culture in many media. While the Disney versions of Snow White, Alice, Peter, et al. were indeed present in the park's fantasy sector, they were accompanied by the Big Eight's versions of medieval castles, chivalrous knights, and devilish pirates. All of these elements conjoined to bring the realm to life. As an artist, Walt Disney possessed the ability to tap into mainstream culture as a means of enriching his personal vision, and thus Fantasyland benefited from its reflection of classical Hollywood.[126]

Epilogue

Walt Disney became a beloved national celebrity in the 1950s, thanks to his highly visible duties as the avuncular host of the *Disneyland* TV series. His dream-world-come-true in Anaheim was an overwhelming success, and the company he founded in 1923 experienced a surge in motion picture output, both animated and live-action.

The park defied efforts to describe it. Critics and journalists persisted in calling it an amusement park. Not until the end of the 1950s did the phrase "theme park," initially in quotation marks, come into widespread use. Typical of attempts to define the park was an article in *Disneyland Holiday* magazine in 1957 that asked, "What Is Disneyland?" The writer decided it was "the happiest place on earth."[1] Another intriguing question—"Is Disneyland Art?"—was posed in the same year by an article in an L.A. newspaper. The answer was yes: "The perfection of every visual effect in the entire Magic Kingdom shows the taste and skill of some gifted and imaginative artist."[2] That unnamed genius was Walt.

Disney always regarded Disneyland as a work in progress. Whenever "I see things that aren't right," he told columnist Hedda Hopper, "I can change them, but I've not been able to do that with pictures. This is the compensation I get out of Disneyland."[3] He also recognized the importance of adding new attractions to draw visitors back for repeat visits. Thus, to use a favorite term of his in the 1950s and 1960s, he was constantly "plussing" the park.[4]

It was primarily in Fantasyland that specific narratives based on Disney animations were recreated for guests to experience, notably the adventures of Snow White, Peter Pan, and Mr. Toad. Not ready for the park's opening, the Alice in Wonderland attraction debuted in 1958. On the other hand, Tomorrowland proved to be the realm most in need of periodic updating. Ideas initiated in the early 1950s came to fruition with the Monsanto House of the Future and the Flying Saucers ride. Disney's ambitious dream of futuristic transportation materialized with the installation of the Disneyland-Alweg Monorail, America's first daily operating monorail, as part of the 1959 Tomorrowland expansion.[5] That year also saw the Submarine Voyage, an alternative to the 20,000 Leagues Under the Sea exhibit.

As we have seen throughout this book, there was a clear pattern of thematic appropriation in Disneyland's usurpation of standard Hollywood movie genres in its division of the park into five realms. However, in the late 1950s, Disney turned to his own recent live-action films as sources for themed rides. When at last he yielded to the pressure for a thrill ride, the result was the Matterhorn Bobsleds on the boundary between Fantasyland and Tomorrowland, inspired by the Disney live-action movie *Third Man on the Mountain* (1959). An elaborate Grand Canyon Diorama, installed in a tunnel along the route of the Disneyland Railroad, was based on the Disney Studio documentary *The Grand Canyon* (1959). Walt's live-action film *Swiss Family Robinson* (1960) spawned a walk-through treehouse attraction in Adventureland.

Some years after Disney's death, a new twist emerged when park designers openly collaborated with other studios to conceive rides incorporating specific characters and plots from non–Disney movies. Notably, George Lucas contributed recognizable elements from two popular franchises to create Star Tours in 1987 and the Indiana Jones Adventure in 1995. The adaptation of storylines from other studios accelerated to the point that today there are entire non–Disney "lands" within Disney parks—for example, Pandora: The World of Avatar at Disney's Animal Kingdom, and Star Wars: Galaxy's Edge at both Disneyland and Disney's Hollywood Studios in Orlando.

Duplicating the Disney Magic

In the postwar years, a boom in leisure-time pursuits and vacation travel, made possible by construction of interstates crisscrossing the continent and the creation of new highways circumventing big cities, boosted tourism to national parks, historic sites, and amusement parks. Disneyland injected new life into the park business. "Imitation Disneylands," *Time* magazine remarked in 1959, "are shooting up across the country." The article cited entrepreneur C.V. Wood, Disney's first general manager, who subsequently lent his expertise to a dozen like-minded wonderlands scattered throughout the U.S.[6] After a slow decline over the first half of the twentieth century, the number of parks rose from about 400 in 1954 to almost twice that number in 1967.[7] They copied not only the Disneyland concept of theming, but elements like the enclosing wall, single entrance, and hub-and-spoke layout. At the same time, older parks and even venues like museums and historic houses were pressured to make themselves more welcoming and entertaining à la Disneyland.

Hedda Hopper chided the Big Eight for not rushing to follow Walt's lead: "For years I've been howling for the studios to do something for millions of tourists who come to our town expecting to see how pictures are made.... Our moguls sat on their minds and hands. All, that is, except Walt Disney, who up and built himself a Disneyland that turned out to be one of the greatest tourist attractions in the world."[8] Universal Studios, which had operated the first Hollywood studio tour, reopened its gates in 1956 to admit Tanner Gray Line Motor Tours onto the premises. In 1959 Universal created its own bus tour and five years later instituted a two-hour tram tour, which gave guests a chance to disembark and observe soundstages and standing sets firsthand. Employing Universal's method, in 1966 Warner Bros. opened its backlot to visitors, and for a limited time MGM contracted with bus companies for tours. Twentieth Century–Fox initiated a walking tour, later changed to a pricey VIP tour.[9] But as studio-bound film production slowed, the fate of the great backlots, and their accessibility to the public, increasingly hung in the balance.

Filmland's Decline

The seven-year period in which Disneyland gradually came into being, from late August 1948 to mid–July 1955, coincided with a crucial moment for Tinseltown. The Hollywood Antitrust Case of 1948 (*United States v. Paramount Pictures*) broke up the monopolistic system of vertical integration that allowed the major studios to impose distribution of their films through their own theater chains. The introduction of smaller, more mobile cameras and sensitive sound equipment all but eliminated the need for the controlled environments provided by the soundstage and backlot, rendering on-location shooting possible anywhere in the world. The concurrent rise of independent film companies, working on their own or in partnership with the studios, posed another direct threat.

The major studios and the "studio system" of overseeing all aspects of film production reached a commercial peak in the 1940s. Production of theatrical features declined sharply from a total of 432 in 1951 to 354 in 1953, and to a low of 303 in 1954.[10] This resulted in significant layoffs at the studios, including the downsizing of art departments, which, fortunately for Walt, redounded to his benefit. Because the number of films being made was smaller, theater owners relied increasingly on rereleases, which in the pre–VCR era gave renewed life to classical Hollywood cinema.

Movie patronage also declined, due to mass migration from cities to suburbia and the lack in small towns or exurban residential areas of movie theaters comparable in size or grandeur to metropolitan movie palaces. Average weekly theater attendance in 1948 was ninety million. In 1953, it sank to about forty-six million, and to forty million by 1959.[11] One-third of the country's cinemas were shuttered in the 1950s; in 1951 alone, some 700 movie theaters were torn down or converted to other uses.[12] The make-up of movie audiences also changed, with the rise of teen films like *Rebel Without a Cause* and *Gidget*. The Cold War pushed the motion picture industry into areas not previously explored, exemplified by a spate of sci-fi horror films echoing subliminal societal anxieties.[13] As movies with mature content thrived, openly challenging bourgeois moral standards with explicit treatments of violence and sex, the number of family films diminished. By 1960, Disney had the reputation as the only producer of family fare in Hollywood left standing.

None of these factors, however, hurt as much as the ascendancy of television, which became the prime locus of family viewing. It was free, and you could eat dinner, enjoy the beverage of your choice, take your shoes off, and dress as you pleased, all in the comfort of your own home. American households counted 250,000 television sets in 1948. In 1949, the number rose to one million, and by 1952 fifteen million.[14] In 1960, nine out of ten homes had at least one set. Though TV hastened the demise of the big studios, it did accomplish two worthwhile things: like the theatrical rerelease of films, it exposed a younger generation to Westerns, adventure movies, and other generic mainstays of old Hollywood; and it reinvigorated Golden Age classics through afternoon and late-night airings and at holiday time. As Frank Capra declared regarding the quintessential small-town film: "It was television. TV. Films didn't die and disappear anymore. They never went out of circulation. Instead, they went to TV and kept right on playing. They were as alive in '57 or '67 or '77 as they had been in 1947. I woke up one morning, and the whole world was watching *It's a Wonderful Life*."[15]

Hollywood was slow to adapt to the challenge of its electronic competitor. The initial reaction was: if the tube was small, the movie screen would simply be bigger. Widescreen formats gained ground alongside immersion techniques like Cinerama. Historical or Biblical spectacles like *The Robe*, *The Bridge on the River Kwai*, and *Ben-Hur* tended to prevail over American themes. Cinematic epics like these revived attendance until the novelty wore off and ticket sales continued to fall. An article in *The Wall Street Journal*, "Hollywood & TV: Studios Plunge into Television," published a few days before Disneyland's opening, acknowledged, "The success of the Disneyland show is generally credited hereabouts with convincing the laggards among the major studios to get into TV."[16] Like Disney, their initial broadcasts drew on film properties stored away in the vault: Warner Bros., for example, planned a limited series based on three popular pictures—*Casablanca*, *Kings Row*, and *Cheyenne*.

The final blow came in the 1960s in the form of the dismemberment and sale of the studios to corporate conglomerates. Universal survived by reintroducing its profitable studio tour, but other studios, desperate for cash, began to tear down and sell off their fabled backlots. Fox demolished the old standing sets in 1961, selling its valuable property to make way for the retail and office complex, Century City, leasing back eighty acres for its own use (Fig. 35).[17] Other losses were the result of a natural hazard that had long plagued backlots: fire. In 1952, two separate blazes at Warner Bros. leveled parts of the backlot and soundstages.[18] In 1969, MGM announced plans to sell off chunks of its property. Debbie Reynolds, one of the few stars who promoted the historic value of the studio, attempted to find buyers for Lot 3. "My idea," she said, "was to turn it into a Disneyland-type amusement park."[19] This was sadly ironic. By repurposing a backlot as a theme park, serious thought was being given to preserving studio sets that had originally inspired Disneyland! Despite Debbie's efforts, the fabled Lot 3 succumbed to the bulldozers in 1972.

Figure 35. Demolition of the Twentieth Century–Fox backlot, 1961 (Bison Archives and HollywoodHistoricPhotos.com).

Meanwhile, the Mickey Rooney, Judy Garland, or Jimmy Stewart type small-town film, which hit its stride in the 1940s, lost momentum in the 1950s, through the tired recycling of clichéd tropes and cotton-candy nostalgia, at a time when a modern, more "with it" suburban family lifestyle was emerging.[20] Similarly, with rare exceptions (John Wayne, Glenn Ford) the old-fashioned horse opera suffered from over-familiar plots and recycled scenery, though it did gain new ground in a different format, with the advent of the "adult" Western, and, ultimately, in TV series like *Gunsmoke* and *Maverick*.

Walt Disney took Hollywood's moribund archetypes and resurrected them as themed attractions and "lands" that the public could physically enter and explore. As the new guardian and promoter of patriotism and American values, he transmuted old cinematic themes to a new medium, the destination theme park. Thus, Walt assumed the mantle previously borne by Zanuck and Mayer. Disneyland breathed new life into the sorts of cultural mythology that the moguls once championed. In short, the legacy of Tinseltown's Golden Age endured through Disneyland.

The Burbank Backlot

As a producer of cartoons, Walt did not need a backlot for film production. After Disneyland opened, however, he began building backlot sets at his own studio, once again creating a Main Street, Residential Street, and Western Street, but this time for live-action filming. For this purpose, he hired yet another art director, Carroll Clark, who had enjoyed an illustrious career at RKO until its demise. Clark collaborated with set decorator Emile Kuri, whom we have already seen working at Disneyland and the Disney Studio.[21] The need for standing sets arose as Walt committed to live-action movies and television shows, starting with *Zorro* in 1957. The following year saw a Western Street designed to accommodate several TV productions. It was redressed as a small-town, turn-of-the-century main street for the feature film *Toby Tyler, or Ten Weeks with a Circus* (1960). The Residential Street set featured four houses specially constructed for *The Absent-Minded Professor* (1960), and Business Street repeated the Main Street formula but brought it into the contemporary world for *The Ugly Dachshund* (1966) and *Follow Me Boys* (1966).[22]

Another twist of fate occurred thirty years later. MGM missed the boat when it failed to follow Disney and Universal's lead in creating a theme park, but the Disney Company under Michael Eisner, seeking to expand park properties at Walt Disney World during the 1980s Disney Renaissance, inked a deal that granted use of MGM's name and films to create a new theme park, the Disney-MGM Studios. Designed to compete with Universal Studios, which was developing its own backlot theme park in Orlando, the Disney venue opened in 1989 with facilities for shooting motion pictures and television shows.[23] It was essentially a faux studio lot, entered via a Hollywood Boulevard that echoed the Magic Kingdom's Main Street, U.S.A., leading to a hub from which different realms branched out in various directions. In an example of art imitating life—imitating art imitating life!—park designers conjured a Disneyfied version of the MGM backlot, with recreated sets from classics like *Singin' in the Rain* and *The Wizard of Oz*. Much more visibly than Disneyland, the Disney-MGM Studios theme park celebrated Golden Age Hollywood and some of the silver screen's truly all-time great films.

Three-quarters of a century after Walt Disney jotted down a score of disjointed ideas for a kiddieland in his studio's backyard, his vision of an amusement park as a cinematic backlot has conquered the world in ways he could never have imagined. It's safe to say that as long as there is a Disneyland, there will always be Hollywood. "Hooray for Disneyland!"

Chapter Notes

Preface

1. "Father Goose," *Time*, 64:26, Dec. 27, 1954, 42.

2. Unlike the amusement parks of the day, which catered to a local and regional population, Disneyland drew its audience from across the U.S. and ultimately the globe; Brendan Richard, Kelly Kaak, and Marissa Orlowski, "Theme Park Tourism," in *The SAGE International Encyclopedia of Travel and Tourism*, ed. Linda L. Lowry (Thousand Oaks: SAGE, 2017), 1219. Disneyland fast became the number one travel destination in the American West, and park publicity promoted the names of foreign heads of state who desired to visit (including Soviet leader Nikita Khrushchev, unsuccessfully); Steven Watts, *The Magic Kingdom: Walt Disney and the American Way of Life* (New York: Houghton Mifflin, 1997), 394; Ira Wolfert, "Walt Disney's Magic Kingdom," *Reader's Digest*, 76, Apr. 1960, 152.

3. "And Now: Disneyland the Dream Come True," *The Westerner*, no. 69, Aug. 1955, 7–9; "Newest Travel Lure: Disneyland," *Travel*, 104:1, July 1955, 16–19. Although Disneyland publicity in 1955 referred to the five sectors as "themed," the term theme park was not used until 1957, when *Billboard* began applying it in its "Parks—Kiddielands—Rinks" section; e.g., "New Animal Farm Prepares for Opening," *Billboard*, April 29, 1957, 68. Walt Disney, in his final filmed appearance, the *EPCOT* film of October 1966, called the proposed Orlando Magic Kingdom an "amusement theme park" and a "theme park." For an overview of theming, see Margaret J. King and J. G. O'Boyle,

"The Theme Park: The Art of Time and Space," in *Disneyland and Culture: Essays on the Parks and Their Influence*, ed. Kathy Merlock Jackson and Mark I. West (Jefferson: McFarland, 2011), 5–18.

4. Florabel Muir, "Walt's Wonderland," *New York Daily News*, July 10, 1955, 70. Likely a quote from a press release, this description of the park, which appeared in part within the script for "The Disneyland Story," the first *Disneyland* TV show, broadcast on October 27, 1954, was much used in publicity and news stories as early as 1952; "Walt Disney Make-Land Project Planned Here," *Burbank Review*, Mar. 27, 1952, A1. See also "Here's Your First View of Disneyland," *Look*, 18:22, Nov. 2, 1954, 82–84, 86; "A New Concept in Family Entertainment: Disneyland," promotional brochure, Disneyland, Inc., 1955; "Disneyland: 160 Acres of Fun," *Hudson Family Magazine*, 1:3 1955, 8–10; "Newest Travel Lure: Disneyland," 17. In October 1955 Hollywood correspondent Bob Thomas toured the park with Walt Disney, whose childlike delight with his "dream come true" impressed the reporter; Bob Thomas, "Guest Columnist: Walt Fascinated as Child on Magic Kingdom Visit," *Disneyland News*, 1:4, Oct. 10, 1955, 4. Like many authors, I use Walt Disney's given name frequently in this text to differentiate him from both his brother Roy Disney and the company they founded in 1923.

5. Gary S. Cross and John K. Walton, *The Playful Crowd: Pleasure Places in the Twentieth Century* (New York: Columbia University Press, 2005), chap. 1. Disney toured Coney Island with actor Richard Todd in August 1953; Michael Barrier, *The Animated Man: A Life of Walt Disney*

(Berkeley: University Press of California, 2007), 242.

6. See "The Modern Amusement Park," *Street Railway Review*, Jan. 15, 1906, 58. This article is notable for its estimate of 970 "summer amusement parks," in operation in the U.S., described as suitable not only for male patrons but also women and children. Many parks contained much desired features like band pavilions and restaurants.

7. Hedda Hopper, "Dream of Disneyland Still Being Realized," *Los Angeles Times*, July 9, 1957, A8.

8. Walt's parents' first home in Kansas City was at 2706 East 31st Street, about three miles north of an even more famous venue that Walt likely frequented when he lived in Kansas City in 1911–17 and 1919–23: Electric Park, at East 46th and The Paseo. See Brian Burnes, Robert W. Butler, and Dan Viets, *Walt Disney's Missouri: The Roots of a Creative Genius* (Kansas City: Kansas City Star Books, 2002), 51; Neal Gabler, *Walt Disney: The Triumph of the American Imagination* (New York: Knopf, 2006), 19; Watts, *Magic Kingdom*, 384; and Mary Jo Draper, *Kansas City's Historic Midtown Neighborhoods* (Charleston: Arcadia Publishing, 2015), 89.

9. "In Walt Disney's magic kingdom there is nothing to convey the feeling you get at most amusement parks—that you're watching a nervous breakdown and being invited to share it. There are no barkers selling tickets, no 'Hurry! Hurry! HURRY!'"; Wolfert, "Walt Disney's Magic Kingdom," 152.

10. A few days before the opening, the *New York Times* stated, "The appellation 'amusement park' is inadequate, for [Disneyland] has no such banalities as rollercoasters, Ferris wheels and dodge-'ems in a milieu of honky tonk. In concept, it is an integrated juvenile world of fantasy"; Gladwin Hill, "Disneyland Gets Its Last Touches, *New York Times*, July 9, 1955, 32.

11. Norma Lee Browning, "Disney's Future World Is Soon to Come," *Chicago Tribune*, Oct. 25, 1966, 37.

12. This Memorandum, dated August 31, 1948, was addressed to veteran Disney animation art director Dick Kelsey. See Michael Broggie, *Walt Disney's Railroad Story: The Small-Scale Fascination That Led to a Full-Scale Kingdom* (Pasadena:

Pentrex, 1997), 88–91; Gabler, *Walt Disney*, 485, 764 (n.), cites the term Mickey Mouse Village. We do not know exactly when Disney first began thinking about an amusement park, but during the planning of the Burbank studio in 1939, he proposed erecting houses for employees on an unused tract of land across Riverside Drive. Animator Ward Kimball recalled Disney saying, "We will build them kind of like *Snow White*-type cottages [across the street from the studio] and they will have kind of a Disney-theme." Kimball mentioned this to Joe Hale, who repeated what he said in an interview with Didier Ghez. While it is tempting to regard this comment as Disney's first inkling of themed architecture based on a film, it is uncertain whether he would have used the expression "Disney-theme" in 1939. See Didier Ghez, *Walt's People: Talking Disney with the Artists Who Knew Him*, vol. 11 (Bloomingdale: XLibris, 2011), 529. For more on the "Snow White cottages," see J.B. Kaufman, *The Fairest One of All: The Making of Walt Disney's* Snow White and the Seven Dwarfs (San Francisco: Walt Disney Family Foundation Press, 2012), 251. Disney routinely ascribed the impetus for the park to his weekend afternoons with his young daughters (Diane, b. 1933, Sharon, b. 1936), when he regretted, c. 1940, the lack of family-friendly venues; Wolfert, "Walt Disney's Magic Kingdom," 144.

13. The Memorandum has been much quoted in the literature. See Bob Thomas, *Walt Disney: An American Original* (New York: Hyperion, 1994), 218–19; Broggie, *Walt Disney's Railroad Story*, 88–91. On the creation of Disneyland, see Randy Bright, *Disneyland: Inside Story* (New York: Abrams, 1987), chap. 1; Karal Ann Marling, "Imagineering the Disney Theme Parks," in *Designing Disney's Theme Parks: The Architecture of Reassurance*," ed. Karal Ann Marling (Montreal: Canadian Center for Architecture, 1997), 29–79 (also 219–22 for a chronology); Barrier, *Animated Man*, chap. 8.

14. "Walt Disney Make-Believe Land Project," A1; "Walt Disney Plans Park for Children," *Los Angeles Times*, Mar. 28, 1952, A10.

15. "Walt Disney's Radio Interview for the New York World's Fair (1964)," www.youtube.com/watch?v=PuonSVNCpZE.

Objections to the original name, Walt Disney, Inc., resulted in the change to WED. The unit was renamed Walt Disney Imagineering in 1986. Thus, the terms "Imagineer" and "Imagineering" are used sparingly in this book.

16. "Walt Disney Builds Half-Pint History," *Popular Science*, 162, Feb. 1953, 118–19.

17. Lillian Disney and Isabella Taves, "I Live with a Genius," *McCall's*, 80, Feb. 1953, 107.

18. For early art directors, see Jeff Kurtti, *Walt Disney's Imagineering Legends and the Genesis of the Disney Theme Park* (New York: Disney Editions, 2008).

19. Widely reproduced; see Bruce Gordon and David Mumford, *A Brush with Disney: An Artist's Journey Told through the Words and Works of Herbert Dickens Ryman* (Santa Clarita: Camphor Tree Publications, 2000), 144–45.

20. Financing was achieved through an arrangement between Walt Disney Productions, American Broadcasting-Paramount Theaters, Western Printing and Lithographing Company, and Walt himself.

21. Karal Ann Marling, "Disneyland, 1955: Just Take the Santa Ana Freeway to the American Dream," *American Art*, 5:1/2, Winter-Spring, 1991, 168–207.

22. Eric Avila, "Popular Culture in the Age of White Flight: Film Noir, Disneyland, and the Cold War (Sub)Urban Imaginary," *Journal of Urban History*, 31:1 (Nov. 2004): 3–22. Acquisition of the seventeen small farms that made up the Anaheim site began in December 1953. Construction commenced in July 1954, one year before the park's projected opening.

23. Muir, "Walt's Wonderland," 71.

24. Terms like "guest" and "cast member," not yet standard in Disneyland's first year, will be used sparingly here; leaflet, *Your Disneyland: A Guide for Hosts and Hostesses* (Anaheim: Disneyland, Inc., 1955). See Jim Korkis, *The Unofficial Disneyland 1955 Companion: The Anecdotal Story of the Birth of the Happiest Place on Earth* (Theme Park Press, 2016), 102.

25. Although the term Magic Kingdom is the name of the first of the four parks at Walt Disney World in Florida (opened in 1971), the term was consistently used from 1955 for the California park.

26. Disney's staff examined recreation grounds nationwide in summer and fall 1954. Herb Ryman's *Aerial View of Disneyland* includes a separate themed space called Lilliputian Land between Fantasyland and Tomorrowland. Coney Island's Dreamland had a "city" of little people called Lilliputia.

27. Before Disney announced his *Disneyland* TV show and theme park, British writers frequently used the term "Disneyland" to indicate the studio and its world of animated characters. See for example the children's book, *The Disneyland Omnibus* (London: Collins, 1945); Robert Neuman, "Toad, Alice and Peter: From England to Disney-Land and Back Again," in *Interpreting and Experiencing Disney: Mediating the Mouse*, ed. Priscilla Hobbs (London: Intellect, 2021), chap. 3, n. 2.

28. On Disney's love of miniature objects, see Wolf Burchard, *Inspiring Walt Disney: The Animation of French Decorative Arts* (New York: The Metropolitan Museum of Art, 2021), 31–41.

29. On Disney's miniature railroad, see Broggie, *Walt Disney's Railroad Story*, chaps. 8–12.

30. The Imagineers, *Walt Disney Imagineering: A Behind the Dreams Look at Making the Magic Real* (New York: Hyperion, 1996): 90.

31. "$17,000,000 Project: Disneyland to Combine Fair, Museum, Kidland," *Billboard*, Feb. 19, 1955, 57, 63.

32. "Disneyland Designers," no. 7 in the series "Disney Family Album," Disney Channel, 1984. On Hench, see Charlie Haas, "Disneyland Is Good for You," *New West*, Dec. 4, 1978, 13–19; Watts, *Magic Kingdom*, 435–40.

33. Bob Gurr in *Walt: The Man behind the Myth*, directed by Jean-Pierre Isbouts (Walt Disney Family Foundation, 2001).

34. "Silk-Screen Signage: Disneyland Ride Posters," *"E" Ticket*, no. 31 (Spring 1999): 16–21.

35. Stephen M. Fjellman, *Vinyl Leaves: Walt Disney World and America* (Boulder: Westview Press, 1992), 257.

36. J.P. Telotte, *The Mouse Machine: Disney and Technology* (Urbana: University of Illinois Press, 2008), chap. 6; idem., "Theme Parks and Films: Play and Players," in *Disneyland and Culture: Essays on the Parks and Their Influence*, ed. Kathy

Merlock Jackson and Mark I. West (Jefferson: McFarland, 2011), 171–82. Todd James Pierce uses the expression "cinematic theme park" in the sense of the visitor being inside a movie and a Hollywood set: *Three Years in Wonderland: The Disney Brothers, C.V. Wood, and the Making of the Great American Theme Park* (Jackson: University Press of Mississippi, 2016), 5–6, 135–37, 207–08, 253–54. See also Brian Sibley, "Disneyland: The Greatest Walk-Through Cartoon Ever Drawn," *Animator* (Spring 1986): 16–19.

37. Christopher Finch, *The Art of Walt Disney: From Mickey Mouse to the Magic Kingdoms* (New York: Abrams, 1973), 392–93, 415.

38. Some observers argue for an analogy with live theater: Wolfert, "Walt Disney's Magic Kingdom," 144; Suzanne Rahn, "The Dark Ride of Snow White: Narrative Strategies at Disneyland," in *Disneyland and Culture: Essays on the Parks and Their Influence*, ed. Kathy Merlock Jackson and Mark I. West (Jefferson: McFarland, 2011), 87–88; others with television and its instant channel-flipping access to different subjects: Marling, "Disneyland, 1955," 201–06.

39. Gabler, *Walt Disney*, 553; Edwin Schallert, "Disney Spending $2,000,000 on New Dreams for Playland," *Los Angeles Times*, May 13, 1956, sect. 4, 1, 4.

40. Likely penned by a staff member, but reflecting Walt's point of view; Alfred Morgan Evans, *Walt Disney: Disneyland, World of Flowers* (Burbank: Walt Disney Productions, 1965), 3.

41. Thomas M. Pryor, "Hollywood Double Entente," *New York Times*, Mar. 11, 1954, X5.

42. Robert S. Sennett, *Hollywood Hoopla: Creating Stars and Selling Movies in the Golden Age of Hollywood* (New York: Billboard Books,1998).

43. Thomas, *Walt Disney*, 218.

44. As one of the few scholars with full access to the Imagineering archives, Marling, "Imagineering," made Disneyland a legitimate art historical subject; Watts, *Magic Kingdom*; Deborah Philips, *Fairground Attractions: A Genealogy of the Pleasure Ground* (London: Bloomsbury Academic, 2012), discusses the literary and theatrical origins of fun park attractions; Lauren Rabinovitz, *Electric*

Dreamland: Amusement Parks, Movies, and American Modernity (New York: Columbia University Press, 2012), focuses on the early ties between parks and movies; Cross and Walton, *Playful Crowd*, chap. 5, provides an excellent historical appraisal of Disneyland.

45. For example, Steven Watts says Disneyland "attracted hordes of eager visitors with a combination of fairy tale images derived from Disney's earlier animated masterpieces and sanitized historical images from his live-action films": "Walt Disney: Art and Politics in the American Century," *Journal of American History* 82:1 (June 1995): 108. Similarly: "Disney rejected the old cluster of mechanical rides and circus sideshows [of the amusement park] for carefully reproduced sets from his movies. ... In fact, the object was not primarily to transport the visitors to a historical site or even to evoke the sense of being in such a place, but to propel them into a story, peopled with familiar characters from a Disney movie"; Cross and Walton, *Playful Crowd*, 175–76.

46. Gabler, *Walt Disney*, 499.

47. Bethanee Bemis, "Mirror, Mirror for Us All: Disney Theme Parks and the Collective Memory of the American National Narrative," *The Public Historian* 42:1 (Feb. 2020): 54–79.

48. A. Bowdoin Van Riper, ed., *Learning from Mickey, Donald, and Walt: Essays on Disney's Edutainment Films* (Jefferson: McFarland, 2011).

49. Quoted in Muir, "Walt's Wonderland," 70.

50. Watts, *Magic Kingdom*, xvi.

51. Karal Ann Marling with Donna R. Braden, *Behind the Magic: 50 Years of Disneyland* (Dearborn: The Henry Ford, 2005), 33.

52. Disney, introducing the project (unrealized) for Liberty Street, a recreation of Boston, c. 1775; "The Liberty Story," *Disneyland* ABC-TV series; aired May 29, 1957.

53. Hopper, "Dream of Disneyland," A8.

54. R.S., "Disneyland Dedication from Coast," *New York Times*, July 18, 1955, 41.

55. Wiley Lee Umphlett, *Mythmakers of the American Dream: The Nostalgic Tradition in Popular Culture* (Lewisburg: Bucknell University Press, 1983), 140.

56. David E. James, *Allegories of*

Cinema: American Film in the Sixties (Princeton: Princeton University Press, 1989), 25.

57. Robert Sklar, *Movie Made America: A Cultural Story of American Movies* (New York: Vintage Books, 1975), 196–97. Of course, many moviemakers were less concerned with inculcating ideals than with making a profit by way of sensational subjects, as demonstrated by the Hays Code, in effect from the 1930s to the 1950s, as a self-censorship device intended to elevate moral content.

58. George F. Custen, *Twentieth Century's Fox: Darryl F. Zanuck and the Culture of Hollywood* (New York: BasicBooks, 1997), 190.

59. Vivian Sobchack, *Screening Space: The American Science Fiction Film* 2d ed. (New Brunswick: Rutgers University Press, 1997): 65. As Jane Marie Gaines and Cornelia Herzog put it, "Familiarity gets overcoded as authenticity": "The Fantasy of Authenticity in Western Costume," in *Back in the Saddle Again: New Essays on the Western*, ed. Edward Buscombe and Roberta E. Pearson (London: BFI, 1998), 174.

60. Pierce, *Three Years in Wonderland*; Korkis, *Unofficial Disneyland 1955 Companion*; Alastair Dallas, *Inventing Disneyland: The Unauthorized Story of the Team that Made Walt Disney's Dream Come True* (Orlando: Theme Park Press, 2018). See also Marcy Carriker Smothers, *Walt's Disneyland: A Walk in the Park with Walt Disney* (Los Angeles: Disney Editions, 2021). For a synthesis of previous scholarship, see Richard Snow, *Disney's Land: Walt Disney and the Invention of the Amusement Park That Changed the World* (New York: Scribner, 2019).

61. Several decades of academic writings on Disneyland and Walt Disney World have introduced a corpus of theoretical concepts: the theme park as hyperreality (Umberto Eco, *Travels in Hyperreality: Essays* [London: Picador, 1987]; Jean Baudrillard, *Simulations* [New York: Semiotext(e), 1983]); Disneyland as Utopia (Louis Marin, "Disneyland: A Degenerate Utopia," *Glyph* no. 1 [1977], 50–66; Priscilla Hobbs, *Walt's Utopia: Disneyland and American Mythmaking* [Jefferson: McFarland, 2015]); and the modernist notion of cinematization (Telotte, *Mouse Machine*).

62. Edited by Marty Sklar, who would rise to oversee Imagineering, *The Disneyland News* was both a "prop" complementing Main Street theming as a home-town newspaper, and a promotional tool for visitors to share with friends back home. See Korkis, *Unofficial Disneyland 1955 Companion*, 121–22. A special bonus awaited visitors to The Print Shop in the Opera House on Town Square, according to an ad in the paper: "Extra! Get your name in headlines in The Disneyland News: Imprinted while you wait!"; *Disneyland News*, 1:4, Oct. 10, 1955, 5.

Introduction

1. The first five studios in this list were vertically integrated, that is, owned their own theater chains and controlled distribution.

2. The terms are used by Bill Ballantine in an interview with Disney in "The Wonderful World of Walt Disney," *Vista II* (Winter 1966–67): 30–32; reprinted in Kathy Merlock Jackson, ed., *Walt Disney: Conversations* (Jackson: University Press of Mississippi. 2006), 135.

3. In a well-known anecdote, Walt described how a young fan asked him, if he did not draw Mickey Mouse or invent the stories, what indeed did he do at the studio? Disney replied by comparing himself to a bee, who flitted from one department to another, providing input at each stop; Robert de Roos, "The Magic Worlds of Walt Disney," *National Geographic*, 124:2, Aug. 1963, 162. Disney's staff described him as an orchestra conductor who assembled his musicians but did not bring sheet music; he was revered for his ability to nurture talents his artists did not realize they possessed. See comments by Bob Gurr in *Walt: The Man Behind the Myth*, directed by Jean-Pierre Isbouts (Walt Disney Family Foundation, 2001).

4. On Disney's managerial style, see Kathy Merlock Jackson, *Walt Disney: A Bio-Bibliography* (Westport: Greenwood Press, 1993), 106–07, 144–54; Steven Watts, *The Magic Kingdom: Walt Disney and the American Way of Life* (New York: Houghton Mifflin, 1997), chap. 20.

5. Eric Avila, "Popular Culture in the Age of White Flight: Film Noir,

Disneyland, and the Cold War (Sub)Urban Imaginary," *Journal of Urban History* 31:1 (Nov. 2004): 10.

6. Quoted (as "Hitchcock used to say") by Peter Bogdanovich in *Who the Devil Made It: Conversations with Legendary Film Directors* (New York: Ballantine Books, 1998), 699.

7. Bob Thomas, *Walt Disney: An American Original* (New York: Hyperion, 1994), 278.

8. Thomas Schatz, *The Genius of the System: Hollywood Filmmaking in the Studio Era* (New York: Pantheon Books, 1988), 11.

9. In 1939 alone, in one "swell foop," Shirley Temple presented Walt with an honorary Oscar, and seven smaller ones, for *Snow White and the Seven Dwarfs*.

10. Eric Smoodin, *Snow White and the Seven Dwarfs* (London: Palgrave Macmillan, 2012), 36–37.

11. Michael Barrier, *The Animated Man: A Life of Walt Disney* (Berkeley: University of California Press, 2007), 204–05; Neal Gabler, *Walt Disney: The Triumph of the American Imagination* (New York: Knopf, 2006), 518–19.

12. Peter Lev, *Twentieth Century-Fox: The Zanuck-Skouras Years, 1935–1965* (Austin: University of Texas Press, 2013), 43–49; George F. Custen, *Twentieth Century's Fox: Darryl F. Zanuck and the Culture of Hollywood* (New York: Basic Books, 1997). Animator Ward Kimball commented on Walt's relationship with Zanuck and the other tycoons: "The Wonderful World of Walt Disney," in Walter Wagner, ed., *You Must Remember This* (New York: Putnam, 1975); reprinted in Jackson, *Walt Disney Bio-Bibliography*, 148.

13. Don Eddy, "The Amazing Secret of Walt Disney," *American Magazine*, 160:2, Aug. 1955, 29, 110–15; Steven Clark and Rebecca Cline, *The Walt Disney Studios: A Lot to Remember* (Los Angeles: Disney Editions, 2019), 44–45.

14. Neal Gabler, *An Empire of Their Own: How the Jews Invented Hollywood* (New York: Doubleday, 1998).

15. Walt Disney, "Give Me the Movies," *Norfolk Virginian Pilot*, Sept. 2, 1938, sec. 2, 5.

16. Walt Disney, "Film Entertainment and Community Life," *Journal of the American Medical Association* 167:11 (July 12, 1958): 1342.

17. Gabler, *Walt Disney*, 77; Barrier, *Animated Man*, 265; Thomas, *Walt Disney*, 69–71.

18. June 1, 1924; Profiles in History, auction, May 14, 2011, lot 450.

19. Gladwin Hill, "Hollywood Is Shifting Her Civic Scenery," *New York Times*, May 8, 1955, 37.

20. Mark Shiel, *Hollywood Cinema, and the Real Los Angeles* (London: Reaktion, 2012), 56.

21. Stephanie Barron and Sheri Bernstein, *Reading California: Art, Image, and Identity, 1900–2000* (Berkeley: University of California Press, 2000), 134, where the phrase characterizes both California and Hollywood.

22. *Los Angeles Times* publisher Harry Chandler erected the Hollywoodland sign in 1923 as an advertisement for a real estate scheme. For the obscure origins of Hollywood's name, see Shiel, *Hollywood Cinema*, 46. Also Jeffrey Charles and Jill Watts, "(Un)Real Estate: Marketing Hollywood in the 1910s and 1920s," in *Hollywood Goes Shopping*, ed. David Desser and Garth S. Jowett (Minneapolis: University of Minnesota Press, 2000), 253–76; Leo Braudy, *The Hollywood Sign: Fantasy and Reality of an American Icon* (New Haven: Yale University Press, 2011).

23. Rufus Steele, "Behind the Screen: How the 'Movie' Is Made in the Valley of the New Arabian Nights," *Ladies Home Journal*, 32, Oct. 1915, 16; quoted in Shelley Stamp, "It's a Long Way to Filmland," in *American Cinema's Transitional Era: Audiences, Institutions, Practices*, ed. Charlie Keil and Shelley Stamp (Berkeley: University of California Press, 2004), 335.

24. "News of the Screen: Culver City-Hollywood Ends Dispute over Name," *New York Times*, Oct. 5, 1937, "Amusements," 29.

25. H. W. Little, "No Movie Was Ever Made in Hollywood," *Los Angeles Times*, May 30, 1937, 115; cited by Shiel, *Hollywood Cinema*, 195.

26. For early history and theory of the backlot, see Brian Jacobson, *Studios Before the System: Architecture, Technology, and the Emergence of Cinematic Space* (New York: Columbia University Press, 2015), chap. 5.

27. "As much as it's possible, now-a-days, everything is shot on the lot.

Forests, ships, country lands, mountains, canals, and all, are built up and tricked so that what, on the screen, may cover miles of ground, in reality only occupies a few acres of the back lot, or a few hundred square feet of the stage"; William Cameron Menzies, lecture, University of Southern California, Los Angeles, CA, 1929; reprinted in William Cameron Menzies, "Pictorial Beauty in the Photoplay," in *Hollywood Directors 1914–1940*, ed. Richard Koszarski (New York: Oxford University Press, 1976), 246. A further incentive to reuse backlot sets occurred during World War II, when the U.S. government restricted spending on materials for new sets.

28. Rudy Behlmer, ed., *Memo from Darryl F. Zanuck: The Golden Years at Twentieth Century-Fox* (New York: Grove, 1993), 17–18; italics added.

29. "Fox to Spend Half Million," *Los Angeles Times*, Nov. 14, 1925, A7.

30. Catherine Sullivan, "The Artist in Hollywood," *American Artist*, 14, Sept. 1950, 43.

31. Julie Lugo Cerra and Marc Wanamaker, *Movie Studios of Culver City* (Charleston: Arcadia, 2011), chap. 2.

32. Robert G. Duncan, "The Ince Studios," *Picture-Play Magazine*, Dec. 1915, 25, cited in Aida Hozic, *Hollyworld: Space, Power, and Fantasy in the American Economy* (Ithaca: Cornell University Press, 2001), 57.

33. "Great White Studio Where Pictures with Lion Brand Are Made," *Los Angeles Times*, July 25, 1923, 8–9, with an early photo of backlot stage flats seen from the rear.

34. "[Gibbons] has virtually recreated the world on the eighty acres that comprise Metro-Goldwyn-Mayer": Morton Eustis, "Designing for the Movies: Gibbons of MGM," *Theatre Arts Monthly*, 1937, 793.

35. John Drinkwater, *The Life and Adventures of Carl Laemmle* (New York: G. P. Putnam's Sons, 1931), 173. In the 1930s, Laemmle owned the Oswald the Lucky Rabbit cartoon series that Walt produced for one year in 1927, before he went on to create Mickey Mouse.

36. Drinkwater, *Laemmle*, 180.

37. Randy Bright, *Disneyland: Inside Story* (New York: Abrams, 1987), 96; Todd James Pierce, *Three Years in Wonderland:*

The Disney Brothers, C. V. Wood, and the Making of the Great American Theme Park (Jackson: University Press of Mississippi, 2016), 212–13.

38. Jacobson, *Studios before the System*, 192f.

39. "A City Built as a Background for Pictures," *Washington Herald*, May 23, 1915, 11.

40. Sam Gennawey, *Universal vs. Disney: The Unofficial Guide to American Theme Parks' Greatest Rivalry* (Birmingham: Keen Communications, 2015), 5.

41. "A City Built as a Background," 11.

42. Drinkwater, *Laemmle*, 175–76.

43. Jacobson, *Studios before the System*, 192–200.

44. Denise M. McKenna, "The City That Made the Pictures Move," Ph.D. diss., New York University (2008), 73–74.

45. Hozic, *Hollyworld: Space, Power, and Fantasy*, 10. Robbins Barstow's film, *Disneyland Dream*, may be viewed in online postings.

46. In a rare aperçu from 1930, in the photo book *Hollywood as It Really Is*, British author Erwin Debries made a connection between the Hollywood backlot and the streets of Hollywood itself, lined with "the most weird buildings. Red-tiled bungalows in the Spanish Mexican style alternate with the plainest new American types of building. Banks like marble renaissance palaces stand alongside glaringly painted Dutch houses, near which real windmills are turning." Even more remarkably, Debries extended the analogy to include a typical fun fair: "The streets of Hollywood are as much a patchwork as the scenery in its studios, and more like an amusement park..."; Erwin Debries, *Hollywood as It Really Is* (London: Routledge, 1930), viii.

47. *Life in Hollywood*, directed by Maurice Kline (Martin Murray Productions, 1947); posted by Prelinger Archives, San Francisco, on archive.org.

48. Shiel, *Hollywood Cinema*, 139–41, 195–204.

49. Quoted by Ward Kimball, in Thomas, *Walt Disney*, 218.

50. Thomas M. Pryor, "Land of Fantasia Is Rising on Coast," *New York Times*, May 2, 1954, 86; "A Wonderful World: Growing Impact of the Disney Art," *Newsweek*, Apr. 18, 1955, 60. Disneyland publicity continually emphasized the "personages

from the arts, television and motion pictures [who] were daily visitors at the Anaheim playland," where they were visible to park guests. See for example "Celebrities Relax at Magic Kingdom," *Disneyland News*, 1:4, Oct. 10, 1955, 7; "Magic Kingdom Top Southern California Attraction," *Disneyland News*, 1:4, Oct. 10, 1955, 1, 9, which cites actors James Stewart, Natalie Wood, Margaret O'Brien, and Jerry Lewis.

51. On the history of art direction in the classical period, see Juan Antonio Ramirez, *Architecture for the Screen: A Critical Study of Set Design in Hollywood's Golden Age*, trans. John F. Moffitt (Jefferson: McFarland, 2004); Beverly Heisner, *Hollywood Art: Art Direction in the Days of the Great Studios* (Jefferson: McFarland, 1990); Jane Barnwell, *Production Design: Architects of the Screen* (London: Wallflower, 2004); Lucy Fischer, ed., *Art Direction and Production Design* (New Brunswick: Rutgers University Press, 2015), chap. 1–3.

52. Arthur Millier, "Art Directors Would Show Films How to Save Money," *Los Angeles Times*, July 2, 1933, A1.

53. "Movie Illusions: Hollywood Technicians Create Reality inside Studios," *Life*, 17:6, Jan. 8, 1945, 71–72. "In the 50 years or so since the motion picture was invented, its technicians have turned out an ever more convincing series of illusions. This ability to make its audiences believe that they are looking at a real Sahara or a real battle has done much to place Hollywood in its pre-eminent technical position over its British, French and Russian rivals."

54. Sullivan, "Artist in Hollywood," 46.

55. Cedric Gibbons, "The Art Director," in *Behind the Scenes: How Films Are Made*, ed. Steven Watts (London: A. Barker, 1938), 41. MGM, following a stipulation in Gibbons' contract, credited him as art director on nearly all of the films—over two thousand features and shorts—produced during his tenure at the studio. This has tended to obscure the names of those who worked under him and were for the most part the actual designer. He is best remembered as the creator of the Oscar statuette: Howard Gutner, *MGM Style: Cedric Gibbons and the Art of the Golden Age of Hollywood* (Guilford: Lyons Press, 2019). For an early effort to reclaim the legacy of MGM's chief designers, see

John Hambley and Patrick Downing, *The Art of Hollywood* (London: Thames Television, 1979). See also D.W.C., "Meet the Set Designer: The Less He Is Noticed, the Better—So Says Van Nest Polglase of RKO," *New York Times*, Aug. 16, 1935, X4.

56. Laurence Irving, *Designing for the Movies: The Memoirs of Laurence Irving* (Lanham: Scarecrow Press, 2005): 109. He went on to say, "Disney was certainly the most fulfilled artist in Hollywood. Success had not cooled his boyish enthusiasms. He wore the mantle of his independence with a flourish."

57. These more finished drawings measured around 18 by 24 inches; Sullivan, "Artist in Hollywood," 42–43. For an illustrated survey of the creative process directed at a lay audience, see "Movie Making: It Is a Complex Business of Machines and Technicians," *Life*, 18:2, Jan. 8, 1945, 69–77; also, Ralph Flint, "Cinema's Art Directors: Little Known to the Public, They Are Back Stage, Among the Lords of the Screen," *New York Times*, Nov. 22, 1931, X7 (135).

58. Sullivan, "Artist in Hollywood," 44.

59. Gibbons, "Art Director," 45–46. Few contemporary publications treat in detail the process of movie set design; see Edward Carrick, *Designing for Films* (London: The Studio Publications, 1949).

60. "Movie Illusions," 78.

61. "Movie Illusions," 70–71.

62. Hill, "Hollywood Is Shifting," 37.

63. Ed Ainsworth, "Disneyland Readied by 'Mr. Magic,'" *Los Angeles Times*, June 23, 1955, A1. On Walt Disney's collection of miniature objects, see Eddy, "Amazing Secret," 46.

64. "A Look at Disneyland from a Construction and Maintenance Standpoint," *Construction Equipment Operation and Maintenance*, 9:5, Sept.-Oct. 1956, 6; advertisement for the Red Wagon Inn, *Disneyland News*, 2:2, Aug. 1956, 7.

65. David Bordwell, *Classical Hollywood Cinema* (New York: Routledge, 2015), 100. Silent-movie director D. W. Griffith confirmed that verisimilitude was a prerequisite in the design of the elaborate sets: "In dealing with an historical subject ... which is placed in a certain distant period of history, months and sometimes years of research work of a regular department is given to obtaining the correct

idea of the manners, customs, costumes, and settings of the period in which you are placing your story." One of the intertitles of *The Birth of a Nation* (1915) specifically calls attention to the veracity of a scene: "AN HISTORICAL FACSIMILE of the State House of Representatives of South Carolina as it was in 1870"; Fischer, *Art Direction and Production Design*, 31.

66. Gibbons, "Art Director," 44–45.

67. See Fred Anderson, "The Warner Bros. Research Department: Putting History to Work in the Classic Studio Era," *Public Historian* 17:1 (Winter 1995): 51–69; Steven Bingen, *Warner Bros.: Hollywood's Ultimate Backlot* (Lanham: Taylor Trade, 2014), 65–66; Steven Bingen, Stephen X. Sylvester, and Michael Troyan, *M-G-M: Hollywood's Greatest Backlot* (Solana Beach: Santa Monica Press, 2011), 59; Steven Bingen, *Paramount: City of Dreams* (Guildford: Taylor Trade, 2017), 232–36; Michael Troyan, Stephen X. Sylvester, and Jeffrey P. Thompson, *Twentieth Century Fox: A Century of Entertainment* (Guilford: Lyons Press, 2017), 83–89.

68. Louis Van den Ecker, "A Veteran's View of Hollywood Authenticity," *Hollywood Quarterly*, 4:4, Summer, 1950, 324–25.

69. Gibbons, "Art Director," 47–48. See also Frank S. Nugent, "Property Man: New Style," *New York Times*, Nov. 25, 1934, X5.

70. "It is a handicap of the camera that it does not photograph what the mind sees. If, for instance, you photograph a romantic location such as a picturesque European street, you will have an accurate reproduction—minus the atmosphere, texture, and color. Hence it is always better to substitute a set that is the impression of that street as the mind sees it, slightly romanticized, simplified, and over-textured": William Cameron Menzies, "Cinema Design," *Theatre Arts Monthly*, 13:9, Sept. 1929, 676, 681.

71. Ramirez, *Architecture for the Screen*, chap. 5.

72. Gibbons, "Art Director," 47.

73. Menzies, "Pictorial Beauty in the Photoplay," 246.

74. George P. Erengis, "Cedric Gibbons," *Films in Review*, 16, 1965, 230.

75. Hedda Hopper, "Hollywood Sets Would Fool Mother Nature: Scenic Experts Make Land, Sea and Sky Look More Realistic Than Reality," *Los Angeles Times*, Nov. 26, 1939, C3.

76. Mark Monahan, "Film-makers on Film: Ken Adam," *Telegraph*, Jan. 14, 2006; Film-makers on film: Ken Adam (telegraph.co.uk)

77. Erengis, "Cedric Gibbons," 226. Gibbons took the same approach in recreating the Palace of Versailles for *Marie Antoinette* (1938): "To duplicate so well known, and dramatically unsuitable, an edifice in Culver City would have been folly. The actual Palace has no 'main' entrance of any importance, the principal entry being at the far end, the wrong end, of a long wall. There is no stairway of any consequence inside the structure that would befit any of the Louis, let alone Norma Shearer. And the 300-foot-long Hall of Mirrors would photograph like a very glittery tunnel. So, from a collection of 12,000 photographs made by an MGM crew that had spent a year in France, Gibbons and William Horning built 98 interior and exterior sets to depict revolutionary France. No one quibbled because they had not slavishly reproduced a single room at Versailles" (230).

78. Custen, *Twentieth Century's Fox*, 15; Boris Kachka, "The Unreal World," *New York Times Magazine*, Sept. 24, 2017, 143–48. Gabrielle Esperdy makes the point that the use of secondary sources for inspiration often resulted in simplification and exaggeration: "From Instruction to Consumption: Architecture and Design in Hollywood Movies of the 1930s," *Journal of American Culture* 30:2 (June 2007): 205.

Chapter 1

1. As host of "The Disneyland Story," the first episode of the *Disneyland* TV series, broadcast by ABC, October 27, 1954; much repeated in publicity and publications. See for example Public Relations Department, "A Visit to Disneyland," *Walt Disney's Magic Kingdom Disneyland*, opening day press kit (Anaheim: Disneyland, Inc., 1955; facsimile reprint, Disneyland Press & Publicity, 2005), 1; Richard Snow, *Disney's Land: Walt Disney and the Invention of the American Amusement Park That Changed the World* (New York: Scribner, 2019), 158.

2. Wayne Franklin, for instance, calls Disneyland's Main Street "the epitome of commercialism" in his foreword to Richard Francaviglia, *Main Street Revisited: Time, Space, and Image-Building in Small-Town America* (Iowa City: University Press of Iowa, 1996), xii. For an excellent characterization of the space, see Deborah Philips, *Fairground Attractions: A Genealogy of the Pleasure Ground* (London: Bloomsbury Academic, 2012), chap. 11. She makes the connection with Hollywood movies in a brief paragraph and focuses instead on consumerism. For a review of critical approaches, including Main Street as a simulacrum, which I do not address here, see Stephen Rowley, *Movie Towns and Sitcom Suburbs: Building Hollywood's Ideal Communities* (Basingstoke: Palgrave Macmillan, 2015), chap. 4.

3. For the business side of Main Street, see Dave Mason, "The Merchants of Main Street," *Frontier Magazine*, 5:4, July-Aug. 2003, 16–18f; and Todd James Pierce, *Three Years in Wonderland: The Disney Brothers, C. V. Wood, and the Making of the Great American Theme Park* (Jackson: University Press of Mississippi, 2016), 139-48.

4. This was not, of course, every American's idea of a happier time. For a recent critique of Main Street's failings, see media historian Susan Douglas's remarks in online publicity for the PBS series, *American Experience: Walt Disney*, where she calls the park "a fake view of America … [that] sought to keep marginalized people in their place"; YouTube, "Interview: Walt Disney's America," clip, season 27, episode 8 (Sept. 2015). I treat problems of racial and ethnic stereotyping, and marketing toward Black patrons, in chapters 2 and 3.

5. Richard W. Longstreth, *The Buildings of Main Street: A Guide to American Commercial Architecture* (Walnut Creek: AltaMira Press, 2000), 24–35.

6. Richard Francaviglia, "Main Street U.S.A.: A Comparison/Contrast of Streetscapes in Disneyland and Walt Disney World," *Journal of Popular Culture* 15:1 (Summer 1981): 143.

7. I am indebted to Mark Licht, who shared his vivid recollections of experiencing the wonders of Main Street as a child in 1955-56.

8. For a comprehensive overview of Main Street as an idea and a place, see Miles Orvell, *The Death and Life of Main Street: Small Towns in American Memory, Space, and Community* (Chapel Hill: University of North Carolina Press, 2012). For a complex contemporary view, see Robert S. Lynd and Helen Merrell Lynd's *Middletown* books; for example, *Middletown: A Study in Contemporary American Culture* (New York: Harcourt Brace, 1929). See also the photo essay by Margaret Bourke-White, "Muncie, Ind. Is the Great U.S. 'Middletown,'" *Life*, 2:19, May 10, 1937, 15–25.

9. Eric Avila, *Popular Culture in the Age of White Flight: Fear and Fantasy in Suburban Los Angeles* (Berkeley: University of California Press, 2006), chap. 4.

10. Griffin Smith, Jr., "Small-Town America: An Endangered Species?" *National Geographic*, 175:2, Feb. 1989, 188–89. Around the time of early suburban development, the pastoralist benefits of small-town life were promoted by *The City*, a film created for the 1939 New York World's Fair (posted on YouTube); for the film's connections with Tomorrowland's Autopia, see chap. 4.

11. Francaviglia, *Main Street Revisited*, chap. 3.

12. This chapter expands my essay: Robert Neuman, "Disneyland's Main Street, USA, and Its Sources in Hollywood, USA," in *Disneyland and Culture: Essays on the Parks and Their Influence*, ed. Kathy Merlock Jackson and Mark I. West (Jefferson: McFarland, 2011), 37–58; originally published in *Journal of American Culture* 31:1 (2008): 83–97.

13. Marcy Carriker Smothers, *Walt's Disneyland: A Walk in the Park with Walt Disney* (Los Angeles: Disney Editions, 2021), 50, 53.

14. "Turn Back the Clock: Complete American Small Town of 1900 Era Reproduced Here," *Disneyland News*, 1:1, July 1955, 3.

15. "Main Street Is Historic Replica," *Disneyland News* 1:1, July 1955, 3.

16. Jack Jungmeyer, "Under the Gaslight," *Disneyland News*, 1:1, July 1955, 3. On the intersection between nostalgia and commerce, see Per Strömberg, "Et in Chronotopia Ego: Main Street Architecture as a Rhetorical Device in Theme Parks and Outlet Villages," in *A Reader in*

Themed and Immersive Spaces, ed. Scott A. Lukas (Pittsburgh: ETC Press, 2016), 83–93.

17. Jack E. Janzen, "Main Street: Walt's Perfect Introduction to Disneyland," *"E" Ticket*, no. 14 (Winter 1992–93): 24–33. For a detailed look at the shops, wares, and personnel, see Jeff Koenig, *The 55ers: The Pioneers Who Settled Disneyland* (Irvine: Bonaventure Press, 2019), 91-154.

18. "Main Street's Market Captures Feel of the Past," *Disneyland News*, 1:11, May 1956, 4.

19. The word "weenie" was used to signify a plot device in silent films. See Martha Bayless, "Disney's Castles and the Work of the Medieval in the Magic Kingdom," in *The Disney Middle Ages: A Fairy-Tale and Fantasy Past*, eds. Tison Pugh and Susan Aronstein (New York: Palgrave Macmillan, 2012), 47, 55 nn. 16–17. Also Karal Ann Marling, "Disneyland 1955: Just Take the Santa Ana Freeway to the American Dream," *American Art*, 5:1/2, Winter-Spring, 1991, 197: "Disney placed great stock in what he called the "weenie" [sic] theory of crowd movement whereby an eye-catching object—a "weenie," like the castle at the end of Main Street—pulls the guest in that direction, past the prompts and cues that make up the visual script along the way. Each Disneyland visitor thus becomes an actor in a drama arranged, like a movie, in an edited sequence of sights and sounds."

20. Orvell, *Death and Life of Main Street*, 10–11.

21. On Main Street's strolling barbershop quartet, the Dapper Dans, see Gage Averill, *Four Parts, No Waiting: A Social History of American Barbershop Harmony* (New York: Oxford University Press, 2003), 144–46. For Italian immigrant Sam Iezza, "one of the few organ grinders left, a reminder of an earlier era," his monkey Josephine, and vintage Monalari barrel organ, visible on the "Dateline Disneyland" park premiere telecast, see "Happy Pair: When Sam Grinds Josephine Dances," *Disneyland News*, 1:4, Oct. 1955, 4.

22. "In the Good Old Summertime: 'Good Old Days' Relived by Park Band Concerts," *Disneyland News*, 2:3, Sept. 1955, 17; "Music Makers March: The Disneyland Band Story," *Disneyland News*, 1:11, May 1956, 10; Koenig, *The 55ers*, 108–17.

23. Sam Abbott, "Disneyland Sets New Designs for Rides, Exhibit Layouts," *Billboard*, June 26, 1954, 80.

24. "Fashions of Yesterday in Main Street Parade," *Disneyland News*, 1:9, March 10, 1956, 1. For the Fall 1955 meeting of the Southern California Horseless Carriage Club in the park, see "Disneyland Visited by Southern California Group," *Horseless Carriage Gazette* 17:6, Nov.-Dec. 1955, 24–25.

25. Francaviglia, *Main Street Revisited*, 147–51.

26. Francaviglia, "Main Street U.S.A.," 156; Karal Ann Marling, "Imagineering the Disney Theme Parks," in *Designing Disney's Theme Parks: The Architecture of Reassurance*, ed. Karal Ann Marling (Montreal: Canadian Centre for Architecture, 1997), 89–90.

27. Steven Watts, *The Magic Kingdom: Walt Disney and the American Way of Life* (New York: Houghton Mifflin Company, 1997), 22. Among many other writers who claim Main Street was patterned after Marceline's Kansas Street, see Christopher Finch, *Walt Disney's America* (New York: Abbeville Press, 1978), 49; Katherine Greene and Richard Greene, *The Man behind the Magic: The Story of Walt Disney* (New York: Viking, 1991), 124; Brian Burnes, Robert W. Butler, and Dan Viets, *Walt Disney's Missouri: The Roots of a Creative Genius* (Kansas City: Kansas City Star Books, 2002), 34–35; Sharon Zukin, *Landscapes of Power: From Detroit to Disney World* (Berkeley: University of California Press, 1991), 222.

28. Burnes, Butler, and Viets, *Walt Disney's Missouri*, 24.

29. Walt Disney, "The Marceline I Knew," *Marceline News*, Sept. 2, 1938, 1. On Disney's tendency to mythologize his early life, see Watts, *Magic Kingdom*, 4-7, 14, 22–23.

30. The *Tour Guide of Marceline, Missouri, Walt Disney's Home Town* (Kansas City: Eisterhold Associates, 2001), 6, 26, claims that during his 1946 trip Disney filmed the entire length of Main Street while researching the town in anticipation of creating a theme park (undocumented); he was not planning Disneyland at this time. See also Smothers, *Walt's Disneyland*, 59. For a cautious view and a survey of Disney's trips back to Missouri, see

Burnes, Butler, and Viets, *Walt Disney's Missouri*, 166. In his 1966 biography of Disney, Bob Thomas mentions that during a pre-opening tour of Main Street, Walt told him "This is exactly like the small-town streets I remember from my boyhood." I suspect that Thomas was merely folding the Marceline legend into his narrative: *Magician of the Movies: The Life of Walt Disney* (New York: Grosset & Dunlap, 1966), 158; (Theme Park Press, 2016 repr.), 144. Thomas opened his obituary of Walt by calling him "a Missouri farm boy"; "Walt Disney Dies; 'Genius' of Films," *Atlanta Constitution*, Dec. 16, 1966, 1.

31. Arthur Gordon, "Walt Disney," *Look*, 19:15, July 26, 1955, 29.

32. Diane Disney Miller and Pete Martin, "My Dad Walt Disney," *Saturday Evening Post*, 229:20, Nov. 17, 1956, 70. Martin largely penned the text, based on interviews with Walt. The title of the final installment hints further at the connection but without any follow-up: "Conclusion: Small Boy's Dream Come True: In Disneyland Walt Re-created the World of His Boyhood," *Saturday Evening Post*, 229:2, Jan. 5, 1957, 24, 80–82.

33. Hedda Hopper, "Hope, Lollobrigida Will Do London Film," *Los Angeles Times*, July 5, 1956, B8.

34. Walt Disney, *Disneyland* (Verona: Mondadori, 1964), 28-31. The Marceline myth became official history; see for example The Imagineers, *The Imagineering Field Guide to Disneyland* (New York: Disney Editions, 2008), 24-25. In 1989 senior designer John Hench alleged in an interview that Disney, in considering shop types for Disneyland in 1953, recalled businesses in Marceline: Marling, "Imagineering," 60, undocumented.

35. "An Interview with Harper Goff," *"E" Ticket*, no. 14 (Winter 1992-93): 7.

36. Kathy Merlock Jackson, *Walt Disney: A Bio-Bibliography* (Westport: Greenwood Press, 1993), 48-49; Michael Broggie, *Walt Disney's Railroad Story: The Small-Scale Fascination That Led to a Full-Scale Kingdom* (Pasadena: Pentrex, 1997), 88-91.

37. Marling, "Imagineering," 39-42, 52-54.

38. "Walt Disney Make-Believe Land Project Planned Here," *Burbank Daily Review*, Mar. 27, 1952, A.1; Michael Barrier, *The Animated Man: A Life of Walt Disney* (Berkeley: University of California Press, 2007), 233-34.

39. Jim Korkis, *The Unofficial Disneyland 1955 Companion: The Anecdotal Story of the Birth of the Happiest Place on Earth* (Theme Park Press, 2016), 19.

40. Thomas M. Pryor, "Disney To Enter TV Field in Fall," *New York Times*, Mar. 30, 1954, 24; Thomas M. Pryor, "Hollywood Double Entente," *New York Times*, Apr. 11, 1954, X5; Karal Ann Marling, "Disneyland, 1955: Just Take the Santa Ana Freeway to the American Dream," *American Art* 5:1/2, Winter-Spring 1991, 188, 203.

41. Thomas M. Pryor, "Land of Fantasia Is Rising on Coast," *New York Times*, May 2, 1954, 86.

42. "A Wonderful World: Growing Impact of the Disney Art," *Newsweek*, 45:16, Apr. 18, 1955, 60.

43. Woodrow Wirsig, "Companionably Yours: Disneyland," *Woman's Home Companion*, 81, June 1954, 12.

44. "New Disney Show Listed for Radio," *New York Times*, Nov. 25, 1955, 55; "New Radio Show Broadcast from Disneyland," *Disneyland News*, 1:6, December 16, 1955), 1; Bruce Gordon and David Mumford, *Disneyland: The Nickel Tour*, 2d ed. (Santa Clarita: Camphor Tree, 2000), 102-03.

45. Neal Gabler, *Walt Disney: The Triumph of the American Imagination* (New York: Knopf, 2006), 12. On Walt Disney's lifelong passion for trains and its impact on Disneyland, see Broggie, *Walt Disney's Railroad Story*; for an overview of Disney features and shorts that include trains, see Dana Amendola, *All Aboard: The Wonderful World of Disney Trains* (Los Angeles: Disney Editions, 2015).

46. Illustrated in Jeff Kurtti and Bruce Gordon, *The Art of Disneyland* (New York: Disney Editions, 2006), 9; "Main Gate," *"E" Ticket*, no. 14 (Winter 1992-93): 3.

47. Illustrated in Herbert Dickens Ryman, Bruce Gordon, and David Mumford, *A Brush with Disney: An Artist's Journey* (Santa Clarita: Camphor Tree Publishers, 2000), 144-45.

48. Karal Ann Marling with Donna R. Braden, *Behind the Magic: Fifty Years of Disneyland* (Dearborn: The Henry Ford, 2005), 40-41; Marling, "Imagineering," 59.

49. Marling, "Imagineering," 89; also Francaviglia, "Main Street U.S.A.," 147,

152; Finch, *Walt Disney's America* (1978), 63.

50. Watts, *Magic Kingdom*, 437; Gabler, *Walt Disney*, 497.

51. Emanuel Levy, *Small-Town America in Film: The Decline and Fall of Community* (New York: Continuum, 1991), 16. For a subgenre of the type, see Noel Brown, *The Hollywood Family Film: A History, from Shirley Temple to Harry Potter* (London: I. B. Tauris, 2012), especially chap. 3.

52. Marling, *Behind the Magic*, 38.

53. Levy, *Small-Town America*, 265-70; Kenneth MacKinnon, *Hollywood's Small Towns: An Introduction to the American Small-Town Movie* (Metuchen: Scarecrow Press, 1984), 191-98.

54. John Hench with Peggy Van Pelt, *Designing Disney: Imagineering and the Art of the Show* (New York: Disney Editions, 2003), 10. For a discussion of Wilder's play in the context of Main-Street iconography, see Orvell, *Death and Life of Main Street*, 114–21.

55. Nezar AlSayyad, *Cinematic Urbanism: A History of the Modern from Reel to Real* (New York: Routledge, 2006), 57.

56. Illustrated in Marling, "Imagineering," 59.

57. Francaviglia, *Main Street Revisited*, 176; Watts, *Magic Kingdom*, 13; Mark I. Pinsky, "The Gospel According to Disney," *Orlando Sentinel*, August 8, 2004, G1, G4.

58. Rowley, *Movie Towns and Sitcom Suburbs*, 27-28.

59. Rowley, *Movie Towns and Sitcom Suburbs*, 25-26. See also Steven Jacobs, *The Wrong House: The Architecture of Alfred Hitchcock* (Rotterdam, 010 Publishers, 2007), 92-101. The invasion of the small town by a malevolent character also underlies the plot of the Orson Welles film, *The Stranger* (1946).

60. New England Street on the Twentieth Century-Fox backlot purportedly stood in for Deeds' Mandrake Falls house; AFI Catalog of Feature films online: *Mr. Deeds Goes to Town*; Michael Troyan, Stephen X. Sylvester, and Jeffrey P. Thompson, *Twentieth Century Fox: A Century of Entertainment* (Guilford: Lyons Press, 2017), 288–93. The train station sequence appears to have been filmed in an actual rural station.

61. Randy Bright, *Disneyland: Inside Story* (New York: Abrams, 1987), 68.

62. Janzen, "Main Street: Walt's Perfect Introduction," 30–31; "Visualizing Disneyland with: Sam McKim," "*E*" *Ticket*, no. 18 (Spring 1994): 8-11; Barrier, *Animated Man*, 226–27.

63. "Harder than Movie Set: Nostalgic Main Street Designed by Rubottom," *Disneyland News*, 1:3, Sept. 1955, 15.

64. "Planning the First Disney Parks: A Talk with Marvin Davis," "*E*" *Ticket*, no. 28 (Winter 1997): 10-13. Notice the bright colors of the store fronts in the rare photo of the model. For studio research libraries, see Troyan, Sylvester, and Thompson, *Twentieth Century Fox*, 83–85; Fred Andersen, "The Warner Bros. Research Department: Putting History to Work in the Classic Studio Era," *Public Historian* 17:1 (Winter 1995): 51–69.

65. Juan Antonio Ramirez, *Architecture for the Screen: A Critical Study of Set Design in Hollywood's Golden Age*, trans. John F. Moffit (Jefferson: McFarland, 2004), 54–66, 81–96.

66. Steven Bingen, Stephen X. Sylvester, and Michael Troyan, *M-G-M: Hollywood's Greatest Backlot* (Solana Beach: Santa Monica Press, 2011), 143. Steven Spielberg on forced perspective: "Funny thing about movies: They make everything look bigger. Actors look bigger. They make directors seem bigger. But we're not. They're really not"; Anthony Breznican, "Steven Spielberg's Secret World," *Entertainment Weekly*, no. 1421, July 1, 2016, 38.

67. Gabler, *Walt Disney*, 533.

68. Gladwin Hill, "Disneyland Gets Its Last Touches," *New York Times*, July 9, 1955, 32.

69. Ira Wolfert, "Walt Disney's Magic Kingdom," *Reader's Digest*, 76, Apr. 1960, 145–46.

70. Bingen, Sylvester, and Troyan, *M-G-M*, 143; Francaviglia, *Main Street Revisited*, 147.

71. "Park Brick Work Varied," *Disneyland News*, 1:3, Sept. 1955, 19.

72. Ramirez, *Architecture for the Screen*, 86.

73. Disney, *Disneyland*, 29.

74. "Red Wagon Inn Presents History with Fine Food," *Disneyland News*, 2:1, July 1956, 6-7.

75. Elaine Woo, "Emile Kuri: Oscar-Winning Designer Worked on Disneyland," *Los Angeles Times*, Oct. 13, 2000,

B8. Kuri was responsible for the Victorian interior of the Disney family apartment on the second floor of the Fire Station: Smothers, *Walt's Disneyland*, 34–35.

76. Richard Neupert, "Painting a Plausible World: Disney's Color Prototypes," in *Disney Discourse: Producing the Magic Kingdom*, ed. Eric Smoodin (New York: Routledge, 1994), 106–17. Through contractual arrangements, Natalie M. Kalmus, wife of Herbert Kalmus, the developer of Technicolor, closely oversaw the studios' use of the technique; see her essay "Colour," in *Behind the Screen: How Films Are Made*, ed. Steven Watts (London: A. Barker, 1938), 117–27.

77. Hench, *Designing Disney*, 108–11; Mildred Houghton Comfort, *Walt Disney, Master of Fantasy* (Minneapolis: Denison, 1968), 145.

78. The Imagineers, *Walt Disney Imagineering: A Behind the Dreams Look at Making the Magic Real* (New York: Hyperion, 1996), 100–01.

79. James Curtis, *Between Flops: A Biography of Preston Sturges* (New York: Harcourt, Brace, Jovanovitch, 1982), 178. Among other films, the set represented the mythical town of Rivers End in *Meet Dr. Christian*, 1939. For the Paramount Ranch and Tom Sawyer Street, see Steven Bingen, *Paramount: City of Dreams* (Guilford: Taylor Trade, 2017), 283–92.

80. The transition from horse-drawn traffic to motorized vehicles took place earlier in cities than in small towns. The presence of both modes in a movie signified a rural locale.

81. AlSayyad, *Cinematic Urbanism*, 45–70; Jeanine Basinger, *The It's a Wonderful Life Book* (New York: Alfred A. Knopf, 1994), 23–27.

82. Michael Willian reconstructs the plan and location of the shops of Genesee Street: *The Essential It's a Wonderful Life: A Scene-by-Scene Guide to the Classic Film* (Chicago: Chicago Review Press, 2006), 9.

83. Richard Shale, *Donald Duck Joins Up: The Walt Disney Studio during World War II* (Ann Arbor: UMI Research Press, 1982), 38–40.

84. Bingen, Sylvester, and Troyan, *M-G-M*, 154–65; see 290–93 for extensive lists of films shot on these sets.

85. Scott Eyman, *Lion of Hollywood: The Life and Legend of Louis B. Mayer*

(New York: Simon and Schuster, 2005), 323–27.

86. Neal Gabler, *An Empire of Their Own: How the Jews Invented Hollywood* (New York: Doubleday, 1998), 119.

87. Mickey Rooney, *Life Is Too Short* (New York: Villard, 1991), 76.

88. MacKinnon, *Hollywood's Small Towns*, 19.

89. Hugh Fordin, *The Movies' Greatest Musicals: Produced in Hollywood USA by the Freed Unit* (New York: Frederick Unger, 1984), 95–96; Bingen, Sylvester, and Troyan, *M-G-M*, 236–39.

90. Beth Genné, "Vincente Minnelli's Style in Microcosm: The Establishing Sequence of 'Meet Me in St. Louis,'" *Art Journal* 43:3 (Fall 1983): 252.

91. To achieve authenticity, Alfred Hitchcock chose Second Empire as the style for the house in *Psycho* (1960), because it typified California domestic architecture. Once the film was released, however, the style became popular in the horror movie genre; Jacobs, *Wrong House*, 127–29.

92. Bob Thomas, *Walt Disney: An American Original* (New York: Hyperion, 1994), 278; Smothers, *Walt's Disneyland*, 59.

93. Troyan, Sylvester, and Thompson, *Twentieth Century Fox*, 288–93, 304–08, 653–54. For the City Streets section of RKO's 40-Acres backlot, where exteriors for such period films as *The Magnificent Ambersons* (1942) were shot, see Steven Bingen, *Hollywood's Lost Backlot: 40 Acres of Glamour and Mystery* (Guilford: Lyons Press, 2019), 116, 173–90.

94. George F. Custen, *Twentieth Century's Fox: Darryl F. Zanuck and the Culture of Hollywood* (New York: BasicBooks, 1997), 14–15, 199–205, 342–47; Peter Lev, *Twentieth Century-Fox: The Zanuck-Skouras Years, 1935–1965* (Austin: University of Texas Press, 2013), 118–26.

95. For Midwest Street on the Warner Bros. backlot, see Steven Bingen, *Warner Bros.: Hollywood's Ultimate Backlot* (Lanham: Taylor Trade, 2014), 167–75, 250–52. On the use of sets in *Kings Row* (Warner Bros., 1942) to denote class distinctions, see Charles Affron and Mirella Jona Affron, *Sets in Motion: Art Direction and Film Narrative* (New Brunswick: Rutgers University Press, 1995), 77–81.

96. Leonard Maltin, *The Disney Films* (New York: Hyperion, 1995), 88-89.

97. Amendola, *All Aboard*, 55–57. One of the songs composed for the movie, but not used, celebrated townsfolk going out to greet the train: "Ridin' on the 'Ninety-Nine'"; Russell Schroeder, *Disney's Lost Chords* (Robbinsville: Voigt Publications, 2007): 1:86–90.

98. *Walt Disney's Main Street Coloring Fun* (Racine: Whitman Publishing, 1955).

99. "Reviewer Finds Main St. Cinema Movies Live Up to Advance Bill," *Disneyland News*, 1:3, Sept. 1955, 18–19.

100. Jimmy Starr, "Guest Columnist: Starr Finds Laughter, Glee for Kids at Disneyland," *Disneyland News*, 1:3, Sept. 1955, 2; "Movie Memories: Main Street Now Boasts 'Show Business' Exhibit," *Disneyland News*, 1:10, Apr. 1956, 8.

101. "'Magic Kingdom' Hosts Entertainment Figures, Film, TV Personalities," *Disneyland News*, 1:9, Mar. 10, 1954, 1, 4. See also "Celebrities Enjoy Disneyland," *Disneyland News*, 1:3, Sept. 1955, 4.

102. "Hollywood Comes to Disneyland," *Disneyland News*, 1:9, Mar. 10, 1956, 7.

103. "'Magic Kingdom' Guests Will Meet Celebrities," *Disneyland News*, 1:9, Mar. 10, 1956, 4.

104. "Disney Artists Paint Visitors," *Disneyland News*, 1:3, Sept. 1955, 16–17.

105. Brown, *Hollywood Family Film*, 88–95.

Chapter 2

1. "Welcome to Disneyland," first park brochure (Disneyland, Inc.), 1955.

2. *The Story of Disneyland* (Racine: Western Printing, 1955), [3, 8].

3. *Disneyland: A Complete Guide* (Racine: Western Printing, 1956), 18. Also, consider the narration of Disney's Cinemascope travelogue in the *People and Places* series, *Disneyland, U.S.A.*, which evokes a living history museum (1956).

4. "No other nation has taken a time and place from its past and produced a construct of the imagination equal to America's creation of the West"; "Sooner or later, virtually everyone who has written about the West refers to 'the myth'"; David H. Murdoch, *The American West: The Invention of a Myth* (Reno: University of Nevada Press, 2001), vii, 13.

5. Please note: such terms as "Indian," "Injun," "redskins," "savages," "savagery" and "natives" appear here and elsewhere in this book only as they were used by Walt Disney and his contemporaries, or in publicity and in literature about Disneyland or Disney films.

6. "Visitors to See Historic West," *Disneyland News*, 1:2, Aug. 1955, 8.

7. The name Frontier Street appears during pre-opening development. I retain it here to designate this area. See for example GWS Auctions, "Artifacts of Hollywood and Music," Lot 19B, Disney H. Ryman "Frontier Street" Concept Art, online auction, March 26, 2022.

8. "[The entire theme park] was an elaborate set where Disney's films could be further dramatized, and where the park's visitors could actually take part in the drama they had seen on movie and television screens"; Richard Francaviglia, "Frontierland as an Allegorical Map of the American West," in *Disneyland and Culture: Essays on the Parks and Their Influence*, ed. Kathy Merlock Jackson and Mark I. West (Jefferson: McFarland, 2011), 70. Francaviglia, 61, explores the cartographic metaphor, calling the realm "a three-dimensional mental map of the West."

"Based largely on a multitude of Western film images—including his own *The Living Desert* (1954), *The Vanishing Prairie* (1954), and *Davy Crockett* (1955)—as well as Walt's midwestern memories and stories gathered from his father-in-law, who had been a sheriff in Idaho Territory, Frontierland was an amalgam of many mythic Wests constructed to unfold like a movie"; "[Frontierland's buildings] all came straight from Hollywood rather than from the messy West"; Michael Steiner focuses on the mythic power of the frontier and Disney as "its most effective merchandiser" in "Frontierland as Tomorrowland: Walt Disney and the Architectural Packaging of the Mythic West," *Montana: The Magazine of Western History*, 48:1, Spring 1998, 4, 11–12.

"Frontierland provides the clearest connection between Hollywood movie sets and the intended effect of Disneyland"; Karal Ann Marling makes incisive observations in brief: Karal Ann Marling with

Donna R. Braden, *Behind the Magic: 50 Years of Disneyland* (Dearborn: The Henry Ford, 2004), 76.

See also Deborah Philips, "Consuming the West: Main Street USA," *Space and Culture* 5:29 (2002): 33: "Both Main Street and Frontierland make reference to an idea of the Wild West derived from the Hollywood Western." Philips calls Main Street the frontier town and does not investigate Frontierland.

9. For *The Covered Wagon*, see David Lusted, *The Western* (New York: Pearson, 2003), 129–33.

10. "Disneyland: The First Twelve Months," *"E" Ticket*, no. 28 (Winter 1997): 20–35.

11. For an examination of the personal values Walt invested in his television and movie Westerns from 1955 to 1960, see J. G. O'Boyle, "'Be Sure You're Right, then Go Ahead': The Early Disney Westerns," *Journal of Popular Film & Television* 24:2 (Summer 1996): 70–81.

12. Lusted, *The Western*, 18–20; Stephen McVeigh, *The American Western* (Edinburgh: Edinburgh University Press, 2007), chaps. 1–2. Jackson interpreted the closing of the frontier in 1890 as the end of the first phase of American development.

13. Neal Gabler, *Walt Disney: The Triumph of the American Imagination* (New York: Knopf, 2006), 13, accepts this as fact; Cody's career was waning by the time of Walt's period in Marceline.

14. Walt Disney, "Frontierland," *True West*, 5:5, May-June 1958, 10–11. Articles signed by Walt were usually written or polished by his staff; this one possesses a strong personal quality.

15. "Walt Disney's Background Apparent on TV Series," *Disneyland News*, 1:2, Aug. 1955, 20. For a more reliable account of the westward move, see Gabler, *Walt Disney*, 7–8.

16. For Buffalo Bill's contribution, see Murdoch, *American West*, 40–42; and Joy S. Kasson, "Life-like, Vivid, and Thrilling Pictures: Buffalo Bill's Wild West and Early Cinema," in *Westerns: Films through History*, ed. Janet Walker (New York: Routledge, 2013), 109–30.

17. Quoted in Jean Narboni and Tom Milne, ed., *Godard on Godard* (New York: Viking Press, 1972), 117.

18. Three examples of such films are *Daniel Boone* (1936), starring George O'Brien and John Carradine; *Northwest Passage* (1940), with Spencer Tracy and Robert Young; and *The Kentuckian* (1955), starring and directed by Burt Lancaster.

19. Lusted, *The Western*, 128–35

20. Jane Marie Gaines and Charlotte Cornelia Herzog, "The Fantasy of Authenticity in Western Costume," in *Back in the Saddle Again: New Essays on the Western*, ed. Edward Buscombe and Roberta E. Pearson (London: BFI, 1998), 172–81.

21. Richard Slotkin, "Prologue to a Study of Myth and Genre in American Movies," *Prospects* 9 (Oct. 1984): 425.

22. The folklore of the West appeared in early literary form, for example, in articles in the *Overland Authority* in the 1860s and Mark Twain's description of mining towns in *Roughing It* of 1872. Artists Frederick Remington and Charles Russell fashioned the imagery of the Old West. The dime novel, born in 1860, and the Wild West magazine coexisted with more exalted Western fiction, of which Owen Wister's *The Virginian* (1902) and the novels of Zane Grey affirmed a host of stereotypes, from the frontier town to the dance-hall girl, that would permeate endless Western movies. For a survey of sources of the Western genre, see Lusted, *The Western*, chap. 3; Richard Aquila, ed., *Wanted Dead or Alive: The American West in Popular Culture* (Urbana: University Press of Illinois, 1996), chaps. 1–3.

23. "Because the history of the American West is itself known primarily through its mythologization in popular literary and cinematic forms, the test of 'authenticity' involves a measuring of each new production against both 'real history' and an elaborate set of traditional myths, conventions, and illusions about history"; Slotkin, "Prologue to a Study," 421. The author expands his argument in Richard Slotkin, *Gunfighter Nation: The Myth of the Frontier in Twentieth-Century America* (Norman: University Press of Oklahoma, 1998), part 3, "Colonizing a Mythic Landscape: Movie Westerns, 1903–1948." See also Jeremy Agnew, *The Old West in Fact and Film: History versus Hollywood* (Jefferson: McFarland, 2012), chap. 1.

24. "The cinema inherited an already pre-determined set of ideas and images [and] the generic forms of the Western

were fixed from the outset, despite some interesting early variations. Working within a genre, filmmakers are not as free as they think they are, or as critics think they are, to choose a more 'accurate' or ideologically 'correct' type of representation. Genre locks in certain images to the exclusion of others"; Edward Buscombe, "*Injuns!*" *Native Americans in the Movies* (London: Reaktion, 2006), 19–20.

25. Similar claims of authenticity were made for the films shot on location for broadcast on the *Disneyland* TV program. See: "Walt Disney's Background Apparent on TV Series," *Disneyland News*, 1:2, Aug. 1955, 20.

26. Patrick came on board in November 1954 and through research contributed to further development of the sector; "Edison's Inventions a Problem but Patrick's Solutions Work," *Disneyland News*, 1:2, Aug. 1955, 8.

27. Including episodes of *Tales of Wells Fargo* (1957), *Cimarron City* (1959), *Laramie* (1959–60), *Overland Trail* (1960), *Riverboat* (1960–61), *Frontier Circus* (1961–62), *The Tall Man* (1962), *Destry* (1964), and *The Virginian* (1962–69).

28. Paul F. Anderson, "Disneyland Illustrator Extraordinaire: A Visit with Sam McKim," *Persistence of Vision* no. 5 (1993): 56; "Visualizing Disneyland with Sam McKim," *"E" Ticket*, no. 18 (Spring 1994): 8–21. See also Jeff Kurtti, *Walt Disney's Imagineering Legends and the Genesis of the Disney Theme Park* (New York: Disney Editions, 2008), 14–17.

29. Drawings are reproduced in Karal Ann Marling, "Imagineering the Disney Theme Parks," in *Designing Disney's Theme Parks: The Architecture of Reassurance*, ed. Karal Ann Marling (Montreal: Canadian Centre for Architecture, 1997), 109–11; Kurtti and Gordon, *Art of Disneyland*, 36, 42. For McKim, see Kurtti, *Walt Disney's Imagineering Legends*, 14–17.

30. Public Relations Department, "Building a Dream," *Walt Disney's Magic Kingdom Disneyland*, Opening Day Press Kit (Anaheim: Disneyland, Inc., 1955; facsimile reprint, Disneyland Press & Publicity, 2005), 4.

31. "Edison's Inventions a Problem," 8.

32. Public Relations Department, "Building a Dream," 2.

33. For a consideration of how sets and props convey meaning in the Western, see Robert S. Sennett, *Setting the Scene: The Great Hollywood Art Directors* (New York: Abrams, 1994), 134–41.

34. "Disneyland Antique Collectors Find U.S., Canadian Items," *Disneyland News*, 1:2, Aug. 1955, 17, which calls the park "a paradise for antique collectors."

35. The Ghost Town at Knott's Berry Farm is an acknowledged source. "[Disneyland] started with Walt asking me, 'Have you ever been to Knott's Berry Farm ... it's fun isn't it? ... I have been thinking that I'd like to have something like that'"; quoted in "An Interview with Harper Goff," *"E" Ticket*, no. 14 (Winter 1992–93): 7.

36. Marling, "Imagineering," 47–52; Bruce Gordon and David Mumford, *Disneyland: The Nickel Tour* (Santa Clarita: Camphor Tree, 2000), 8.

37. For the full text, see Michael Broggie, *Walt Disney's Railroad Story: The Small-Scale Fascination That Led to a Full-Scale Kingdom* (Pasadena: Pentrex, 1997), 88–91.

38. "Walt Disney Make-Believe Land Project Planned Here," *Burbank Daily Review*, Mar. 27, 1952, A1; "Walt Disney Plans Park for Children," *Los Angeles Times*, Mar. 28, 1952, A10.

39. "Welcome to Disneyland," 1955.

40. John G. Cawelti, *The Six-Gun Mystique Sequel* (Bowling Green: Bowling Green State University Popular Press, 1999), 24. The quote concerns literature, but pertains equally to other media.

41. Slotkin, "Prologue to a Study," 424.

42. E. J. Stephens and Marc Wanamaker, *Early Warner Bros. Studios* (Charleston: Arcadia, 2010), 71.

43. Stephen Bingen, Stephen X. Sylvester, and Michael Troyan, *M-G-M: Hollywood's Greatest Backlot* (Solana Beach: Santa Monica Press, 2011), 224–35.

44. Michael Troyen, Stephen X. Sylvester, and Jeffrey Paul Thompson, *Twentieth Century Fox: A Century of Entertainment* (Guilford: Lyons Press, 2017), 343–49.

45. Steven Bingen, *Warner Bros.: Hollywood's Ultimate Backlot* (Lanham: Taylor Trade, 2014), 234–35.

46. Steven Bingen, *Paramount: City of Dreams* (Guilford: Taylor Trade, 2017), 203–11.

47. Bingen, *Warner Bros.*, 175–85, 218–23.

48. Harold O. Wright, "Man Who Bought a Ghost Town," *Desert*, July 1953, 14–18.

49. "Movie Illusions: Hollywood Technicians Create Reality inside Studios," *Life*, 17:6, Aug. 7, 1944, 78.

50. "Frontierland: Explore the Lost 'Rainbow Mine,'" *Disneyland News*, Extra Edition, [May] 1956, 2–3; "Disneyland Art Director ... Bill Martin," *"E" Ticket*, no. 20 (Winter 1994–95): 10–11.

51. "Disneyland: Welcome to Disneyland," newspaper advertising insert, July 15, 1955, 5.

52. Hedda Hopper, "Walt Disney's Fete 250 at Fabulous Disneyland," *Chicago Daily Tribune*, July 16, 1955, 17.

53. Diana C. Reep, "See What the Boys in the Back Room Will Have: The Saloon in Western Films," in *Beyond the Stars*, vol. 4, *Locales in American Popular Film*, ed. Paul Loukides and Linda K. Fuller (Bowling Green: Bowling Green State University Popular Press, 1993), 204–20.

54. Elliott West, *The Saloon on the Rocky Mountain Mining Frontier* (Lincoln: University of Nebraska Press), 1996, chaps. 2, 4, especially p. 40; Robert Clyde Allen, *Horrible Prettiness: Burlesque and American Culture* (Chapel Hill: University Press of North Carolina, 1991), 73–75.

55. I am unaware of the origins of the story that Goff designed the saloon interior for *Calamity Jane* and, following Walt's directive, copied his own plans for the Frontierland interior. See Gordon and Mumford, *Disneyland: Nickel Tour*, 58; Marling, "Imagineering," 105, among others. Goff, a former movie set designer, had left Warner's before *Calamity Jane* was produced and was working for Walt as early as 1951. The film credits Art Direction to John Beckman. See Todd James Pierce, blog, "Golden Horseshoe—Girlie Club Edition," Disneyhistoryinstitute.com, May 7, 2012. For Goff, see Kurtti, *Walt Disney's Imagineering Legends*, 2–5.

56. For historical décor, see Richard Erdoes, *Saloons of the Old West* (New York: Knopf, 1979), chap. 4.

57. "Disneyland: Welcome to Disneyland," 5.

58. "Golden Horseshoe 'Saloon' Presents Light, Gay Revue," *Disneyland News*, 1:3, Sept. 1955, 8, 18; "The Four Young Ladies of the Golden Horseshoe," *Disneyland News*, 2:1, June 1956, 4.

59. David Price, *Cancan!* (London: Cygnus Arts, 1998), 168–69; Erdoes, *Saloons of the Old West*, 171–72.

60. Henry Nash Smith. *Virgin Land: The American West as Symbol and Myth* (Cambridge: Harvard University Press, 1950), 3.

61. *Disneyland, U.S.A. (People and Places)*, directed by Hamilton Luske (1956: Buena Vista).

62. For the Pony Farm and anecdotes about the early rides, including accidents leading to the elimination of stagecoaches in 1957, see David Koenig, *The 55ers: The Pioneers Who Settled Disneyland* (Irvine: Bonaventure Press, 2019), 198–208. For the dude ranch, which anticipated aspects of Frontierland, see Earl S. Pomery, *In Search of the Golden West: The Tourist in Western America* (Lincoln: University of Nebraska Press, 2010), 167–72.

63. For a complete description of the attraction, see "Frontierland Stage Coach Rides Again! Century-Old Transportation a Slice of Living History," *Disneyland News*, 1:8, Feb. 1956, 10–11. The article praises the assemblage of historic vehicles and emphasizes their accessibility to park patrons as opposed to being museum exhibits.

64. "Disneyland: Welcome to Disneyland," [18]; Sam Gennawey, *The Disneyland Story: The Unofficial Guide to the Evolution of Walt Disney's Dream* (Birmingham: Keen, 2014), 78–79.

65. Gladwin Hill, "Disneyland Reports on Its First Ten Million," *New York Times*, Feb. 2, 1958, X1, 7.

66. "Conestogas Once Tops," *Disneyland News*, 1:2, Aug. 1955, 8, discusses the origins of the wagon in the Conestoga Valley of Lancaster County, Pennsylvania, and its use to transport thousands of migrants through the Allegheny Mountains.

67. McVeigh, *American Western*, 66–67.

68. Quote from William K. Everson, *A Pictorial History of the Western Film* (Secaucus: The Citadel Press, 1969), 110.

69. On the question of authenticity in movie "Indian" attacks on wagon trains, see Gregory F. Michno and Susan J. Michno, *Circle the Wagons! Attacks on*

Wagon Trains in History and Hollywood Films (Jefferson: McFarland, 2009), 96–99.

70. See the extensive list with summaries in Michno and Michno, *Circle the Wagons!*, Appendix A: The Wagon Train Movies, 201–13.

71. Bob Thomas, "51 Acres of Disney's Studios Are Crammed with Ideas," *Reading Eagle*, March 15, 1955, 18.

72. Leonard Maltin, *The Disney Films* (New York: Hyperion, 1995), 138–40.

73. The company changed its name from Van Noy Railway Hotel and News Company in July 1917; "Articles of Incorporation," *Fort Wayne Journal-Gazette*, July 10, 1917, 11; Van Noy-Interstate into New Building," *Walden's Stationer*, 44:9, Jan. 1921, 74.

74. Broggie, *Walt Disney's Railroad Story*, chaps. 8–15; Dana Amendola, *All Aboard: The Wonderful World of Disney Trains* (Los Angeles: Disney Editions, 2015), chap. 4.

75. "Where Do the Stories Come From?" *Disneyland* television program, aired April 4, 1956; Bill Cotter, *The Wonderful World of Disney Television: A Complete History* (New York: Hyperion, 1997), 173. Walt Disney viewed this cartoon with columnist Bob Thomas in the Mickey Mouse Club Theater in Fantasyland: Bob Thomas, "Guest Columnist: Walt Fascinated as Child on Magic Kingdom Visit," *Disneyland News*, 1:4, Oct. 10, 1955, 4.

76. Broggie, *Walt Disney's Railroad Story*, chaps. 18–19.

77. *Story of Disneyland* [3]; *Disneyland, U.S.A.* (*People and Places*).

78. Walt gave the original station movie set to Kimball; see chap.1; also Broggie, *Disney's Railroad Story*, 267. In Herb Ryman's *Aerial View of Disneyland* (1953), one train passes by Frontierland directly behind one of two riverboats, while a second train leaves the Main St. Station.

79. On the railroad as film icon representing progress and civilization, see Vivian Sobchack, *Screening Space: The American Science Fiction Film* (New Brunswick: Rutgers University Press, 1997), 67–68.

80. Brian Garfield, *Western Films: A Complete Guide* (New York: Da Capo Press, 1982), 146–47; Agnew, *Old West*, 20–23. Walt Disney acknowledged *Union Pacific* in an interview with DeMille; "Lux Radio Theater," Dec. 26, 1938; archiv.com.

81. "'Glamor Girl of Rails' Portrays 'General' in 'Locomotive Chase,'" *Disneyland News*, 1:9, Mar. 1956, 11. The Andrews Raid is also the subject of the Buster Keaton silent film, *The General* (1926).

82. George Sidney, audio commentary, *The Harvey Girls*, DVD (Warner Home Video, 2002).

83. The tune was released in many cover versions six months before the movie, enjoying a long life on the charts, and won the Academy Award for Best Song. The historic rail line, chartered in 1859, only went as far as Colorado in its early days, but lyricist Johnny Mercer, for the sake of a rhyme, had the train running all the way to "Cali-for-ni-ay."

84. "'Mark Twain' River Steamer Docks Again," *Disneyland News*, 1:2, Aug. 1955, 8.

85. Disney, "Frontierland," 10, 12.

86. On the connections between Twain and Disney, see Brian Burnes, Robert W. Butler, and Dan Viets, *Walt Disney's Missouri: The Roots of a Creative Genius* (Kansas City: Kansas City Star Books, 2002), 154–55.

87. Public Relations Department, "Building a Dream," 4.

88. Hugh Fordin, *The Movies' Greatest Musicals: Produced in Hollywood USA by the Freed Unit* (New York: Frederick Ungar, 1984), 336–42; Bingen, Sylvester, and Troyen, *M-G-M*, 220–21, 245–48.

89. For the design and construction, see "Disneyland's Queen of the River, the Mark Twain," "*E*" *Ticket*, no. 15 (Spring 1993): 16–27; Stewart Robinson, "Mark Twain," *Motor Boating*, 96:6, June 1956, 43, 115–17. For the Fox studio's *Little Old New York* (1940) Zanuck ordered two replicas of Robert Fulton's paddle steamer, the *Clermont*, so that one could be destroyed by fire; Hedda Hopper, "Hollywood Sets Would Fool Mother Nature: Scenic Experts Make Land, Sea and Sky Look More Realistic Than Reality," *Los Angeles Times*, Nov. 26, 1939, C3.

90. Smith, *Virgin Land*, 11.

91. "They [the attractions] were an early form of virtual reality—'movie' in which the audience could walk around, interact, and integrate their own stories"; Margaret J. King, "The Audience in the Wilderness: The Disney Nature Films," *Journal*

of Popular Film and Television 24:2 (Summer, 1996): 62–63. Like most writers, she acknowledges the theme park's relationship to film, but does not explore it. Other relevant True-Life films are *Beaver Valley* (1953) and *The Vanishing Prairie* (1954).

92. Reep, "See What the Boys in the Back Room Will Have," 206.

93. Leon J. Janzen, "Corriganville Movie Ranch," *"E" Ticket*, no. 8 (Winter 1989–90): 29–31. In an interview with the present author (2021) Mark Licht recounted his childhood memories of visiting the ranch in the 1950s.

94. "Movie Illusions," 72–73.

95. "Green Emphasizes Spring throughout Realms of Park," *Disneyland News*, 1:2, Aug. 1955, 17.

96. "See the Beauties of the Rainbow Desert," *Disneyland News*, 2:2, Aug. 1956, 3. For a description of the Painted Desert, renamed the Rainbow Desert in Summer 1956, see "Frontierland Area Site of New Attraction," *Disneyland News*, 2:2, Aug. 1956, 1, 3.

97. "Firm of Evans and Reeves Does Record Landscaping," *Disneyland News*, 1:3, Sept. 1955, 9.

98. Quoted in Frank Jensen, "Mohab—Movie Town," *Salt Lake Tribune Home Magazine*, Nov. 26, 1961, 5–6, which details the cost and mechanics of shooting a major movie on location.

99. "Monument Valley has now come to signify Ford, Ford has come to be synonymous with the Western, the Western signifies Hollywood cinema, and Hollywood stands for America. Thus, through a kind of metonymic chain, Monument Valley has come to represent America itself"; Edward Buscombe, "Inventing Monument Valley," in *Fugitive Images: From Photography to Video*, ed. Patrice Petro (Bloomington: Indiana University Press, 1995), 87–108, especially 93, 103. See also Peter Cowie, *John Ford and the American West* (New York: Harry N. Abrams, 2004).

100. John Herron, "John Ford, Thomas Hart Benton, and the American Frontier," in *American Epics: Thomas Hart Benton and Hollywood*, ed. Austen Barron Bailly (New York: Prestel, 2015), 50–51. The arches and balancing rocks also owe a debt to geological formations in Arches National Park, Utah.

101. "Tom Sawyer Island," *"E" Ticket*,

no. 37 (Spring 2002): 14–28; Mark I. West, "Tom Sawyer Island: Mark Twain, Walt Disney, and the Literary Playground," in *Disneyland and Culture: Essays on the Parks and Their Influence*, ed. Kathy Merlock Jackson and Mark I. West (Jefferson: McFarland, 2011), 101–06.

102. "Scenes from 'Tom Sawyer's Island,'" *Disneyland News*, 2:1, July 1956, 4. For a tour of the island taken with Walt Disney, see Ira Wolfert, "Walt Disney's Magic Kingdom," *Reader's Digest*, 76, Apr. 1966, 146. Walt is credited with the layout of the island; Marcy Carriker Smothers, *Walt's Disneyland: A Walk in the Park with Walt Disney* (Los Angeles, Disney Editions, 2021), 94, 101.

103. In the early planning stages for Disneyland, the island remained unnamed as various proposals were floated. There was a concept for Mickey Mouse and Minnie Mouse Island, a place to which all Mouseketeers would travel for official induction into the Mickey Mouse Club, being broadcast on television. Or it might be called Treasure Island, in reference to the Disney live-action film (1950). Another idea, which takes up Walt's love for miniatures, was to build on the shoreline, visible from the *Mark Twain*, small replicas of great American river sites, such as Natchez, West Point, and Mount Vernon. See "Your Tanner Grey Line Tour to Disneyland," brochure, Tanner Gray Line Motor Tours, 1955; Sam Abbot, "Disneyland Sets New Designs for Rides, Exhibit Layouts," *Billboard*, June 26, 1954, 80.

104. Disney, "Frontierland," 10–11, 13. In the early 1940s Disney gave his daughter Diane copies of the Tom Sawyer and Huck Finn stories in the editions illustrated by Norman Rockwell.

105. "1956 Hannibal MO Gift Presented to Walt Disney, Disneyland, Tom Sawyer Island," online sale listing, Saturday's Toys, March 2013.

106. Joe Adamson, *Byron Haskin* (Metuchen: Scarecrow Press, 1984), 168. In 1944 Warner Bros. produced a biopic, *The Adventures of Mark Twain*, which combined elements of Twain's biography with imagery from his stories; the young Sam Clemens was played by Dickie Jones, the voice of Disney's *Pinocchio* four years earlier.

107. The production team received

special mention in the reviews: "'Tom Sawyer' Notable Screen Story of Youth," *Los Angeles Times*, Mar. 24, 1938, A11.

108. Hedda Hopper, "Curtiz Will Direct Roman in 'Serenade,'" *Los Angeles Times*, June 7, 1950, B6.

109. Ronald Haver, *David O. Selznick's Hollywood* (New York: Bonanza Books, 1985), 213–14, 220–21, 370. Notice the exceptional reproduction of fifteen dramatic stills from the cave sequence, p. 221. MGM produced a successful movie of *The Adventures of Huckleberry Finn* in 1939, starring Mickey Rooney. From 1943 through the mid-1950s the Freed Unit worked on a musical version of *Huckleberry Finn*, at one point considering Danny Kaye and Gene Kelly as the King and the Duke, but that production was ultimately shelved. In the end, MGM would release the non-musical *Adventures of Huckleberry Finn*, directed by Michael Curtiz, in 1960.

110. Robert Irwin, "The Failure of Tom Sawyer and Huckleberry Finn on Film," *Mark Twain Journal* 13:4 (Summer 1967): 9–11; Kate Newell, "'You Don't Know about Me without You Have Read a Book': Authenticity in Adaptations of *Adventures of Huckleberry Finn*," *Literature/Film Quarterly* 41:4 (Oct. 2013): 303–16; Mary Allen Abbott, "A Guide to the Discussion of the Technicolor Photoplay of *The Adventures of Tom Sawyer* as Produced by David O. Selznick," *Photoplay Studies* 4:2 (Feb. 1938): 1–16.

111. Perry June Frank, "The Adventures of Tom Sawyer on Film: The Evolution of an American Icon," PhD diss., George Washington University, 1991, 287.

112. "Tom Sawyer Island To Have Old West Fort, Secret Cave," *Disneyland News*, Extra Ed., [May] 1956, 1; Leon J. Janzen, "Exploring the Caves of Tom Sawyer Island," *"E" Ticket*, no. 7 (Summer 1989): 26–29.

113. "Creating the Disney Landscape: An Interview with Bill Evans," *"E" Ticket*, no. 23 (Spring 1996): 9. The influence of Selznick's *Adventures of Tom Sawyer* is apparent in the colorful Disneyesque musical adaptation created by Richard and Robert Sherman, *Tom Sawyer* (1973); Injun Joe falls to his death in the cave sequence, filmed in an actual underground cavern. In 2007, following the

success of the Disney Company's *Pirates of the Caribbean* series, the island was rethemed as Pirates Lair on Tom Sawyer Island, with Dead Man's Grotto taking the place of Injun Joe's Cave.

114. Rudy Behlmer, ed., *Memo from David O. Selznick: The Creation of* Gone with the Wind *and Other Motion Picture Classics* ... (New York: Modern Library, 2000), 121.

115. Frank S. Nugent, "The Screen," *New York Times*, Feb. 18, 1938, L23.

116. Tom Nabbe, *From Disneyland's Tom Sawyer to Disney Legend: The Adventures of Tom Nabbe* (Theme Park Press, 2015).

117. "Welcome to Disneyland," 1955.

118. The quote is by Karl Ann Marling in describing costuming in films by John Ford and others; "Thomas Hart Benton's *Boomtown*: Regionalism Redefined," *Prospects* 6 (Oct. 1981): 120. On the reality effect in costume, see Gaines and Herzog, "The Fantasy of Authenticity in Western Costume." Also, Warwick Frost and Jennifer Laing, *Imagining the American West through Film and Tourism* (London: Routledge, 2017), chap 13.

119. Ray White, "The Good Guys Wore White Hats: The B western in American Culture," in *Wanted Dead or Alive: The American West in Popular Culture*, ed. Richard Aquila (Champaign: University of Illinois Press, 1998), 135.

120. For the career of Jim Lindsey, a former stunt rider, see "Stage Coach Driver Jim Finds Hazards Are Not All in the Desert," *Disneyland News*, 1:8, Feb. 1956, 10–11.

121. "Walt Disney's Frontierland," *TV Guide*, 3:3, Jan. 15, 1955, 8–9.

122. Hedda Hopper, "Disney Brings Native American Folklore Characters to Public as Film Heroes," *Los Angeles Times*, May 9, 1948, C1.

123. "World Visitors Enjoy Disneyland; Guests from Foreign Nations, All Parts of America Include Hollywood Stars," *Disneyland News*, 1:2, Aug. 1955, 1.

124. Walt Disney, "Frontierland," 11; "Gunfights Liven Lucky's Day—Delight Frontierland Watchers," *Disneyland News*, 2:3, Sept. 1956, 5, 10. For Sheriff Bill Lacy, see "Frontierland's Sheriff Finds Action a-Plenty," *Disneyland News*, 1:4, Oct. 10, 1955, 10, 15. For Sheriff Lucky, Black Bart,

and Pecos Bill, see "Wally Boag Tells of Frontierland," *"E" Ticket*, no. 15 (Spring 1993): 8–9; Koenig, *The 55ers*, 218–21. The shoot-out was recorded in the *Disneyland, U.S.A.* featurette.

125. Lusted, *The Western*, 90, 152, referring to the cowboy gunfighter; Agnew, *Old West*, 159–60.

126. "Frontierland Sign Recalls Old Scout," *Disneyland News*, 1:2, Aug. 1955, 23.

127. Gabler, *Walt Disney*, 93.

128. For an analysis of the Crockett shows and their impact on television programming, see J. P. Telotte, *Disney TV* (Detroit: Wayne State University Press, 2004), chap. 2. For Disney's approach to the Western, see O'Boyle, "'Be Sure You're Right.'"

129. The second series of Crockett films, "Davy Crockett's Keelboat Race" and "Davy Crockett and the River Pirates," aired on November 16 and December 14, 1955, respectively. The final TV programs were combined to make a second, less successful theatrical release, *Davy Crockett and the River Pirates*, which premiered simultaneously with the celebration of Disneyland's first year of operation on July 18, 1956.

130. In October 1955, the museum's name changed to the Davy Crockett Arcade.

131. "Crockett Museum Features Products of Old Mexico," *Disneyland News*, 2:2, Aug. 1956, 8; "Leather Shop Opens in Crockett Museum," *Disneyland News*, 2:3, Sept. 1956, 3.

132. "Rifle Assn. Exhibit in Crockett Arcade," *Disneyland News*, 4:1, Oct. 10, 1955, 15; "In Crockett Arcade: Ancient Arts Still Flourish," *Disneyland News*, 4:1, Oct. 10, 1955, 6, on Indigenous crafts. See also "Disneyland's Davy Crockett," *"E" Ticket*, no. 33 (Spring 2000): 34–41. The Mike Fink Keel Boats ride, based on the second Crockett TV series, opened on Dec. 25, 1955: "Keelboater King Rivals Davy Crockett in TV Race," *Disneyland News*, 4:1, Oct. 10, 1955, 5.

133. Daniel Kothenschulte, "A Comic Opera of the Wild Woods," in *The Walt Disney Film Archives: The Animated Movies, 1921–1968*, ed. Daniel Kothenschulte (Cologne: Taschen, 2016), 282–93. Benton had painted set designs for Westerns

filmed in New Jersey by Rex Ingram in 1914–17. Later, as a muralist, Benton was one of those artists who created the iconography of the Old West, as in the mural *A Social History of Missouri: Pioneer Days and Early Settlers* for the Missouri State Capitol in Jefferson City (1936); Erika Doss, *Benton, Pollock, and the Politics of Modernism* (Chicago: University of Chicago Press, 1991), 42–43.

134. According to Buddy Ebsen: Paul F. Anderson, *The Davy Crockett Craze: A Look at the 1950s Phenomenon and Davy Crockett Collectibles* (Hillside: R&G Productions, 1997), 17.

135. Margaret J. King, "The Recycled Hero: Walt Disney's Davy Crockett," in *Davy Crockett: The Man, the Legend, the Legacy, 1786–1986*, ed. Michael Lofaro (Knoxville: University of Tennessee Press, 1985), 141–45. For Disney's use of Crockett as a weapon against the Cold War, see Steven Watts, *The Magic Kingdom: Walt Disney and the American Way of Life* (New York: Houghton Mifflin, 1997), 287–302, 313–22.

136. Norman Bruce, "A Newly Discovered Silent Film: An Article on *Davy Crockett*," in *Davy Crockett: The Man, the Legend, the Legacy, 1786–1986*, ed. Michael Lofaro (Knoxville: University of Tennessee Press, 1985), 125–36.

137. Broggie, *Walt Disney's Railroad Story*, 90.

138. Public Relations Department, "A Visit to Disneyland," *Walt Disney's Magic Kingdom Disneyland*, opening day press kit (Anaheim: Disneyland, Inc., 1955; facsimile reprint, Disneyland Press & Publicity, 2005), 4. See the concept sketch by Bruce Bushman, 1954, shown in the first *Disneyland* TV program: Kurtti and Gordon, *Art of Disneyland*, 35.

139. Edwin Schallert, "Disney Spending $1,000,000 on New Dreams for Playland," *Los Angeles Times*, May 13, 1956, sect. 4, 1, 4.

140. "A Visit to Frontierland's Indian Village," *Disneyland News*, 2:2, Aug. 1956, 4–5. See also "Authentic Long House Newest Addition to Indian Village," *Disneyland News*, 2:3, Sept. 1956, 8, which opens with the standard claim: "An almost extinct art is currently being revived at Disneyland as part of the interesting and educational show at Frontierland's Indian

Village." Walt Disney specifically commented on the authenticity of proposed villages of different tribes: Thomas, "Guest Columnist," 4.

141. "Tom Sawyer Island," 1–2.

142. Disney, "Frontierland," 13; "Tom Sawyer Island," 1.

143. Lusted, *The Western*, 132–33, 138. The literature on Indigenous peoples in the movies is abundant. For an introduction, see Agnew, *Old West*, chap. 12; Bob Herzberg, *Savages and Saints: The Changing Image of American Indians in Westerns* (Jefferson: McFarland, 2008).

144. "Animated 'Hiawatha' Feature in Preparation by Disney," *Boxoffice*, 53:5, May 29, 1948, 31; Edwin Schallert, "Walt Disney Commences Scouting for 'Hiawatha,'" *Los Angeles Times*, Nov. 22, 1948, 27; Kothenschulte, "Comic Opera," 286–87.

145. On Disney's view toward Native Americans, see Douglas Brode, *Multiculturalism and the Mouse: Race and Sex in Disney Entertainment* (Austin: University of Texas Press, 2005), chap. 1.

146. In his essay on Frontierland, Walt was conflicted in describing the presentation of Native Americans, balancing the notion of authenticity with the duality of noble vs. savage: Disney, "Frontierland," 12.

147. Koenig, *The 55ers*, 222–25. The Indian Village closed in 1971, and the Indigenous presence steadily decreased.

148. "Wooden Indian Identifies Main Street Tobacco Shop," *Disneyland News*, 1:9, Mar. 10, 1956, 8.

149. See n. 102 above.

150. On the history of New Orleans Street and the issue of race, see Florian Freitag, *Popular New Orleans: The Crescent City in Periodicals, Theme Parks, and Opera, 1875–2015* (New York: Routledge, 2020), 144–54. Walt passed through New Orleans on the way to the *Song of the South* premiere: Ralph McGill, "Critter Company To Arrive Today To Kindle Light of Remus Stories," *Atlanta Constitution*, Nov. 10, 1946, 14A. Harper Goff researched park ideas in New Orleans; Gabler, *Walt Disney*, 495. On the Casa de Fritos and its mascot, the Frito Kid, see Koenig, *The 55ers*, 210–11.

151. "Food Flavors Southwest Atmosphere," *Disneyland News*, 2:1, June 1956, 7. The quote is from the MGM documentary short, *The Old South* (1940).

152. "Atmosphere, Fine Food Make Dining Tops at Disneyland," *Disneyland News*, 2:7, Jan. 1957, 4–5.

153. Ruth P. Shellhorn, "Disneyland: Dream Built in One Year through Teamwork of Many Artists," *Landscape Architecture* 46:3 (Apr. 1956): 130. See also "Landscaper Shellhorn Supervises Planting," *Disneyland News*, 1:2, Aug. 1955, 20; David Koenig, blog, "The Secret Plans of Disneyland," micechat.com, June 28, 2018; Kelly Comras, *Ruth Shellhorn* (Athens: University of Georgia Press, 2016).

154. "Disneyland: Welcome to Disneyland," [7].

155. Ida Jeter, "*Jezebel* and the Emergence of the Hollywood Tradition of a Decadent South," in *The South and Film*, ed. Warren French (Jackson: University Press of Mississippi, 1981), 31.

156. Steven Bingen, *Hollywood's Lost Backlot: 40 Acres of Glamour and Mystery* (Guilford: Lyons Press, 2019), 136–50; Bingen, Sylvester, and Troyen, *M-G-M*, 196–97; Troyan, Sylvester, and Thompson, *Twentieth Century Fox*, 244–47.

157. "Mardi Gras Dedicates New Orleans Street," *Disneyland News*, 1:3, Sept. 1955, 11.

158. "Disneyland: Ronnie and Vickie Enjoy a Day of Fun in Kiddies' Paradise," *Ebony*, 11:5, Mar. 1956, 63–65; "A Day with a Mouseketeer in Disneyland," *Hue*, Sept. 1956, 10–12. On Black visitors, see Susan Sessions Pugh, *Are We There Yet? The Golden Age of American Family Vacations* (Jackson: University Press of Mississippi, 2008), 115. On race and ethnicity at Disneyland, see Eric Avila, *Popular Culture in the Age of White Flight: Fear and Fantasy in Suburban Los Angeles* (Berkeley: University of California Press, 2006), 132–44.

159. It is not clear whether the tapping youth was a regular cast member on New Orleans Street. H. Wayne Schuth includes "black children dancing" in his list of New Orleans stereotypes: "The Image of New Orleans on Film," in *The South and Film*, ed. Warren French (Jackson: University Press of Mississippi, 1981), 241. In the mid-1960s a pair of Black youths worked in Disneyland's New Orleans Square; Dave DeCaro, blog, "Teddy and Kenny, the Shoeshine Boys," davelandblog.blogspot.com, Jan. 15, 2013; "Teddy, Disneyland's Shoeshine Boy," May 20, 2013. During

the inauguration of the sector, Walt and the mayor of New Orleans were photographed having their shoes shined; Ethel S. Goodstein, "Southern Outposts in the Magic Kingdom: The South as a Regional Sub-text in Disney's American Spectacle," *Visual Resources* 14:3 (1999): 318 n. 11.

160. Koenig, *The 55ers*, 209; Arthur F. Marquette, *Brands, Trademarks, and Good Will: The Story of the Quaker Oats Company* (New York: McGraw-Hill, 1967), 137, 157–58; M. M. Manring, *Slave in a Box: The Strange Career of Aunt Jemima* (Charlottesville: University Press of Virginia, 1998), 74–78, 162–71.

161. "Days of Old South Relived in Aunt Jemima's Kitchen," *Disneyland News*, 2:2, Aug. 1956, 6–7. Disney had previously presented the Mammy stereotype in the *Silly Symphony* short, *Broken Toys* (1935).

162. "Needed: A Negro Legion of Decency," *Ebony*, 2:4, Feb. 1947, 36. Also criticized was the film's portrayal of Toby, the Black child; elsewhere Walt described him using the common racist word, "Pickaninny" (Watts, *Magic Kingdom*, 279). See the classic study, Donald Bogle, *Toms, Coons, Mulattoes, Mammies, and Bucks: An Interpretive History of Blacks in American Films* (New York: Continuum, 1994), especially 3–18, 135–36.

163. "Life of Story-Telling Genius Retold in 'Song of the South,'" *Disneyland News*, 1:8, Feb. 1956, 2. On the troubled history of *Song of the South*, see Jason Sperb, *Disney's Most Notorious Movie: Race, Convergence, and the Hidden Histories of* Song of the South (Austin: University of Texas Press, 2012), 1–16, 32–85.

164. In 2020 Quaker Oats retired the Jemima character. In 2021 the Disney Company announced the redevelopment of its Splash Mountain attractions, replacing *Song of the South* theming with its 2009 film, *The Princess and the Frog*.

165. George F. Custen, *Twentieth Century's Fox: Darryl F. Zanuck and the Culture of Hollywood* (New York: BasicBooks, 1997), 319; Troyan, Sylvester, and Thompson, *Twentieth Century Fox*, 346–47.

166. William Boddy, "'Sixty Million Viewers Can't Be Wrong': The Rise and Fall of the Television Western," in *Back in the Saddle Again: New Essays on the Western*, ed. Edward Buscombe and Roberta E. Peterson (London: BFI, 1998), 116–37. The

huge success of Davy Crockett and, more generally, of the TV Western led ABC to pressure Disney to produce more Western programming, which he resisted, despite his support for the frontier narrative in the park; see Cotter, *Wonderful World of Disney Television*, 64–66.

167. Smith, *Virgin Land*, especially chap. 22. See Peter Stanfield, *Hollywood, Westerns, and the 1930s: The Lost Trail* (Exeter: University of Exeter Press, 2001), 8–12; Francaviglia, "Frontierland as an Allegorical Map," 67–70. Priscilla Hobbs, *Walt's Utopia: Disneyland and American Mythmaking* (Jefferson: McFarland, 2015), 179–80, discusses Frontierland in terms of Manifest Destiny, a concept connoting imperialism. For the classic discussion of Walt and the Cold War, see Watts, *Magic Kingdom*, 287–95, 347–50, and passim.

168. Smith, *Virgin Land*, 3, repeats the much-quoted question posed by French settler, St. John de Crèvecoeur.

169. "Walt Disney's Background Apparent," 20.

Chapter 3

1. *Welcome to Disneyland*, first park brochure (Disneyland, Inc.), 1955. Please note: such terms as "savage," "savages," and "cannibals" appear here and elsewhere in this book only as they were used by Walt Disney and his contemporaries, or in publicity and in literature about Disneyland or Disney and Hollywood films.

2. Walt Disney called the Jungle Cruise "the most popular attraction in Disneyland": Bob Thomas, "Guest Columnist: Walt Fascinated as Child on Magic Kingdom Visit," *Disneyland News*, 1:4, Oct. 10, 1955, 4. For a history of the "land," see "The Adventureland Story," "E" *Ticket*, no. 39 (Spring 2003): 16–33; Justin Arthur, "Beyond the Backside of Water: Journey of the World-Famous Jungle Cruise," *Disney Twenty-Three*, 13:2, Summer, 2021, 10–13; David John Marley, *The Jungle Cruise: The Wild History of Walt's Favorite Ride* (Theme Park Press: 2021); Michael Goldman, *The Making of Disney's Jungle Cruise* (Los Angeles: Disney Editions, 2021). On the concept of adventure tourism, see Jennifer Laing and Warwick Frost, *Explorer*

Travellers and Adventure Tourism (Bristol: Channel View, 2014).

3. "Island Trade Store Offers Wares of Orient, Oceana," *Disneyland News*, 1:6, Dec. 10, 1955, 11; *Picture Souvenir Book of Disneyland in Natural Color* (Boston: American Souvenir Company, 1955; facsimile reprint, New York: Disney Editions, 2005), [8]. For the Hawaiian music performed on the Adventureland terrace, see "Lovely Elana Provides Enchanting Island Songs," *Disneyland News* 1:4, Oct. 10, 1955, 15.

4. "Celebrities Enjoy Disneyland," *Disneyland News*, 1:3, Sept. 1955, 4.

5. For a discussion of sources, see Deborah Philips, *Fairground Attractions: A Genealogy of the Pleasure Ground* (London: Bloomsbury Academic, 2012), chap. 7.

6. Richard B. Jewell categorizes the jungle genre as a sub-category of the adventure film: *The Golden Age of Cinema: Hollywood, 1929–45* (Malden: Blackwell, 2007), 206–07.

7. Marcy Carriker Smothers, *Walt's Disneyland: A Walk in the Park with Walt Disney* (Los Angeles: Disney Editions, 2021), 76–82; Walt's ideal was a seven-minute boat ride.

8. See the early concept layout by Marvin Davis in Jeff Kurtti, *Walt Disney's Imagineering Legends and the Genesis of the Disney Theme Park* (New York: Disney Editions, 2008), 35; on Davis's career, 34–39.

9. The Neptune feature endured in descriptions of the Jungle Cruise in magazines published after Disneyland's opening: Guillaume Hanoteau, "Une ville qui s'appelle Disney," *Paris Match*, no. 335, Aug. 27-Sept. 3, 1955, 41; "Newest Travel Lure: Disneyland," *Travel*, 104:1, July 1955, 19.

10. "Here's Your First View of Disneyland," *Look*, 18:22, Nov. 2, 1954, 82–83; also reproduced in Jeff Kurtti and Bruce Gordon, *The Art of Disneyland* (New York: Disney Editions, 2006), x–xi.

11. "Tropical Designer Reveals: Goff Takes Up New Hobbies," *Disneyland News*, 1:2, Aug. 1955, 6, 18. For his recollections on creating the ride, see "An Interview with Harper Goff," *"E" Ticket*, no. 14 (Winter 1992–93): 8–11.

12. See for example Jim Korkis, *The Vault of Walt, Volume 2* (Theme Park Press: 2013), 177; Chris Strodder, *The Disneyland Encyclopedia* (Solana Beach: Santa Monica Press, 2012), 233; Sam Gennawey, *The Disneyland Story: The Unofficial Guide to the Evolution of Walt Disney's Dream* (Birmingham: Keen, 2014), 72.

13. Hibler's narration confuses crocodiles with alligators.

14. For a short history of the travelogue in Africa, see Kenneth M. Cameron, *Africa on Film: Beyond Black and White* (New York: Continuum, 1994), chap. 3.

15. J. B. Kaufman, *South of the Border with Disney: Walt Disney and the Good Neighbor Program, 1941–1948* (New York: Disney Editions, 2009), 226 n. 136.

16. "Camera Crews Cover the Earth," *Disneyland News*, 1:12, June 1956, 8.

17. "Milotte Photographic Team Shoots True Life Features," *Disneyland News*, 1:2, Aug. 1955, 6.

18. "Tropical Designer Reveals," 6, 18.

19. "Milotte Photographic Team," 6; "'African Lion' Hailed by New York Critics," *Disneyland News*, 1:4, Oct. 10, 1955, 12–13. In a period when Walt's interest in animation was waning, the *True-Life Adventures* offered the promise of a new genre of storytelling: "People & Places Reveal 'Blue Men of Morocco,'" *Disneyland News*, 2:1, July 1956, 9. Of the seventeen *People and Places* documentaries that Disney filmed across the globe, only one focuses on Africa: *Blue Men of Morocco* deals with a nomadic Muslim tribe.

20. For Disney's transformation of the safari genre (defined as a film in which animals are captured or shot) and the travelogue, and for the impact of Disney's animated classics, *Dumbo* and *Bambi*, see Derek Bousé, *Wildlife Films* (Philadelphia: University of Pennsylvania Press, 2000), 37–57, 62–70, 132–47.

21. *Disneyland: A Complete Guide* (Racine: Western Printing, 1956), [22].

22. I have adapted and amended the categories of stereotypes proposed by Kevin Dunn, "Lights … Camera … Africa: Images of Africa and Africans in Western Popular Films of the 1930s," *African Studies Review* 39 (Apr. 1996): 149–75.

23. Dana Benelli argues for calling *Trader Horn* a hybrid film, in which the story is often interrupted by travelogue segments: "Hollywood and the

Travelogue," *Visual Anthropology* 15:1 (2002): 3–16.

24. For the American idea of Africa created by the *Tarzan* films, see Cameron, *Africa on Film*, chap. 2.

25. "A great deal of the credit is due to the expert work of the camera men, Charles Clarke and Clyde de Vinna. Their photography helps in lending a veneer of veracity to this highly imaginative affair. … The action is shown with such conviction that how it was accomplished would be apt to baffle anybody. Just as one might hazard that Tarzan is struggling with a stuffed lion, one sees that the animal has a full-toothed jaw"; Mordaunt Hall, "Life in the Jungle: 'Tarzan and His Mate' a Marvel of Camera Work," *New York Times*, Apr. 29, 1934, X3.

26. Steven Bingen, Stephen X. Sylvester, and Michael Troyen, *M-G-M: Hollywood's Greatest Backlot* (Solana Beach: Santa Monica Press, 2011), 222–23.

27. Tim Onosko, "Made in Hollywood, USA: A Conversation with A. Arnold Gillespie," *Velvet Light Trap* no. 18 (1978): 47.

28. Studio publicity claimed that Weissmuller did his own stunts: "'Tarzan' Weissmuller Goes for Real Ride on Rhinoceros' Back," *Chicago Daily Tribune*, Mar. 14, 1934, 8. In an extensive interview, director W. S. Van Dyck set down rules for filming wild animals in a narrative: "You may say what you like about temperamental actors in Hollywood, but, believe it or not, wild animals are ten times as bad"; "Picturing Wild Beasts," *New York Times*, May 27, 1932, X5.

29. Rudy Behlmer, "Tarzan, Hollywood's Greatest Jungle Hero," part 1, *American Cinematographer*, 68:1, Jan. 1987, 43.

30. *The Story of Disneyland* (Racine: Western Printing, 1955), [3].

31. "Mattey Designs Animals Seen in Jungle Journey," *Disneyland News*, 1:2, Aug. 1955, 4.

32. Didier Ghez, ed., *Walt's People: Talking Disney with the Artists Who Knew Him*, vol. 14 (Orlando: Theme Park Press, 2014), 273–81; "Disney's Mechanized Magic," *"E" Ticket*, no. 25 (Winter 1996): 6–19; "Chris Mueller," *"E" Ticket*, no. 25 (Winter 1996): 34–39. See also Tom McHugh, "Walt Disney's Mechanical

Wonderland," *Popular Mechanics*, 108:5, Nov. 1957, 138–43, 230. I am unable to confirm the legend that Mattey worked on the *Tarzan* beasts for MGM.

33. "Sound Effects Add Realism to Disneyland," *Radio and Television News*, Aug. 1956, 52–53.

34. Mordaunt Hall, "The Screen," *New York Times*, March 28, 1932, 11.

35. *New York Evening Post*, excerpted from *Literary Digest* (April 16, 1932); quoted in David Fury, *Kings of the Jungle: An Illustrated Reference to "Tarzan" on Screen and Television* (Jefferson: McFarland, 1994), 70.

36. Robert W. Fenton, *Edgar Rice Burroughs and Tarzan: A Biography of the Author and His Creation* (Jefferson: McFarland, 2003), 136.

37. For a chronology of *Tarzan* sets on the MGM backlot, see Bingen, Sylvester, and Troyen, *M-G-M*, 116–19, 128, 146–47, 168–69, 226–27, 241–44. When MGM lost interest in *Tarzan* and the rights reverted to producer Sol Lesser, Weissmuller moved to the RKO Forty Acres backlot, where, in an extremely confined space, art directors and greensmen created a jungle bordered by a creek that, aided by matte paintings, served another six movies with the Olympic champion; Steven Bingen, *Hollywood's Lost Backlot: 40 Acres of Glamour and Mystery* (Guilford: Lyons Press, 2019), 122–25.

38. Hedda Hopper, "Hollywood Sets Would Fool Mother Nature," *Los Angeles Times*, Nov. 26, 1939, C3. On Hollywood landscapes, see also Juan Antonio Ramirez, *Architecture for the Screen: A Critical Study of Set Design in Hollywood's Golden Age*, trans. John F. Moffitt (Jefferson: McFarland, 2004), 72–76.

39. T.S., "A Kipling Jungle Is Re-created," *New York Times*, March 8, 1942, 14–15.

40. "Creating the Disney Landscape: An Interview with Bill Evans," *"E" Ticket*, no. 23 (Spring 1996): 4–15.

41. Korkis, *The Vault of Walt, Volume 2*, 175; see Randy Bright, *Disneyland: Inside Story* (New York: Abrams, 1987), 69–73.

42. Public Relations Department, "Building a Dream," *Walt Disney's Magic Kingdom Disneyland*, opening day press kit (Anaheim: Disneyland, Inc., 1955; facsimile reprint, Disneyland Press & Publicity, 2005), 5.

43. "Green Emphasizes Spring throughout Realms of Park," *Disneyland News*, 1:2, Aug. 1955, 17.

44. Weldon D. Woodson, "Through the Jungles of Disneyland," *American Forests*, Jan. 1956, 20–22.

45. Hopper, "Hollywood Sets," C3; Morgan Evans, *Walt Disney: Disneyland: World of Flowers* (Burbank: Walt Disney Productions, 1965), 57, 60.

46. Mae Tinée, "'Tarzan' Offers Movie Thrills for All Ages," *Chicago Daily Tribune*, Apr. 8, 1932, 19.

47. Rudy Behlmer, "Tarzan and M-G-M: The Rest of the Story," part 2, *American Cinematographer*, 68:2, Feb. 1987, 42.

48. Brady Earnhart, "A Colony of the Imagination: Vicarious Spectatorship in MGM's Early *Tarzan* Talkies," *Quarterly Review of Film and Video* 24:4 (2007): 346.

49. Edwin Schallert, "Man of the Jungle and Jane Here," *Los Angeles Times*, Apr. 23, 1934, 8.

50. Behlmer, "Tarzan and M-G-M," 42.

51. "Stanley's Exploits in Search for Livingston [sic] Brought to Life by Adventureland Boat Trip," *Disneyland News*, 1:2, Aug. 1955, 6.

52. Dunn, "Lights … Camera … Africa," 166.

53. William Beinart and Dominique Schafer, "Hollywood in Africa 1947–62: Imaginative Construction and Landscape Realism," in *Wild Things: Nature and the Social Imagination*, ed. William Beinart, Karen Middleton, and Simon Pooley (Cambridge: White Horse Press, 2013), 47. See also Michael J. Anderson, "*Hatari!* and the Hollywood Safari Picture," *Senses of Cinema* no. 52 (Sept. 2009) (online journal).

For the conventions recycled on film, see Sarah Steinbock-Pratt, who posits, "The medium of photography belied the creative process. Photographs and film present themselves—rather than drawings or verbal descriptions—as objective truth. Furthermore, the images to which people were exposed tended to fit within the preexisting discourse"; "The Lions in the Jungle: Representations of Africa and Africans in American Cinema," in *Africans and the Politics of Popular Culture*, ed. Toyin Falola and Augustine Agwuele (Rochester: University of Rochester Press, 2009), 214.

54. For example, Karal Ann Marling with Donna R. Braden, *Behind the Magic: 50 Years of Disneyland* (Dearborn: The Henry Ford, 2004), 82, who calls *The African Queen* "one of Walt Disney's personal favorites."

55. For the extraordinary story of the film's creation, see Rudy Behlmer, *Behind the Scenes: The Making of …* (Hollywood: Samuel French, 1990), chap. 13; Katharine Hepburn, *The Making of "The African Queen," or How I Went to Africa with Bogart, Bacall, and Huston and Almost Lost My Mind* (New York: Alfred A. Knopf, 1987); and the documentary *Embracing Chaos: Making* The African Queen, directed by Eric Young (Paramount Home Entertainment, 2010).

56. Bruce Gordon and David Mumford, *Disneyland: The Nickel Tour* (Santa Clarita: Camphor Tree, 2000), 61.

57. Behlmer, *Behind the Scenes*, 234, 250.

58. Hepburn, *Making of*, 93–97.

59. Cameron, *Africa on Film*, 28–30.

60. Advertisement, *New York Times* (Nov. 5, 1950), quoted in "Bwana Metro Makes a Piksha," *Africa on Film: Myth and Reality*, ed. Richard A. Maynard (Rochelle Park: Hayden Book Company, 1974), 48.

61. "Stanley's Exploits," 6. For a photograph of the Jungle Cruise natives during installation, see "Disney's Mechanized Magic," 6. Critical comments on race in Disney parks have been brief; see for example Stacy Warren, "The City as Theme Park and the Theme Park as City: Amusement Space, Urban Form, and Cultural Change," Ph.D. diss., University of British Columbia, 1993, 163. In January 2021 the Walt Disney Company announced that it would upgrade the Jungle Cruise to remove offensive stereotypes.

62. Scott Tracy Griffin, *Tarzan on Film* (London: Titan Books, 2016), 46.

63. Julia Kershow, "Capturing Africa: Sightseeing through the Tarzan Cycle of the 1930s," *Athanor* 36 (2018): 80.

64. Guido Abbattista, ed., *Moving Bodies, Displaying Nations: National Cultures, Race and Gender in World Expositions Nineteenth to Twentieth First Century* (Trieste: EUT Edizione Università di Trieste, 2014).

65. Philips, *Fairground Attractions*, 155–60; Lauren Rabinovitz, *Electric*

Dreamland: Amusement Parks, Movies, and American Modernity (New York: Columbia University Press, 2012), 120.

66. Clara Henderson, "'When Hearts Beat like Native Drums': Music and the Sexual Dimensions of the Notions of 'Savage' and 'Civilized' in *Tarzan and His Mate*," *Africa Today* 48:4 (Winter 2001): 91–124; Dunn, "Lights … Camera … Africa," 154–55, 163–64; Sarah Steinbock-Pratt, "Lions in the Jungle," 214–36.

67. Chesly Manly, "Witchcraft, Sexual Evils, Paganism Run Riot in Africa: Natives Commit Ritual Murders and Cannibalism despite City Veneer of Civilization," *Chicago Tribune*, June 15, 1958, 1, 10; Jarred Staller, *Converging on Cannibals: Terrors of Slaving in Atlantic Africa, 1509–1670* (Athens: Ohio University Press, 2019).

68. It is widely accepted that the design of Disney's Evil Queen in *Snow White and the Seven Dwarfs* was influenced by Helen Gahagan's ice goddess character in *She*: J. B Kaufman, *The Fairest One of All: The Making of Walt Disney's* Snow White and the Seven Dwarfs (San Francisco: Walt Disney Family Foundation Press, 2012), 78, 173 n. 84.

69. Todd James Pierce points out the similarity between the accoutrements worn by Adventureland's cannibals and the (anachronistic) cannibals portrayed in Disney's *20,000 Leagues under the Sea*; the same design team worked on both; blog, "How Could I Have Missed This?" disneyhistoryinstitute.com, Feb. 27, 2012.

70. Jerry Hulce, "Dream Realized—Disneyland Opens," *Los Angeles Times*, July 18, 1955, A1.

71. David Koenig, *The 55ers: The Pioneers Who Settled Disneyland* (Irvine: Bonaventure Press, 2019), 167–68.

72. Cameron, *Africa on Film*, 71–73.

73. "Disneyland: Ronnie and Vickie Enjoy a Day of Fun in Kiddies' Paradise," *Ebony* 11:5, Mar., 1956, 63–65. At the time of the 1959 expansion, the ABC television network special, "Kodak Presents Disneyland '59," noted that the park had played "host to fifteen million visitors, to kings and presidents, to almost one in every ten Americans, to people of every race and creed."

74. Andrew A. Erish, *Col. William N. Selig, the Man Who Invented Hollywood* (Austin: University of Texas Press, 2012), 111, 114–17, 128–29.

75. Jeffrey Wayne Maulhardt, *Images of America: Jungleland* (Charleston: Arcadia, 2011), 7–8, 25.

Chapter 4

1. For example, Deborah Philips, *Fairground Attractions: A Genealogy of the Pleasure Ground* (London: Bloomsbury Academic, 2012), 202–08; Gary S. Cross and John K. Walton, *The Playful Crowd: Pleasure Places in the Twentieth Century* (New York: Columbia University Press, 2005), 184; Priscilla Hobbs, *Walt's Utopia: Disneyland and American Mythmaking* (Jefferson: McFarland, 2015), 158–59; Alex Wright, *The Imagineering Field Guide to Disneyland: An Imagineer's-Eye Tour* (New York: Disney Editions, 2008), 110–11.

2. Futuristic narratives were not a genre that the studio engaged in. Therefore, when the *Disneyland* TV series was launched, there was no backlog of theatrical productions in the vault that could be aired under the thematic heading of Tomorrowland. In the series' first year, there was just one Tomorrowland show, "Man in Space."

3. Jack Holland, "Walt Disney: The Man Who Won't Sell You Short," *TV-Radio Life*, 31:3, Mar. 4, 1955, 5.

4. Many passing references to Tomorrowland's movie connections exist in print; see for example, Philips, *Fairground Attractions*, 202–203, which is otherwise excellent regarding the legacy of literature and world's fairs. Despite the title, other issues prevail in Scott Bukatman, "There's Always Tomorrowland: Disney and the Hypercinematic Experience," *October* 57 (Summer 1991): 55–78.

5. "Motion Picture Exhibition Techniques at Disney's Tomorrowland," *Business Screen Magazine*, 16:6, Sept. 15, 1955, 37, 44.

6. "Walt Disney Plans Park for Children," *Los Angeles Times*, Mar. 28, 1952, A10.

7. "Planning the First Disney Parks: A Talk with Marvin Davis," *"E" Ticket*, no. 28 (Winter 1997): 14–15. For early design sketches, which incorporate the streamlined motifs of the Art Moderne style of the 1930s and even the "lily pad" columns of Frank Lloyd Wright's Johnson Wax

Administration Building (1936–39), see Jeff Kurtti, Vanessa Hunt, and Paul Wolski, *The Disney Monorail: Imagineering a Highway in the Sky* (Los Angeles: Disney Editions, 2020), 44–67.

8. Bob Thomas, *Walt Disney: An American Original* (New York: Hyperion, 1994), 268.

9. "Clock of the World Symbolizes Tomorrowland Future Theme," *Disneyland News*, 1:3, Sept. 1955, 18; "Tomorrowland Clock of the World," *"E" Ticket*, no. 45 (Summer 2007): 24–29.

10. "Tomorrowland's Food Service: Here Today!" *Disneyland News*, 2:4, Oct. 1956, 7. For midcentury futurist architecture, see Alan Hess, *Googie Redux: Ultramodern Roadside Architecture* (San Francisco: Chronicle Books, 2004).

11. "Tomorrowland Exhibits Show World of the Future," *Disneyland News*, 1:2, Aug. 1955, 4, 18.

12. Thomas M. Pryor, "Cine-Miracle Joins Big Screen's Big Parade," *New York Times*, July 3, 1955, X5; quoted in "Motion Picture Exhibition Techniques," 38. See also Thomas M. Pryor, "Disney Presents Movies-in-Round," *New York Times*, June 28, 1955, 23.

13. "'Around the West' Movie Draws Rave Reviews," *Disneyland News*, 1:3, Sept. 1955, 16.

14. Randy Bright, *Disneyland: Inside Story* (New York: Abrams, 1987), 89–91; Jim Korkis, *The Revised Vault of Walt: Unofficial, Unauthorized, Uncensored Disney Stories Never Told* (Orlando: Theme Park Press, 2012), 151–59.

15. The Circarama filming system consisted of eleven 16mm Cine Kodak cameras, chosen for their lighter weight compared to the standard 35 mm camera, facing outwards on a platform and mounted on the top of a Rambler station wagon.

16. "360 Degrees: Super-Wide Screen Shows Travel Film in Circarama," *Disneyland News*, 1:3, Sept. 1955, 16; "Motion Picture Exhibition Techniques," 41.

17. For an interpretation of *A Tour of the West* as a combination of road trip and celebration of consumerism and free enterprise, see Sarah Nilson, "America's Salesman: The USA in Circarama," in *Learning from Mickey, Donald, and Walt: Essays on Disney's Edutainment Films*, ed.

A. Bowdoin Van Riper (Jefferson: McFarland, 2011), 326–53.

18. Jennifer Lynn Peterson, "'The Nation's First Playground': Travel Films and the American West," in *Virtual Voyages: Cinema and Travel*, ed. Jeffrey Ruoff (Durham: Duke University Press, 2006), 79–98.

19. Tom Gunning, "Landscape and the Fantasy of Moving Pictures: Early Cinema's Phantom Rides," in *Cinema and Landscape*, ed. Graeme Harper and Jonathan Rayner (Bristol: Intellect, 2010), 33–70.

20. *Chicago Railroad Fair: Official Guide Book* [Chicago: The Fair, 1949, 10].

21. Thomas Belton, *Widescreen Cinema* (Cambridge: Harvard University Press, 1992).

22. A trimmed-down version of *Napoléon*, without the climactic three-screen effect, toured the United States on a limited basis. Disney was in New York City on February 11, 1929, when it opened at the Fifty-Fifth Street Playhouse.

23. Alastair Dallas, *Inventing Disneyland: The Unauthorized Story of the Team That Made Walt Disney's Dream Come True* (Orlando: Theme Park Press, 2018), 196–98.

24. David R. Smith, "The Sorcerer's Apprentice: Birthplace of *Fantasia*," *Millimeter* 4:2 (Feb. 1976): 66.

25. Michael Broggie, *Walt Disney's Railroad Story: The Small-Scale Fascination That Led to a Full-Scale Kingdom* (Pasadena: Pentrex, 1997), 130–31; Bruce Gordon and David Mumford, *Disneyland: The Nickel Tour* (Santa Clarita: Camphor Tree, 2000), 154; Jeff Kurtti, *Walt Disney's Imagineering Legends and the Genesis of the Disney Theme Park* (New York: Disney Editions, 2008), 97.

26. Leslie Iwerks and John Kenworthy, *The Hand Behind the Mouse: An Intimate Biography of the Man Walt Disney Called "The Greatest Animator in the World"* (New York: Disney Editions, 2001), 185–87, 198–99. Jeff Kurtti surmises that Walt attended the premiere engagement of *This Is Cinerama* in April 1953 at the Warner Hollywood Theatre; Kurtti, *Walt Disney's Imagineering Legends*, 97 n. 8.

27. Bright, *Disneyland: Inside Story*, 89–91. Both Iwerks and Walt's names appear as "Inventors" on the application

for the patent, filed on the year anniversary of Circarama's opening, July 17, 1956, but Broggie alone is listed as technical advisor in contemporary reports: "Motion Picture Exhibition Techniques," 38. Drawings for the patent show the battery of eleven cameras mounted on an automobile roof, the circular auditorium, and the location of the projectors on cantilevers; Stacey V. Jones, "Circarama Patented," *New York Times*, July 2, 1960, 38. Iwerks received the Herbert T. Kalmus Gold Medal from the Society of Motion Picture and Television Engineers (SMPTE) for technical achievements that included Circarama.

28. Norman C. Lipton, "Disneyland's Circarama: Where the Movie Screen Surrounds You," *Popular Photography*, Dec. 1955, 96; "Disney Shows 360-Deg. Film Screen Process," *Los Angeles Times*, June 28, 1955, A1.

29. "AMC Exhibit Unique," *Nash News*, 19:4, Aug.-Sept. 1955, 1–2.

30. Pryor, "Cine-Miracle Joins," X5.

31. Lipton, "Disneyland's Circarama," 185.

32. Zofia Trafas, "Designed for Impact: Widescreen and 360-Degree Cinematic Interiors at the Postwar World's Fair," *Interiors*, 3:1–2, 2012, 143–67. A second Circarama film, *America the Beautiful*, of sixteen minutes duration, premiered at the World's Fair in Brussels in 1958 and then replaced *A Tour of the West* at Disneyland in 1960, when sponsorship changed to Bell Telephone. In June 1960 a new format, called Circle-Vision, featured a 35 mm system of projecting onto nine slightly curved panels, which eliminated much of the distortion in the first version. Arguably the most long-lived 360-degree films are those in Disney theme parks, particularly the ones in the Canada and China Pavilions in the world's-fair-like World Showcase at EPCOT.

33. "Motion Picture Exhibition Techniques," 41–42; "Diorama Model Builders Faced Unique Problems," *Disneyland News*, 1:6, Dec. 10, 1955, 13.

34. *In the World beneath Us: What Happens?* brochure, [Richfield, 1955]; Richfield Presents Geological History," *Disneyland News*, 1:3, Sept. 1955, 15; "Motion Picture Exhibition Techniques," 41–42.

35. "Motion Picture Exhibition Techniques," 43–44.

36. Story meeting notes, April 17, 1954, quoted by David R. Smith, "They're Following Our Script: Walt Disney's Trip to Tomorrowland," *Future* (May 1978): 55–56; reprinted in *The Walt Disney Film Archives: The Animated Movies, 1921–1968*, ed. Daniel Kothenschulte (Cologne: Taschen, 2016), 490–99.

37. *Your Tanner Gray Line Tour to Disneyland*, brochure, Tanner Gray Line Motor Tours, 1955; *The Story of Disneyland* (Racine: Western Printing, 1955), [22]. A placard outside the ride touted, "A factual and thrilling ride through space at 13,716 miles per hour! Experience the "feel" of space travel—see the Earth below and the heavens above as you pass space station Terra, coast around the Moon and return to planet Earth...."

38. David R. Smith, "Walt Disney's Conquest of Space," *Starlog*, 3, May 1978, 30–33; Don Hahn, *Yesterday's Tomorrow: Disney's Magical Mid-Century* (Los Angeles: Disney Editions, 2017), 95; Todd James Pierce, *The Life and Times of Ward Kimball: Maverick of Disney Animation* (Jackson: University Press of Mississippi, 2019), 191.

39. "Noted Rocket Moon Authorities Contribute Skills to Space Ride," *Disneyland News*, 1:2, Aug. 1955, 2. For descriptions of the ride, "Space Travel: The Trip to the Moon, Disneyland Style," *Disneyland News*, 1:9, Mar. 10, 1956, 10–11; "Feeling of Space Journey Accompanies Trip to the Moon," *Disneyland News*, 2:7, Jan. 1957, 6.

40. As noted by contemporaries, von Braun possessed a movie-star charisma. He even had a Hollywood agent: Michael J. Neufeld, *Von Braun: Dreamer of Space, Engineer of War* (New York: Vintage Books, 2008), 286–87.

41. For example, "What Are We Waiting For?" *Collier's*, Mar. 22, 1952, 23, which stressed political urgency: "It is now possible to establish an artificial satellite or 'space station' in which man can live or work far beyond the earth's atmosphere. ... The first nation to do so will control the earth." See Randy Liebermann, "The *Collier's* and Disney Series," in *Blueprint for Space: Science Fiction to Science Fact*, ed. Frederick I. Orway and Randy Liebermann (Washington, DC: Smithsonian Institution Press, 1992): 135–46. For another early example in the popular

media, see Jack Coggins and Fletcher Pratt, *Rockets, Jets, Guided Missiles, and Space Ships* (New York: Random House, 1951), with a forward by Willy Ley.

42. "Disneyland: Welcome to Disneyland," newspaper advertising insert, July 1955, [10].

43. "Rocket Trip to Moon Blasts Off for Realistic Space Ride," *Disneyland News*, 1:2, Aug. 1955, 16; "Motion Picture Exhibition Techniques," 43–44. For the script of the captain's intercom talk, see "Disneyland's Rocket to the Moon," *"E" Ticket*, no. 24 (Summer 1996): 18–31. For clips of the Briefing Room film and scanner view of the blast off, see "Dateline Disneyland," the park's televised premiere, July 17, 1955.

44. Ira Wolfert, "Walt Disney's Magic Kingdom," *Reader's Digest*, 76, Apr. 1960, 149–50.

45. Another antecedent was Hale's Tours, a franchised ride developed shortly after the turn of the century, that simulated train travel. Installed in Kansas City's Electric Park in 1905, it may have impressed Disney in his teens, when he lived in the "Paris of the Plains," from 1911 to 1917. Screens at the front and back of Hale's make-believe railroad car showed the landscape slipping by, as the carriage rocked on "rails" and electric fans blew air at the audience. The contraption was so popular that it was duplicated at over 500 urban locations and amusement parks worldwide. An important ingredient of what would later be termed "motion simulation" was the *frisson* felt by "passengers" that technology might go awry and cause a fatal mishap; Lauren Rabinovitz, *Electric Dreamland: Amusement Parks, Movies, and American Modernity* (New York: Columbia University Press, 2012), chap. 3.

46. For the historical precedents, see Philips, *Fairground Amusements*, chap. 9.

47. David A. Kirby, "The Future Is Now: Diegetic Prototypes and the Role of Popular Films in Generating Real-World Technological Development," *Social Studies of Science* 40:1 (Feb. 2010): 58. Pal went on to produce three more futuristic films: *When Worlds Collide* (1951), *War of the Worlds* (1953), and *Conquest of Space* (1955), the latter based on a book co-authored by Willy Ley.

48. Helen Gould, "Scientific Films Staging Comeback," *New York Times*, May 21,

1950, X4: "Far from portraying the more fantastic space excursions of Buck Rogers or even H. G. Wells, the studios are in step with science … [and] might even be said to be prodding science along."

49. "Rocket to the Moon," *Life*, Jan. 17, 1949, 67–73; the article is unsigned, and the "V-2 rocket engineers" who believed in the possibility of space travel are unnamed, although von Braun was surely among them. George Pal also consulted with a team of scientists who could lend credibility to his project. Willy Ley collaborated on *Destination Moon* with astronomical view painter and special effects designer, Chesley Bonestell, who created the movie's lunar sets.

50. Gail Morgan Hickman, *The Films of George Pal* (South Brunswick: A. S. Barnes, 1977); Bradley Schauer, "The Greatest Exploitation Special Ever: *Destination Moon* and Postwar Independent Distribution," *Film History* 24:1 (2015): 1–28.

51. Bosley Crowther, "Two New Features Arrive," *New York Times*, June 28, 1950, 32.

52. Edwin Schallert, "Space Ship Flight Dazzling Success," *Los Angeles Times*, Aug. 10, 1950, A8: "One gains the impression that it is as authentic as a technical advisor on art in the skies can make it. Chesley Bonestell wins this particular credit.…" See also Thomas E. Stimson, Jr., "Rocket to the Moon: No Longer a Fantastic Dream," *Popular Mechanics*, May 1950, 89–94, 230, 236.

53. "Disneyland's Rocket to the Moon," 26–27.

54. Smith, "They're Following Our Script," 57; Neufeld, *Von Braun*, 285.

55. "Hollywood Will Reach Moon First," *Los Angeles Times*, Dec. 11, 1949, E1, 3.

56. By now, Ward was truly one of Walt's fair-haired boys. In an interview in 1956, with Pete Martin, the *Saturday Evening Post* writer and co-author with Diane Disney Miller of a forthcoming biography of Diane's father, Walt confirmed Kimball's status. See Diane Disney Miller and Pete Martin, *The Story of Walt Disney* (New York: Dell, 1959), 155. The interview with Martin took place in May or June 1956.

57. "Introducing Disneyland," *TV Radio Mirror*, Dec. 1954, 62–65; "Walt

Disney's Tomorrowland," *TV Guide*, Jan. 1955, 8–9; "Disney Plans TV Trip to the Moon," *Popular Science*, Nov. 1955, 99–101; J. P. Shandley, "TV: A Trip to the Moon," *New York Times*, Dec. 29, 1955, 41; Pierce, *Life and Times of Ward Kimball*, chaps. 12–13; J. P. Telotte, "Animating Space: Disney, Science, and Empowerment," *Science Fiction Studies* 35:1 (Mar. 2008): 48–59; J. P. Telotte, *The Mouse Machine: Disney and Technology* (Urbana: University of Illinois Press, 2008), 104–112; Sven Grampp, "Picturing the Future in Outer Space at the Dawn of the Space Race: Disney's *Tomorrowland* (USA 1955–56) and *Road to the Stars* (USSR 1957)," *Repositorium Medienkulturforschung* 8 (2015): 1–29.

58. Smith, "They're Following Our Script," 56.

59. A. Bowdoin Van Riper, "The Promise of Things to Come: *Disneyland* and the Wonders of Technology, 1954–1958," in *Learning from Mickey, Donald, and Walt*, ed. A. Bowdoin Van Riper (Jefferson: McFarland, 2011), 84–102.

60. "Limited animation" refers to the use of shortcuts to avoid traditional time-consuming cel animation. The Cartoon Modern aesthetic dates to Disney's inspirational artists of the late 1940s, like Mary Blair, who encouraged a simpler, flatter style that opposed the high realism of Golden-Age animation. Rival studios, like UPA, embraced these changes, partly for economic reasons, and considerable stylization appeared in 1950s Disney shorts and the feature film, *Sleeping Beauty*. See "Walt Disney's Man in Space: Ward Kimball," *"E" Ticket*, no. 24 (Summer 1996): 12; Amid Amidi, *Cartoon Modern: Style and Design in Fifties Animation* (San Francisco: Chronicle Books, 2006).

61. Gary Westfahl, *The Spacesuit Film: A History, 1918–1969* (Jefferson: McFarland, 2012), 24.

62. Kimball confirmed that the two teams worked separately, but that Disney asked them to collaborate, and the attraction designers borrowed elements from the TV series. Regarding the sci-fi ruins, he stated, "If that's also in the TWA Rocket to the Moon ride, they may have gotten it from our shows. I only saw that attraction once, back when it opened"; "Walt Disney's Man in Space: Ward Kimball,"

14–16. For comments on cultural context and the relationship between the park and television Tomorrowlands, see Catherine L. Newell, "The Strange Case of Dr. von Braun and Mr. Disney: Frontierland, Tomorrowland, and America's Final Frontier," *Journal of Religion and Popular Culture* 25:3 (Fall 2013): 416–29. In "Man and the Moon" the ship is constructed at the space station, where the moon journey begins.

63. "The TWA Rocket: Technically Speaking," *"E" Ticket* no. 29 (Spring 1998): 32–39. Toy models of rockets, planes, and cars were demonstrated in a nearby fenced enclosure: "A Visit to Hobbyland: Models Demonstrated in Tomorrowland Show," *Disneyland News*, 1:4, Oct. 10, 1955, 14.

64. "Disneyland's Rocket to the Moon," 27–28; Hench indicated, "There is a little of the V2 rocket in its design."

65. "Disneyland's Rocket to the Moon," 68.

66. The rationale was that the *Luna* would be fueled by atomic power; Robert A. Heinlein, "The Making of *Destination Moon*," *Starlog*, no. 6, June 1977, 23 n. 2. See Newell, "The Strange Case of Dr. von Braun," 423; Ron Miller, "The Spaceship as Icon: Designs from Verne to the Early 1950s," in *Blueprint for Space: Science Fiction to Science Fact*, ed. Frederick I. Ordway and Randy Liebermann (Washington, DC: Smithsonian Institution Press, 1992), 49–68.

67. Vivian Sobchack, *Screening Space: The American Science Fiction Film* (New Brunswick: Rutgers University Press, 1997), 68–69.

68. Gould, "Scientific Films Staging Comeback," X4.

69. "Disneyland's Rocket to the Moon," 27–29. Von Braun understood the persuasiveness of a sleek, futuristic style as a means of selling space exploration to the American public. According to Neufeld, *Von Braun*, 285–90, von Braun's contribution to the Rocket to the Moon attraction consisted of consulting on the plans, compared to more extensive involvement with the Disneyland television shows. See also Howard E. McCurdy, *Space and the American Imagination* (Washington, DC: Smithsonian Institution Press, 1997), 43. The space fantasy *Project Moon Base* (1953), co-scripted by Robert A. Heinlein, shows

the influence of *Destination Moon* despite its cheesy elements.

70. The *Luna* influenced other media as well. A single-stage spaceship, coated in white paint with cherry-red trim, graces the cover of *Objectif Lune* (1953) in the Belgian cartoonist Hergé's classic comic book series, *Les Aventures de Tintin*; the English-language version (1959) was named *Destination Moon*. Garry Apgar kindly pointed out this connection.

71. *Picture Souvenir Book of Disneyland in Natural Color* (Boston: American Souvenir Company, 1955; facsimile reprint, New York: Disney Editions, 2005), [22].

72. "Space Station X-1 Gives Outer Space View of U.S.," *Disneyland News*, 2:4, Oct. 1956, 2.

73. Erkki Huhtamo, *Illusions in Motion: Media Archaeology of the Moving Panorama and Related Spectacles* (Cambridge: MIT Press, 2013).

74. "Painting the Backdrops," *New York Times*, Sept. 28, 1941, 4X; Richard M. Isackes and Karen L. Maness, *The Art of the Hollywood Backdrop* (New York: Regan Arts, 2016). McConnell oversaw a staff of eight artists. Most of his work was filmed in black and white, but he painted in color because it facilitated design decisions, and actors preferred color's greater naturalism.

75. "Motion Picture Art Work on Exhibition," *Disneyland News*, 1:2, Aug. 1955, 4; "Movie Art Directors Show Making of Motion Picture," *Disneyland News*, 1:3, Sept. 1955, 19. The society, founded in 1937, became the Art Directors Guild in 1998.

76. "Walt Disney Make-Believe Land Project Planned Here," *Burbank Review*, Mar. 27, 1952, A1. Coney Island's 1903 ride at Luna Park, 20,000 Leagues under the Sea, simulated an underwater voyage to the North Pole. For Verne's impact on science fiction writing and film as well as theme park attractions, see Philips, *Fairground Attractions*, 192–98.

77. Steven Clark and Rebecca Cline, *The Walt Disney Studios: A Lot to Remember* (Los Angeles: Disney Editions, 2016), 88–91.

78. Smith, D23 blog, News and Features, "In a League of Their Own," d23.com, Dec. 3, 2009.

79. "Famed Craft Nautilus Shown at Disneyland," *Los Angeles Times*, Aug. 17, 1955, A26; "Sea Monsters on *Disneyland*," *Atlanta Journal and Atlanta Constitution*, Jan. 6, 1955, 7E.

80. "Captain Nemo's Submarine: Nautilus Recovered from Davy Jones Locker, Placed on Exhibit," *Disneyland News*, 1:3, Sept. 1955, 9; Jack E. Janzen, "Disneyland's *20,000 Leagues under the Sea* Exhibit, "*E*" Ticket, no. 5 (Summer 1998): 16–29.

81. "An Interview with Harper Goff," "*E*" Ticket, no. 14 (Winter 1992–93): 4–5.

82. Cynthia J. Miller and A. Bowdoin Van Riper, "'In God's Good Time': *20,000 Leagues under the Sea* and Cold War Culture," in *It's the Disney Version! Popular Cinema and Literary Classics*, ed. Douglas Brode and Shea T. Brode (Lanham: Rowman & Littlefield, 2016), 93–104.

83. *The Story of Disneyland*, [22].

84. Mark Langer, "Why the Atom Is Our Friend: Disney, General Dynamics and the USS Nautilus," *Art History* 18:1 (Mar. 1995): 63–96.

85. Heinz Haber, *Our Friend the Atom: A Tomorrowland Adventure* (Syracuse: Singer, 1956), 46–48; Hahn, *Yesterday's Tomorrow*, 102–05.

86. Andrew Huebner, "Lost in Space: Technology and Turbulence in Futuristic Cinema of the 1950s," *Film & History* 40:2 (Fall 2010): 6–26.

87. Telotte, *Mouse Machine*, chap. 4; J. P. Telotte, "Science Fiction as 'True-Life Adventure': Disney and the Case of *20,000 Leagues under the Sea*," *Film & History* 40:2 (Fall 2010): 66–79.

88. "Guests Praise 'Fascinating' Sub Interior," *Disneyland News*, 1:3, Sept. 1955, 9.

89. Gordon and Mumford, *Disneyland: Nickel Tour*, 108–09. Visiting the Art Corner with Bob Thomas, Walt recalled his early art training in Chicago: Bob Thomas, "Guest Columnist: Walt Fascinated as Child on Magic Kingdom Visit," *Disneyland News*, 1:4, Oct. 10, 1955, 4.

90. "Thrills Await Drivers on 1986 Freeway," *Disneyland News*, 1:2, Aug. 1955, 4; "The Autopia: Disneyland's 'Expressway of the Future,'" "*E*" Ticket, no. 27 (Summer 1997): 12–27; Gordon and Mumford, *Disneyland: Nickel Tour*, 73–76.

91. "A Look at the Car of Tomorrow: Autopia Car Built Special for 'Freeway of the Future,'" *Disneyland News*, 1:8, Feb. 1956, 7; "Bob Gurr's Main Street

GurrMobiles," *"E" Ticket*, no. 27 (Summer 1997): 8–11; Lester Nehamkin, "Disneyland's Autopia," *Rod and Custom*, Nov. 1955, 11–15; "Roadsters in Disneyland," *Hot Rod*, Oct. 1955, 62–63.

92. "County Girds for Disneyland Rush," *Los Angeles Times*, July 10, 1955, OC1.

93. Mark Shiel, *Hollywood Cinema and the Real Los Angeles* (London: Reaktion, 2012), 100–111.

94. A quarter of a century later, Walt, in his last filmed appearance, the *EPCOT* film (October 1966), introduced a similar concept for an ideal community within the larger domain of his Florida Project.

95. Eric Avila, *Popular Culture in the Age of White Flight: Fear and Fantasy in Suburban Los Angeles* (Berkeley: University of California Press, 2006), 203. In 1956 President Eisenhower signed the Federal Aid Highway Act, earmarking $25 billion for the establishment of an interstate road system and improvement of existing roads.

96. Norman Bel Geddes, *Magic Motorways* (New York: Random House, 1940), 4. On the preceding page, the author states that Futurama was "the most popular show of any Fair in history."

97. Hedda Hopper, "Disney the Great!" *Chicago Daily Tribune*, Jan. 30, 1955, F22; Hahn, *Yesterday's Tomorrow*, 106–11.

98. Russell Schroeder, *Disney's Lost Chords* (Robbinsville: Voigt Publications, 2007), 196–99.

Chapter 5

1. Bob Thomas, after touring the newly inaugurated park with its creator, wrote that Walt "confessed" that Fantasyland was "his favorite realm"; Bob Thomas, "Guest Columnist: Walt Fascinated as a Child on Magic Kingdom Visit," *Disneyland News*, 1:4, Oct. 10, 1955, 4. See also *The Story of Disneyland* (Racine: Western Printing, 1955), [11]. For the literary, theatrical, and cinematic background of fairy tales as elements of amusement parks, and for Disney's appropriation of European children's stories, see Deborah Philips, *Fairground Attractions: A Genealogy of the Pleasure Ground* (London: Bloomsbury Academic, 2012), chap. 4.

2. "Disneyland Art Director … Bill Martin," *"E" Ticket*, no. 20 (Winter 1994–95): 10–12. Martin collaborated with Disney studio artists Bruce Bushman, Ken Anderson, and Claude Coats; Jeff Kurtti, *Walt Disney's Imagineering Legends and the Genesis of the Disney Theme Park* (New York: Disney Editions, 2008), 39–42. For the development of Fantasyland, see Alastair Dallas, *Inventing Disneyland: The Unauthorized Story of the Team That Made Walt Disney's Dream Come True* (Orlando: Theme Park Press, 2018), 127–31; "Disneyland," *McCall's*, 82:4, Jan. 1955, 8–11.

3. Sam Gennawey, *The Disneyland Story: The Unofficial Guide to the Evolution of Walt Disney's Dream* (Birmingham: Keen Communications, 2014), 85–89. "Dark ride" is a term used for indoor amusement park rides in which guests are conveyed in a moving vehicle, such as a car or a boat, on a track through a specially lit space, accompanied by special effects and music.

4. The names of these classic Fantasyland rides vary slightly in early guidebooks and publicity. Today's parkgoers may be more familiar with the Toad ride than with the Disney film. See Robert Neuman, "Disney's Final Package Film: The Making and Marketing of *The Adventures of Ichabod and Mr. Toad* (1949)," *Animation: An Interdisciplinary Journal* 14:2 (2019): 149–63.

5. Bruce Bushman, a Disney animation layout artist and sketch artist for *20,000 Leagues under the Sea*, produced drawings for the Alice in Wonderland Walk Thru; Matt Crandell, blog, "Bruce Bushman Concept Brownline of Alice Walkthru" (multiple posts) *vintagedisneyalice.blogspot.com*, 2010.

6. Storybook Land developed out of the Hollywood studios' use of architectural models and miniatures; Jack E. Janzen, "Storybook Land," *"E" Ticket*, no. 11 (Summer 1991): 6–19.

7. "Disneyland: Welcome to Disneyland," newspaper advertising supplement [July 1955], 2.

8. Priscilla Hobbs, *Walt's Utopia: Disneyland and American Mythmaking* (Jefferson: McFarland, 2015), chap. 6; Gary S. Cross and John K. Walton, *The Playful Crowd: Pleasure Places in the Twentieth Century* (New York: Columbia University

Press, 2005), 175–80; Susan Aronstein, "Pilgrimage and Medieval Narrative Structures in Disney's Parks," in *The Disney Middle Ages: A Fairy-Tale and Fantasy Past*, ed. Tison Pugh and Susan Aronstein (New York: Palgrave Macmillan, 2012), 62–66; Suzanne Rahn, "The Dark Ride of Snow White: Narrative Strategies at Disneyland," in *Disneyland and Culture: Essays on the Parks and their Influence*, ed. Kathy Merlock Jackson and Mark I. West (Jefferson: McFarland, 2011), 87–100; Jack E. Janzen, "The Original Snow White Dark Ride," *"E" Ticket*, no. 13 (Summer 1992): 16–25; "Mr. Toad's Wild Ride," *"E" Ticket*, no. 20 (Winter 1994–95): 20–33; "Disney's Peter Pan's Flight," *"E" Ticket*, no. 26 (Spring 1997): 10–25; "Alice in Wonderland," *"E" Ticket*, no. 31 (Spring 1999): 24–37.

9. Karal Ann Marling, "Imagineering the Disney Theme Parks," in *Designing Disney's Theme Parks: The Architecture of Reassurance*, ed. Karal Ann Marling (Montreal: Canadian Centre for Architecture, 1997), 70.

10. "Planning the First Disney Parks: A Talk with Marvin Davis," *"E" Ticket*, no. 28 (Winter 1997): 13–14.

11. Michael Broggie, *Walt Disney's Railroad Story: The Small-Scale Fascination That Led to a Full-Scale Kingdom* (Pasadena: Pentrex, 1997), 88–91.

12. "Walt Disney Make-Believe Land Project Planned Here," *Burbank Review*, Mar. 27, 1952, A1; "Walt Disney Plans Park for Children," *Los Angeles Times*, Mar. 28, 1952, A10.

13. Illustrated in Jeff Kurtti and Bruce Gordon, *The Art of Disneyland* (New York: Disney Editions, 2006), vi–vii; attributed to Goff, dated 1951.

14. Illustrated in Marling, "Imagineering," 51, attributed to Harper Goff; Randy Bright, *Disneyland: Inside Story* (New York: Abrams, 1987), 43.

15. In 1937, Disney erected a reduced version of the Dwarfs' House in the forecourt of the Carthay Circle Theatre. According to one of Walt's most trusted, senior unit directors, Wilfred Jackson, the boss was talking about a park even then. Another old hand, director Ben Sharpsteen, similarly remembered Walt, in 1940, saying he "was thinking of creating displays of Disney characters in their fantasy surroundings on land adjacent to the studio," as "something to show visitors." See Kurtti and Gordon, *Art of Disneyland*, vi; Neal Gabler, *Walt Disney: The Triumph of the American Imagination* (New York: Knopf, 2006), 484.

16. Ed Ainsworth, "Disneyland Readied by 'Mr. Magic,'" *Los Angeles Times*, June 23, 1955, A1.

17. Davis claimed, "I did a hundred and thirty-three different drawings and designs, because we had no idea where the Park was going to be or anything to begin with"; "Planning the First Disney Parks," 10; Marling, "Imagineering," 60–64, 68–70. The Main Street elevation was drawn in July 1953.

18. "Planning the First Disney Parks," 10–11; see the similar text in Jeff Kurtti, *Sleeping Beauty Castle: Building the Most Magical Castle on Earth* (New York: Sterling Innovation, 2014; in the "Build Sleeping Beauty Castle" kit), 26. An aerial photo of Schloss Neuschwanstein appeared on the cover of a special issue of *Life* devoted to "Germany: A Giant Awakened" a year before the park opened (May 10, 1954); Wolf Burchard, *Inspiring Walt Disney: The Animation of French Decorative Arts* (New York: The Metropolitan Museum of Art, 2021), 187, 192. Later in 1955, Davis married his research assistant, Marjorie Sewell Bowers, Lillian Disney's niece. See Michael Barrier, blog, "Richard Todd and Walt Disney, July 1952," *MichaelBarrier. com*, Jan. 30, 2010.

19. For these four drawings, see "Disneyland 'Sleeping Beauty's Castle' Architectural Plans Group (Walt Disney, 1953)," Lot 94412, Heritage Auctions, July 1–2, 2014; the fourth elevation is reproduced in Kurtti, *Sleeping Beauty Castle*, 27. See also Broggie, *Walt Disney's Railroad Story*, 200. See also the definitive elevation drawing of the courtyard, labeled *Castle North Elevation*, signed by Roland E. Hill and dated Feb. 12, 1955; Burchard, *Inspiring Walt Disney*, 187, 192.

20. A façade for the Snow White ride in this drawing, with turrets, Gothic arcade, and spiraling stair tower inspired in part by châteaux like Azay-le-Rideau or Blois in France's Loire Valley, was never built due to time and financial constraints.

21. Davis's view of the courtyard side of the Castle essentially duplicated in reverse

the front, eliminating only the Neuschwanstein-inspired towers that framed the Main-Street-facing entrance.

22. A late addition to the skyline, the "chapel," a small structure with pointed Gothic windows, flying buttresses, a chevron-patterned roof, and a spire, followed French prototypes like Viollet-le-Duc's proposal for the remodeling of the Château de Pierrefonds, also a source for Sleeping Beauty Castle's ring of fortified towers. For Pierrefonds, see Chris Brooks, *The Gothic Revival* (London: Phaidon, 1999), 350–53.

23. Early descriptions refer to the "shimmering pastel-colored castle." See "Disneyland: 160 Acres of Fun," *Hudson Family Magazine*, 1:3, 1955, 10.

24. William Cameron Menzies, "Pictorial Beauty in the Photoplay," in *Hollywood Directors, 1914–1940*, ed. Richard Koszarski (New York: Oxford University Press, 1976), 243; "Picture Paradise: Photographic Subjects Many at Magic Kingdom," *Disneyland News*, 2:4, Oct. 1956, 10.

25. Reproduced in The Imagineers, *Walt Disney Imagineering: A Behind the Dreams Look at Making the Magic Real* (New York: Hyperion, 1996), 16–17.

26. Reproduced in The Imagineers, *Walt Disney Imagineering*, 57. I focus on the chronology of the drawings because Ryman's second drawing is often considered as evidence of his authorship for the castle's design, despite the apparent dating: Kurtti, *Sleeping Beauty Castle*, 27; Marling, "Imagineering," 70; The Imagineers, *Walt Disney Imagineering*, 57; Burchard, *Inspiring Walt Disney*, 187.

27. Ryman later noted that his drawing was indebted to designs previously produced by Walt's team: "Marvin and Dick and Harper Goff had done a lot of preliminaries and groundwork on other parks that Walt had conceived of, which were very small things. So all of this was sort of put into the hopper." He added, "Whenever I went to the park, I was very aware of the contributions I had made, as I'm also aware of contributions by Bill Martin, Marvin Davis, John Hench, Ken Anderson, and all who were playing in Disney's orchestra." See Herbert Dickens Ryman, Bruce Gordon, and David Mumford, *A Brush with Disney: An Artist's Journey*

(Santa Clarita: Camphor Tree, 2000), 147–48.

28. Eyvind Earle appears in a photo painting the roofs of the large model; there was debate regarding whether the roofs should be brightly colored, as recommended by Earle, or blue to resemble French slate, as suggested by Herb Ryman. Earle was concurrently working on *Sleeping Beauty*.

29. The seven-inch model may also be seen in a photo used to illustrate an interview with Marvin Davis published in 1997. "Here's the model," Davis remarked: "Planning the First Disney Parks," 10–11, 19. For photos of Walt, see "Flair and Versatility: A Visit to Walt's Original W.E.D. Model Shop with Harriet Burns," *"E" Ticket*, no. 44 (Summer 2006): 30, 37.

30. Harriet Burns recalled making "several small models of the Castle for Walt"; "Flair and Versatility," 30. For Joerger and Burns, see the special issue, "Walt's Model Shop," *"E" Ticket*, no. 44 (Summer 2006): 2–17, 28–41; Kurtti, *Walt Disney's Imagineering Legends*, 79–87.

31. "Introducing Disneyland," *TV Radio Mirror*, Dec. 1954, 63.

32. Bright, *Disneyland: Inside Story*, 87.

33. "Planning the First Disney Parks," 10–11.

34. Charles Affron and Mirella Jona Affron, *Sets in Motion: Art Direction and Film Narrative* (New Brunswick: Rutgers University Press, 1995), 157.

35. The classic study of European influence on Disney is Robin Allan, *Walt Disney and Europe: European Influences on the Animated Feature Films of Walt Disney* (Bloomington: Indiana University Press, 1999); for castles, see 15, 47, and passim.

36. Jeff Kurtti, *The Art of Tangled* (San Francisco: Chronicle Books, 2010), 131.

37. The Disney castle became the production logo of the Walt Disney Pictures division of the company in 1985, a status it has held through various permutations.

38. J. P. Telotte, "Flatness and Depth: Classic Disney's Medieval Vision," *The Year's Work in Medievalism* 30 (2015): 5–6. As Telotte observes, castles also provided settings in other studios' cartoon shorts.

39. See for example James Bacon, "$17 Million Disneyland Opens Gates to Young, Old Alike," *Great Bend* (Barton, KA) *Tribune*, July 18, 1955, 18 (Associated Press

wire story); "Motion Picture Exhibition Techniques at Disney's Tomorrowland," *Business Screen Magazine*, 16:6, Sept. 15, 1955, 37. See also Charles Solomon, *Once upon a Dream: From Perrault's* Sleeping Beauty *to Disney's* Maleficent (New York: Disney Editions, 2014), 106–07.

40. Kathleen Coyne Kelly, "Disney's Medievalized Ecologies in *Snow White and the Seven Dwarfs* and *Sleeping Beauty*," in *The Disney Middle Ages: A Fairy-Tale and Fantasy Past*, ed. Tison Pugh and Susan Aronstein (New York: Palgrave Macmillan, 2012), 190–95.

41. Didier Ghez, *They Drew as They Pleased: The Hidden Art of Disney's Golden Age, the 1930s* (San Francisco: Chronicle Books, 2015), 128–33, 152–55.

42. Chris Nichols writes that Cinderella and Robin Hood were considered as namesakes for the castle (source not cited): *Walt Disney's Disneyland* (Cologne: Taschen, 2018), 133.

43. Janzen, "The Original Snow White Dark Ride," 24–25.

44. "Disney Got Start with $40 in 1923, Realizes Dream in $17 Million Park," *Disneyland News*, 1:2, Aug. 1955, 23; "Movie Art Directors Show Making of Motion Picture," *Disneyland News*, 1:3, Sept. 1955, 19.

45. "Mickey Mouse's Fabulous New Playground," *Fortnight*, Nov. 17, 1954, 19.

46. Public Relations Department, "A Visit to Disneyland," *Walt Disney's Magic Kingdom Disneyland*, opening day press kit (Anaheim: Disneyland, Inc., 1955; facsimile reprint, Disneyland Press & Publicity, 2005), 3.

47. *Story of Disneyland*, [11, 21].

48. Floribel Muir, "Walt's Wonderland," *New York Daily News*, July 10, 1955, 70. See also "Chaos in Disneyland," *Fortnight*, Aug. 1955, 40; "Newest Travel Lure: Disneyland," *Travel*, 104:1, July 1955, 18.

49. For Earle's artwork, see "Sleeping Beauty Castle," *Walt Disney's Mickey Mouse Club Magazine*, Feb. 1957, 8–9. On early versions of the walk-through, see Jack E. Janzen, "Sleeping Beauty Castle," *"E" Ticket*, no. 10 (Winter 1990–91): 4–12; "Castle Comments," *"E" Ticket*, no. 11 (Summer 1991): 22–24. The attraction closed in 2001 and a revamped version opened in 2008.

50. Cedric Gibbons, "The Art Director,"

in *Behind the Screen: How Films Are Made*, ed. Stephen Watts (New York: Dodge, 1938), 46. On the use of plaster to simulate stone, brick, and wood, see Edward Carrick, *Designing for Films* (London: The Studio Publications, 1949), 90–91.

51. According to Jim Korkis, an early plan by Marvin Davis is labeled Robin Hood Castle: *The Unofficial Disneyland 1955 Companion* (Theme Park Press, 2016), 146.

52. Robert S. Sennett, *Setting the Scene: The Great Hollywood Art Directors* (New York: Abrams, 1994), 39–41; Beverly Heisner, *Hollywood Art: Art Direction in the Days of the Great Studios* (Jefferson: McFarland, 1990), 161–63.

53. "Robin Hood: A Tale of Mirth and Joyousness in the Land of Fancy," *Landscape Architecture*, 29, July 1938, 200–01.

54. Hedda Hopper, "Robert Newton Will Portray Friar Tuck," *Los Angeles Times*, Feb. 15, 1951, A10. Although Bobby Driscoll and Luana Patten are considered Disney's earliest contract players, evidence suggests that James Baskett, who played Uncle Remus in *Song of the South*, may share that distinction; Hedda Hopper, "Looking at Hollywood," *Los Angeles Times*, Jan. 24, 1945, 9.

55. Hedda Hopper, "Animated Cartoons Prove Complicated Business," *Los Angeles Times*, May 11, 1952, E1.

56. "Dateline Disneyland," advertisement, *TV Guide*, July 16–22, 1955, A8. Two adjacent castle features, the moat and the portcullis, were also publicized. See for example, the photo caption, "Fantasyland begins at this seventy-foot-high reproduction of a medieval castle, complete with a portcullis and a moat," accompanying Gladwin Hill, "Disneyland Gets Its Last Touches," *New York Times*, July 9, 1955, 32.

57. "Facts You Will Want to Know about 'Ivanhoe,'" *Tallahassee Democrat*, Nov. 10, 1952, 6; "'Ivanhoe' Filmed in Actual Locale of Scott's Story," *Los Angeles Times*, Oct. 28, 1952, B7.

58. Celestine Sibley, "Elizabeth Taylor Is What Hollywood Does for Ivanhoe," *Atlanta Journal and Constitution*, July 27, 1952, SM10.

59. "An 80-foot high King Arthur castle will be built in the 'fantasy' section of Disneyland": Aline Mosby, "Disney Amusement Park Delight for Children," *San*

Mateo Times, May 12, 1954, 22. See also Ainsworth, "Disneyland Readied by 'Mr. Magic,'" A28.

60. *Atlanta Journal*, December 19, 1966, 30, drawing by editorial cartoonist Lou "Eric" Erickson; cited by Kevin J. Harty, "Walt in Sherwood, or the Sheriff of Disneyland: Disney and the Film Legend of Robin Hood," in *The Disney Middle Ages: A Fairy-Tale and Fantasy Past*, ed. Tison Pugh and Susan Aronstein (New York: Palgrave Macmillan, 2012), 133.

61. "$17,000,000 Project: Disneyland to Combine Fair, Museum, Kidland," *Billboard*, Feb. 19, 1955, 68: "The Merry-Go-Round will have a King Arthur and His Knights design."

62. Reproduced in Alex Wright, *The Imagineering Field Guide to Disneyland: An Imagineer's-Eye Tour* (New York: Disney Editions, 2008), 82; "King Arthur Carrousel," *"E" Ticket*, no. 35 (Spring 2001): 6–17. See also "Disneyland: Welcome to Disneyland," newspaper advertising supplement [July 1955]. On the inner canopy, medallions hold alternating busts of jesters and princesses in Renaissance garb.

63. "Steeds Prance to Caliope [sic] Tunes," *Disneyland News*, 1:2, Aug. 1955, 5.

64. John Conner, "King Arthur and the Carrousel," *Walt Disney's Mickey Mouse Club Annual*, ed. Walt Disney (Racine: Whitman, 1956), 98–99.

65. Other studios followed suit with animated shorts incorporating knights and jousting, such as Paramount's *Wotta Knight* (1947) with Popeye, and the Bugs Bunny classics from Warner Bros., *Knights Must Fall* (1949) and *Knight-Mare Hare* (1955).

66. On Disney's *The Sword in the Stone*, see Brian Sibley, "A Most Befuddling Thing," in *The Walt Disney Film Archives: The Animated Movies, 1921–1968*, ed. Daniel Kolthenschulte (Cologne: Taschen, 2016), 548–55; Rob Grossedge, "*The Sword in the Stone*: American *Translatio*," in *The Disney Middle Ages: A Fairy-Tale and Fantasy Past*, ed. Tison Pugh and Susan Aronstein (New York: Palgrave Macmillan, 2012), 115–31.

67. Edwin Schallert, "Disney Again to Wed Cartoons, Live Action; Montgomery Does Ranger," *Los Angeles Times*, July 22, 1950, 9.

68. A. H. Weiler, "By Way of Report," *New York Times*, May 29, 1949, X5; Bob Thomas, "51 Acres of Disney's Studios Are Crammed with Ideas," *Reading Eagle*, March 15, 1955, 18. The project with Todd was dropped due to waning interest in Disney's live-action British movies. The impetus for *The Sword in the Stone* finally came in the form of a script and storyboards produced by story man and concept artist Bill Peet.

69. Susan Aronstein, "Higitus! Figitus! Of Merlin and Disney Magic," in *It's the Disney Version! Popular Cinema and Literary Classics*, ed. Douglas Brode and Shea T. Brode (Lanham: Rowman & Littlefield, 2016), 129. *The Sword in the Stone* focuses on the education of young Arthur ("Wart") and concludes with the incident at the stone.

70. The much-debated existence of Arthur and his Knights of the Round Table had three principal literary sources: Thomas Malory's prose retelling of the legend, *Le Morte d'Arthur* (1485), the poet Alfred, Lord Tennyson's *Idylls of the King* (1859–85), and T. H. White's twentieth-century series of novels on the subject. See Philips, *Fairground Amusements*, chap. 3.

71. Zia Isola, "Defending the Domestic: Arthurian Tropes and the American Dream," in *King Arthur in Popular Culture*, ed. Elizabeth S. Sklar and Donald L. Hoffman (Jefferson: McFarland, 2002), 26.

72. The Pyle books are *The Story of King Arthur and His Knights* (1903), *The Story of the Champions of the Round Table* (1905), *The Story of Sir Launcelot and His Companions* (1907), and *The Story of the Grail and the Passing of Arthur* (1910); see Jeanne Fox-Friedman, "Howard Pyle and the Chivalric Order in America: King Arthur for Children," *Arthuriana* 6:1 (Spring 1996): 77–95; Barbara Tepa Lupack with Alan Lupack, *Illustrating Camelot* (Woodbridge: Brewer, 2008).

73. Jason Tondro, "Camelot in Comics," in *King Arthur in Popular Culture*, ed. Elizabeth S. Sklar and Donald L. Hoffman (Jefferson: McFarland, 2002), 170–71.

74. Rebecca A. Umland and Samuel J. Umland, *The Use of Arthurian Legend in Hollywood Film: From Connecticut Yankees to Fisher Kings* (Westport: Greenwood Press, 1996), 74–84.

75. Bosley Crowther, "The Screen in Review," *New York Times*, Jan. 8, 1954, 17.

76. Edwin Schallert, "Chivalry Epic to Be Massive," *Los Angeles Times*, Dec. 13, 1953, E1, E4.

77. "Premiere for 'Knights of Round Table' Set," *Los Angeles Times*, Dec. 22, 1953, 2.

78. Schallert, "Chivalry Epic," E4.

79. Newspaper advertisement, *Asheville Citizen*, Apr. 18, 1954, 14.

80. "5 Real Castles for 'Valiant,'" *Atlanta Journal Constitution*, Aug. 23, 1953, 8B.

81. Michael Troyan, Stephen X. Sylvester, and Jeffrey P. Thompson, *Twentieth Century Fox: A Century of Entertainment* (Guildford: Lyons Press, 2017), 359–60. See the description of the fiery battle scene at the mock castle in William H. Brownell, Jr., "Comics Come Alive," *New York Times*, Nov. 1, 1953, X7.

82. Fox's TV airing of *Valiant*'s premiere preceded Walt's use of the same publicity gimmick; "Film Premiere on KTTV (11) Tonight," *Los Angeles Times*, Apr. 2, 1954, 30.

83. "These tent-like tournament things shaded the queue areas, gave everything a festive carnival flavor and didn't cost much at all": "Disneyland Art Director ... Bill Martin," 10. See also Karal Ann Marling with Donna R. Braden, *Behind the Magic: 50 Years of Disneyland* (Dearborn: The Henry Ford, 2005), 65.

84. Brian R. Price, "In the Lists: The Arthurian Influence in Modern Tournaments of Chivalry," in *King Arthur in Popular Culture*, ed. Elizabeth S. Sklar and Donald L. Hoffman (Jefferson: McFarland, 2002), 197–208.

85. David Crouch, *Tournament* (London: Hambledon, 2006), 118–19.

86. Kevin J. Harty, "Robin Hood on Film: Moving Beyond a Swashbuckling Stereotype," in *Robin Hood in Popular Culture: Violence, Transgression, and Justice*, ed. Thomas Hahn (Cambridge: Brewer, 2000), 91. The quote by Dwan comes from the February 1923 issue of *Motion Picture Magazine*.

87. Sidney Lanier, *The Boy's King Arthur* (New York: Scribner's Sons, 1922), facing 246.

88. Jean Froissart, *Chroniques*, 4:1 (The Harley Froissart), c. 1470–72; British Library, Harley 4379 f. 43.

89. Paul Creswick, *Robin Hood* (New York: Scribner, 1917). See also the colorful tents in N. C. Wyeth's illustration, "Sir Nigel Sustains England's Honor in the Lists," in Arthur Conan Doyle, *The White Company* (New York: Cosmopolitan, 1933). The tournament sequence was filmed at the former Busch Gardens in Pasadena.

90. Rudy Behlmer, *The Adventures of Robin Hood* (Madison: University of Wisconsin Press, 1979), 39–40. Critics called the film "a richly produced, bravely bedecked, romantic and colorful show," "beautifully done in Technicolor without its looking like an overpainted postcard"; quoted in Behlmer, *Adventures of Robin Hood*, 36.

91. Halsey Raines, "The England of 'Ivanhoe' Comes Alive Again," *New York Times*, Aug. 26, 1951, X5.

92. Edwin Schallert, "'Ivanhoe' Director Finds Chain Armor Weighty Problem," *Los Angeles Times*, Oct. 21, 1951, D4, 10.

93. Edwin Schallert, "'Ivanhoe' Cinema Spectacle of Medieval Combat, Romance," *Los Angeles Times*, Oct. 10, 1952, B9.

94. "Ivanhoe," *Monthly Film Bulletin*, 19:216, Jan. 1, 1952, 106.

95. The comic-book style of the film, based on Hal Foster's Sunday newspaper strips (debuted in 1937), was dubbed by critics "a transcript of the funnies" and "the adventures of a Hollywood Viking among the Knights of the Round Table": Bosley Crother, "The Screen in Review," *New York Times*, Apr. 7, 1954, 40; Penelope Houston, "Cinema," *The Spectator*, May 7, 1954, 542–43.

96. Menzies, "Pictorial Beauty in the Photoplay," 244.

97. David Koenig, *The 55ers: The Pioneers Who Settled Disneyland* (Irvine: Bonaventure Press, 2019), 231, 248–52; Dallas, *Inventing Disneyland*, 188–89.

98. "Merlin's Wizardry Lives on in Fantasyland Shop," *Disneyland News*, 2:4, Oct. 1956, 8. See also "Merlin's Magic Fascinating Fun," *Disneyland News*, 1:11, May 1956, 11. For medieval street sets, see Juan Antonio Ramirez, *Architecture for the Screen: A Critical Study of Set Design in Hollywood's Golden Age*, trans. John F. Moffitt (Jefferson: McFarland, 2004), 105–06, 142. The Sword in the Stone Ceremony held in the castle courtyard, in

which a child, overseen by a cast member dressed as Merlin, pulls Excalibur from an anvil to become king or queen for a day, was instituted in 1983 as part of the New Fantasyland.

99. "Knights of the Round Table," advertisement, *Disneyland News*, 1:2, Aug. 1955, 9.

100. Bruce Gordon and David Mumford, *Disneyland: The Nickel Tour* (Santa Clarita: Camphor Tree, 2000), 79.

101. Koenig, *The 55ers*, 253–54.

102. Advertisement, *Disneyland News*, 1:2, Aug. 1955, 5; "Disneyland Food Offers Sure Appetite Booster," *Disneyland News*, 1:4, Oct. 10, 1955, 8; "Pirate's Galleon Offers Atmosphere, Seafood," *Disneyland News*, 1:4, Oct. 10, 1955, 13.

103. According to Neil Rennie, silent films regenerated the genre of "literary pirates" as "antipirates, displaced gentlemen." By the early 1920s, the "cinematic pirate" was "ready for the big screen." See Neil Rennie, *Treasure Neverland: Real and Imaginary Pirates* (Oxford: Oxford University Press, 2013), 226.

104. Antonio Sanna, *Pirates in History and Popular Culture* (Jefferson: McFarland, 2018), 20.

105. For the literary tradition and its impact on Stevenson and Barrie, foreshadowing cinema and theme parks, see Philips, *Fairground Attractions*, chap. 8. For the cinematic pirate, see Rennie, *Treasure Neverland*, chap. 7; Brian Taves, *The Romance of Adventure: The Genre of Historical Adventure Movies* (Jackson: University Press of Mississippi, 1993), 25–30. On the popularity and political symbolism of these films, see Richard E. Bond, "Piratical Americans: Representations of Piracy and Authority in Mid-Twentieth-Century Swashbucklers," *Journal of American Culture* 33:4 (Dec. 2010): 309–21.

106. Rennie, *Treasure Neverland*, chap. 4.

107. David Cordingly and John Falconer, *Pirates: Fact & Fiction* (New York: Artabras, 1992), 69.

108. Merle Johnson, *Howard Pyle's Book of Pirates* (New York: Harper, 1921), frontispiece, facing 36; Rudy Behlmer, "High Style on the High Seas," part 1, *American Cinematographer*, 73:4, Apr. 1992, 34; Rudy Behlmer, "*The Black Pirate*

Weighs Anchor," part 2, *American Cinematographer*, 73:5, May 1992, 34–40.

109. Jeffrey Richards, *Swordsmen of the Screen: From Douglas Fairbanks to Michael York* (London: Routledge, 1977), 162. A contemporary reviewer sensed the debt to literary tradition: "'The Black Pirate,' Douglas Fairbanks's natural color picture, is a subject of intense beauty, with situations that remind one of Robert Louis Stevenson's 'Treasure Island' tinged with Sir James M. Barrie's whimsicality"; Mordaunt Hall, "Fairbanks's Pirate Film Whimsical and Beautiful," *New York Times*, Mar. 14, 1926, 183.

110. Rudy Behlmer, "*The Sea Hawk* Sets Sail," part 1, *American Cinematographer* 77:7 (July 1996): 86–90; part 2, 77:8 (Aug. 19, 1996): 88–92. For a first-person account of motion-picture ship-building, see Carrick, *Designing for Films*, 14, 44–45, 80–81. Movie-makers were so clever at building "ships" that scholars often misread the visual evidence. For example, Nathan Holmes misidentifies a shot in *The Sea Hawk* of two miniature models as full-scale ships; "Curtiz at Sea: *Captain Blood*, *The Sea Hawk*, *The Sea Wolf*, and *The Breaking Point*," in *The Many Cinemas of Michael Curtiz*, ed. R. Barton Palmer and Murray Pomerance (Austin: University of Texas Press, 2018), 113. And Beverly Heisner mistakenly claims that *Mutiny on the Bounty* (1935) was filmed entirely on a real ship (*Hollywood Art*, 79), but according to director/actor Charles Laughton, "When I saw the picture I could not even remember what was shot in the studio and what was shot at sea" (Carrick, *Designing for Films*, 81).

111. Steven Bingen, Stephen X. Sylvester, and Michael Troyen, *M-G-M: Hollywood's Greatest Backlot* (Solana Beach: Santa Monica Press, 2011), 118.

112. Rennie, *Treasure Neverland*, 226–31.

113. Michael Singer, *Disney Pirates: The Definitive Anthology* (Los Angeles: Disney Editions, 2017), 21–25; Joe Adamson, *Byron Haskin* (Metuchen: Scarecrow Press, 1984), 166–85; Scott Allen Nollen, "Walt Disney and Robert Louis Stevenson: Haskin's *Treasure Island* or Stevenson's *Kidnapped*?" in *It's the Disney Version! Popular Cinema and Literary Classics*, ed. Douglas Brode and Shea

T. Brode (Lanham: Rowman & Littlefield, 2016), 61–70.

114. "Film Reviews," *Focus: A Film Review,* 3:8, Aug. 1950, 235.

115. A sense of Walt's fascination with pirates may be reflected in the major role they played in the 1960 film, *Swiss Family Robinson.* In addition, an episode in the *Disneyland* series, "Davy Crockett and the River Pirates," was aired Dec. 14, 1955.

116. Jill P. May, "James Barrie's Pirates: *Peter Pan*'s Place in Pirate History and Lore," in *J. M. Barrie's* Peter Pan *In and Out of Time: A Children's Classic at 100,* ed. Donna R. White and C. Anita Tarr (Lanham: Scarecrow Press, 2006), 69–78; Philips, *Fairground Attractions,* 180.

117. On Stevenson and Barrie's contributions to pirate lore, see Rennie, *Treasure Neverland,* chap. 6.

118. Frederick C. Szebin, "*Peter Pan* Escapes Cinematic Neverland," *American Cinematographer,* 76:10, Oct. 1995, 97–101.

119. A. W. [A. H. Weiler], "At the Capitol," *New York Times,* Dec. 25, 1952, 34.

120. Martin's assistants were Oswald Runnison and Fred Stoos. See "Disneyland Art Director … Bill Martin," 11.

121. Mindy Johnson, *Tinker Bell: An Evolution* (New York: Disney Editions, 2013), 38, 108. For the televised animation, Disney artists used a simpler version of the fairy, typical of the Cartoon Modern style that reads clearly on the black-and-white tube.

122. Moore Raymond, "Disney Has Made Tinker Bell a Little Tinker," *Sunday Dispatch,* Apr. 19, 1953. For the critical reaction to *Peter Pan,* see Robert Neuman, "Toad, Alice and Peter: From England to Disney-Land and Back Again," in *Interpreting and Experiencing Disney: Mediating the Mouse,* ed. Priscilla Hobbs (Bristol: Intellect, 2021), chap. 3.

123. The association between Tinker Bell and the castle endures in the current Walt Disney Pictures logo, in which a stream of pixie dust arcs over the castle. In 2009 the company initiated its successful Tinker Bell franchise by creating a backstory for the character and giving her a speaking voice. For the mid-1950s revival of Disney's most famous creation, see "In a New Role: Mickey Mouse Makes Debut as Full Time TV Star," *Disneyland News,* 1:4, Oct. 10, 1955, 2.

124. Johnson, *Tinker Bell,* 124.

125. "Peter Pan," *What's On in London,* Apr. 17, 1953, n.p.

126. Steven Watts, *The Magic Kingdom: Walt Disney and the American Way of Life* (New York: Houghton Mifflin, 1997), xvi.

Epilogue

1. "What Is Disneyland?" *Disneyland Holiday* 1:1, Spring, 1957, 2.

2. John Garth, "Is Disneyland Art?" "Disneyland News," souvenir edition, supplement to *The Argonaut,* July 26, 1957, 12–15.

3. Hedda Hopper, "Dream of Disneyland Still Being Realized," *Los Angeles Times,* July 9, 1957, A8.

4. Bob Thomas, *Walt Disney: An American Original* (New York: Hyperion, 1994), 244.

5. Jeff Kurtti, Vanessa Hunt, and Paul Wolski, *The Disney Monorail: Imagineering a Highway in the Sky* (Los Angeles: Disney Editions, 2020).

6. "Disneyland & Son," *Time,* 73, June 29, 1959, 54. See also Ira Wolfert, "Walt Disney's Magic Kingdom," *Reader's Digest,* 76, Apr. 1960, 152: "The success of [Disneyland] has put a ferment into the amusement-park business everywhere."

7. Gary S. Cross and John K. Walton, *The Playful Crowd: Pleasure Places in the Twentieth Century* (New York: Columbia University Press, 2005), 252–56.

8. Hedda Hopper, "New Studio Tours Generate Goodwill," *Los Angeles Times,* Aug. 11, 1964, C8. Likewise, Hedda Hopper, "Movie Mogul Takes Cue from Disneyland," *Chicago Tribune,* Aug. 11, 1964, A1.

9. Sam Gennawey, *Universal vs. Disney: The Unofficial Guide to American Theme Parks' Greatest Rivalry* (Birmingham: Keen, 2015), 27–28.

10. David Kenyon Webster, "Hollywood Producers Concentrate on Fewer, More Lavish Pictures, *Wall Street Journal,* July 13, 1954, 1. For an examination of these changes at one particular studio, see Peter Lev, *Twentieth Century-Fox: The Zanuck-Skouras Years, 1935–1965* (Austin: University of Texas Press, 2013), chap. 4.

11. For changes in movie-going habits, see John Belton, *Widescreen Cinema*

(Cambridge: Harvard University Press, 2014), 80.

12. Ronald Haver, *David O. Selznick's Hollywood* (New York: Bonanza, 1985), 416.

13. Stuart Samuels, "The Age of Conspiracy and Conformity: *Invasion of the Body Snatchers*," in *American History/American Film: Interpreting the Hollywood Image*, ed. John E. O'Connor and Martin A. Jackson (New York: Continuum, 2016), 203–17.

14. For the impact of television, see Noel Brown, *The Hollywood Family Film: A History, from Shirley Temple to Harry Potter* (London: I. B. Tauris, 2012), 88–95.

15. Quoted in Jeanine Basinger, *The* It's a Wonderful Life *Book* (New York: Alfred A. Knopf, 1994), 68.

16. David Kenyon Webster, "Hollywood & TV: Studios Plunge into Television," *Wall Street Journal*, July 6, 1955, 1.

17. Lev, *Twentieth Century-Fox*, 183–84.

18. Steven Bingen, *Warner Bros.: Hollywood's Ultimate Backlot* (Lanham: Taylor Trade, 2014), 29–30.

19. Steven Bingen, Stephen X. Sylvester, and Michael Troyan, *M-G-M: Hollywood's Greatest Backlot* (Solana Beach: Santa Monica Press, 2011), 271, 275, 282. In 1977 an effort to convert the surviving Lot 2 into a theme park also failed.

20. Brown, *Hollywood Family Film*, 82.

21. Michael L. Stephens, *Art Directors in Cinema: A Worldwide Biographical Dictionary* (Jefferson: McFarland, 2008), 57–61.

22. Steven Clark and Rebecca Cline, *The Walt Disney Studios: A Lot to Remember* (Los Angeles: Disney Editions, 2016), 53–55; "Leonard Maltin's Studio Tour," *Walt Disney Treasures: Behind the Scenes at the Walt Disney Studio*, DVD, Walt Disney Home Video, 2002.

23. Gennawey, *Universal vs. Disney*, chap. 6.

Bibliography

Primary Sources up to 1970

Abbot, Sam. "Disneyland Sets New Designs for Rides, Exhibit Layouts." *Billboard,* June 26, 1954, 80.

Adventure in Disneyland by Richfield. Promotional comic book. Richfield Oil, 1955.

"'African Lion' Hailed by New York Critics." *Disneyland News,* 1:4, Oct. 10, 1955, 12–13.

Ainsworth, Ed. "Disneyland Readied by 'Mr. Magic.'" *Los Angeles Times,* June 23, 1955, A1.

Alexander, Jack. "The Amazing Story of Walt Disney." *Saturday Evening Post,* part 1, Oct. 31, 1953, 24–25, 80, 84–86, 90, 92; part 2, Nov. 7, 1953, 26–27, 99–100.

"AMC Exhibit Unique." *Nash News,* 19:4, Aug.–Sept. 1955, 1–2.

"Anaheim Chosen as Cite [sic] of Disneyland." *Billboard,* May 8, 1954, 46.

"'Around the West' Movie Draws Rave Reviews." *Disneyland News,* 1:3, Sept. 1955, 16.

"Atmosphere, Fine Food Make Dining Tops at Disneyland." *Disneyland News,* 2:7, Jan. 1957, 4–5.

Bacon, James. "Disneyland Unable to Cope with First-Day Visitors." *Corpus Christi Caller-Times,* July 18, 1955, 30.

———. "$17 Million Disneyland Opens Gates to Young, Old Alike." *Great Bend* (Barton, KA) *Tribune,* July 18, 1955, 18.

Bagley, Dick. "Disneyland Progresses." *Miniature Locomotive,* 2:15, Sept.-Oct. 1954, 4.

Berg, Louis. "Walt Disney's New Ten Million Dollar Toy." *This Week Magazine,* Sept. 19, 1954, 8–9, 15.

"Camera Crews Cover the Earth." *Disneyland News,* 1:12, June 1956, 8.

"Captain Nemo's Submarine: Nautilus Recovered from Davy Jones Locker, Placed on Exhibit." *Disneyland News,* 1:3, Sept. 1955, 9.

Carrick, Edward. *Designing for Films.* London: The Studio Publications, 1949.

"Celebrities Enjoy Disneyland." *Disneyland News,* 1:3, Sept. 1955, 4.

"Celebrities Relax at Magic Kingdom." *Disneyland News* 1:4, Oct. 10, 1955, 7.

"Chaos in Disneyland." *Fortnight,* Aug. 1955, 39–41.

"Le chemin de fer du 'Disneyland.'" *La vie du rail,* no. 545, April 19, 1956, 5–7.

Chicago Railroad Fair: Official Guide. Chicago: The Fair, 1949.

"A City Built as a Background for Pictures." *Washington Herald,* May 23, 1915, 11.

"Clock of the World Symbolizes Tomorrowland Future Theme." *Disneyland News,* 1:3, Sept. 1955, 18.

"Conestogas Once Tops." *Disneyland News,* 1:2, Aug. 1955, 8.

Connor, John. "King Arthur and the Carrousel." In *Walt Disney's Mickey Mouse Club Annual,* edited by Walt Disney. Racine: Whitman, 1956.

Cook, Lois. "Disneyland Visited by Southern California Group." *Horseless Carriage Gazette,* 17:6, Nov.-Dec. 1955, 24–25.

"County Girds for Disneyland Rush." *Los Angeles Times,* July 10, 1955, OC1.

Craig, Lee. "Celebrity Throng at Premiere." *Long Beach Independent,* July 18, 1955, 1, 5.

"Crockett Museum Features Products of Old Mexico." *Disneyland News,* 2:2, Aug. 1956, 8.

"Dateline Disneyland." *TV Guide,* July 16–22, 1955, A8.

"A Day at Disneyland with Spring Byington and Bobby Diamond." *TV Radio Mirror,* 45:5, Apr. 1956, 40–43.

"Days of Old South Relived in Aunt Jemima's Kitchen." *Disneyland News,* 2:2, Aug. 1956, 6–7.

"Diorama Model Builders Faced Unique Problems." *Disneyland News,* 1:6, Dec. 10, 1955, 13.

Disney, Walt. *Disneyland.* Verona: Mondadori, 1964.

———. "Film Entertainment and Community Life." *Journal of the American Medical Association,* 167:11 (July 12, 1958): 1342–45.

———. "Frontierland." *True West,* 5:5, May–June 1958, 10–13.

———. "Give Me the Movies." *Norfolk Virginian Pilot,* Sept. 2, 1938, sec. 2, 5.

———. "The Marceline I Knew." *Marceline News,* Sept. 2, 1938, 1.

"Disney Artists Paint Visitors." *Disneyland News,* 1:3, Sept. 1955, 16–17.

"Disney Credits Four Park Ops." *Billboard,* July 30, 1955, 48.

"Disney Got Start with $40 in 1923, Realizes Dream in $17 Million Park." *Disneyland News,* 1:2, Aug. 1955, 23.

"Disney in TVland." *TV Guide,* Oct. 23, 1954, 4–6.

"Disney Plans TV Trip to the Moon." *Popular Science,* Nov. 1955, 99–101.

"Disney Shows 360-Deg. Film Screen Process." *Los Angeles Times,* June 28, 1955, A1.

"Disney Talk Sparks Convention Interest." *Billboard,* Dec. 4, 1954, 59.

"Disneyland." *Life,* 39:7, Aug. 15, 1955, 39–42.

——— *McCall's,* 82:4, Jan. 1955, 8–11.

——— *Modern Screen,* Aug. 1955, 42–44.

——— *Motion Picture Daily,* July 18, 1955, 9.

——— *My Weekly Reader,* 33:1, Sept. 12–16, 1955.

Disneyland, U.S.A.: People and Places. Press book. Walt Disney Productions, 42 min. Released Dec. 20, 1956.

Disneyland: A Complete Guide. Racine: Western Printing, 1956.

Disneyland: A Dream Come True. Brochure promoting park sponsors. Racine: Western Printing, 1955.

"Disneyland: A New Fairyland." *My Weekly Reader,* 24:30, May 2–6, 1955, 132.

"Disneyland & Son." *Time* 73, June 29, 1959, 54.

"Disneyland Antique Collectors Find U.S., Canadian Items." *Disneyland News,* 1:2, Aug. 1955, 17.

"Disneyland: First Anniversary Souvenir Pictorial." Newspaper advertising supplement, [July 1956].

"Disneyland Food Offers Sure Appetite Booster." *Disneyland News* 1:4, Oct. 10, 1955, 8.

"Disneyland Gates Open." *New York Times,* July 19, 1955, 22.

"Disneyland Grand Opening Is Scheduled for July 18: Preview Getting 90-Min. Telecast." *Hollywood Reporter,* May 19, 1955, 8.

"Disneyland Issue." *Coca-Cola: The Refresher,* Sept. 1955.

——— *Overture,* Sept. 1955.

——— *The Westerner,* Aug. 1955.

"Disneyland: 160 Acres of Fun." *Hudson Family Magazine,* 1:3, 1955, 8–10.

"Disneyland: Ronnie and Vickie Enjoy a Day of Fun in Kiddies' Paradise." *Ebony,* 11:5, Mar. 1956, 63–65.

The Disneyland Story. Burbank: Disneyland, Inc., Sept. 3, 1954; reprinted in *Remembering Disneyland: An Exhibition and Auction* (Sherman Oaks: Van Eaton Galleries, 2017), 4, cat. 1; also, facsimile reprint, portfolio of concept art, Dave Smith, D23 Official Disney Fan Club, Gold Membership Gift, 2015.

"Disneyland: The Magic Children's Playground …" *The Sphere,* July 30, 1955, 164.

"Disneyland to Combine Fair, Museum, Kiddieland." *Billboard,* Feb. 19, 1955, 57, 68–69.

"Disneyland: Welcome to Disneyland." Newspaper advertising supplement, [July 1955].

"Disney's Railway." *Model Engineer,* 113:2844, Nov. 14, 1955.

D.W.C. "Meet the Set Designer: The Less He Is Noticed, the Better—So Says Van Nest Polglase of RKO." *New York Times,* Aug. 16, 1935, X4.

Eddy, Don. "The Amazing Secret of Walt Disney." *American Magazine,* 160:2, Aug. 1955, 28–29, 110–15.

"Edison's Inventions a Problem but Patrick's Solutions Work." *Disneyland News,* 1:2, Aug. 1955, 8.

Erengis, George P. "Cedric Gibbons." *Films in Review*, 16, 1965, 217–32.

Eustis, Morton. "Designing for the Movies: Gibbons of MGM." *Theatre Arts Monthly*, 1937, 783–98.

Evans, Morgan. *Walt Disney: Disneyland: World of Flowers*. Burbank: Walt Disney Productions, 1965.

"Fairyland of Yesterday and Tomorrow." *Popular Mechanics*, 102:6, Dec. 1954, 118–19.

"Fashions of Yesterday in Main Street Parade." *Disneyland News*, 1:9, Mar. 10, 1956, 1.

"Father Goose." *Time*, 64:26, Dec. 27, 1954, 42–46.

"Firm of Evans and Reeves Does Record Landscaping." *Disneyland News*, 1:3, Sept. 1955, 9.

Flint, Ralph. "Cinema's Art Directors: Little Known to the Public, They Are Back Stage, Among the Lords of the Screen." *New York Times*, Nov. 22, 1931, X7 (135).

"Food Flavors Southwest Atmosphere." *Disneyland News*, 2:1, June 1956, 7.

"The Four Young Ladies of the Golden Horseshoe." *Disneyland News*, 2:1, June 1956, 4.

"Fox to Spend Half Million." *Los Angeles Times*, Nov. 14, 1925, A7.

"Frontierland: Explore the Lost 'Rainbow Mine'" *Disneyland News*, Extra Edition, [May] 1955, 2–3.

"Frontierland Sign Recalls Old Scout." *Disneyland News*, 1:2, Aug. 1955, 23.

"Frontierland Stage Coach Rides Again! Century-Old Transportation a Slice of Living History." *Disneyland News*, 1:8, Feb. 1956, 10–11.

"Frontierland's Sheriff Finds Action a-Plenty." *Disneyland News*, 1:4, Oct. 10, 1955, 10, 15.

Garth, John. "Is Disneyland Art?" "Disneyland News," souvenir edition, supplement to *The Argonaut*, July 26, 1957, 12–15.

Gibbons, Cedric. "The Art Director." In *Behind the Scenes: How Films are Made*, edited by Steven Watts, 41–50. London: A. Barker, 1938.

Gillette, Don Carle. "The Disneyland Story: A Unique Amusement Park Yields More Pleasure than Profit." *Barron's National Business and Financial Weekly*, 36:4, Jan. 23, 1956, 9, 29f.

"'Glamor Girl of Rails' Portrays 'General' in 'Locomotive Chase.'" *Disneyland News*, 1:9, Mar. 1956, 11.

"Golden Horseshoe 'Saloon' Presents Light, Gay Revue." *Disneyland News*, 1:3, Sept. 1955, 8, 18.

Gordon, Arthur. "Walt Disney." *Look*, 19:15, July 26, 1955, 28–35.

"Great White Studio Where Pictures with Lion Brand Are Made." *Los Angeles Times*, July 25, 1923, 8–9.

"Green Emphasizes Spring Throughout Realms of Park." *Disneyland News*, 1:2, Aug. 1955, 17.

"Guests Praise 'Fascinating' Sub Interior." *Disneyland News*, 1:3, Sept. 1955, 9.

Haber, Heinz. *Our Friend the Atom: A Tomorrowland Adventure*. Syracuse: Singer, 1956.

Hall, Mordaunt. "Life in the Jungle: 'Tarzan and His Mate' a Marvel of Camera Work." *New York Times*, Apr. 29, 1934, X3.

Hanoteau, Guillaume. "Une ville qui s'appelle Disney." *Paris Match*, no. 335, Aug. 27-Sept. 3, 1955, 36–48.

"Happy Pair: When Sam Grinds Josephine Dances." *Disneyland News*, 1:4, Oct. 1955, 4.

"Harder Than Movie Set: Nostalgic Main Street Designed by Rubottom." *Disneyland News*, 1:3, Sept. 1955, 15.

Hastings, Don. "All Aboard for Disneyland." *Westways*, 47:7, July 1955, 4–5.

"Here's Your First View of Disneyland." *Look*, 18: 22, Nov. 2, 1954, 82–84, 86, 88–89.

Hill, Gladwin. "Disneyland Gets Its Last Touches." *New York Times*, July 9, 1955, 32.

_____. "Disneyland Reports on Its First Ten Million." *New York Times*, Feb. 2, 1958, X1,7.

_____. "Hollywood Is Shifting Her Civic Scenery." *New York Times*, May 8, 1955, 37.

_____. "A World Walt Disney Created." *New York Times*, July 31, 1955, X1, 7.

Hill, Monica. *Disneyland Stamp Book*. New York: Simon & Schuster, 1956.

Holland, Jack. "Walt Disney: The Man Who Won't Sell You Short." *TV-Radio Life*, 31:3, Mar. 4, 1955, 4–7.

Hopper, Hedda, "Disney the Great!" *Chicago Daily Tribune*, Jan. 30, 1955, F22.

_____. "Disneyland Preview Reveals

Wonderland." *Los Angeles Times*, July 16, 1955, 14.

———. "Dream of Disneyland Still Being Realized." *Los Angeles Times*, July 9, 1957, A8.

———. "Hollywood Sets Would Fool Mother Nature: Scenic Experts Make Land, Sea and Sky Look More Realistic Than Reality." *Los Angeles Times*, Nov. 26, 1939, C3.

———. "Hope, Lollobrigida Will Do London Film." *Los Angeles Times*, July 5, 1956, B8.

———. "Walt Disney's Fete 250 at Fabulous Disneyland." *Chicago Daily Tribune*, July 16, 1955, 17.

Hulce, Jerry. "Dream Realized: Disneyland Opens." *Los Angeles Times*, July 18, 1955, A1.

"In a New Role: Mickey Mouse Makes Debut as Full Time TV Star." *Disneyland News*, 1:4, Oct. 10, 1955, 2.

"In Crockett Arcade: Ancient Arts Still Flourish." *Disneyland News*, 4:1, Oct. 10, 1955, 6.

"In the Good Old Summertime: 'Good Old Days' Relived by Park Bank Concerts." *Disneyland News*, 2:3, Sept. 1955, 17.

In the World Beneath Us: What Happens? Brochure. Richfield, 1955.

"Introducing Disneyland." *TV Radio Mirror*, Dec. 1954, 62–65.

"It's Disneyland Time." *Santa Fe Magazine*, 49:8, Aug. 1955, 8–12.

Johnson, Robert. "Plenty of Walking, Gawking Needed to See 'Disneyland.'" *Memphis Press-Scimitar*, July 18, 1955, 21.

Jungmeyer, Jack. "Under the Gaslight." *Disneyland News*, 1:1, July 1955, 3.

"Keelboater King Rivals Davy Crockett in TV Race." *Disneyland News*, 4:1, Oct. 10, 1955, 5.

"Kids' Dream World Comes True." *Popular Science*, Aug. 1955, 92.

"KODAK Is on 'Main Street' at Disneyland!" *Kodak Movie News*, 3:4, Fall 1955, 1.

"Landscaper Shellhorn Supervises Planting." *Disneyland News*, 1:2, Aug. 1955, 20.

Let's Build Disneyland: Push Out and Put together Book. Racine: Western Printing, 1957.

"Life of Story-Telling Genius Retold in 'Song of the South.'" *Disneyland News*, 1:8, Feb. 1956, 2.

Lipton, Norman C. "Disneyland's Circarama: Where the Movie Screen Surrounds You." *Popular Photography*, Dec. 1955, 37, 96–97, 184–85.

Little, H.W. "No Movie Was Ever Made in Hollywood." *Los Angeles Times*, May 30, 1937, 115.

"A Look at Disneyland from a Construction and Maintenance Standpoint." *Construction Equipment Operation and Maintenance*, 9:5, Sept.-Oct. 1956, 5–8.

"Lovely Elana Provides Enchanting Island Song." *Disneyland News*, 1:4, Oct. 10, 1955, 15.

MacCann, Richard Dyer. "A Couple of Its Most Famous Citizens Talk about Disneyland—and Television." *Christian Science Monitor*, Sept. 3, 1954, sec. 2, 1.

"Magic Kingdom Called Disneyland." *Children's Newspaper* (U.K.), Sept. 25, 1955, 5.

"'Magic Kingdom' Guests Will Meet Celebrities." *Disneyland News*, 1:9, Mar. 10, 1956, 4.

"Magic Kingdom Top Southern California Attraction." *Disneyland News*, 1:4, Oct. 10, 1955, 1, 9.

"Main Street Is Historic Replica." *Disneyland News*, 1:1, July 1955, 3.

"Main Street's Market Captures Feel of the Past." *Disneyland News*, 1:11, May 1956, 4.

"Major Disneyland Additions Revealed!" *Disneyland News*, Extra Edition, [May] 1956, 1–3.

"Mardi Gras Dedicates New Orleans Street." *Disneyland News*, 1:3, Sept. 1955, 11.

"'Mark Twain' River Steamer Docks Again." *Disneyland News*, 1:2, Aug. 1955, 8.

Marley, Mary, "Visit to Disneyland Like Going into Past and Present at Once." *Miami Daily News*, May 1, 1955, 63.

Marx, Arthur. "Trapped in Disneyland." *Saga: True Adventures for Men*, 12:6, Sept. 1956, 40–41.

"Mattey Designs Animals Seen in Jungle Journey." *Disneyland News*, 1:2, Aug. 1955, 4.

McHugh, Tom. "Walt Disney's Mechanical Wonderland." *Popular Mechanics*, 108:5, Nov. 1957, 138–43, 230.

"Meet Davy Crockett." *Look*, 19, July 26, 1955, 36–37.

"Metro Operates Special Bus Line to

Disneyland." *Mass Transportation,* Jan. 1956, 20–21.

"Mickey Mouse's Fabulous New Playground." *Fortnight,* Nov. 17, 1954, 18–19.

Miller, Diane Disney, and Pete Martin. "My Dad Walt Disney" (first of eight serialized articles). *Saturday Evening Post,* 229:20, Nov. 17, 1956, 25–27, 130–34.

Millier, Arthur. "Art Directors Would Show Films How to Save Money." *Los Angeles Times,* July 2, 1933, A1.

"Milotte Photographic Team Shoots True Life Features." *Disneyland News,* 1:2, Aug. 1955, 6.

Mosby, Aline. "Disney Amusement Park Delight for Children." *San Mateo Times,* May 12, 1954, 22.

———. "Disneyland Made Its Debut Sunday in a 'Confused Mess.'" *Madera Daily News Tribune,* July 18, 1955, 3.

"Motion Picture Art Work on Exhibition." *Disneyland News,* 1:2, Aug. 1955, 4.

"Motion Picture Exhibition Techniques at Disney's Tomorrowland." *Business Screen Magazine,* 16:6, Sept. 15, 1955, 37–44.

"The Mouse That Turned to Gold." *Business Week,* July 9, 1955, 72–74.

"Movie Art Directors Show Making of Motion Picture." *Disneyland News,* 1:3, Sept. 1955, 19.

"Movie Illusions: Hollywood Technicians Create Reality inside Studios." *Life,* 17:6, Jan. 8, 1945, 69–77.

"Movie Making: It Is a Complex Business of Machines and Technicians." *Life,* 18:2, Aug. 7, 1944, 71–79.

"Movie Memories: Main Street Now Boasts 'Show Business' Exhibit." *Disneyland News,* 1:10, Apr. 1956, 8.

Muir, Florabel. "Walt's Wonderland." *New York Daily News,* July 10, 1955, 70–71.

Nehamkin, Lester. "Disneyland's Autopia." *Rod and Custom,* Nov. 1955, 11–14, 62, 66.

A New Concept in Entertainment: Disneyland. Brochure. Disneyland, Inc., 1955.

"New Disney Show Listed for Radio." *New York Times,* Nov. 25, 1955, 55.

"Newest Travel Lure: Disneyland." *Travel,* 104:1, July 1955, 16–19.

"Noted Rocket Moon Authorities Contribute Skills to Space Ride." *Disneyland News,* 1:2, Aug. 1955, 2.

Official Road Map to Disneyland. Brochure. Anaheim: Richfield, 1955.

Penny, Bert. "Heigh Ho! Heigh Ho! Let's Load the Car and Go: Disneyland." *Buick Magazine,* 18:7, May 1957, 2–4.

"People & Places Reveal 'Blue Men of Morocco.'" *Disneyland News,* 2:1, July 1956, 9.

Picture Souvenir Book of Disneyland in Natural Color. Boston: American Souvenir Company, 1955; facsimile reprint. New York: Disney Editions, 2005.

"Pirate's Galleon Offers Atmosphere, Seafood." *Disneyland News,* 1:4, Oct. 10, 1955, 13.

Pryor, Thomas M. "Cine-Miracle Joins Big Screen's Big Parade." *New York Times,* July 3, 1955, X5.

———. "Disney Presents Movies-in-Round." *New York Times,* June 28, 1955, 23.

———. "Disney to Enter TV Field in Fall." *New York Times,* Mar. 30, 1954, 24.

———. "Hollywood Double Entente." *New York Times,* Mar. 11, 1954, X5.

———. "Land of Fantasia Is Rising on Coast." *New York Times,* May 2, 1954, 86.

———. "West Coast Activities." *New York Times,* July 3, 1955, X9.

Public Relations Department. *Walt Disney's Magic Kingdom Disneyland.* Opening day press kit. Anaheim: Disneyland, Inc., 1955; facsimile reprint, Disneyland Press & Publicity, 2005.

"Rare Antiques in Disneyland." *The American Home,* 56:4, Sept. 1956, 14–15.

"Red Wagon Inn Presents History with Fine Food." *Disneyland News,* 2:1, July 1956, 6–7.

"Reviewer Finds Main St. Cinema Movies Live Up to Advance Bill." *Disneyland News,* 1:3, Sept. 1955, 18–19.

Rhodes, Douglas Nelson. "Disneyland: Fabulous New Magic Kingdom." *Nash Airflyte Magazine,* July 1955.

"Rifle Assn. Exhibit in Crockett Arcade." *Disneyland News,* 4:1, Oct. 10, 1955, 15.

"Roadsters in Disneyland." *Hot Rod,* Oct. 1955, 62–63.

"Rocket Trip to Moon Blasts Off for Realistic Space Ride." *Disneyland News,* 1:2, Aug. 1955, 16.

R.S. "Disneyland Dedication from Coast." *New York Times,* July 18, 1955, 41.

"Scenes from 'Tom Sawyer's Island.'" *Disneyland News,* 2:1, July 1956, 4.

Schallert, Edwin. "Disney Spending

$1,000,000 on New Dreams for Play-land." *Los Angeles Times,* May 13, 1956, sect. 4, 1, 4.

"See the Beauties of the Rainbow Desert." *Disneyland News,* 2:2, Aug. 1956, 3.

Senn, John. "A Look at Disneyland." *Magic Circle,* 9:3, June 1956, 3–6.

Shandley, J. P. "TV: A Trip to the Moon," *New York Times,* Dec. 29, 1955, 41.

Shellhorn, Ruth P. "Disneyland: Dream Built in One Year Through Teamwork of Many Artists." *Landscape Architecture,* 46:3, April 1956, 125–36.

[Sklar, Martin A.] *Disneyland.* Verona: Mondadori, 1964.

———. *Walt Disney's Disneyland.* Burbank: Walt Disney Productions, 1969.

"Sound Effects Add Realism to Disneyland." *Radio and Television News,* Aug. 1956, 52–53.

"Space Station X-1 Gives Outer Space View of U.S." *Disneyland News,* 2:4, Oct. 1956, 2.

"Space Travel: The Trip to the Moon, Disneyland Style." *Disneyland News,* 1:9, Mar. 10, 1956, 10–11.

Spencer, Dick, III. "The Horse Is King in Wonderful Disneyland." *Western Horseman,* 22:7, Sept. 1957, 22–23, 68–69.

"Stage Coach Driver Jim Finds Hazards Are Not All in the Desert." *Disneyland News,* 1:8, Feb. 1956, 10–11.

"Stanley's Exploits in Search for Livingston [sic] Brought to Life by Adventureland Boat Trip." *Disneyland News,* 1:2 Aug. 1955, 6.

Starr, Jimmy. "Guest Columnist: Starr Finds Laughter, Glee for Kids at Disneyland." *Disneyland News,* 1:30, Sept. 1955, 2.

"Steeds Prance to Caliope [sic] Tunes." *Disneyland News,* 1:2, Aug. 1955, 5.

The Story of Disneyland. Racine: Western Printing, 1955. The first official souvenir guidebook.

Sullivan, Catherine. "The Artist in Hollywood." *American Artist,* 14, Sept. 1950, 42–46.

Thomas, Bob. "Disney TV Shows to Teach Children." *Miami Daily News,* Mar. 16, 1955, 148.

———. "51 Acres of Disney's Studios Are Crammed with Ideas." *Reading Eagle,* Mar. 15, 1955, 18.

———. "Guest Columnist: Walt

Fascinated as Child on Magic Kingdom Visit." *Disneyland News,* 1:4, Oct. 10, 1955, 4.

———. "160-acre Fairyland called Disneyland Opens: $17 Million Wonderland in California." *Pittsburgh Post-Gazette,* July 18, 1955.

———. "22,000 Guests Dazzled by Fantastic Disneyland." *Hartford Courant,* July 18, 1955, 10.

———. "Walt Disney's Fantastic Amusement Park Is Almost Completed Near Los Angeles." *Daily Press* (Newport News), May 11, 1955, 6.

"360 Degrees: Super-Wide Screen Shows Travel Film in Circarama." *Disneyland News,* 1:3, Sept. 16, 1955, 16.

"Thrills Await Drivers on 1986 Freeway." *Disneyland News,* 1:2, Aug. 1955, 4.

Tinée, Mae. "'Tarzan' Offers Movie Thrills for All Ages." *Chicago Daily Tribune,* Apr. 8, 1932, 19.

"Tom Sawyer Island to Have Old West Fort, Secret Cave." *Disneyland News,* Extra Edition, [May] 1956, 1.

"Tomorrowland's Exhibits Show World of the Future." *Disneyland News,* 1:2, Aug. 1955, 4, 18.

"Tomorrowland's Food Service: Here Today!" *Disneyland News,* 2:4, Oct. 1956, 7.

"Tropical Designer Reveals: Goff Takes Up New Hobbies." *Disneyland News,* 1:2, Aug. 1955, 8–11.

"Turn Back the Clock: Complete American Small Town of 1900 Era Reproduced Here." *Disneyland News,* 1:1, July 1955, 3.

"Viaggio nel paese dei balocchi." *Oggi,* 11:31, Aug. 4, 1955, 32–35.

"Visit to Disneyland." *Panorama,* Spring 1955, 4–5.

"A Visit to Frontierland's Indian Village." *Disneyland News,* 2:2, Aug. 1956, 4–5.

"A Visit to Hobbyland: Models Demonstrated in Tomorrowland Show." *Disneyland News,* 1:4, Oct. 10, 1955, 14.

"Visitors to See Historic West." *Disneyland News,* 1:2, Aug. 1955, 8.

"Walt Disney Builds Half-Pint History." *Popular Science,* 162, Feb. 1953, 118–19.

"Walt Disney Make-Believe Land Project Planned Here." *Burbank Review,* Mar. 27, 1952, A1.

"Walt Disney Opens New Park but Guests Call It Confused Mess." *Russell Daily News,* July 18, 1955, 1.

"Walt Disney Plans TV Show." *Hollywood Reporter,* Jan. 11, 1954, 1, 4.

Walt Disney Takes You to Disneyland: A Musical Tour of the Magic Kingdom. With Walt Disney and Disneyland Concert Orchestra. Released 1956. Disneyland Records, 4004, LP.

"Walt Disney's Background Apparent on TV Series." *Disneyland News,* 1:2, Aug. 1955, 20.

Walt Disney's Main Street Coloring Fun. Racine: Whitman Publishing, 1955.

"Walt Disney's Tomorrowland"; "Walt Disney's Fantasyland"; "Walt Disney's Frontierland"; "Walt Disney's Adventureland." Series of four articles, *TV Guide,* 3:1–4, Jan. 1–22, 1955.

WED Enterprises. *Disneyland: Where you Leave Today. .. and Visit the World of Yesterday and Tomorrow.* Burbank: Disneyland, Inc., [Sept.] 1953.

Welcome to Disneyland. First park brochure. Disneyland, Inc., 1955.

"What Is Disneyland?" *Disneyland Holiday,* 1:1, Spring 1957, 2.

Winecoff, Nat. *The Disneyland Story.* Burbank: Disneyland, Inc., Apr. 20, 1954.

Wirsig, Woodrow. "Companionably Yours: Disneyland." *Woman's Home Companion,* 81, June 1954, 12.

Wolfert, Ira. "Walt Disney's Magic Kingdom." *Reader's Digest,* 76, Apr. 1960, 144–147, 149–50, 152.

"A Wonderful World: Growing Impact of the Disney Art." *Newsweek,* 45:16, Apr. 18, 1955, 60, 62–64.

Woodson, Weldon D. "Through the Jungles of Disneyland." *American Forests,* Jan. 1956, 20–22.

"World Visitors Enjoy Disneyland: Guests from Foreign Nations, All Parts of America Include Hollywood Stars." *Disneyland News,* 1:2, Aug. 1955, 1.

Your Guide to Disneyland. Brochure. Bank of America, 1955.

Your Tanner Gray Line Guide to Disneyland. Brochure. Los Angeles: Tanner Gray Line Motor Tours, 1955.

Secondary Sources from 1970

Affron, Charles, and Mirella Jona Affron. *Sets in Motion: Art Direction and Film Narrative.* New Brunswick: Rutgers University Press, 1995.

Agnew, Jeremy. *The Old West in Fact and Film: History versus Hollywood.* Jefferson: McFarland, 2012.

"Alice in Wonderland." *"E" Ticket,* no. 31 (Spring 1999): 24–37.

Allan, Robin. *Walt Disney and Europe: European Influences on the Animated Feature Films of Walt Disney.* Bloomington: Indiana University Press, 1999.

Amendola, Dana. *All Aboard: The Wonderful World of Disney Trains.* Los Angeles: Disney Editions, 2015.

Anderson, Fred. "The Warner Bros. Research Department: Putting History to Work in the Classic Studio Era." *Public Historian* 17:1 (Winter 1995): 51–69.

Anderson, Paul F. "Disneyland Illustrator Extraordinaire: A Visit with Sam McKim." *Persistence of Vision* 5 (1993): 47–54.

"The Autopia: Disneyland's 'Expressway of the Future.'" *"E" Ticket,* no. 27 (Summer 1997): 12–27.

Avila, Eric. *Popular Culture in the Age of White Flight: Fear and Fantasy in Suburban Los Angeles.* Berkeley: University of California Press, 2006.

Barnwell, Jane. *Production Design: Architects of the Screen.* London: Wallflower, 2004.

Barrier, Michael. *The Animated Man: A Life of Walt Disney.* Berkeley: University Press of California, 2007.

Basinger, Jeanine. *The* It's a Wonderful Life *Book.* New York: Alfred A. Knopf, 1994.

Behlmer, Rudy. *The Adventures of Robin Hood.* Madison: University of Wisconsin Press, 1979.

———. *Behind the Scenes: The Making of....* Hollywood: Samuel French, 1990.

———. "*The Black Pirate* Weighs Anchor." Part 2. *American Cinematographer,* 73:5, May 1992, 34–40.

———. "High Style on the High Seas." Part 1. *American Cinematographer,* 73:4, April 1992, 34–40.

———. "*The Sea Hawk* Sets Sail." Part 1. *American Cinematographer,* 77:7, July 1996, 86–90.

———. "Tarzan and M-G-M: The Rest of the Story." Part 2. *American Cinematographer,* 68:2, Feb. 1987, 34–44.

———. "Tarzan, Hollywood's Greatest Jungle Hero." Part 1. *American Cinematographer,* 68:1, Jan. 1987, 38–44.

———, ed. *Memo from Darryl F. Zanuck: The Golden Years of Twentieth Century-Fox.* New York: Grove, 1993.

Belton, Thomas. *Widescreen Cinema.* Cambridge: Harvard University Press, 1992.

Benelli, Dana. "Hollywood and the Travelogue." *Visual Anthropology* 15:1 (2002): 3–16.

Bingen, Steven. *Hollywood's Lost Backlot: 40 Acres of Glamour and Mystery.* Guilford: Lyons Press, 2019.

———. *Paramount: City of Dreams.* Guilford: Taylor Trade, 2017.

———. *Warner Bros.: Hollywood's Ultimate Backlot.* Lanham: Taylor Trade, 2014.

Bingen, Steven, Stephen X. Sylvester, and Michael Troyan. *M-G-M: Hollywood's Greatest Backlot.* Solana Beach: Santa Monica Press, 2011.

"Bob Gurr's Main Street GurrMobiles." *"E" Ticket,* no. 27 (Summer 1997): 8–11.

Bonner, Marcel, and Stephen Daly. "Remembering Fred Joerger." *"E" Ticket,* no. 44 (Summer 2006): 6–17.

Braudy, Leo. *The Hollywood Sign: Fantasy and Reality of an American Icon.* New Haven: Yale University Press, 2011.

Bright, Randy. *Disneyland: Inside Story.* New York: Abrams, 1987.

Broggie, Michael. *Walt Disney's Railroad Story: The Small-Scale Fascination That Led to a Full-Scale Kingdom.* Pasadena: Pentrex, 1997.

Brown, Noel. *The Hollywood Family Film: A History, from Shirley Temple to Harry Potter.* London: I. B. Tauris, 2012.

Burchard, Wolf. *Inspiring Walt Disney: The Animation of French Decorative Arts.* New York: The Metropolitan Museum of Art, 2021.

Burnes, Brian, Robert W. Butler, and Dan Viets. *Walt Disney's Missouri: The Roots of a Creative Genius.* Kansas City: Kansas City Star Books, 2002.

Buscombe, Edward. *"Injuns!" Native Americans in the Movies.* London: Reaktion, 2006.

Cameron, Kenneth M. *Africa on Film: Beyond Black and White.* New York: Continuum, 1994.

Cerra, Julie Lugo, and Marc Wanamaker. *Movie Studios of Culver City.* Charleston: Arcadia, 2011.

Cotter, Bill. *The Wonderful World of Disney Television: A Complete History.* New York: Hyperion, 1997.

"Creating the Disney Landscape: An Interview with Bill Evans." *"E" Ticket,* no. 23 (Spring 1996): 4–15.

Cross, Gary S., and John K. Walton. *The Playful Crowd: Pleasure Places in the Twentieth Century.* New York: Columbia University Press, 2005.

Custen, George F. *Twentieth Century's Fox: Darryl F. Zanuck and the Culture of Hollywood.* New York: BasicBooks, 1997.

Dallas, Alastair. *Inventing Disneyland: The Unauthorized Story of the Team That Made Walt Disney's Dream Come True.* Orlando: Theme Park Press, 2018.

"Disneyland Art Director … Bill Martin." *"E" Ticket,* no. 20 (Winter 1994–95): 10–19.

Disneyland: The First Quarter Century. Burbank: Walt Disney Productions, 1979.

"Disneyland: The First Twelve Months." *"E" Ticket,* no. 28 (Winter 1997): 20–35.

"Disneyland's Davy Crockett." *"E" Ticket,* no. 33 (Spring 2000): 34–41.

"Disneyland's Queen of the River, The Mark Twain." *"E" Ticket,* no. 15 (Spring 1993): 16–27.

"Disneyland's Rocket to the Moon." *"E" Ticket,* no. 24 (Summer 1996): 18–31.

"Disney's Peter Pan's Flight." *"E" Ticket,* no. 26 (Spring 1997): 10–25.

Dunn, Kevin. "Lights … Camera … Africa: Images of Africa and Africans in Western Popular Films of the 1930s." *African Studies Review* 39 (Apr. 1996): 149–75.

Erish, Andrew A. *Col. William N. Selig, the Man Who Invented Hollywood.* Austin: University of Texas Press, 2012.

Esperdy, Gabrielle. "From Instruction to Consumption: Architecture and Design in Hollywood Movies of the 1930s." *Journal of American Culture* 30:2 (June 2007): 198–211.

Finch, Christopher. *The Art of Walt Disney: From Mickey Mouse to the Magic Kingdoms,* New York: Abrams, 1973.

———. *Walt Disney's America.* New York: Abbeville Press, 1978.

Fisher, Lucy, ed. *Art Direction and Production Design.* New Brunswick: Rutgers University Press, 2015.

"Flair and Versatility: A Visit to Walt's Original W.E.D. Model Shop with

Harriet Burns." *"E" Ticket,* no. 44 (Summer 2006): 28–41.

Francaviglia, Richard. "Frontierland as an Allegorical Map of the American West." In *Disneyland and Culture: Essays on the Parks and Their Influence,* edited by Kathy Merlock Jackson and Mark I. West, 59–86. Jefferson: McFarland, 2011.

_____. *Main Street Revisited: Time, Space, and Image-Building in Small-Town America.* Iowa City: University of Iowa Press, 1996.

_____. "Main Street U.S.A.: A Comparison/Contrast of Streetscapes in Disneyland and Walt Disney World." *Journal of Popular Culture* 15:1 (Summer 1981): 141–56.

Freitag, Florian. *Popular New Orleans: The Crescent City in Periodicals, Theme Parks, and Opera, 1875–2015.* New York: Routledge, 2020.

French, Warren, ed. *The South and Film.* Jackson: University Press of Mississippi, 1981.

Fury, David. *Kings of the Jungle: An Illustrated Reference to "Tarzan" on Screen and Television.* Jefferson: McFarland, 2003.

Gabler, Neal. *An Empire of Their Own: How the Jews Invented Hollywood.* New York: Doubleday, 1998.

_____. *Walt Disney: The Triumph of the American Imagination.* New York: Knopf, 2006.

Gaines, Jane Marie, and Charlotte Cornelia Herzog. "The Fantasy of Authenticity in Western Costume." in *Back in the Saddle Again: New Essays on the Western,* edited by Edward Buscombe and Roberta E. Pearson, 172–81. London: BFI, 1998.

Gennawey, Sam. *The Disneyland Story: The Unofficial Guide to the Evolution of Walt Disney's Dream.* Birmingham: Keen, 2014.

_____. *Universal vs. Disney: The Unofficial Guide to American Theme Parks' Greatest Rivalry.* Birmingham: Keen, 2015.

Ghez, Didier, ed. *Walt's People: Talking Disney with the Artists Who Knew Him.* Vol. 14. Orlando: Theme Park Press, 2014.

Gordon, Bruce, and David Mumford. *Disneyland: The Nickel Tour.* Santa Clarita: Camphor Tree, 2000.

Gutner, Howard. *MGM Style: Cedric*

Gibbons and the Art of Hollywood.* Guilford: Lyons Press, 2019.

Hambling, John, and Patrick Downing. *The Art of Hollywood.* London: Thames Television, 1979.

Haver, Ronald. *David O. Selznick's Hollywood.* New York: Bonanza Books, 1985.

Heisner, Beverly. *Hollywood Art: Art Direction in the Days of the Great Studios.* Jefferson: McFarland, 1990.

Hench, John, with Peggy Van Pelt. *Designing Disney: Imagineering and the Art of the Show.* New York: Disney Editions, 2003.

Hepburn, Katharine. *The Making of "The African Queen," or How I Went to Africa with Bogart, Bacall, and Huston and Almost Lost My Mind.* New York: Alfred A. Knopf, 1987.

Herzberg, Bob. *Savages and Saints: The Changing Image of American Indians in Westerns.* Jefferson: McFarland, 2008.

Hobbs, Priscilla. *Walt's Utopia: Disneyland and American Mythmaking.* Jefferson: McFarland, 2015.

Hozic, Aida. *Hollyworld: Space, Power, and Fantasy in the American Economy.* Ithaca: Cornell University Press, 2001.

The Imagineers. *Walt Disney Imagineering: A Behind the Dreams Look at Making the Magic Real.* New York: Hyperion, 1996.

"An Interview with Harper Goff." *"E" Ticket,* no. 14 (Winter 1992–93): 4–11.

Irving, Laurence. *Designing for the Movies: The Memoirs of Laurence Irving.* Lanham: Scarecrow Press, 2005.

Iwerks, Leslie, and John Kenworthy. *The Hand Behind the Mouse: An Intimate Biography of the Man Walt Disney Called "The Greatest Animator in the World."* New York: Disney Editions, 2001.

Jackson, Kathy Merlock. *Walt Disney: A Bio-Bibliography.* Westport: Greenwood Press, 1993.

_____, and Mark I. West, eds. *Disneyland and Culture: Essays on the Parks and Their Influence.* Jefferson: McFarland, 2011.

Jacobson, Brian. *Studios Before the System: Architecture, Technology, and the Emergence of Cinematic Space.* New York: Columbia University Press, 2015.

Janzen, Jack. "Disneyland's 20,000 Leagues under the Sea Exhibit." *"E" Ticket,* no. 5 (Summer 1998): 16–29.

_____. "Main Street: Walt's Perfect

Introduction to Disneyland." *"E" Ticket,* no. 14 (Winter 1992–93): 24–31.

———. "The Original Snow White Dark Ride." *"E" Ticket,* no. 13 (Summer 1992): 16–25.

———. "Sleeping Beauty Castle." *"E" Ticket,* no. 10 (Winter 1990–91): 4–12.

———. "Storybook Land." *"E" Ticket,* no. 11 (Summer 1991): 6–19.

Janzen, Leon J. "Corriganville Movie Ranch." *"E" Ticket,* no. 8 (Winter 1989–90): 29–31.

Kershow, Julia. "Capturing Africa: Sightseeing through the Tarzan Cycle of the 1930s." *Athanor* 36 (2018): 79–87.

King, Margaret J. "The Recycled Hero: Walt Disney's Davy Crockett." In *Davy Crockett: The Man, the Legend, the Legacy, 1786–1986,* edited by Michael A. Lofaro, 137–58. Knoxville: University of Tennessee Press, 1985.

Koenig, David. *The 55ers: The Pioneers Who Settled Disneyland.* Irvine: Bonaventure Press, 2019.

Korkis, Jim. *The Unofficial Disneyland 1955 Companion: The Anecdotal Story of the Birth of the Happiest Place on Earth.* Theme Park Press, 2016.

Kurtti, Jeff. *Sleeping Beauty Castle: Building the Most Magical Castle on Earth.* New York: Sterling Innovation, 2014; in the "Build Sleeping Beauty Castle" kit.

———. *Walt Disney's Imagineering Legends and the Genesis of the Disney Theme Park.* New York: Disney Editions, 2008.

———, and Bruce Gordon. *The Art of Disneyland.* New York: Disney Editions, 2006.

———, Vanessa Hunt, and Paul Wolski. *The Disney Monorail: Imagineering a Highway in the Sky.* Los Angeles: Disney Editions, 2020.

Lev, Peter. *Twentieth Century-Fox: The Zanuck-Skouras Years, 1935–1965.* Austin: University of Texas Press, 2013.

Levy, Emanuel. *Small-Town America in Film: The Decline and Fall of Community.* New York: Continuum, 1991.

Lusted, David. *The Western.* New York: Pearson, 2003.

MacKinnon, Kenneth. *Hollywood's Small Towns: An Introduction to the American Small-Town Movie.* Metuchen: Scarecrow Press, 1984.

Maltin, Leonard. *The Disney Films.* New York: Hyperion, 1995.

Marling, Karal Ann. "Disneyland, 1955: Just Take the Santa Ana Freeway to the American Dream." *American Art,* 5:1/2, Winter-Spring, 1991, 168–207.

———, ed. *Designing Disney's Theme Parks: The Architecture of Reassurance.* Montreal: Canadian Centre for Architecture, 1997.

Marling, Karal Ann, with Donna R. Braden. *Behind the Magic: 50 Years of Disneyland.* Dearborn: The Henry Ford, 2005.

Menzies, William Cameron. "Pictorial Beauty in the Photoplay." In *Hollywood Directors 1914–1940,* edited by Richard Koszarski, 238–51. New York: Oxford University Press, 1976.

"Mr. Toad's Wild Ride." *"E" Ticket,* no. 20 (Winter 1994–95): 20–33.

Neuman, Robert. "Disneyland's Main Street, USA, and Its Sources in Hollywood, USA." In *Disneyland and Culture: Essays on the Parks and Their Influence,* edited by Kathy Merlock Jackson and Mark I. West, 37–58. Jefferson: McFarland, 2011.

———. "Disney's Final Package Film: The Making and Marketing of The Adventures of Ichabod and Mr. Toad (1949)." *Animation: An Interdisciplinary Journal* 14:2 (2019): 149–63.

———. "Now Mickey Mouse Enters Art's Temple: Walt Disney at the Intersection of Art and Entertainment." *Visual Resources* 14, no. 3 (1999): 249–261.

———. "Toad, Alice and Peter: From England to Disney-Land and Back Again." In *Interpreting and Experiencing Disney: Mediating the Mouse,* edited by Priscilla Hobbs, chap. 3. London: Intellect, 2021.

Nichols, Chris. *Walt Disney's Disneyland.* Cologne: Taschen, 2018.

O'Boyle, J. G. "'Be Sure You're Right, then Go Ahead': The Early Disney Westerns." *Journal of Popular Film and Television* 24:2 (Summer 1996): 70–81.

Orvell, Miles. *The Death and Life of Main Street: Small Towns in American Memory, Space and Community.* Chapel Hill: University of North Carolina Press, 2012.

Philips, Deborah. *Fairground Attractions: A Genealogy of the Pleasure Ground.* London: Bloomsbury Academic, 2012.

Pierce, Todd James. *Three Years in Wonderland: The Disney Brothers, C. V. Wood, and the Making of the Great American Theme Park.* Jackson: University Press of Mississippi, 2016.

"Planning the First Disney Parks: A Talk with Marvin Davis." *"E" Ticket,* no. 28 (Winter 1997): 8–19.

Rabinovitz, Lauren. *Electric Dreamland: Amusement Parks, Movies, and American Modernity.* New York: Columbia University Press, 2012.

Rennie, Neil. *Treasure Neverland: Real and Imaginary Pirates.* Oxford: Oxford University Press, 2013.

Rowley, Stephen. *Movie Towns and Sitcom Suburbs: Building Hollywood's Ideal Communities.* Basingstoke: Palgrave Macmillan, 2015.

Ryman, Herbert Dickens, Bruce Gordon, and David Mumford. *A Brush with Disney: An Artist's Journey.* Santa Clarita: Camphor Tree, 2000.

Schatz, Thomas. *The Genius of the System: Hollywood Filmmaking in the Studio Era.* New York: Pantheon Books, 1988.

Sennett, Robert S. *Setting the Scene: The Great Hollywood Art Directors.* New York: Abrams, 1994.

Shiel, Mark. *Hollywood Cinema and the Real Los Angeles.* London: Reaktion, 2012.

Slotkin, Richard. "Prologue to a Study of Myth and Genre in American Movies." *Prospects* 9 (Oct. 1984): 407–32.

Smothers, Marcy Carriker. *Walt's Disneyland: A Walk in the Park with Walt Disney.* Los Angeles: Disney Editions, 2021.

Snow, Richard. *Disney's Land: Walt Disney and the Invention of the Amusement Park That Changed the World.* New York: Scribner's, 2019.

Sobchack, Vivian. *Screening Space: The American Science Fiction Film.* New Brunswick: Rutgers University Press, 1997.

Steiner, Michael. "Frontierland as Tomorrowland: Walt Disney and the Architectural Packaging of the Mythic West." *Montana: The Magazine of Western History,* 48:1, Spring 1998, 2–17.

Stephens, E. J., and Marc Wanamaker. *Early Warner Bros. Studios.* Charleston: Arcadia, 2010.

Strodder, Chris. *The Disneyland Encyclopedia.* Solana Beach: Santa Monica Press, 2012.

Strömberg, Per. "Et in Chronotopia Ego: Main Street Architecture as a Rhetorical Device in Theme Parks and Outlet Villages." In *A Reader in Themed and Immersive Spaces,* edited by Scott A. Lukas, 83–93. Pittsburgh: ETC Press, 2016.

Thomas, Bob. *Walt Disney: An American Original.* New York: Hyperion, 1994.

"Tom Sawyer Island." *"E" Ticket,* no. 37 (Spring 2002): 14–28.

"Tomorrowland Clock of the World." *"E" Ticket,* no. 45 (Summer 2007): 24–29.

Troyan, Michael, Stephen X. Sylvester, and Jeffrey P. Thompson. *Twentieth Century Fox: A Century of Entertainment.* Guilford: Lyons Press, 2017.

Van Riper, A. Bowdoin, ed. *Learning from Mickey, Donald, and Walt: Essays on Disney's Edutainment Films.* Jefferson: McFarland, 2011.

"Visualizing Disneyland with Sam McKim." *"E" Ticket,* no. 18 (Spring 1994): 8–21.

"Wally Boag Tells of Frontierland." *"E" Ticket,* no. 15 (Spring 1993): 8–9.

"Walt Disney's Man in Space: Ward Kimball." *"E" Ticket,* no. 24 (Summer 1996): 4–17.

Watts, Steven. *The Magic Kingdom: Walt Disney and the American Way of Life.* New York: Houghton Mifflin, 1997.

White, Donna R., and C. Anita Tarr. *J. M. Barrie's* Peter Pan *In and Out of Time: A Children's Classic at 100.* Lanham: Scarecrow Press, 2006.

Wright, Alex. *The Imagineering Field Guide to Disneyland: An Imagineer's-Eye Tour.* New York: Disney Editions, 2008.

Index

Page numbers in **bold italics** indicate pages with illustrations

261

Index   265

Marshal's Office (Frontierland) 66
Martin, Bill 3, 69, 79, 157, 160, 182, 186, 194, 242*n*27
Martin, Pete 40
Mary Poppins (film, 1964) 18, 49, 130
Mason, James 18, 148, 181
Matterhorn Bobsleds attraction (Fantasyland) 163, 197, 200
Mattey, Robert A. (Bob) 111, 150
Mayer, Louis B. 11, 14, 54, 204
McAfee, Harry 46
McDaniel, Hattie 93
McKim, Sam 46, 65
Medieval films 165, 170–77, 180–86
Meet Me in St. Louis (film, 1944) 54–57, *55*, 59
Méliès brothers 140
Melody Time (film, 1948) 62–63, 74, 80, 86, 88
Memorandum, August 1948 2–3, 5, 40, 66, 74, 127, 160, 186, 208
Menzies, William Cameron 30, 48, 84, 185
Merlin (legendary figure) 186, 245*n*98
Merlin's Magic Shop (Fantasyland) 177, 186
MGM (Metro-Goldwyn-Mayer) 6, 13–14, 16, 19, 21–22, *21*, 26, 31, 36, 46, 53–56, 67, 70, 75–77, 82, 92, 103, 105, 108–9, *110*, 111, 113–14, 116, 119, 121, 162, 172, 175–76, 180–81, 185, 191–92, 201–5; Andy Hardy Street *21*, 22, 53–54, 56; Jungle and Lake 112; Lot 1 22; Lot 1 lake 112, 191; Lot 2 22, 53, 109, 112, 248*n*19; Lot 3 *21*, 22, 54, *55*, 67, 77–78, *78*, 109, 112, 203; Lot 4 109; Lot 6 112; St. Louis Street 22, 54, *55*, 56, 57, 67; Small Town Square *21*, 22, 54; Tarzan Lake *21*, 112
MGM Studio Tour (theatrical short, 1925) 24
Mickey Mouse (character) 1, 6, 9, 17, 57, 111, 123, 125, 134, 165–66, 196, 247; cartoon shorts 15–17, 63
Mickey Mouse Club (TV, 1955–59) 14, 196, 226*n*103
Mickey Mouse Club Circus 152
Mickey Mouse Club Theater (Fantasyland) 157, *178*, 225*n*75
Mickey Mouse Park 3, 40, 127, 148
Mickey's Gala Premier (cartoon short, 1933) 17
Mickey's Man Friday (cartoon short, 1935) 123
Midget Autopia (Tomorrowland) 152
Mike Fink Keel Boats attraction (Frontierland) 66
Miller, Diane Disney 40
miniaturization and models 3, 5, 27–28, 47, 69, 76–77, 99, 111, *145*, 148–49, 152, 155, 162–63, 165, 174, 189, 192, 194–95, 209*n*28, 214*n*63, 226*n*103, 240*n*6, 242*n*29
Minnelli, Vincente 54–57, *55*
The Miracle of Morgan's Creek (film, 1944) 51
Mr. Deeds Goes to Town (film, 1936) 45–46

Mr. Toad's Wild Ride attraction (Fantasyland) 8, 157, *178*, 182, 199
Mogambo (film, 1953) 116, 121–22
Monorail (Tomorrowland) 127, 195, 199–200
Monsanto House of the Future (Tomorrowland). 127, 199
Monument Valley *73*, 79–80, 130, 226*n*99
Moonliner (Tomorrowland) 129, 136, *137*, 139, 141, 143–45
movie stars and celebrities 7–8, 24, 58–59, 86, 213*n*50
Mueller, Chris 111, 150
music 35, 38, 70, 92–93, 102, 139, 143, 177

The Naked Jungle (film, 1953) 118–19, *118*
Negro Motorist Green-Books 93
Neuschwanstein Castle, Bavaria 161–64, 169, 241*n*18, 241*n*21
New Orleans in film 91–93
New Orleans Square 42, 91, 195
New Orleans Street (Frontierland) 62, 91–92
New York World's Fair (1939) 131, 154, 216*n*10
The Nifty Nineties (cartoon short, 1941) 57
nostalgia 33, 36, 42, 56, 60, 95

Oakley, Annie 63
Oh, What a Knight! (cartoon short, 1928) 165
Okey, Jack 52
Opening Day (July 17, 1955) 13, 57, 62, 77, 96, 126, 128, 168, 172, 178, 187; *see also* "Dateline Disneyland"
Opera House (Town Square) 36, 41, 70
O'Sullivan, Maureen 108, 114
Our Town (film, 1940) 43–44
Out of Scale (cartoon short, 1951) 74

Pack Mules attraction (Frontierland) 62, 72, *72*, 85
Painted Desert (Frontierland) 62, 72, 79, 80–81
Pal, George 140–41, 237*n*49
panoramas 58, 146–47
Paramount Pictures 6, 13, 16, 29, 57, 65, 68, 73, 75, 82, 112, 118, *118*, 123, 132, 149, 196, 201 Paramount Ranch 50, *50*; Tom Sawyer Street 50, *50*
Parker, Fess 87, 94
Parker, Max 25
parking lot 153
Patrick, George 65
Pendleton Woolen Mills Dry Goods Store (Frontierland) 66, *67*
Penny Arcade (Main Street) 37–38
People and Places films 99, 103–104, 130, 133, 173, 231*n*19
Peter Pan (film, 1924) 193, 195–96
Peter Pan (film, 1953) 63, 90, 160, 187, 191, 193–97